NEMESIS

NEMESIS

ALCIBIADES AND THE FALL OF ATHENS

DAVID STUTTARD

 Harvard University Press

CAMBRIDGE, MASSACHUSETTS

LONDON, ENGLAND | 2018

First Printing

Library of Congress Cataloging-in-Publication Data
Names: Stuttard, David, author.
Title: Nemesis : Alcibiades and the fall of Athens / David Stuttard.
Description: Cambridge, Massachusetts : Harvard University Press,
    2018. | Includes bibliographical references and index.
Identifiers: LCCN 2017045399 | ISBN 9780674660441
    (hardcover : alk. paper)
Subjects: LCSH: Alcibiades—Biography. | Greece—History—
    Peloponnesian War, 431–404 B.C.
Classification: LCC DF230.A4 S78 2018 | DDC 938/.05092 [B]—dc23
LC record available at https://lccn.loc.gov/2017045399

To my wife, Emily Jane

CONTENTS

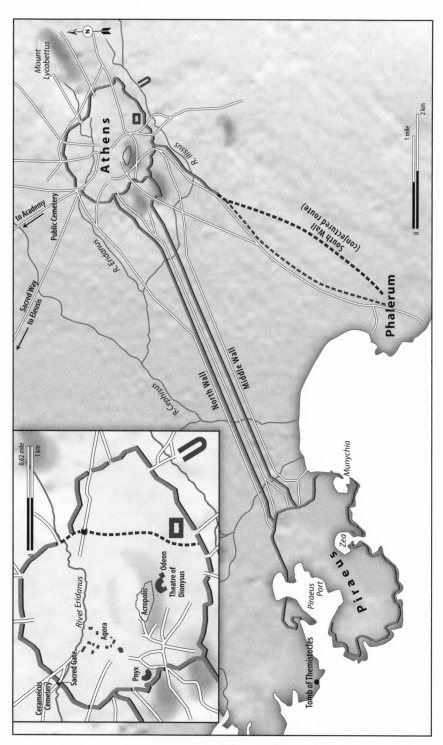

Athens and Piraeus. Inset shows city of Athens.

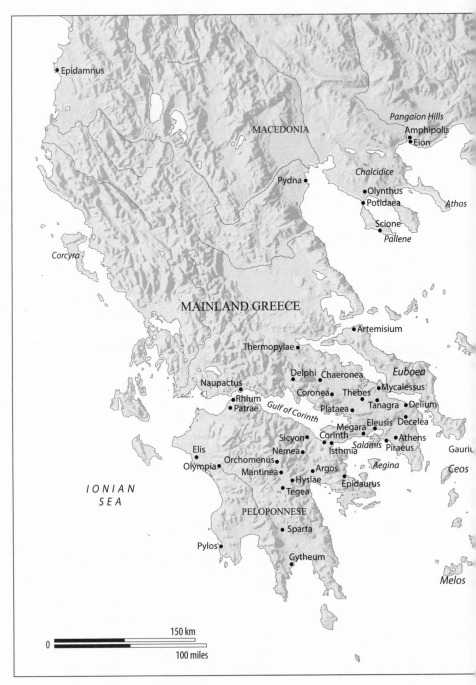

Epidamnus

MACEDONIA

Pangaion Hills
Amphipolis
Eion

Chalcidice
Pydna
Olynthus
Potidaea
Athos
Scione
Pallene

Corcyra

MAINLAND GREECE

Artemisium

Thermopylae

Delphi Chaeronea
Naupactus
Coronea Thebes Mycalessus
Rhium Euboea
Patrae Gulf of Corinth
Plataea Tanagra Delium
Megara Eleusis Decelea
Sicyon Corinth
Nemea Salamis Piraeus Athens
Elis Isthmia Gauriu
Orchomenus Aegina
Olympia Argos Ceos
Mantinea Hysiae Epidaurus
Tegea

IONIAN
SEA

PELOPONNESE

Sparta

Pylos

Gytheum

Melos

0   150 km

    100 miles

Greece, Macedonia, Thrace, and Asia Minor

BLACK
SEA

BOSPORUS

THRACE

Abdera

Selymbria
Bisanthe •Perinthus Byzantium •Chrysopolis
•Chalcedon

PROPONTIS or
SEA OF MARMARA

Proconnesus

Cardia
•Pactye
Aegospotami
Thracian Chersonese •Lampsacus •Cyzicus
Sestus• HELLESPONT
Cynossema• •Abydus
•Dardanus •Dascyleum
•Rhoetium
•Troy

N

Eresus
•Mytilene
Lesbos

Arginusae

ASIA MINOR

Melissa•

AEGEAN
SEA

•Cyme
•Phocaea

•Sardis

Chios •Erythrae •Smyrna
Chios •Clazomenae
•Teos
Colophon• •Notium
•Ephesus
•Magnesia
Samos Samos• •Aphrodisias
ndros Meander Plain
•Andros •Miletus
•Teichiusa
Delos •Iasus

•Halicarnassus

Cos •Cnidus

Rhodes

EA OF CRETE

Attica and environs

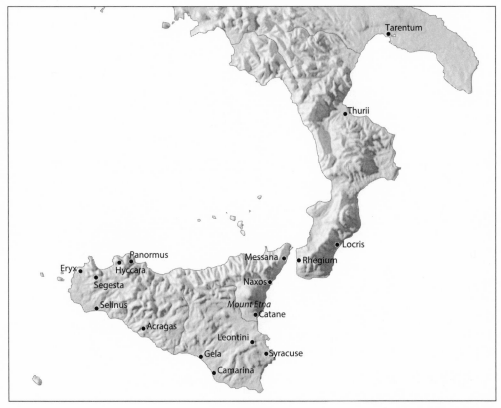

Sicily and Magna Graecia

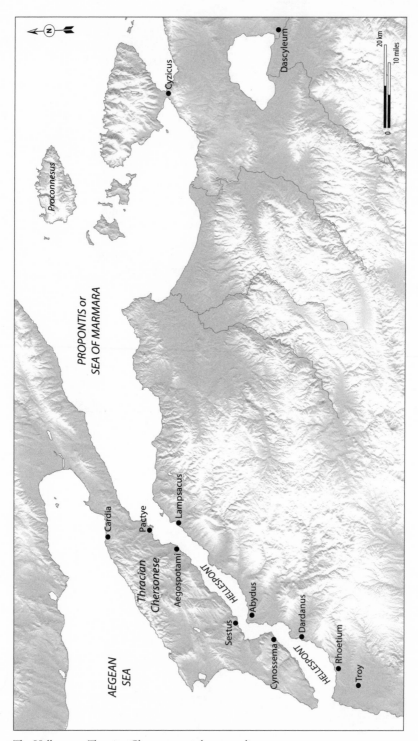

The Hellespont, Thracian Chersonese, and surrounding areas

Alcibiades' Family Tree

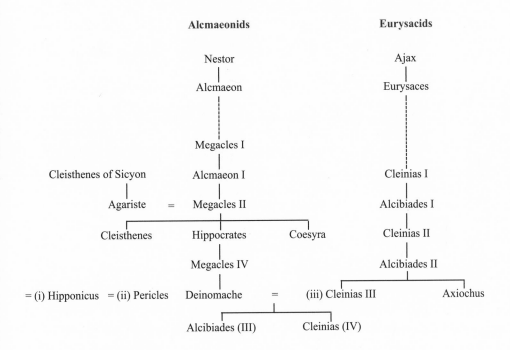

NEMESIS

INTRODUCTION

PINNING DOWN PROTEUS

> Then, may your hearts be strong and brave. Hold firm, no matter how
> he struggles, no matter what he does to try to slip from you! For he
> will try! He will take on every kind of shape of every creature on the
> earth, in water and in the dazzling air. Keep firm hold nonetheless!
> Grasp onto him more tightly!
>
> Homer, *Odyssey*, 4.115–19[1]

IN THE EARLY HOURS of an autumn night in 404 BC, in the
Persian compound at Melissa on the high Anatolian plain of central Asia
Minor, Alcibiades awoke to the acrid stench of smoke. At first he may have
thought that he was still plunged in a nightmare, for recently strange images had plagued his sleep. Just days before, he dreamt he had been lying
paralyzed and frozen, wrapped in the clothes of his mistress, the beautiful
Timandra, while, weeping, she rubbed rouge into his cheeks. Now, though,
as he crossed the room and flung open the door, the wall of heat which met
him from the blazing brushwood stacked around the threshold showed
clearly that this was no dream.[2]

What happened next reads like the stuff of fiction. Yet, though Greek
and Roman sources differ slightly in their details, they agree on the core
facts. Hurriedly Alcibiades returned to where Timandra was still lying naked

1

in a muss of tousled sheets, and urgently awoke her. Efficiently he dragged the mattress from the bed and heaved it heavily to where the fire was fiercest, while Timandra piled thick blankets all around to staunch the flames. Then he took stock. For now, the fire was curbed but the danger was not over. If he were not aware already of the peril he was in, snippets of reports that he had heard in the past weeks had alerted Alcibiades to real and present plots against his life, and now his weapons had gone missing. With no real knowledge of who was waiting in the darkness, Alcibiades needed to think fast.[3]

In the past he had survived because he did the unexpected—not only in the field of politics, but in battle, too. At Selymbria on the Propontis (the Sea of Marmara), when he found himself outnumbered, facing bristling ranks of enemy foot-soldiers, had he not bluffed his way to victory simply through his dazzling belief in his invincibility? Surely, with his luck, he could achieve the same here now.

So, wrapping a cloak around his left arm as a shield, he snatched the dagger which a friend had lent him just the night before. Then, with a last look at Timandra, he turned towards the door before, screaming his war-cry, he leapt over the still-smouldering bedding, and ran wildly out into the night. Plutarch tells how his enemies turned tail and fled, too terrified to engage with this berserker. But then the archers drew and fired; the spearmen launched their javelins; and Alcibiades fell dying on the darkened earth.

Their job done, the assassins melted back into the night. Only Timandra stayed. The fire quenched, she somehow dragged the heavy corpse back inside the house, where she wrapped it in her clothing and performed last loving rites. Then, in this strange land far from his beloved Athens, with the few who had stayed loyal to him, she buried Alcibiades.

Alcibiades' dramatic—almost filmic—death was a fitting end to an entirely unconventional life, a life that fascinated his contemporaries and captivated later generations. Enviably well-connected, strikingly handsome, immensely rich, intensely charismatic, unashamedly louche, and, like the Homeric hero Achilles, motivated by the ambition "always to be best and to surpass all others," in his lifetime Alcibiades attracted not just passionate admirers but bitter enemies jealous of his easy charm and his political success, suspicious of where his energies might lead him. And in a society driven by a moral code that advocated helping friends while harming enemies by every means imaginable, this would prove very dangerous indeed. Throughout his life, the rumour mill of his native Athens and the wider world ground out tales of his duplicity and decadence that mired him in controversy and threatened to destroy him. Meanwhile Alcibiades himself, adept at self-promotion, countered them with testimonies of his patriotic probity, until it was impossible for anyone to know with any certainty where the truth really lay. For later generations the problem was compounded by the bias of what evidence survived, so that the sources that we have today must be approached with caution.[4]

So, what are those sources, and how should they be treated by a modern biographer? The majority are literary, and some were written or begun during Alcibiades' lifetime. Chief among these is the *History* of Thucydides, which focuses on the first twenty years of the Peloponnesian War, fought between Athens (and her empire) and Sparta (and her allies). Until comparatively recently, Thucydides was lauded as an exemplary historian, forensic, detached, reliable; but modern scholarship has shown that he was, in fact, highly selective, using his narrative as a vehicle with which to explore morality, being especially interested in "the nature of power, and the effect of conflict on social values." For him, then, Alcibiades was, in part, an intriguing case study. But he may have been more than that. It is now widely accepted that Thucydides (who was in exile for many of the years about which he wrote) may have based certain episodes of his *History* on interviews with Alcibiades himself, and that his account may thus represent Alcibiades' own "spin" on some of the key events of his political life. Which means two things. On the one hand, Thucydides' evidence, once considered to be of unimpeachable value, must now be treated with greater circumspection. On the other, it may contain material that is the closest we will ever come to an autobiographical account of some of the most important moments in Alcibiades' life.[5]

Contemporary, too, are the comedies of Aristophanes, written and performed before audiences of Athenian citizen-voters throughout most of Alcibiades' adulthood. Absurdist, stylized, and highly political, Aristophanes' comedies contained hard-hitting social commentary, often choosing leading figures—the celebrities of Athens—as their targets. From the very start, these included Alcibiades and his social circle. Sometimes Alcibiades was identified by name as the butt of Aristophanes' humour; at other times (such as in *Clouds*) he provided the model for leading characters. But always his presence is felt to a greater or lesser degree. And this was true not just of Aristophanes. Other playwrights, too, appear to have been fascinated by Alcibiades' character. As the fourth-century-AD Greek rhetorician Libanius commented, "What play did not include Alcibiades [hidden] among its *dramatis personae?* Did not Eupolis and Aristophanes present him on stage? It was thanks to him that comedy was successful." But it is precisely because the plays of Aristophanes and Eupolis *were* comedies that they furnish us with such unreliable evidence. They were written not to provide historians with objective source material, but to raise laughs and win first prize at the competitive festivals of Dionysus, and to do so they were more than ready to exaggerate and distort, to slander and invent, to tap into the most scurrilous and unsubstantiated gossip of the day. So, like Thucydides' *History,* Aristophanes' comedies must be navigated with great care. While they undoubtedly contain evidence for how Alcibiades was perceived by some of his contemporaries, there is no certainty that this perception was always grounded in fact. Yet again, Alcibiades' presence can be felt, but at the same time there is a distinct sense of the absence of the real and rounded man.[6]

This is true, too, of the works of another contemporary author, the much younger philosopher Plato. Like Alcibiades, Plato was a student of Socrates, another of Athens' contentiously divisive "celebrities," whose posthumous reputation he was keen to salvage. Less than five years after Alcibiades' death, Socrates was executed, having been found guilty on two counts: of not believing in the gods of Athens and of corrupting the city's young men. His trial was essentially political. Many of the young men in question had led the savage oligarchical regime of the Thirty, which had been imposed on Athens by Sparta at the end of the Peloponnesian War, and some (such as the notorious Critias) had at one time or another been friends or supporters of Alcibiades. It was partly Plato's ambition to clear his mentor's name by scotching any suggestion that Socrates was a malign influence on the *jeunesse dorée* of Athens, and demonstrating that it was in spite and not because of his teaching that they behaved the way they did. So, when we find Alcibiades in Socrates' company in the *Symposium* and other dialogues, including two that are named from him, we must be aware of Plato's agenda: if only Alcibiades had given himself over to Socrates' teaching, his fate and that of Athens could have been very different.

Nor is Plato alone here. Xenophon, too, who may once have served under Alcibiades, was a friend of Socrates; his writings, too, reflect a desire to exculpate his mentor. Both his *Memorabilia,* a collection of Socratic conversations, and his *Hellenica,* the history of his times, must be read with this in mind.[7]

Also from the years immediately after Alcibiades' death come a series of forensic speeches, one written by Isocrates to be delivered by Alcibiades' son, two written by Lysias to be made against him. Taken together, these, more than any other documents, demonstrate the deep polarity that existed between Alcibiades' supporters and his opponents, especially as they rely on the juries' prejudicial memories of Alcibiades to influence their reactions. While Isocrates paints Alcibiades as a noble (if misunderstood) hero, Lysias vilifies him as a scheming traitor. Both exaggerate for their own ends—speeches in Athenian courts of law appealed to the emotions as much as to hard evidence—and neither should be taken at face value. Yet, they do bring in details of Alcibiades' life and background that we would otherwise not have, and that the authors would probably have hesitated to include if they were demonstrably false. Once more, however, the real Alcibiades seems to lurk just out of sight in the shadows—as he does in another speech, this time by his fellow aristocrat, the pusillanimous Andocides, accused of complicity in the scandal of the mutilation of the Herms and profanation of the Mysteries in 415, who escaped execution only by treacherously pointing the finger at others.

Even in his lifetime, then, and its immediate aftermath, the reality of Alcibiades was elusive. Different people saw in him different things, rather like the blind men in the famous Indian parable, each of whom examines a different part of an elephant in isolation.

As time went on, the problems were compounded. When the first-century BC Sicilian, Diodorus, with his interest in the rise and fall of empires, wrote his compendious *Library of History,* he was in the main content to draw unquestioningly on earlier historians such as the now-lost fourth-century Ephorus (himself a student of Isocrates). Also in the first century, the Roman polymath Cornelius Nepos chose Alcibiades as the subject of a brief biography, while a hundred or so years later the philosopher Plutarch paired the Greek Alcibiades with the Roman Coriolanus as part of his series of *Parallel Lives,* which sought to draw lessons by observing the similarities between representatives of the two cultures. But neither Nepos nor Plutarch were biographers in our sense of the word. Instead, Plutarch especially—by judicious selection and arrangement of his material—used his subjects as moral exemplars, through which to explore his own philosophical ideas. By his own admission, he intermingled the lives of those whom he considered to be good men with those whom he considered bad, and, while even Plutarch could not resist Alcibiades' charm, it is not unlikely that he felt he fell into the latter category.[8]

By the time the third-century-AD rhetorician Athenaeus wrote his "Partying Professors" (*Deipnosophistae*), seven hundred years had passed since the death of Alcibiades, but still he continued to fascinate, and the professors in question trade anecdotes and quotations galore from works of literature that have since been lost, and many of them provide otherwise unrecorded details. But, again, few should be taken at face value. For by now the evidence trail was not just cold but deeply muddied. Complicating matters was the trend in schools of rhetoric to set students the task of writing speeches to defend or prosecute figures from Greek history. Unsurprisingly, one of their favourite subjects was Alcibiades, and it is still uncertain whether a speech such as Andocides' *Against Alcibiades* is a genuine oration from around 415 or the product of a later rhetorician.

Alongside these works of literature can be placed epigraphic evidence. Surviving inscriptions, for example, help place Alcibiades by the Sea of Marmara in around 410, and his granddaughter in Cerameicus Cemetery some fifty years later. Of the greatest interest, however, are the so-called Attic Stelae. First published in the 1950s, these fragmentary inscriptions contain details of property confiscated from those, including Alcibiades, who were condemned for having profaned the Eleusinian Mysteries in 415. The details that survive provide a vivid picture of the lifestyle and possessions of members of his circle. At the same time, ongoing archaeology continues to unearth new evidence.

Even from this brief overview it can be seen that any study of Alcibiades requires not just a vigorous sifting of the available material, but a firm resolve to steer a course through the shoals and shifting sandbanks of contradictory evidence. This inevitably means that, unless we are to hem every statement round with caveats and scholarly apparatus (all of which, being contrary to the spirit of Alcibiades himself, would impede the flow and skew the reader's perception of his character), to create a coherent narrative we are sometimes forced to make hard choices over which precise path to follow. For this book is written not for the specialist but for the general reader with an interest in the many areas of human experience with which Alcibiades' biography intersects: politics and society, religion and philosophy, ambition and betrayal, and the drama of a life lived to the fullest by a subject who often seems to have been making up the rules as he went along.

There can be no denying the drama of Alcibiades' life, either in general or in specifically Greek terms. Its arc is that of the quintessential tragic hero who, from a position of great power, engineers his own destruction thanks to bad choices or flawed character. This was the pattern of many an Athenian tragedy, and one with which Alcibiades would have been totally familiar, having watched from his seat in the Theatre of Dionysus as the plays of Aeschylus and Sophocles unfolded. Like the playwrights, he would have known the maxim, "Nothing in Excess" (*mēden agan*), carved in huge letters on the marble façade of Apollo's temple at Delphi (built by his own ancestors), and recognized the orthodoxy of the formula that vaunting ambition, hubris, an assault on the laws of cosmic order, led to the gods' anger (*phthonos*) and punishment (*nemesis*). And yet, the product of an age of growing rationalism, when sophistic scientists were questioning long-held beliefs, he refused to be pinned down by stifling social niceties and tried to break the mould—only to be broken himself.

Perhaps the character from Greek drama whom Alcibiades most resembled, and who can shed most light for us on how contemporaries viewed him, was the protagonist of a tragedy that Alcibiades himself never saw. In 405, a year before the fall of Athens, when Alcibiades was in exile, Euripides' last plays were staged. They included *Bacchae,* an exploration of the destructive power of Dionysus, the god of theatre, wine, and transformation. It tells how, after many years spent in Asia, Dionysus returns to Greece, where many of the ruling class refuse to recognize his power. As a result, the cruel, charismatic god first infatuates them, then destroys them. It could almost be—indeed, perhaps it was—a parable about Alcibiades, a reflection of his amoral influence on Athens. For, like Dionysus, Alcibiades was beautiful yet merciless, a shape-shifter who (like a chameleon, says Plutarch) could transform himself to suit whatever the circumstance demanded, a determined figure cutting a lone furrow, followed by a crowd of ardent devotees. There are some today who have even gone so far as to suggest he was a psychopath.[9]

But, if the god is indeed intended to remind the audience of Alcibiades, it is the effect that *Bacchae*'s Dionysus has on those around him that is most telling, and that perhaps brings us closer than any other surviving work of literature to Alcibiades' impact on Athens and her democracy. Confident, seductive, with flashes of wry humour, he captivates not just the on-stage characters, but the theatre audience as well, subtly, and with apparent lack of effort, bringing them onside, inspiring them to see the world from his specific point of view, before leaving them stunned, bewildered by his audacity, and questioning just how they have allowed themselves to be so led astray. If modern readers can see Alcibiades in Dionysus, how much more could his contemporaries?[10]

The charismatic politician subverting the democracy, inciting a pliant People to follow him in a direction that, under other circumstances, they would hesitate to go, is a figure familiar throughout history. Familiar, too, are the circumstances which allow such a demagogue to thrive: economic turbulence, a crisis of national confidence, and war, to name a few. In some respects the story of Alcibiades, his rise to influence during the uneasy Peace of Nicias, and his call to arms in the ensuing phase of the Peloponnesian War fit neatly into this mould. However, what sets him apart and causes him still to fascinate today are not only his responses to the setbacks that he experienced at almost every step of the way, but how many of the Athenian voting public continued to believe in him despite suffering the consequence of his betrayals, how, knowing that he was the architect of their defeat, they still yearned to have him lead them, and, in the end, how his life both shaped and mirrored the fortunes of his city.

For, to appreciate the life of Alcibiades, we must also explore what was perhaps the most ambitious social experiment that had yet been undertaken anywhere on the globe: Athenian democracy. Its Greek name proclaimed its nature. *Demos* meant "the People" (specifically the majority, poorer citizens), while *kratos* meant "power": in other words, "people power," or, as one modern commentator has put it, summarizing the views of richer Athenians, "the dictatorship of the proletariat." Formed in the aftermath of tyranny, this democracy was already at its most radical when Alcibiades was born: a militia of (male) citizens, up to sixty thousand strong, each one of whom could vote on the affairs of state, while being subject to appointment, usually by lot, to every civic office imaginable, from sewage supervisor to chief magistrate. Yet even such an apparently egalitarian regime was subject to the influence of class and wealth, as aristocrats and (increasingly) industrialists, wooing the electorate through ostentatious public displays, redefined their relationship with the People and competed for influence. With no defined political parties, Athenian politics relied on popularity and patronage as much as statesmanship and skill. This was the culture in which Alcibiades grew up, and that he subsequently sought to lead.[11]

But what makes Alcibiades unique among his contemporaries is that his experience was not confined to his native city, but embraced many of the diverse cultures of his age. None of his contemporaries was as comfortable as he was, not just in democratic Athens but in the military barracks of the Spartans, the scented pleasure gardens of the Persians, or the crenellated towers of Thrace. And not only was he comfortable there, he managed to assimilate such varied ways of life that he could interact with alien societies with the ease of a native, advising and doing business with their leading lights, apparently carving out a role as an indispensable member of their communities. Alcibiades' life, then, allows us to explore many of the distinct civilizations that made up what we can all too easily refer to as the homogenous "Ancient World," reminding us that, far from being settled, Greek culture was in a state of flux, subject to constant and often unforeseen influences both at home and abroad.

As a guide to follow through the politics and social mores of the late fifth century BC Alcibiades is perhaps not the most reliable. But, since he was mercurial, if it is to try to do him justice, his biography cannot be too scholarly or dry. I hope that, in the pages that follow, the journey will prove not just instructive but entertaining, too, as befits such an extraordinary figure, a man whom the Romans called the bravest of the Greeks.[12]

PROLOGUE

A FAMILY DIVIDED

> Great exploits spark great envy, and the saying is true: good fortune,
> flowering for all time, brings with it not just happiness but tragedy.
>
> Pindar, *Pythian*, 7.19–22

ON A LATE SUMMER'S DAY in 447, two small boys, brothers of perhaps four and five years old, stood at the threshold of one of the most influential houses in all Athens. They must have been bewildered. Just a few days earlier, the pattern of their lives had been abruptly shattered when a report reached the city of how its army had been ambushed in the Muse-haunted foothills of Mount Helicon. But it was not the number of casualties which had rocked the household, appalling though they were. Nor that among the dead was the Athenian general, Tolmides. Rather, the news which smashed into the family's lives like a lightning-bolt was that, cut down at Coronea, his lifeblood drenching the dry soil, had been the brave and handsome Cleinias, the father of these little boys. The younger shared their father's name, Cleinias ("The Famous One"), while the elder was named after their paternal grandfather: Alcibiades ("Great Strength").[1]

The reason they had come to this strange, forbidding house was that, with their father dead, the law dictated that his household be dissolved. With commendable foresight, Cleinias had made provision for his sons' future should he die. They would be entrusted to a guardian, who would shape their lives now that he could do so no longer. But their mother, Deinomache ("Terrifying in Battle"), was unable to go with them. Other arrangements must be made for her. In many ways, a well-bred woman was considered as dependent as a child, so now that she was widowed, she must be returned to the protection of her closest male relative—or swiftly married to another man. So in all probability the grieving Deinomache took her fragrant chests of sumptuous dresses and her boxes glittering with jewels, and returned to her childhood home, the cool, well-columned mansion of her father, to live out the rest of her life cloistered in the bosom of her family.[2]

And what a family it was. One of the richest and most famous—certainly the most notorious—of all the old Athenian families, the Alcmaeonids had been for centuries at the pulsing heart of power. Proud aristocrats, they traced their lineage back to the Trojan War and to Nestor, King of Pylos, whose great-grandson Alcmaeon ("Strong Endeavour") had helped conquer Boeotian Thebes before forging south to Athens, where he founded a dynasty. Already by the seventh century, when the city was being governed by a group of elite families, Alcmaeonids were serving in the highest echelons of government. By 632, one of their number, Megacles I ("Great Fame"), held the coveted rank of Archon Eponymus, the leading magistrate after whom the year was named. But if his heart swelled with pride at his appointment, the stark responsibilities of power would soon almost destroy not only him but his whole family.[3]

Politics in Athens were always personal and messy. And in the year that Megacles I was Archon, Cylon, an ambitious young aristocrat, tried to stage a coup. A swaggering Olympic victor and son-in-law of the overlord of nearby Megara, Cylon whispered his ambitions to the oracle at Delphi, which advised him: "Seize Athens during the great festival of Zeus." For Cylon this could mean but one thing: he should plan his coup to coincide with the Olympic Games. So, that August, with his partisans, Cylon clattered onto the Acropolis, at that time the seat of power, cleared it of all opposition and proclaimed himself *tyrannos,* tyrant, the title given to a de facto (if unconstitutional) sole ruler.

The Athenians, however, were not so easily subdued. They laid siege to the Acropolis, and soon the sweltering heat of August took its toll on the conspirators. Too late, Cylon realized that he had misinterpreted the oracle.

It surely meant a different festival! Somehow he managed to escape, and his supporters, desperately weak from thirst and hunger, begged for clemency. Megacles I offered them safe passage from the Acropolis, but despite his oath the rebels did not entirely trust him. They tied a long rope to the Temple of Athene Polias ("Athene Who Guards the City"), along which the goddess' protecting energy might flow, and keeping hold of it they stumbled down the ramp towards the city. Then, by the chasm where the avenging Furies were believed to crouch, the rope broke. Doubtless, this was a sign from heaven! Athene had abandoned them! The citizens' anger erupted in a hail of rocks. Skulls cracked. Blood sprayed. Not even those conspirators who clung tight to the altars were allowed to live. The butchery was total.

But in the weeks that followed, ghostly apparitions were seen gliding through the nighttime streets. Sacrifices went awry. Entrail interpreters muttered darkly of a city defiled. Old men remembered how in legend Alcmaeon the dynast had transgressed primordial taboos, when he murdered his own mother, how the Furies maddened and pursued him, how death met him in squalid ambush. So now as Athens seethed with fear, thinking itself polluted by the killing of the suppliants, priests pointed trembling fingers at not just Megacles I but all his family. The Alcmaeonids fled. Not even their dead were allowed to remain. Their bones were disinterred and thrown out far across the border. And for all future generations the Alcmaeonids were held to be a family accursed. Which, for the Greeks, was no small matter. In their mythology, the dynasties of Oedipus and Agamemnon, similarly blighted by a curse, not only tore themselves apart, but undermined the very fabric of their cities. To consort with such people, then, represented a real danger. To allow them into government could be disastrous.[4]

For the Alcmaeonids, however, exile and an eternal curse were merely obstacles to be overcome. Within a generation they were back, recalled to Athens in 594 by the fearless general-cum-lawgiver-cum-poet Solon, a triumph which Megacles I's son, another Alcmaeon (I), capped a mere two years later by winning the prestigious chariot race at the Olympic Games of 592, the first Athenian to do so. Horses and chariots were the preserve of the aristocratic elite, and the Alcmaeonids loved the sport of racing more than any other. But the costs were astronomical. Where did the money come from? Rumours abounded. One told of a journey which Alcmaeon

I once made to Sardis, to the court of the fabulously wealthy Lydian King Croesus. When Croesus, ever generous, offered his guest as much gold as he could carry, Alcmaeon put on the tallest, widest boots that he could find, and packed them tight with gold dust; in the folds of his capacious robes he carried more; he even ladled gold dust into his hair and beard and crammed his mouth with it. When Croesus saw him, lumbering bloated from the treasury, he was so delighted that he presented Alcmaeon with double the amount.[5]

At home Alcmaeon's ingenuity (and wealth) won him a generalship. He commanded the Athenian contingent when an allied army, led by Cleisthenes, the tyrant of Sicyon, fought for control of the Delphic oracle, ultimately winning victory through biological warfare: the allies introduced hellebore into the enemy's water supply, causing debilitating diarrhea, which forced surrender.[6]

Now on a par with kings, Alcmaeon celebrated when his son, also called Megacles (II), married his old ally Cleisthenes' daughter, Agariste. Again the rumours swirled. Cleisthenes, they said, had tested Agariste's suitors for a full year, and it looked as though another Athenian would win: Hippocleides, a member of the powerful Philaid dynasty. But at the final banquet, tunic-clad and fired by alcohol, Hippocleides was inspired to leap onto a table and dance, at one point standing on his head and waving his legs lustily. The Greeks being strangers to underwear, Cleisthenes was unimpressed, Hippocleides was dismissed in shaming silence, and Megacles II won Agariste's hand.[7]

The next generations of Alcmaeonids strode even further centre stage. Despite the best efforts of social reformers such as Solon, by the mid-sixth century Athens was again in turmoil, as its most powerful families competed for supreme control. By 555, Megacles II recognized that he could not win, threw his support behind his rival, Peisistratus, and bolstered his position by giving his daughter, Coesyra, to Peisistratus in marriage. It was not a success. Peisistratus refused to father children, baulking at the thought that they would inherit the Alcmaeonid curse; Coesyra complained of the deviant sex acts which he insisted she perform. Peisistratus was forced to flee. But in 546, he returned at the head of a great army, defeated Megacles II near Marathon, and installed himself once more as Athens' tyrant, a position he still held at his death in 528.[8]

Some Alcmaeonids may have reached an understanding with Peisistratus. Others trooped off once more into exile. At Delphi, in the wake of a devastating fire, they funded the restoration of the Temple of Apollo, thereby ingratiating themselves with the priests and earning their support against the family of Peisistratus. At last their investment paid off. In 514, Peisistratus' son and successor, Hippias, responded to the assassination of his brother by instigating a reign of terror. The time was ripe for intervention. Just four years later, Megacles II's son, Cleisthenes (named after his maternal grandfather), rode into Athens at the head of a liberating army. Hippias and his family made a hasty exit east to Persia, whose power was rapidly expanding, and where they found refuge at the court of the Great King.[9]

Yet even now the Alcmaeonids were not home and dry. Citing the family curse, a rival backed by Sparta forced Cleisthenes from Athens. But it was the briefest of exiles. The new regime was so repressive that the Athenian People rose up, drove out the Spartan puppet, and recalled Cleisthenes, who shrewdly recognized that times had changed. For while rich men might still hold power in Athens, to retain that power they clearly needed the agreement and support of the People. Which was why he set out to change the constitution.[10]

Later Athenians hailed Cleisthenes' reforms as the birth of their democracy. They were certainly far-reaching. There had always been tensions between not just Athens' powerful families but the rural, coastal, and urban poor. Now, to counter these and build political coherence, Cleisthenes created a new social structure in which every citizen belonged to one of ten new tribes, each named from ancient heroes and made up of smaller units, "demes," located in the city, countryside, and coast. At the same time he extended membership of both legal and legislative bodies to a wider range of social classes. And not just that. From now on, most of the key positions would be filled by lot, with every tribe being represented equally. At the constitution's legislative heart was the Popular Assembly (which met several times a month to debate motions put forward by the Council, itself made up of fifty men chosen at random from each tribe); while at its ideological heart was the concept of *isonomia,* equality (for male citizens at least) before the law.[11]

Among the only offices to which Cleisthenes allowed appointment to be made by merit were those of the ten generals, top military commanders who must be equally proficient on both land and sea (though even here, as far as possible, each tribe elected one general). The wisdom of this departure from the norm could soon be seen, for by the start of the fifth century, the Greek world was fighting for survival.[12]

The Persian Empire had expanded west at an alarming rate, devouring the nations on its borders. With the fall of Croesus' Lydia, the Persians reached Ionia and the ribbon of Greek city-states strung out along the Aegean's Asiatic coast. It was a powerful enemy and an alluring friend. In 507, when Sparta threatened Athens shortly after Cleisthenes had been restored, the Athenians sought Persia's help. The Persians agreed. On one condition. When they came to negotiate with their satrap, the provincial governor now based at Croesus' old capital, Sardis, the Athenians must bring with them jars of their native earth and water. And so they did. Only to realize too late that, by doing so, they had symbolically made themselves subjects of Persia. Cleisthenes himself may have headed the legation. At any rate, in addition to being cursed, the Alcmaeonids were now accused of "medizing," of sympathizing with the Medes (as the Athenians called the Persians).[13]

Events moved quickly. While Athens claimed that it had never meant to surrender its independence, Ionia, inspired by Athens' brave new democratic experiment, rose up against its Persian masters. Beginning in 499, the rebellion quickly spread—south to Cyprus, north to the Hellespont and Byzantium. But the Greek states were no match for the Persian juggernaut. Ephesus fell. City after city followed. At last only Miletus held out. And then, just five years after the revolt began, it, too, was crushed, and the Persians turned their eyes towards the Greek mainland. Three times they launched invasions against Greece, each one more deadly than the last. In 492, their first fleet foundered in a storm off the rocky cape of Athos in the north Aegean Sea. In 490, their second army scrambled for their ships at Marathon when the Athenians, devastatingly outnumbered but daringly led by the brilliant Miltiades, charged with the dawn and slaughtered them by the thousand. Only the third invasion force, ten years later, seemed likely to succeed. Smashing through the Spartan shield line at Thermopylae and acquitting themselves well against the allied fleet at Artemisium, the Persians took Athens and torched the city. But within days the Athenian general, bull-necked Themistocles, had lured the invaders to defeat in the choppy seas at Salamis, and the next year, at Plataea, the Greeks won a great victory that sent the Persians limping home for the last time.[14]

In the years that followed, Athens blossomed, first as the leader of the Delian League, set up by Greek states for their mutual protection against Persia, then, thanks to her fragile scruples and strong navy (which policed the League to her advantage), as the head of an Empire. In this new dispensation the Alcmaeonids bloomed, too. Cleisthenes' nephew, Megacles IV, shrugged off the latest accusations of medizing (it was said the family had flashed a shield signal to the Persians at Marathon), and settled down to enjoy his wealth and racing.[15]

For a man like Megacles IV, the great circuit of international sporting festivals was a chance to show off his wealth and charisma. At the Olympic Games—and other games held at Isthmia near Corinth, at Nemea, and at Delphi—his horses thundered round the hippodrome to the raucous cheers of thousands of spectators. Already in 486 (in a lull between Persian invasions), he had been able to commission the great praise-poet Pindar to commemorate his victory in the four-horse chariot race at Delphi, blazoning the glory of the Alcmaeonids and lauding the dynasty's freshly proclaimed piety in rebuilding the temple of Apollo:

> Athens' mighty city is the fairest prelude to the song,
> which the Alcmaeonids, their family powerful far and wide,
> can set as the foundation of this paean to their horses.
> For what city or what household
> can you name,
> more shining in the whole of Greece?
> In every land men speak of these Athenians, Apollo,
> and how they beautified your shrine at Delphi.
> Five victories at Isthmia,
> one—wonderful!—at the Olympic Games of Zeus,
> and two at Delphi—yours and your ancestors'—
> inspire my song.
> My heart leaps at this new success.
> But even so I sorrow.
> Great exploits spark great envy, and the saying is true:
> good fortune, flowering for all time, brings with it
> not just happiness but tragedy.[16]

Stark though those last lines are, they encapsulate a common classical belief: too much success, too much prosperity, or even too much happiness is dangerous. It can lead to hubris, the transgression of the limits which the gods place on humanity. And sooner or later that mortal hubris would be punished by *nemesis,* divine retribution. Much better, then, to steer a path of moderation, as the pithy dictum inscribed beneath the pediment of the Alcmaeonids' Temple of Apollo at Delphi proclaimed: *mēden agan,* nothing in excess.[17]

Yet it was for riches and racing, not for moderation that the Alcmaeonids lived, and Megacles IV made sure his children knew it. He instilled in his son a love of horses, so that in 436, in keeping with the family tradition, he, too, won the Olympic chariot race. As for his daughter, Deinomache, when she reached the cusp of puberty and was old enough for marriage, he chose as her husband Hipponicus. That his name meant "Horse Victory" was by-the-by. What really mattered was that Hipponicus was the richest man in Athens, if not all Greece.[18]

But, beautiful and brooding, Deinomache was not entirely made for married life. When she had borne two sons and heirs, Hipponicus divorced her. Not that this mattered much to Megacles IV. She had already given him two grandsons. She had already bound Hipponicus tightly to him. Instead, he saw the divorce as an opportunity to forge strong ties with another powerful figure, an up-and-coming politician, the son, it happened, of a female Alcmaeonid cousin. Such blood-ties did not disturb the Greeks, for whom the mother was nothing but the incubator of the father's seed. Rather, the allure of marrying a daughter to a relative was that the dowry stayed in the family. And, when that relative was Pericles, the prospect of close marriage-ties was irresistible.

Intensely charismatic and a mesmerizing orator, by the early 450s, when the nuptials took place, Pericles was fast consolidating his position not just as Athens' leading statesman but as the champion of the Alcmaeonids. For much of the 460s, Cimon, son of Miltiades, the hero of Marathon and leader of the rival Philaid dynasty, had dominated politics, pursuing a rigorously anti-Persian and pro-Spartan foreign policy. But in 464, his grip on power unravelled when he tried to help the Spartans quell a slave revolt. Suspicious of the motives of his democratic task force, Sparta humiliated the Athenians by ordering them off her land, and when Cimon returned home he found that his enemies had amended the constitution, under-mining his allies among the city's establishment and placing more power in the hands of the People. Now in 460, with Cimon forced abroad, Pericles was goading Sparta, stoking the coals of war, provoking a conflict which he hoped would end in the lasting supremacy of Athens.[19]

But while he could bend the People to his will, even the imposing Pericles was no match for Deinomache. They had two sons before agreeing that, as a couple, they were incompatible. And so it was with her consent that, in around 453, Deinomache married for the third and possibly last time, although it was perhaps the first time that she had been consulted. Her new husband would be Cleinias, at around thirty (roughly the age Deinomache was now) an up-and-coming figure on the Athenian political scene, and soon to be the father of our Alcibiades. Like Deinomache, Cleinias was a force to be reckoned with. Sprung from a distinguished lineage, he was ambitious for the future.[20]

Cleinias, too, could trace his family back to a hero of the Trojan War, the bravest of the Greeks after Achilles: Ajax, who fathered his one son, Eurysaces, with a captive Phrygian princess. Like the Alcmaeonids, rehabilitated in the wake of their curse—like, too, the forebears of Hipponicus—Cleinias' family was close to the sixth-century lawgiver Solon. Indeed it was still rumoured that the families of Hipponicus and Cleinias owed some of their great riches to insider trading at the time of Solon's reforms. In 594, told in confidence that Solon meant to cancel all debts owed on land, the two men borrowed heavily and bought up huge tracts of the Athenian countryside. When Solon's law was passed they kept their new estates and refused to repay their creditors.[21]

The family prospered, forging new ties and foreign contacts not only among Athens' natural allies, the Ionian Greeks of Miletus and the Asiatic coast, but in Sparta, too. With one leading Spartan family they cemented the friendship-link of *xenia,* a relationship between individuals and households of different city-states, designed to ensure mutual support and built on a foundation of shared hospitality. And to mark his Spartan links, Cleinias I called his own son by the name of his Spartan *xenos,* Alcibiades (I). Not only that. They were appointed Spartan *proxenoi,* Sparta's official represen-tatives in Athens, whose role ranged from hosting Spartan delegations to backing Spartan interests.[22]

During the Persian invasions, the family rallied with enthusiasm to defend their homeland. Embracing the brilliant advice of the People's advocate, Themistocles, Athens built a fleet of two hundred triremes, a new model of sleek, expensive warships, as graceful as dolphins, as deadly as sharks, which could ram and cripple enemy vessels before nimbly backing off to safety. The family's current head, another Cleinias (II), not only volunteered to finance and captain a trireme and its crew of two hundred men, but in battle with the Persians at Artemisium fought with such panache that he was awarded the *aristeia,* the prize given to the fighter singled out as the best of all the Greeks.[23]

As Pindar warned, however, to be outstanding is to invite envy. Ever since the harsh reign of the tyrant Hippias, the Athenians feared powerful men's ambitions, so, to check them (and also to avoid protracted stalemates between two rival interests), they had instituted the practice of ostracism. Each year they could choose to vote on whether to expel one of their leading politicians from the city for ten years without loss of his prestige or property, after which period he was free to return and resume his former life.[24]

The day of the ostracism was charged and raucous, as citizens jostled in the Agora, each inscribing the name of his chosen candidate on a fragment of broken pottery (*ostrakon* in Greek), queuing to deposit it in the jar that served as ballot box, waiting for the result to be announced—and in 460 it was Alcibiades II, the son of Cleinias II, hero of Artemisium, who felt the People's anger. His family's Spartan connections had been his undoing. Sparta's highhanded action in rejecting the task force sent by Athens to help crush her slave revolt had far-reaching consequences, and the backlash was such that anyone with Spartan ties was seriously suspect. As Spartan *proxenos,* Alcibiades II was a target for the People's wrath. Despite desperately trying to distance himself from Sparta by renouncing the *proxeny,* his views were so clearly at odds with the public mood and policies that there was little he could do. First scapegoated, then ostracized, he sailed east to Asia Minor and the sumptuous trading-city of Miletus, leaving behind the eldest son of his first marriage, Cleinias III, now winning a name for himself as one of most promising young men in Pericles' Athens.

Built at the southern entrance of a wide and shallow bay, Miletus had been ransacked by the Persians at the end of the Ionian Revolt. Since then, though, it had been revitalized. Thoroughly modern now, wide streets criss-crossed the squat peninsula between its two great harbours, a nucleus for trade and enterprise, a melting pot for new ideas. Philosophers had long thrived here: Thales, who used geometry to measure the Egyptian pyramids and astronomy to predict eclipses; Anaximenes, who sought scientific causes for the earth's creation; Anaximander, who first mapped the world. Ideas and speculation fired one friend of the exiled Alcibiades II in particular: Antiochus, who cared so little for tradition that he educated even his daughters to the highest standards. So captivated by these girls was Alcibiades II that he married one and, when his period of ostracism ended, brought both her and her sister, Aspasia, back home with him to Athens.[25]

Things in his absence had moved on. Athens' empire had expanded to include the mainland cities of Boeotia to the north. Moreover, his son, Cleinias III, had formed close links with Pericles. He had not only married Deinomache, Pericles' former wife, but would soon be entrusted to draw up new rules to ensure that tribute paid by city-states in Athens' empire arrived in full and on time. And to cap it all, Alcibiades was now grandfather to two boys, the elder of whom, in accordance to tradition, shared his name.[26]

But dark clouds were massing. In 447, Boeotia rose up in arms, and Athens sent a thousand *hoplites,* heavy infantry, to stamp out the rebellion. A last farewell, and Cleinias III was marching north. At Chaeronea he and his fellow soldiers were victorious, but at Coronea, in maquis of the foothills of Mount Helicon above the shallow Lake Copaïs, the Boeotians ambushed them. Caught in a trap, the Athenians fought on stubbornly, but they had no hope. Close to a temple of Athene, Cleinias and many of his comrades were cut down. Others were rounded up and herded off as captives. Athens' land empire lay in tatters. And in Cleinias's house, plunged into mourning, contingencies, which everyone had hoped would never be required, were hastily put into action.[27]

Deinomache knew what she must do: return to the protection of her father, Megacles IV. But what of her two boys? Because the laws of inheritance, which Solon had set down, forbade anyone to act as a child's guardian who stood to profit from his death, their immediate relations could not care for them. Instead, Cleinias had made it clear that, should he die, he wished his sons to become wards of a close friend, a man who had not only been his own staunchest ally in the cut and thrust of politics, but with whose family his sons shared bonds of blood: Pericles.[28]

Which was why on that late summer day the two boys, Alcibiades (III) and Cleinias (IV), were bundled through the streets of Athens to Pericles' house. Now, until their adulthood, Pericles—and his brother Ariphron, who had agreed to share responsibility—would be accountable for their education, well-being, and upbringing.[29]

No longer would they be delighted by their mother's stories of their ancestors; of how their grandfather had raced his chariot to victory in clouds of dust and pounding hooves; of how, like a golden statue, Alcmaeon had lurched from Croesus' treasury; of how their family had helped to win the Trojan War. Now their future would be shaped by Pericles, a man who, although a blue-blooded aristocrat, eschewed the flamboyant pursuits of his class so that he might be perceived to be a man of the People, a man who, ambitious, ruthless, and self-disciplined, took such pride in his dignity that he never laughed or smiled, a man who ran his household like the tightest ship, a man who was used to being obeyed. As the children left the sun-drenched street and stepped inside that oddly silent house, neither they nor their new guardians could know quite what domestic challenges the next few years would bring.[30]

1

REARING THE LION CUB

> You were instructed by a language teacher, a music master and an
> athletic trainer—not to become a specialist or a professional, but so
> that you might be as educated as a free individual should be.
>
> Plato, *Protagoras,* 312b

IT WAS IN LATE OCTOBER, with the nights drawing in and a
chill already sharpening the air, that Alcibiades officially received his name.
The Athenian calendar was alive with festivals, but the first in which anyone
participated—albeit passively—was the Apaturia, a celebration of the family.
Over three days, members of kinship-groups, or *phratriai,* assembled in local
halls and private houses throughout Attica for rowdy feasts and sacrifice.
On the third day, boys born during the past year were presented by their
fathers to their clan. A sheep or goat was slaughtered, an oath sworn to declare the child's legitimacy, and the infant's name was entered in the family
register. Then the celebrations began. It was not for nothing that the next
day was known as Epibda, the day of reckoning, hangover day.[1]

So now for the first time, with his father and his family crowding round,
the name was written down: Alcibiades Cleiniou Scambonides, Alcibiades,
the son of Cleinias, of the deme Scambonidae—a name rooted to the very
core of Athens. For, not only was the family of proud Athenian stock, the

deme Scambonidae was sited at the city's heart, in the area which embraced two hills: the Pnyx, where the Athenian Assembly was held, and the Hill of the Muses.[2]

Scambos meant "crooked," and the name reflected the neighbourhood, a maze of narrow streets tacking up rocky slopes, alleyways zigzagging towards houses whose rooftops commanded fine views not only of the mountains and the plain of Attica, the city and the sea, but of the sheer walls of the Acropolis. Most evenings, its rock-face would glow rich crimson in the setting sun, while, shimmering on its summit, the great bronze statue of Athene Promachos ("Athene, Who Fights in the Front Line") stood watch, her spear-tip glinting like a living flame against the darkening purple of the sky. But of the temples and shrines that had once adorned the Acropolis, when Alcibiades was born all lay in blackened ruins, burnt by the Persians a generation earlier—a silent memorial, a reminder of lost lives and unfinished business—while such column drums as had survived were ostentatiously built into the citadel's new retaining wall, clearly visible from the Agora below.[3]

As a member of the deme Scambonidae, Alcibiades belonged automatically to the Leontis tribe, named from the mythical—and obscure—Leos. Five generations earlier, when Solon named Attica's new tribes, he sent a list of fifty heroes from Athenian mythology to the oracle at Delphi, from which he asked it to choose ten. But even in Athens there may have been some who had never heard of Leos. His only claim to fame was that, a minor herald, he had saved King Theseus from being killed in ambush. For the Leontis tribe, though, this was not enough, so they invented a sequel to the story, in which Leos' daughters performed an enduring act of noble patriotism, sacrificing themselves fearlessly to save their war-torn country.[4]

Of course, the five-year-old Alcibiades can have had no memory of his first Apaturia, but even for a little boy the realities of war and patriotic sacrifice were all too starkly clear. With his father, Cleinias, killed in the ambush at Coronea, and his mother, Deinomache, forced to return to her childhood home without her children, Alcibiades and his younger brother were hustled off to the house of their new guardian, Pericles.

But Pericles had other matters on his mind. The expedition against Boeotia, in which Cleinias had died, had been disastrous, its defeat ruining any hopes that Athens might have entertained of forming a land empire.

Not only that. Sensing her weakness, disillusioned allies and reluctant members of her maritime empire, too, were rising in revolt—Megara to the west; Euboea to the east—while, in 446, the old enemy, Sparta, with whom Athens had been fighting for the past four years, marched into Attica and laid waste her villages and crops.[5]

A major shift in foreign policy was needed fast. Determined to cling to his position of authority, Pericles led an army to Eleusis just ten miles northwest of Athens, where the Spartan army was encamped. Here, near the site of one of the most sacred sanctuaries in Greece, he entered into secret negotiations with the Spartan king, Pleistoanax, after which the Spartans returned meekly home. Precisely what the two men said cannot be known. In Sparta, Pleistoanax was put on trial for accepting bribes; he was condemned, and exiled. As for Pericles, when he filed his official accounts, he included the extravagant sum of ten talents under the heading, "for necessary purposes." Even so, soon after, reversing its policy of hostility towards Sparta and signing a thirty-year peace treaty, Athens was forced to concede her hard-won mainland territories.[6]

Rebellious allies were brought back into line; stability within the Empire was restored; great revenues continued to pour into Athens' coffers, both from taxation on subject states and from the state silver mines at Laurium in southeast Attica and gold mines in her north Aegean territories; but still Athens' pride was dented. Ambitious personally to re-establish it, Pericles needed to act tirelessly and swiftly. Assembling a doughty core of statesmen and intellectuals, he sent them west to the instep of Italy to found a new town, Thurii, whose citizens, drawn from a diversity of Greek-speaking states, would (he hoped) live in harmony, a blueprint for a brave new Panhellenic world, which would recognize its debt of genesis to Athens.[7]

At the same time, at home he inaugurated a bold new project to rebuild temples sacked by the Persians a generation earlier. It caused a frenzy of patriotic action. To the northeast of the city, the quarries of Mount Pentelicum clanged to the arrhythmic beat of chisel against marble, along rutted roads strong ox-carts laden with rough-hewn stone groaned down towards the city, and high on the Acropolis, where tall cranes towered against the skyline, a forest of columns began to sprout and grow, the exoskeleton of the exquisite jewel-box of a temple which would in time be called the Parthenon. It was the beginning of an ambitious if controversial programme,

Athens: Pericles' vision of a resurgent Athens is encapsulated in the buildings on
the Acropolis. (Photograph by the author.)

inspirational to some, to others threatening. One rival politician, Thucydides
Melesiou, had attacked Pericles in the Assembly on the grounds that he was
misappropriating the tribute paid by Athens' subject states for a vanity
project to further his own career, and causing the Acropolis to look like
nothing so much as a heavily painted courtesan. So deep did divisions run
within Athenian society that an ostracism was declared. Thucydides was condemned and exiled for ten years; Pericles emerged triumphant; but to consolidate and maintain his position as Athens' "first citizen" required every
ounce of energy and focus.[8]

Or perhaps not quite every ounce. A little before Alcibiades and Cleinias arrived on his doorstep, Pericles had welcomed another exotic addition
to his home—the beguiling Aspasia, whom Alcibiades II had brought to

Athens from Miletus, his new wife's sister. With her quicksilver wit, incisive intellect, and melting eyes, Aspasia had captivated Pericles. Which placed him in an awkward situation. In late 451, just months before Aspasia's arrival in the city, he had carried a law effectively preventing marriage between Athenians and foreigners by forbidding any resulting children from becoming citizens. Now, though, and perhaps for one of the only times in his life, passion seriously discomposed the cerebral politician. He had only to meet her, and his devotion to Aspasia became notorious. He could not even leave his house, the rumour-mongers gloated, without embracing her and showering her with kisses—a scandalous situation in a city where most marriages were arranged and love between spouses was rare.[9]

For political enemies and idle gossips alike, the relationship provided endless ammunition. Not that they were content to stick to the facts. In such a male-centric society as Athens, clever, educated women were a threat, an aberration, polar opposites of the submissive wifely norm, and so (the prurient-minded argued) they must be as deviant morally as they were intellectually. Little wonder, then, that Aspasia's reputation suffered as a result. With her name meaning "Joy," it was all too easy to argue that she was nothing but a high-class courtesan, that she ran a brothel, that she slept her way into the upper echelons of Athenian society—and that she was the guiding power behind Pericles' policies. Comic dramatists, whose societal role included pouring as much vituperative scorn upon the mighty as they could, saw in Aspasia an easy target. Where lofty, inapproachable Pericles was their city's Zeus, Aspasia was the wily Hera, queen of gods and men. One comedian waxed eloquent. "The goddess of buggery," he wrote, "gave birth to bitch-faced Aspasia to be [Pericles'] Hera."[10]

Aspasia bore Pericles a son, whom—although he could not take him to the Apaturia for enrolment—he could not resist naming after himself. So, what with the demands of politics and his new-found domestic bliss, Pericles had little time for his two legitimate sons, let alone for Cleinias' orphans. Not that fathers did spend much time with children. Nannies played a much more active role. And young Alcibiades' nanny—originally part of Cleinias' household, with its historical Spartan ties, who accompanied the boys when they left it—was a Spartan slave, Amycla. While Spartan men were notoriously tough, Spartan women were (if anything) even tougher. In the rest of the Greek world, free-born girls from a young age were required to be demure, domestic, deferential. Not so in Sparta. Here alone girls exercised in public, honing their bodies, building their strength, undergoing the rigorous physical training which would enable them to bear staunch, fearless warrior sons. And their iron-hard physique was matched by a merciless lack of maternal sentiment.[11]

Stories about these spitfires abounded. Asked why only Spartan women could control their menfolk, Gorgo (wife of King Leonidas, who fell fighting the Persians at Thermopylae) replied: "Because only Spartan women give birth to proper men." Another, learning that her son had died bravely in battle, quipped, "Yes, he was brave, but Sparta has many better men than he was." And when a Spartan captive, sold into slavery, was asked to list her skills, she retorted: "Being free."[12]

It is unlikely, though, that Amycla had ever enjoyed freedom. Perhaps she was a Helot, one of the oppressed underclass, the indigenous inhabitants of the Spartan territories of Laconia and Messenia, who outnumbered their masters by at least ten to one, and whose revolt just seven years before, in 464, had eventually been put down with the greatest savagery. If so, she may well have been even more embittered and less nurturing than a free-born Spartan woman, for Helots were treated with inhuman cruelty. Each year, the Spartans declared war on them, a technicality which allowed Helots to be arbitrarily killed without fear of sanctions. How Amycla viewed her new charge, Alcibiades, a precocious high-born Athenian with a patrician Spartan name, can only be imagined.[13]

A nanny being a woman, her sphere of influence was confined to the house. When outside, a well-bred boy was supervised by a *paidagogos,* a male slave whose role it was to accompany him to classes, ensure that he did not get up to mischief, and protect him from the wrong kind of attention from the wrong kind of older man. Nurse and *paidagogos,* therefore, played a role akin to that of surrogate parents, but in Alcibiades' case they made for a distinctly odd couple. For, whereas Pericles' choice of Amycla as nanny implies a desire for strict discipline, his choice of *paidagogos* was baffling in the extreme. He assigned the task to Zopyrus, a Thracian slave, who was too old and infirm for any other work.[14]

As a rule Athenians were disdainful of Thracians. They believed them to be unsophisticated, uncouth drinkers of strong wine, whose tattooed bodies clearly proclaimed them to be not only different from but inferior to Greeks.

Which was not to say that merchants and politicians were not prepared to do business with them. Stretching for a march of many days from Macedonia northeast to the Danube, the Thracian kingdoms were vast and wealthy, their revenue at least a match for Athens' Empire. And on the fringes of these Thracian territories, in the north Aegean and on the northern shores of both the Sea of Marmara and the Black Sea, Athenian colonists vied for valuable concessions, mining for gold or farming on the rolling fertile plains, whose grain, shipped through the Bosporus and Hellespont in lumbering convoys, was increasingly relied upon to feed their mother city.[15]

Zopyrus' lot was unenviable, for although it was generally held that a *paidagogos* should at all times be obeyed, Alcibiades was already proving himself headstrong, and with a distinct lack of deference to authority. Or so later stories would record. One concerned a game of knucklebones, popular with children, in which a handful of the pastern bones of sheep or goats were thrown onto the ground, and points awarded according to how they fell. Alcibiades and his friends were playing in a narrow lane. Alcibiades took his throw. But before he could check his score, a heavy cart heaved round the corner. The knucklebones lay directly in its path. It was vital they should not be disturbed! Alcibiades yelled to the driver to stop. To no avail. The cart kept coming. His friends scattered, flattening themselves against the warm stone walls to let the wagon past. Not Alcibiades. Instead he ran into its path and flung himself down on the rutted street in front of it. Only just in time the driver reined in his team. A moment's pause. And then the boys ran shouting to their friend, while onlookers and *paidagogoi* fussed or flapped around him.[16]

Impossible to confirm or disprove, this episode is typical of anecdotes which cling to the young Alcibiades. It is as if dark clouds have opened to let forth a shaft of light, in which, for a moment, the golden boy stands centre stage. Already his character shines through: bold where his companions are timid, imperious where they are yielding, prepared to risk everything, his safety and his life, to get his own way. To win. Classical Greeks believed that personality, shaped in early life, changed little if at all in adulthood—which is perhaps why a cluster of other tales that focus on Alcibiades' precociousness concern specific aspects of his education.[17]

In the fifth century BC, the vast majority of Athenian boys received only the most modest schooling. Although the community was coming to rely increasingly on writing—for recording laws and treaties, posting military call-up lists, and scratching names of candidates for ostracism on bits of broken pottery—many Athenians possessed only very basic literacy. For the most part it was still an oral society. Poetry was sung and recited, but rarely read; decrees were proclaimed by town criers; politics were debated in rousing speeches. So there was little need for peasant farmers, vase-painters, or shoemakers to read or write; for them, education consisted of the passing on of skills.[18]

Not so for the elite. In Greek society these elite were called (primarily, one suspects, by themselves) the *kalokagathoi,* those who are both beautiful (*kaloi*) and noble (*agathoi*), and much of the education of a young male aristocrat was aimed at developing both of these attributes. Nobility was encouraged through exposure not only to inspiring literature (specifically the epic poems of Homer, which boys were expected to copy out and learn by heart) but to the right kind of music, which was believed to embody and have the potential to arouse noble sentiment. Physical beauty, the beauty of the human form, was honed through rigorous exercise, specifically running and wrestling. And in each of these disciplines, if we can believe our sources, Alcibiades asserted his individuality from a young age, while at the same time revealing a disturbing tendency towards bitterness or violence if he did not win or get his own way.[19]

Two anecdotes involve Homer. In one, Zopyrus takes his young charge to an outstandingly qualified schoolmaster, whose boast is that he has made his own edition of the Homeric epics. "If you're so clever that you can correct Homer, what are you doing teaching boys to read?" Alcibiades quips. "Can't you find work at a higher level?" Modern schoolteachers, the butt of similar wisecracks, may sympathize with their classical colleague. Still more with another, the victim of not sarcasm but fists. When slightly older, Alcibiades, out and about one day and perhaps wanting to check a reference, approaches a schoolmaster, asks if he has one of the books of Homer, and (not unsurprisingly, given the bulkiness of manuscripts) receives the answer, "No." Alcibiades' response is to punch the poor man, leave him stunned and helpless, and walk away.[20]

Even when fighting was legitimate, the young Alcibiades chose to play by his own rules. Much of a young aristocrat's time was spent at gymnasia, or fitness schools. Here, oiled and naked, young men sparred, toning flesh and honing muscle, striving to sculpt their bodies into mirror-images of those idealized statues of their gods which presided over much of civic life. Here, too, they talked, discussing everything from gossip to philosophy, avidly absorbing the latest theories of fellow members, scholars, and intellectuals.

There were three public gymnasia, all outside the city walls. Two were reserved for free-born citizens: the Lyceum, situated to the northeast near the Temple of Apollo, the Wolf God (Lycaeus), from which it took its name; and the Academy to the northwest, near the shrine of the hero Academus in a luxuriantly landscaped setting, rippling with streams and fountains, and furnished with not just a running track but leafy walks. A third public *gymnasion,* Cynosarges ("White Dog"), near the walls to the northeast, was for non-citizens. There were also numerous *palaistrai,* wrestling schools, some founded by retired former champions. Strict regulations governed wrestling and, to ensure they were adhered to, referees were armed with long sticks.[21]

For Alcibiades, though, even as a boy, winning was everything, and once, when it seemed he must be thrown, he sank his teeth so hard into his opponent's arm that he almost bit right through it. Blood spurted; Alcibiades broke free; and when the other boy accused him of fighting like a woman, Alcibiades retorted: "Me? No! *I* fight like a lion." A well-known private *palaistra* run by the formidable Sibyrtius was the setting for a rather darker story told of Alcibiades. Here, in the heat of anger, he was said to have struck one of his slave-attendants with a club and killed him. As with so many rumours, it is impossible to know the truth, but Alcibiades' life was to be littered with unpredictable and violent outbursts.[22]

In later years, Alcibiades would be accused of refusing to take part in athletic contests, because to do so meant competing with the low-born and ill-educated. But as a young man, training with his social equals, he put in valuable hours at the *palaistra,* hours which had a pleasing effect on his physique. For, as Alcibiades grew, so did his physical beauty. Soon he was recognized as the handsomest youth in Athens, and it was a reputation he was jealous to uphold. Which brought him into conflict with the third of his three trainers, his music master. As well as singing, boys were trained to play the seven-stringed lyre and the *aulos,* a reed instrument, not unlike the oboe, but which (like the modern Armenian *duduk*) produced a faintly buzzing sound and required considerable puff. Again, Alcibiades was sent to the best tutor: Pronomus, a master of the instrument.[23]

But Alcibiades categorically refused to play it. Many believed it was because it made his cheeks bulge unappealingly. This, though, was not the reason he put forward. Rather, he argued that, although while playing the lyre one could sing or speak, the *aulos* made this impossible. "Leave *auloi* to the Boeotians, bad conversationalists all of them!" Furthermore, to lend gravitas to his argument, he cited Athene and Apollo. Although Athene invented the *aulos*, she, too, refused to play it when she saw how it distorted her features, while lyre-playing Apollo challenged Marsyas, a virtuoso on the *aulos*, to a contest that involved each singing to the accompaniment of his chosen instrument. For Marsyas this was, of course, impossible, and Apollo celebrated his victory by having his rival flayed alive. Whether it was Alcibiades or later biographers who drew these parallels with mythology, even as a boy he was so influential that increasing numbers of his contemporaries, too, refused to pick up the *aulos*, with the result that an instrument, which ever since the Persian Wars had enjoyed an almost faddish popularity among the cultural elite, was dropped from the curriculum.[24]

There may, of course, be another reason for Alcibiades' rejection of the *aulos*, one which would fit perfectly with his character. He may simply have been no good at it. Whatever he did, Alcibiades was determined to win at all costs, and where it was clearly impossible to win, he would rather not take part. With his half-brother Callias, son of Hipponicus, not to mention his friend Critias, well-known for their prowess on the *aulos*, Alcibiades may have realised that he could never compete. Instead, he came up with persuasive arguments why the game was not worth the candle, while at the same time undermining any cachet which his coevals might earn from their musical ability.[25]

Precocious, dangerous, his beauty blossoming, from an early age Alcibiades both basked in the power of his charisma and knew how to manipulate it. For patrician young Athenians, part of their path to maturity involved taking older male lovers. Men between the ages of eighteen and thirty (at which time they usually married) would court boys of around twelve and older in the hope of forming a lasting relationship. This was not only—perhaps not even primarily—sexual, although physical intercourse played a part in it. Rather, the older partner, the *erastes*, was expected to educate the younger, his *eromenos*, integrating him into society, introducing him to his friendship groups, and generally preparing him for adult civic life.[26]

For some, the relationship was the most ideal possible between two human beings. Plato claimed that while a heterosexual union might result in physical children, a homosexual partnership produced spiritual offspring, splendid philosophical ideas, sublime concepts, which a man simply could not share with a woman. For a precociously handsome boy such as Alcibiades, however, it could offer something altogether more basic: a chance to gratify lusts and explore the lengths to which he could manipulate others.[27]

Throughout his life, Alcibiades enjoyed a hard-earned reputation for sexual voracity. Psychologists might put this down to his being essentially parentless from early childhood, to his craving for a father figure, to his longing for a mother's love, to his distrust as an adult of forming lasting bonds when, as a young child, his closest ties had been severed so suddenly and irreversibly. Equally, it could be argued that from a tender age he learned that, through giving or withholding sexual favours, he could wield considerable power, manipulating those apparently stronger or more influential than himself, thereby enhancing his own prestige and reputation.

Once more, poor, feeble Zopyrus could exercise but little control. It was acceptable for a boy to form a strong exclusive bond with one *erastes*. Indeed, the relationship was usually such that the respectable (*kalokagathos*) lover was expected to keep the boy's father or guardian well apprised of his son's progress. Alcibiades, however, had other ideas. Well on his path to manhood, long-haired and handsome, he was the talk of Athens, where his already charismatic personality was irresistible. Now, as throughout his life, men jostled for his favours. As with Aspasia, so with Alcibiades—the rumour mill worked overtime. With gleeful outrage, it was noised abroad that he had run away from home and was living at the house of his lover, Democrates, whose populist name belied great wealth, whose father had been lauded for his beauty, and whose family regularly won equestrian events at the Panhellenic Games. For the horse-mad Alcibiades, Democrates' stud farm would have held attractions at least equal to those of the man himself. But his guardians had no idea where he had gone. Was he in danger? Was he dead? At his wits' end, Ariphron urged Pericles to order the town crier to proclaim that Alcibiades was missing and urge the citizens to search for him. Pericles was more canny. Much better, he argued, to wait. If Alcibiades was dead, it would only hasten the discovery of the inevitable. If he was alive, his reputation would be forever ruined.[28]

This, incidentally, is one of only two times that we hear of Pericles and his brother Ariphron actively intervening in the life of their wards. On the other occasion, Pericles is said to have been so worried that Alcibiades was corrupting his younger brother, Cleinias, that he sent Cleinias to Ariphron to care for. After six months Ariphron returned him. The boy, he complained, was ungovernable. Even Alcibiades was thought to agree. He is recorded as describing Cleinias as "raving mad." Apparently the brothers did not get on, and, unlike Alcibiades, young Cleinias made no impact on Athenian society. Nothing of his adult life is known—or even whether he reached adulthood.[29]

Meanwhile the adolescent Alcibiades, safely back from his adventures with Democrates, continued to toy with a string of admirers, including many who simply wanted to be included in his entourage. Their motives were myriad. Some were captivated by his bewitching personality and beauty; others saw some social benefit in his acquaintance. But there was one man who claimed to see beyond Alcibiades' outward charms directly to his inner soul, who could perceive his brilliance, who knew that life's temptations could lead him astray. Who wished to save him. That man was Socrates.[30]

Born around 469, Socrates was now in his mid-thirties, and already his keen intellect was the talk of Athens. Although he would become famous for his technique of trying to identify universal truths by relentlessly questioning self-acknowledged experts, as a young man his interests may, like those of most earlier and contemporary philosophers, have included astronomy. Certainly it was partly as an astronomer that he would later be lampooned by the prematurely balding comic playwright Aristophanes, while his most famous pupil, Plato, recognized that astronomy was a first step towards enlightenment, forcing the soul to look upwards, turning one's contemplation from the physical to the metaphysical. Now by the mid-430s, Socrates was a familiar sight both on Athens' streets and in her salons, and—for those not at its receiving end—his intellectual dexterity was thrilling to observe. When the great Protagoras of Abdera, a thriving port on the north Aegean's Thracian shores, visited Athens around 434, he announced that he admired Socrates above all others of his generation.[31]

By now Socrates was infatuated with Alcibiades. How the two met is unknown. Alcibiades belonged to precisely the circle of rich young dilettantes to whom the philosopher was attracted, but, intriguingly, it may have been old Zopyrus who first introduced them. Certainly a Zopyrus was known to Socrates, and there is no reason to suppose him to be other than the Thracian tutor. Zopyrus' nickname was "The Physiognomist," for he believed that a person's character, nature, and even fate could be read from facial features. Using his skills, he judged Socrates to be both stupid and fixated on women, a judgement which his subject graciously proclaimed to be correct, adding that he overcame these afflictions only by assiduously exercising the force of reason.[32]

Zopyrus' diagnosis can have come as no surprise, for to his contemporaries the shaggy, shabby Socrates, who trailed round Athens barefoot, staring at the world through bulbous eyes, resembled no one more closely than the mythological Silenus, half man, half horse, thick-lipped, snub-nosed and balding, a priapic slave to drink and sex, the close companion of the wine god, Dionysus. As for Dionysus—young, lithe, and comely, his scented ringlets tumbling in rich profusion across lissom shoulders, "a god" (as the tragedian Euripides would later write) "of terror and of gentle comfort for mankind"—Alcibiades could easily have passed for his earthly incarnation.[33]

Unlike Zopyrus, Socrates claimed that he could see beneath the surface. To Alcibiades' true nature. And, what he saw, he feared. For here, he believed, was a young man who had the capability for either tremendous good or untold destruction. Alcibiades' future, he predicted, would be influenced by his choice of friends, and many of those who now were hanging on his every word, sniggering at his jokes, and bolstering his orphan ego were plainly doing so for purely selfish reasons. So, while Alcibiades joined Athens' gilded youth in hunting expeditions to the scrubby hills and mountains which embraced the olive-silvered plains of Attica, Socrates was stalking his own quarry. And that quarry was Alcibiades.[34]

The nature of their relationship baffled even their contemporaries. Some insisted that it was purely platonic: chaste and non-physical. Others assumed quite naturally that there must have been at least a spark of the erotic in Socrates' attraction to such a divinely handsome youth, especially as he was said to be quite open about his response to the charms of others among his pupils—glimpsing another young man's naked flesh beneath his tunic, he "caught fire" and "could not contain himself," even while remembering a snatch of poetry which advised men to "take care not to come into your lover's presence as a fawn before a lion, lest he catch you as his prey." Later, another poem circulated, said to have been written by Aspasia, in which she not only expressed her delight that Socrates was showing an interest in Alcibiades (whose personality was making such a stamp upon her household), but advised the philosopher how best to woo him.[35]

Occasionally Greek literature offers tantalizing sightings of the maturing Alcibiades, as he enjoys Socrates' company in these formative years. Plato reveals him on the threshold of manhood, his first beard darkening his cheeks, one of a group of young men who have assembled at the house of his half brother, Callias, to pay their respects to Protagoras of Abdera. The courtyard is packed with glitterati: aristocrats, aspiring playwrights, venerable intellectuals, those keen to learn and others keen to advertise their learning.[36]

As well as Socrates, the flamboyant Hippias of Elis is present, a man who claimed to know everything there was to know about anything, and who once appeared at the Olympic Games wearing nothing that he had not made himself. There, too, is Prodicus, a true academic, from sun-drenched Ceos, an island off the southern tip of Attica. Obsessed with the exact use of language, with his resonant, deep voice and rhetorical skills, Prodicus could electrify even the most somnolent of audiences. As a result he was often sent out on diplomatic missions—occasions which he turned to personal advantage, enrolling high-fee-paying students to his seminars and lectures.[37]

When Alcibiades arrives at the gathering, Prodicus is still in bed, lying on a couch in an old storage room, covered in a pile of rugs and blankets. Indeed, Socrates sends Alcibiades to get him up, so that he might join their conversation, and later, when the debate seems about to dissolve in acrimony, Alcibiades intervenes politely yet conclusively to ensure that it continues. At which another of the guests sneers: "Whatever Alcibiades decides to get involved with, he always has to win."[38]

The identity of the guest in question is significant. He is Critias, one of the accomplished *aulos* players whose instrument Alcibiades had once disparaged. Like Alcibiades, Critias was born of an ancient family. His hair worn long after the Spartan fashion in a clear outward sign of his disdain for the Athenian democracy, Critias was a brilliant young poet and playwright, whose writing questioned the existence of the gods. But more crucially, his fortunes—like those of Callias, the owner of the house in which they now were meeting—would become inextricably and fatally intertwined with those of Alcibiades.[39]

For now, though, all eyes were on Protagoras. For in a culture where enquiry and learning were so much in vogue, he represented an exciting and profitable new wave of education—because Protagoras was the first sophist. Which is to say that he taught not just philosophy and rhetoric, but the use of those disciplines to formulate persuasive arguments. And, for the rich and ambitious Athenian, the ability to argue well in the Assembly or law courts was the key to future success. What Protagoras and the other sophists, who quickly jumped on his bandwagon, offered, then, was not just a theoretical education but a deeply practical training, for it was clear to anyone who had seen democracy in action that what convinced the People was not so much rational logic but plausible, beguiling, and seductive eloquence. Indeed, Protagoras boasted, he could teach how to make a weak argument seem much more convincing than a strong one. But all this came at a price. The sophists who toured the Greek world lecturing and tutoring the young elite commanded hefty fees, and so great was the prize they offered—power over the People—that they were never short of wealthy students.[40]

Callias, with whom Protagoras was staying, was said to have spent more money on sophists than the rest of his fellow citizens put together. Indeed, the cast of intellectuals gathered there that day was stellar. But even more luminary were those philosophers, artists, and musicians who clustered around Pericles, infusing the very atmosphere in which Alcibiades was growing up, and casting their influence upon his adolescence.[41]

Pericles, too, was intrigued by Protagoras, attracted not only to his opinion that virtue consists in the smooth-running of the household and in wielding benign political influence through words and deed, but to his religious scepticism. "I can't tell whether or not the gods exist or what they might be like," Protagoras once wrote, "since the question is thorny and human life is short." Rather, "man is the measure of all things, of those which are, that they are, and of those which are not, that they are not." To him, then, morality was subjective. Mankind was incapable of grasping absolute or universal truths.[42]

Even closer to Pericles' heart was Anaxagoras, a man whose supreme rationalism earned him the nickname *"Nous"* ("Mind"). Originally from

Clazomenae, an Ionian city built on an island off the long low isthmus which forms the southern arm of the Gulf of Smyrna, Anaxagoras rejected a life of politics in favour of philosophy. Approaching middle age and attracted by Athens' reputation for free thinking, he settled in the city in the late 460s, when Pericles was first wielding authority. His influence on Pericles (and by extension on his household) was immense.[43]

A genius and polymath, Anaxagoras did much to revolutionize his contemporaries' world view. For him, reason guided the universe. Planets were not divine beings but blazing rocks, the moon's light was a reflection of the sun's, and the sun itself was an object on a massive scale (larger even than the Peloponnese) formed of molten metal. Anaxagoras' scientific worldview was already winning converts—when a meteorite roared through the skies and smashed into the sandy earth at Aegospotami on the northern shores of the Hellespont, what had appeared to be a dazzling heavenly body was discovered to be nothing but a stone.[44]

Meanwhile, others in Pericles' circle were putting new discoveries to other uses. The musicologist Damon was conducting research into the effect which different keys and rhythms have on the human ear, and how these might be used to influence behaviour and decision-making. What worked for music, he suggested, could apply equally effectively to rhetoric, and there were those who suspected that Pericles' bewitching oratory owed more than a little to Damon's teachings.[45]

And worse, the rumour mill suggested. Damon was a dangerous revolutionary, an *éminence grise,* who wished to overthrow the state, who was using Pericles to implement his own subversive policies. Take, for example, the law which had been passed to issue pay for jury service, enabling the poor to judge the rich. Who was behind that, wealthy gossips asked, if not Damon? Such was the weight of suspicion which grew up around the musician, so menacing an influence he seemed, that in the mid-440s he was ostracized.[46]

It was not long before another of Pericles' inner circle was thought similarly suspect. If Damon was a master of harmony in music, the sculptor Pheidias was his equal in the plastic arts, and he, too, was making his mark on the fabric of the state. The creator of the bronze Athene Promachos on the Acropolis, Pheidias had been overseeing the ambitious building project which had galvanized all Attica.[47]

By 438 his awe-inspiring statue of Athene Parthenos (Athene the Virgin)—forty feet high and faced in ivory (for the flesh) and gold (for everything else)—and much of the building housing it, the Parthenon, had been completed and a lavish service of consecration held, probably as part of that August's quadrennial Great Panathenaic Festival. Whether or not the then fourteen-year-old Alcibiades attended we cannot know, but it is at least possible. What is more certain is that he would have been all too aware of the way in which Pericles' enemies used his relationship with Pheidias as a means of undermining him.

Athens was a highly litigious society, and two lawsuits were filed against the sculptor, seeking to attack him on both religious and secular grounds. One was for misappropriating some of the gold earmarked for the statue of the goddess, a charge which was easily refuted since the gold façade had been attached in such a way that it could be removed and weighed.[48]

The other accusation, however, was potentially more dangerous. Although the intelligentsia of Athens were more than prepared to question the nature and even the existence of the gods in private, the vast bulk of citizens remained religiously conservative and superstitious. Even Pericles took great care to be seen to pray before he made a public speech. Since any public act that seemed to cross the bounds of what was acceptable to the gods—indeed anything that could be deemed in the slightest way heretical—might be construed as threatening the well-being of the state, it was well to avoid any doubt. There was an unwritten orthodoxy that no living person might be represented on a building or statue dedicated to the gods. So when it was suggested that one of the figures sculpted on Athene's shield bore an uncanny likeness to Pheidias himself, while another (slightly hidden) looked like Pericles, there erupted an almighty scandal. Especially as Pericles was a member of the cursed Alcmaeonids.

Quite how it all played out is uncertain. Some say that Pheidias was forced into exile, others that he was subsequently executed for impiety. Whatever the fallout, it was a lesson to anyone—not least an adolescent boy—that the People took breaches of religious propriety very seriously, and anyone suspected of profanity might expect the harshest treatment. It was a lesson, too, that in politics any weapon might be used to bring down the enemy.[49]

By the late 430s, as religious conservatives flexed their muscles, and Pericles' enemies, encouraged by the return of Thucydides Melesiou from his ten-year exile, strutted with new-found confidence, there was a flurry of litigation against Pericles and members of his circle. A charge of embezzlement of public funds was brought against him—an episode that led to long hours poring over financial documents, and that reveals another tantalizing moment in the development of the precocious young Alcibiades. An anecdote describes him at the door to Pericles' office, impatient and desperate to see his guardian. Pericles' staff have refused to admit him. They cannot possibly disturb the great politician when he is considering how best to present his accounts before the People. Petulant, Alcibiades turns and stalks away, but not before remarking: "Wouldn't it be better if he considered how not to *have* to present his accounts to the People in the first place?"[50]

This is not the only time, according to his near contemporaries, that the adolescent Alcibiades voices his indifference to the Athenian democracy and law. Once, we see him faced by a troupe of actors, clustering round the comic poet Hegemon, who has been brought to trial in Athens by the islanders of his native Thasos. They are clamouring for Alcibiades to help have him acquitted. Coolly, the young man bids them follow him, and leads them to the heart of the Agora, to the Metrōon, where the public records are housed. There, he requests to see the document outlining the charges against Hegemon, and, when he is presented with it, he calmly wets his finger and rubs it across the papyrus, blurring and erasing the words. The public officials are horrified, but they say nothing out of deference—or fear—of Alcibiades. Besides, we are told, the plaintiff had disappeared.[51]

On another occasion we see Alcibiades debating at some length with Pericles the nature of law and justice. Laws are not just, argues Alcibiades, simply because they have been passed by the powerful majority in the Assembly—especially if by passing them the People can wield unwelcome force against the minority (the propertied classes to which he himself belongs). Wearily, Pericles refuses to concede, instead observing that, "When I was your age, I loved clever arguments, too, and I spent hours splitting hairs as you're doing now." To which Alcibiades cheekily replies: "I wish I'd known you then—when you were at the peak of your powers!"[52]

But it was Pericles' rationalism, and the rationalism of his friends, which provided his political enemies with the easiest of targets. A soothsayer called Diopeithes was put forward to propose a decree, opening up to prosecution anyone who questioned the existence of the gods or who taught scientific astronomy. The bill was passed. Anaxagoras was forced into exile. And Protagoras, too. Many of his books were seized by an angry crowd and burned in the Agora.[53]

Nor was Aspasia exempt. Fuelled by the scurrilous slanders of comic poets who not only questioned her religious beliefs but accused her of procuring free-born Athenian women for Pericles, accusations of impiety were laid against her that led to her being put on trial. Pericles himself made an impassioned speech in her defence, so impassioned that he wept as he delivered it—perhaps the only time that he allowed emotion to better him in public. Aspasia was acquitted, but still ugly rumours coiled around the streets and lanes, as gossips muttered that the woman had cast a spell on Pericles, that she had caused him to go to war before on her behalf, that she was stirring up the seeds of conflict once again.[54]

For by now international politics were indeed becoming fraught. Although the thirty-year peace treaty with Sparta had held, relations with another Peloponnesian city, Corinth, were fast unravelling. Like Athens, Corinth was an important trading state. Her geographical position, close to the isthmus connecting the Peloponnese to mainland Greece, not only meant that she could control the passage of goods and people overland between the north and south, but allowed her to have two booming ports, one on each side of the isthmus, enabling easy access by sea to markets in both the Aegean and Asia Minor to the east and Italy and Sicily to the west. With both Athens and Corinth ambitious for commercial growth, it was inevitable that their interests would lead to war. The only reason for surprise was the nature of the event that triggered it.[55]

Corinth had long resented her colony Corcyra (modern Corfu) for failing to pay her the honours due to a *metropolis* (founding city). In 435, that simmering resentment boiled over into conflict, when the two cities took opposing sides in a civil war in Corcyra's own colony, Epidamnus (modern Dürres). A naval battle saw Corcyra victorious, but Corinth was not prepared to accept defeat. For months her shipyards resounded to the rasp of saws and din of hammers, while, attracted by high wages, oarsmen flocked to sign up from across all Greece. Corcyra feared the worst, but, having for years pursued a policy of political neutrality, she had no allies. The only other state which possessed a navy large and experienced enough to help her counter Corinth was Athens.

And so it was that in the spring of 433, ambassadors from Corcyra addressed the Athenian Assembly. Their arguments were a clever combination of carrot and stick: war between Athens and the Peloponnesians was inevitable; Athens needed to control the sea; she could not allow Corcyra's fleet to fall into Peloponnesian hands; and, besides, having Corcyra as an ally would greatly increase Athens' economic potential, since Corcyra was a vital staging post on any voyage to Italy and Sicily. Despite a Corinthian delegation's warnings of dire consequences, and despite initial hesitations, the Athenian People voted to give Corcyra limited support, and a fleet set sail.[56]

But this was not the only potential cause of discord between Athens and the Peloponnese. After the Battle of Coronea, in which Cleinias was killed, Athens' western neighbour, Megara, had switched sides and allied herself with Sparta. In retaliation, Pericles had passed an economic embargo, forbidding Megara from doing business in any port or market within the Athenian Empire, effectively cutting her off from the entire Aegean Sea. There can be no doubt that the four so-called Megarian Decrees, the first set of economic sanctions in recorded history, were intended to be provocative, to explore how far Athens might assert her dominion of the sea, to test how Sparta and her allies would respond. There can be no doubt either that Pericles was fully aware that both the Decrees and Athens' support of Corcyra could be interpreted as hostile acts. The city was sliding towards war.[57]

It was against this background, in this heightened atmosphere, that Alcibiades' childhood officially came to an end. Some time in 435 or 434, perhaps at the Apaturia festival in late October, Alcibiades was presented once more to the deme, Scambonidae. His parentage was again proclaimed, his age—eighteen—announced, and a solemn vote was cast to enrol him as a voting member of the deme. A short time later, after a meeting of the City Council at which the deme's decision was confirmed, Alcibiades and his coevals gathered on the Acropolis at the sanctuary of the mythological princess Aglaurus, where in the presence of the priestess, Theano, and dressed in full armour, they were enrolled as ephebes, a status they would hold for the next two years.[58]

Key to this ceremony was the oath, which each was required to swear, never to dishonour his armour or abandon a comrade in battle, always to defend the rights of gods and men, to increase and enhance the lands of Athens, to respect authority, obey the laws, and punish any who might try to overthrow the constitution. And to seal the oath, the ephebe called as witness not only an array of terrifying gods, but the very boundaries of Athens, its wheat and barley, vines and olive trees and fig trees. Alcibiades embraced the oath with fervent zeal. And in Theano, the priestess of Aglaurus, who presided at the ceremony, he made a lasting ally.[59]

With the swearing of the oath, Alcibiades became a citizen of Athens, eligible not only to attend the Assembly but to frequent the Agora, the city's municipal heart, to which no Athenian under eighteen was admitted. But before he could exercise full rights, he must first undergo two years of training. Evidence from the next century suggests that, after a tour of the main sanctuaries of Athens, the cohort of ephebes was led down to Piraeus to spend a year manning garrisons and undergoing drills, at the end of which they staged a military display in the theatre. For their second year, they were sent slightly further afield, to one of the frontier forts which ringed rural Attica on its rugged borders with Boeotia and Megara, or perhaps on a windy coastal headland.[60]

These two years as an ephebe were a rite of passage, a time when young men were almost ritually kept apart from the public life of Athens, when they were forced to experience and endure the company of strangers, the rich rubbing shoulders with the poor, the realities of democratic equality before the law thrown into sharp focus. There is no record of how Alcibiades spent this period of his life or whether family connections helped to smooth his path.

But we do gain one glimpse of him around this time. He is in the company of Axiochus, his uncle, who, despite being his father Cleinias' half brother, is only a year or so older than Alcibiades. The two young men (there are perhaps inevitable rumours that they are lovers) have made a voyage east. It is tempting to imagine that their journey has included not only Miletus, home of Axiochus' grandfather (the father of Aspasia), but other cities of Ionia. It is tempting, too, to suppose that no small part of the purpose of the expedition has been to make personal introductions to the nexus of important contacts—business friends and family members—whose cooperation and support will be of such great value to a neophyte politician aspiring to make his mark on the international stage. Certainly, before long, Alcibiades will enjoy close friendships with many rich and powerful Ionians, not just at

Miletus but in nearby Ephesus and other cities of the coast, not to mention the neighbouring islands of Chios, Samos, and Lesbos.[61]

However, it is not here in Ionia, where the ragged silhouettes of mountains glint in the dazzling sun, or on the eastern islands that we now find Alcibiades. Rather, he is in Abydus, a city on the southern shores of the choppy, racing Hellespont, the narrow channel which connects the Sea of Marmara to the Aegean. At Abydus the Hellespont is only a mile wide, and already it is steeped in history and myth. Here the Persian Great King Khashayarsha, known to the Greeks as Xerxes, once commanded that a bridge of boats be built across the channel so that his army might invade Greece on dry land. Here, too, on a headland, opposite Abydus, with the Persians defeated, Pericles' father, Xanthippus, led the captive Persian governor up onto the headland and crucified him, forcing him to look on as his son was stoned to death. And here in legend the lovely Hero, priestess of Aphrodite, once lived in a tower, signaling each night to her lover, Leander, to swim across the seething Hellespont and be with her.[62]

Like Leander, it is love—or rather sex—which has led Alcibiades and Axiochus here, as they round off their tour of the Greek east with some rest and relaxation. They have heard rumours of the beauty of a local courtesan, Medontis, and they wish to visit her. Alcibiades, it is suggested, has fallen in love with her even before he meets her. The two men generously share her favours. Gossips say they sire a daughter by her. And in time the idle talk goes further: when the daughter comes of age, Axiochus and Alcibiades both sleep with her, each pretending as they do so that the other is her father.[63]

But sex tourism to Abydus, educational though it may have been, could be nothing more than a detour on Alcibiades' road to adulthood. In Athens the drums of war were beating more loudly and frenetically than ever, as hostilities with Corinth were approaching a new peak. This time the pretext was the north Aegean town of Potidaea.[64]

Sited on the narrow isthmus of Pallene, the westernmost of the three promontories which form Chalcidice, Potidaea was an anomaly. Founded by Corinth in around 600, it had resisted siege during the last Persian invasion, gone on enthusiastically to join the Delian League, and consequently been subsumed into the Athenian Empire. But it still appointed Corinthian magistrates each year, and kept close links with its *metropolis*.

Recently, though, Athens had issued an ultimatum. In view of the deteriorating international situation, Potidaea was to renounce its ties with Corinth, expel magistrates already in office, agree not to appoint replacements, send hostages to Athens, and—as proof of its passivity—dismantle its town walls. The Potidaeans refused. Not only that, they requested help from Corinth. Two thousand volunteers and mercenaries duly answered the call; and within months all Chalcidice was in revolt.

Ambitious to assert the city's status as the most powerful in the whole Greek world, the Athenian Assembly could entertain just one response. They had already sent a thousand of their heavily armed infantry—their hoplites—to the region, but with the escalation of hostilities this was clearly not enough. So, come the spring of 432, beneath the budding plane trees of the Agora, knots of men were scouring call-up lists nailed onto whitened message boards below the statues of the ten tribal heroes. Two thousand names were there, two hundred for each tribe. And among those written on the roll of the Leontis tribe was Alcibiades Cleiniou Scambonides. The son of Cleinias was going to war.[65]

2

COMING OF AGE

> For a young man, who enjoys the glittering flower of his enchanting
> youth, everything seems wonderful. Men gaze at him in admiration,
> women with desire.

Tyrtaeus, frag. 10 (West), 27–29

NOTHING COULD TRULY PREPARE A MAN for the disorienting
terror of hoplite warfare. Training and military exercises, the braggadocio
of war-scarred veterans, the rousing, reassuring words of generals—they were
all very well. But now for the first time, as well-drilled personal attendants
helped make masters ready for the coming battle, armour was being strapped
on in earnest: over the tunic, the glittering bronze breastplate, hinged at the
shoulders, tied tight with leather thongs along the sides, weighing between
thirty and forty pounds; close-fitting metal greaves bent snug around the
shins and calves; and encasing the head, the helmet, also made of bronze,
five pounds in weight, complete with cheek, nose, and neck guards and occasionally, too, a central ridge supporting a tall horsehair crest.[1]

And slung across the shoulder was a leather baldric into which was slid
a short sword, two feet long. In the right hand, a thrusting spear between
six and eight feet long, its ash or cornel shaft the merest inch in diameter,
topped at one end with an iron spear-head up to a foot in length, and at

the other with a long bronze spike. The spear was heavy, between two and four pounds in weight, but heavier by far—at up to sixteen pounds—was the great round convex shield, roughly three feet in diameter, its wooden core faced in a thin sheet of burnished bronze, and furnished with two leather straps, through one of which the hoplite thrust his left arm, as he gripped the other with his left hand. The shield was not purely for defence. An upward jab, a sideways slice, and its metal rim became a lethal weapon.

Now armed and ready, their helmets for the moment pushed up and back onto the top of their heads, their armour glinting in the still-strong September sun, the hoplites stood in phalanxes five or six men deep, as their general made ritual sacrifice—a sheep or goat, taken from the herds brought specially for this purpose, its throat sliced, its entrails exposed and examined for good omens—and the priests offered prayers for victory. The sacrifice was performed not merely as a piece of flummery. If the priests found anything amiss with the victim's organs—a sure sign that both the offering, and those making it, displeased the gods—battles could be postponed and campaigns abandoned. Only if they found them healthy would the attack begin.[2]

And so, after a long, anxious wait, with the sacrifice completed, and the generals reassured that the gods were on their side, at last the order came. Advance! To a man, the hoplites lowered their helmets. And at once their whole world changed. Vision became tunnelled. Sound became muffled. Now there was only the pounding of blood in ears, the rush of adrenaline magnified, the sweat of anticipation sheening the skin, soaking the tunic and the leather shield-straps, slick on the smooth wooden spear shafts.

As both sides advanced across the rust-red soil, the Athenian phalanxes began to sing, the voices steadier, more confident with every stride, the words well-known and so emboldening—the paean hymn, an anthem for victory to the god Apollo, its melody rising from the roaring throats of three thousand men or more as they first marched, then ran across the scrubby ground to meet the enemy. For this was no meeting of tight ranks, each bristling with long spears, like the later Macedonian phalanxes of Philip II and Alexander the Great. Rather, as Euripides, describing a duel between two hoplites, reminded his theatre audience of seasoned fighters, it was a chaotic confrontation, as unstructured as the crashing of a wave upon the seashore:

Accompanied by the music of an *aulos*-player, hoplite phalanxes clash in battle. (Chigi Vase, seventh century BC. Paul Fearn/Alamy Stock Photo.)

> Like a beacon fire, the trumpet blazed the order for murderous battle, and they ran at one another savagely; like boars with cruelly sharpened tusks, they clashed, and their beards were wet with spittle. As they kept on stabbing with their spears, they crouched beneath their round shields, so that—harmlessly—the iron glanced off. But if one saw the other's eyes above the shield rim, he would stab at him with his spear tip, in his lust to kill him.[3]

A forest of spears jabbing, thrusting, breaking now; the clash of shield on shield; dust; shouting; screams; the sudden impact of a heavy blow; a flash of swords; a blossoming of pain; a jet of blood; a jostling of bodies, before one side collapsed in disarray, and its hoplites fled in panic, while close at their heels the enemy, a pack of bronze men, masked in the anonymity of grim, gleaming helmets, ran in merciless pursuit. "In battle," as one poet proclaimed, "it's the sweetest thing to slice your running enemy full through the midriff."[4]

Which is how it all unfolded on that warm September day at Potidaea, on a narrow spit of land between two lazy seas. A battle like so many others. A skirmish, which so easily might be forgotten. Except for an image which seared itself into the minds of those Athenians who saw it: a young man plunging fearlessly into the heart of the mêlée; a young man fighting with ferocious bravery; a young man falling, wounded on the blood-red soil. And then, within a heartbeat, an older man stood over him, battling the enemy as they swarmed around him, scooping up the young man and supporting him, desperately slicing a path back to safety, an act of almost superhuman strength and fearlessness, which saved the young man's life.[5]

Almost certainly, in that moment, Socrates (for the older man was he) rescued the injured Alcibiades from an all-too-early grave. But when the battle was over and the Athenians proved victorious, when the generals were discussing whom they should honour with the coveted award for bravery, the philosopher refused it, insisting instead that it should go to Alcibiades. And so in a ceremony held before the gathered troops, wounded but triumphant, his beauty not only undiminished but burnished by his brush with death, the son of Cleinias claimed his prize—a suit of armour and a victor's wreath. Already, only twenty years of age, he had equalled in glory his grandfather, Cleinias II, who had won his *aristeia*, his award for bravery, almost fifty years before against the Persians at Artemisium. It was a tremendous accolade, which, in Athens' militaristic society, bestowed on Alcibiades the coveted aura of heroism.[6]

Not that the battle at Potidaea had been quite so momentous. After setting out from Athens, Alcibiades, Socrates, and their messmates under the command of Callias Calliadou had first sailed to Pydna. Here they joined forces with a smaller Athenian army besieging the Macedonian prince, Perdiccas, a former ally, who was now supporting the Peloponnesians, in the hope that they in turn would help him in a bitter struggle with his brother. Terms were reached with Perdiccas. The siege was lifted. And the Athenian army and its baggage train, a lumbering mass of hoplites and servants, cavalry, pack animals, and wagons, set off on a trek of many days past mountains and the shallow restless sea, until at last they headed south towards Chalcidice.[7]

As they approached they learned that a force of Corinthian volunteers had reached Potidaea before them. The city on the isthmus was well guarded. And, at the same time, a second hostile force, swollen by the arrival of the ever-treacherous Perdiccas, who had switched sides yet again, had gathered in Olynthus, a fine new city in the heartland of Chalcidice, to attack the Athenians from the rear, should they dare to march down the short narrow spit to Potidaea.

Calliadou acted quickly. He sent an allied force to distract the enemy at Olynthus, while he and his combined force of three thousand Athenian hoplites marched on Potidaea. In 432, Greek warfare was (for the most part) still fought by old heroic rules. An enemy approach on city walls called for a show of force, and sure enough the Corinthians, together with Potidaea's city militia, drew up en masse to meet them. The ensuing battle (in which Alcibiades was wounded) was hard fought but brief. The right wings of both armies were victorious, but the Corinthians could not follow up their partial victory, as to do so would potentially have cut them off from Potidaea. So, instead, they turned back, racing along the breakwater under a hail of javelins and arrows, until they reached the safety of the city walls.

The Athenians had won, though at a cost. A hundred and fifty of their men lay dead, their general, Calliadou, among them. But undeterred they set to work raising siege walls, first to the north of Potidaea, then—when reinforcements reached them—to the south. Before the blockade was total, the Corinthians slipped out to safety. Which was not an option open to the common citizenry. So, as summer faded into autumn and the bitter winds began to blow from Thrace, the Potidaeans were forced to face the grim realities of siege.[8]

Not just the Potidaeans. The besieging Athenians, too. Still organized by tribe, the hoplites and their attendants encamped as best they could, some in huts made from branches or bits of wood looted from local cottages, others in flimsy shelters of frames stretched with animal hides, still others huddled close together under blankets around spitting, smoking camp fires. Only a very few enjoyed the luxury of tents, but among them was Alcibiades. And it was later said that, flouting the convention that members of different tribes should not live together on campaign, he shared his tent with Socrates. If this were indeed true, perhaps Socrates had been allowed to nurse the wounds the young man had sustained in action, or perhaps, his award for bravery still fresh in the minds of all, Alcibiades was already exploiting his celebrity to bend the rules.[9]

What happened when these two unlikely tent-mates were together was a matter of some speculation. According to Plato, Alcibiades had already tried in vain to seduce the philosopher in Athens, contriving situations whereby Socrates would be obliged to spend the night with him. Once, when he did keep Socrates with him, the older man rebuffed his blatant propositioning and repeated attempts at arousal, and, although the two did sleep on the same couch, they did so as if they were brothers—or father and son. By the time they were on campaign, Alcibiades had no doubt long realised that (in that department at least) Socrates was a lost cause, though it can have done his sense of his own place in history no harm to have shared a tent platonically with an older, respected man. After all, was this not precisely how Homer said Achilles and Patroclus had behaved at Troy?[10]

It was not only Alcibiades who had cause to admire Socrates' heroic fortitude at Potidaea. In the biting winter, heavy frosts and icy winds made conditions on the isthmus almost unbearable. While others wrapped themselves up as best they could, tying felt and sheepskin round their feet, and staying as close to fires as possible, Socrates, dressed only in his usual meagre tunic, walked barefoot across the frozen earth. And when the warmth of summer came again, he was once seen standing stock-still in the morning sun, engrossed in a philosophical problem. By midday his behaviour was attracting comment and, by evening, more than a little curiosity. Some of the soldiers—allies from Ionia—even brought out their bedding and watched through the night. Then, at dawn the next day, Socrates emerged from his reverie, made prayer to the rising sun, and walked away.[11]

Socrates' imperviousness to physical hardship stood him in particularly good stead when he, Alcibiades, and the rest of the army were not infrequently sent to raid the nearby mainland Chersonese. Such missions were essential—not only for acquiring provisions but for maintaining physical fitness and morale, as well as for ensuring that the enemy could not successfully man bases dangerously close to the isthmus. They could, however, be irksome. Often, hoplites found themselves cut off in hostile territory without food. For most this was a source of some distress. But not for Socrates. Somehow, he managed to transcend mere physical needs and live off air.[12]

If only the Potidaeans had succeeded in doing likewise. By the autumn of 430, their situation had turned desperate. Starvation set in. Their food supplies exhausted, there were even reports that, "among other horrors," some of the citizens had resorted to cannibalism. With no real prospects of relief, they could hold out no longer. So they offered to surrender on terms. The Athenian generals agreed, and, with winter drawing in once more, the city gates at last were opened and a pathetic procession shuffled through. The men had been allowed to take one piece of clothing each, the women, two. And no possessions, save what was strictly needed for the journey. The Athenian army occupied the city and enjoyed a well-earned celebration.[13]

Whether Alcibiades was present for the entire duration of the three-year siege, we cannot tell. There is no reason to suggest otherwise. It would have taught him much, not least regarding siege techniques, which were rudimentary, to say the least. Without sophisticated siege engines, if a city did not capitulate, or if it was not betrayed, a besieging army had no real option but to surround and hope to starve it into submission. As Potidaea showed, this could be a lengthy—and expensive—business. This operation alone cost the Athenians two thousand talents, a third of the six thousand talents' war-reserve built up so carefully in peace time and now safely under lock and key in the Parthenon treasury—a significant investment in both time and money for arguably little gain. If Athens were to win the war, it clearly could not rely solely on military exercises such as this. Of equal, if not greater, importance must be diplomacy.[14]

Because it was now official. The Greek world was at war. In the spring of 431, news reached Alcibiades and his comrades up at Potidaea that the international situation had deteriorated so much that even the reluctant Spartans had been persuaded that war was inevitable. But it was Thebes which made the first move, racing to seize Plataea, a neighbouring Boeotian city of great strategic worth, which had close ties with Athens. Their first attempts were botched. Plataea resisted, and now, in 430, it, too, was enduring a seemingly interminable siege. At least the Plataeans could not blame themselves. Unlike the Athenians, who, to their chagrin, found themselves in a very similar position.[15]

As he urged them to face down the Spartans, Pericles, Alcibiades' erst-while guardian, had promised the Athenians that they could easily win through, if they followed his advice to the letter. Enjoying naval supremacy as it did, Athens should not even try to fight the Spartans by land, but rather bring all its people from the countryside into the city, send all its livestock overseas to the allied island of Euboea, rely for food on imports from abroad, and settle down to weather a war which would (in all probability) last no more than four or five years. With varying degrees of reluctance, the Athenians agreed.[16]

So, when, in the spring of 431, between forty and sixty thousand Spartans and their allies marched into Attica, their army was unopposed. Faced with this unprecedented situation, it settled down to destroy as many of the country's ten million olive trees and countless vines as possible, smash farm machinery, torch ripening fields of grain, and prove the harrowing reality of Greek descriptions of such devastating raids—that they turned "crop lands into sheep walks" and forced the normally tree-dwelling cicadas "to sing out of the ground." The Spartans' strategy was, with luck, to provoke Athens' twenty thousand farmers into leaving the protection of their city walls and meeting them in what they were convinced would be a far from equal battle.[17]

Somehow, though, despite seeing palls of black smoke billow, thick and lazy, from their homesteads into pure blue skies, the Athenians held their nerve and stayed put. And within a few weeks the Peloponnesians departed, albeit leaving in their wake a swathe of ruin. Though it *was* only ruin, not total destruction. It takes harder work than even sixty thousand soldiers can exert to kill so many olive trees and vines. In time they would grow back. All Athens had to do was wait. So, as the farmers hiked back home to their small holdings to survey the damage, their hearts may have been heavy, but they could still entertain hope.[18]

Which was why, the next year, buoyed by a stirring speech from Pericles, commemorating the city's fallen, they were prepared to do it all again. Only this time—though they did not know it—they must face another, far more deadly enemy.

In the spring of 430, close to three hundred thousand people packed into Athens and Piraeus: city dwellers sharing homes with country cousins; farmers, peasants, and their families erecting bivouacs on whatever empty spaces they could find—even sacred land—or sleeping rough between the

Long Walls which linked Athens and its port. As the weeks advanced and days turned hotter, the stench of such a great assemblage of humanity, cramped together without sanitation and with barely enough water to drink, let alone to wash in, became ever harder to endure.[19]

And then the rumours started of a strange new sickness spreading through Piraeus. Headaches and chest pains. Coughing blood and vomiting. Pustules, uncontrollable diarrhea, ulcerated bowels. And sleeplessness. A fever so intense that sufferers were climbing into water tanks and cisterns in a vain bid to cool down. And then came the first deaths.[20]

At first they thought the Spartans must have poisoned the wells. But then they learned about the plague—how it had spread so swiftly in the months before through Ethiopia, and Libya and Egypt; how, as the sailing season opened and merchant ships crisscrossed the busy seas, it had reached Ionia and the Aegean islands; and how in time, unerringly, inevitably it had made landfall on the quay sides of Piraeus, the greatest trading hub in the Greek world. And now, within days, it breached the bottle neck of the Long Walls and swept through the crowded streets of Athens. And within weeks it had come to Potidaea.

That summer the Athenians had sent a fresh army north to try to break the siege of Potidaea, but all it did was infect their troops already there. As at home, so, too, at Potidaea: more than a third of the Athenian troops were wiped out by the plague, and after just forty days, the relief force sailed home, leaving the veterans to endure the campaign on their own. There is no word of whether Alcibiades or Socrates fell ill. Some who did recovered, though many suffered subsequently from amnesia or chronic paralysis of their extremities and genitals. In later years, neither Socrates or Alcibiades exhibited any of these symptoms, so perhaps neither caught the plague. Perhaps the two men had already joined their general on campaign elsewhere in the north, for only his detachment escaped contagion. But come the ending of the siege, even they must sail back home.[21]

In normal times, a victorious army sailing into harbour at Piraeus could expect to be met with joyful celebration. Not now. The atmosphere that greeted them was sombre, bleak. This was a plague city. The doctors had no skills to cure the sickness. No prayers, no sacrifices, nothing that the priests could do could stem it either. Incense drifting from altars, the smoke of sacrifice, all was being choked by a deadlier miasma, the fumes of blazing mass pyres, private cremations peremptorily interrupted, as in overwhelming numbers the anonymous corpses of the fetid dead were tossed unceremoniously into hungry, crackling flames. Abandoned by the gods, many turned their backs on religion and morality, and resigned themselves to a brief blaze of hedonism, before facing their untimely death. No one was immune. Not even the most severely virtuous. Not even Pericles.

Within his household it was his eldest son, Xanthippus, who succumbed first. For years, encouraged by his spendthrift wife, the young man had been embroiled in such bitter arguments with Pericles over money that his father had taken him to court. Now, even at the end, they were unreconciled. Next, Pericles' sister died. Then Paralus, the younger of his two sons by Deinomache. As he laid the wreath on the dead body, Pericles, who had tried so hard throughout his life to present a façade of stoic calm, broke down and wept. In sympathy, the People voted to allow him to flout his own law and enrol his one surviving son, born to the Milesian Aspasia, as a full Athenian citizen. Then, in 429, Pericles, too, became infected. As he lay dying, surrounded by his diminished circle, including perhaps Alcibiades, he pleaded that they should remember: "No Athenian ever put on mourning because of me." Few last words can have been so inappropriate.[22]

Perhaps sixty thousand Athenians died from the plague, but even as it continued to eddy across Athens and Piraeus, now abating, now returning in full force throughout the next three years, military, political, and private life went on as best it could. And for Alcibiades, now entering Athenian society for the first time as an adult, each of those spheres of life was there to be embraced.[23]

Despite his war record as a hoplite, it was to the rich cavalry class that Alcibiades truly belonged. A decade earlier, Pericles had increased the size of Athens' cavalry to twelve hundred men, but it was still associated in the minds of many with the aristocratic youth. Since a horse consumes as much as six times the amount of barley that a man eats in one day, and the cost of buying one in the first place could support a family of six for two years, only the wealthy could afford one. For those who struggled, there was some state aid, but a man as rich as Alcibiades had no need of assistance. So, soon after the new administrative year began on July 1, and with his name freshly inscribed in the official register, he sloughed off his hoplite armour and joined the cavalry.[24]

Not that he would never fight on foot again. There could—and would—still be occasion for him to do so, and anyone with ambition to be elected general would need a fine suit of hoplite armour. For such appearances Alcibiades, ever with an eye to impact, made sure that he was dressed in style. Now back in Athens, and perhaps remembering the talismanic value of Achilles' shield, hand-crafted by the god Hephaestus for the epic siege of Troy, he commissioned a new shield of his own.[25]

But unlike that of the Homeric hero, his bore no worthy scenes of a nation in times of peace or war. Instead, shining gold and inlaid in ivory, Alcibiades' shield was emblazoned with the figure of Eros. Wielding the thunderbolt of Zeus. In the minds of some, Eros was the oldest of all gods, revered and respected, the primeval force of generation in the universe. But to others he was a young boy, the initiator of promiscuous lust, the archer-son of Aphrodite, who delighted in sowing mischief in the hearts of all mankind. To a man like Alcibiades, determined to make his mark in politics, yet wedded fast to hedonism, such ambiguity must have been deliciously appealing. And to give his Eros Zeus' thunderbolt added more than just a frisson of the blasphemous.

Equally Homeric was the business of handling horses. Homeric heroes such as Hector were expert riders, adept at breaking horses, and, like them, the Athenian elite adored the beasts. Aristocratic names reflected this—names such as Xanthippus ("Bay Horse"), Hippocrates ("Horse Strength"), Hipponicus ("Horse Victory"), all borne by members of the Alcmaeonid dynasty. And while much time went into training horses for the flat-racing and chariot events at the great Panhellenic Games, much effort was expended, too, on preparing them for war.

Alcibiades' younger contemporary, Xenophon, wrote a treatise on the subject—and another on how a cavalry commander should comport himself. He advises what to look for in buying a horse, how best to rub it down, and how to diagnose infirmities. In an age before horseshoes, he writes of how to toughen hooves in exercise yards surrounded by an iron rim and spread with five wagon loads of round stones "large enough to fit into your hand." He discusses how to train a horse for war by taking it on hunts. And how to train a rider. In one exercise, a horseman pursues another, hurling blunted javelins at him, before catching up with him, stabbing with his spear, and trying to unseat him by first pulling him, and then pushing him away.[26]

But it is when Xenophon is writing about the cavalry displays held regularly in the Agora, down by the sea at Phalerum, or close to the Lyceum and Academy, that he is at his most evocative. He describes squadrons galloping across the flat ground, spears levelled between horses' ears, or, with trumpets blazing, charging each other in mock battle, passing between each others' ranks, wheeling round in tight formation. His readers can almost hear the jangle of the bridles, the thud of hooves, the whinnying of horses, the applause of those gathered on the bleachers to spectate. And Alcibiades took part in such displays, the warm wind in his hair, revelling in the adulation of the crowd.

But it was not just for such ceremonial parades that Alcibiades saddled up. Although Athens' policy was still to hunker down, and for the most part passively to weather Sparta's annual raids on Attica, they did occasionally respond by sending out a rapid-response team to pick off stragglers and ensure that not everything went the enemy's way. And this team was made up exclusively of members of the cavalry.[27]

So, in his first years in the cavalry, Alcibiades and his patrician friends must frequently have found themselves assembling on packed-gravel roads inside the city walls, their horses dancing and snorting in anticipation, before the gates were opened, and they galloped out on lightning attacks. Such were their aggression and frustration at being penned-up, impotent, inside the crowded city, that, when the young men came upon the enemy, they would be merciless. And by reputation, Alcibiades was more merciless than most.

His mania for horses was becoming infamous. So was the money that he spent on them. It was even the subject of a comedy. In 423, at the City Dionysia, the great annual festival of drama to which visitors flocked from every corner of the empire, Aristophanes produced *Clouds,* a biting satire of modern education—in particular of the sophistic movement gripping the rich young men of Athens. Curiously, though, he chose as the chief butt of his cruel jokes not Protagoras or Hippias or any of the foreigners who were truly sophists, but home-grown Socrates, who did all he could to distance himself from them. And to fill the role of one of Socrates' pupils Aristophanes invented a young man called Pheidippides ("Horse-Sparer").[28]

Early in the play it became quite clear who this "Pheidippides" was meant to represent: he was none other than Alcibiades. As the character's father reveals, the youth is an Alcmaeonid. His mother (not named, but clearly a stand-in for Deinomache) is the niece of Megacles, son of Megacles. She is a haughty woman, accustomed to luxury and perfumed with fragrant oils, who whispered to Pheidippides as a boy how, clad in a soft long robe, he would "drive his chariot to town, like Megacles." And while Pheidippides is a very thinly disguised Alcibiades, his father, Strepsiades (whose name means "Twister"), may well represent Alcibiades' guardian, Pericles.[29]

Clouds reveals much about how Alcibiades' family and intellectual circle were perceived by some of his contemporaries—and especially by their enemies. It presents Pheidippides (Alcibiades) as a spendthrift, bleeding the household dry with his purchases of chariots and horses, who is horrified at the idea of spending time indoors with pale-faced academics, instead of sporting with his comrades; Strepsiades (Pericles) as a gullible old man, whose consorting with philosophers leads him to question the existence of the traditional gods; and Socrates, whom Aristophanes does not even bother to disguise, as an amoral charlatan, who twists truth and makes bad arguments persuasive.

At the heart of this black comedy is a scene that encapsulates the tensions of contemporary Athenian society familiar with Protagoras' boast that he could teach how to make weak arguments seem more convincing than strong ones. In it Aristophanes presents, embodied, two types of argument. Rightful Reasoning is elderly. His speech praises traditional education and morality. Wrongful Reasoning, on the other hand, is a young upstart who, in the manner of Socrates himself, refuses to deliver a set speech, instead engaging in debate, picking holes in Rightful Reasoning's arguments, and promising that, thanks to him, whoever commits a crime of any sort will get off scot free. In the end, though, no doubt to the delight of many in the audience, Socrates' "Thinking Factory," as Aristophanes describes it, is burnt to the ground, while the philosopher and his students are stoned and chased out of town for their "crimes against the gods."[30]

An uncompromising reflection of Athenian society in the 420s, *Clouds* makes for uncomfortable reading. For its first audience, it made for uncomfortable viewing, too. It reflects a city bedevilled by schisms between rich and poor, learned and ill-educated, progressive and conservative, young and old. But, in Athens, drama was not just a mirror. It could be a catalyst as well, and, since many of its audience were members of the voting pubic, opinions aired in the Theatre of Dionysus could be incendiary.

In the aftermath of *Clouds,* some suggested that Socrates' reactionary enemies had commissioned Aristophanes to write the play. Their brief to the poet, "whose onely business," one writer (quoted here in a suitably archaic translation) naively supposed, "was to raise mirth," was that he should slander the philosopher on stage, intermingling calumny with "much abusive mirth & pleasant Verses." But, our source goes on, Socrates had been forewarned. He positioned himself in the most conspicuous seat possible. And while the foreign visitors "raised a humme and whisper, every one asking who that Socrates was . . . he rose up, and all the while the Play lasted continued in that posture."[31]

Alcibiades, however, was said to have been furious. It was bad enough that his friend had been so grotesquely burlesqued, or Pericles mocked for his religious scepticism. But that the audience had laughed at him for being a smooth-talking, bullying young wastrel! With stories circulating about his violent temper already beyond a joke, Alcibiades (or so another story went) decided to take matters into his own hands. With a group of his closest friends, he is said to have sought out the judges, who would decide which of the five comedies performed at that year's Dionysia should secure the prize, and painted a graphic picture of the consequences, should Aristophanes be crowned. By the time they left, all concerned could quite confidently predict that, whichever comedy won that year, it would not be *Clouds.*[32]

Whatever the truth of this tale (and it is tenuous), *Clouds* may well have helped sour the previously warm relationship between Alcibiades and Socrates. With his eye on politics and power, the young aristocrat could not afford to be so publicly humiliated by controversial friendships—especially when charges of religious scepticism (or worse) could only reinforce an audience's prejudice about the so-called ancestral curse on the Alcmaeonids. So the erstwhile friends saw less and less of one another. Their comradeship withered. And Alcibiades quietly dropped his old companion.

One of those suspected of persuading Aristophanes to attack Socrates and Alcibiades in *Clouds* was a wealthy Athenian, Anytus. He had strong personal reasons. Alcibiades had once humiliated him, and Socrates (he felt) had once made fun of him. So, true to the Greek code of doing whatever harm one could to enemies, Anytus was determined to pay both back in style. The feud had its roots in petty beginnings. Anytus' father was an enterprising tanner who, thanks to his wits and hard work, had accumulated a great fortune, pulling himself out of poverty until he attained the rank of "horseman."[33]

For the nouveau-riche, politically ambitious Anytus, associating with the blue-blooded Alcibiades could do no harm among the higher echelons of Athens, so he began to curry the young man's favour. Ostentatiously, Anytus asked Alcibiades to dinner and, intending to impress, set out a glittering array of gold and silver cups, and plates, and bowls, all of the most expensive and exquisite workmanship. But Alcibiades knew precisely why he had been invited, and he stayed at home, indulging in some serious drinking with his friends. Then, impressively inebriated, he wove his way to Anytus' house. When he arrived, he refused even to enter the dining room. Instead, leaning nonchalantly against the door jamb for support, he commanded his slaves to seize half the tableware and take it back to his house. As Alcibiades swept off, the guests spluttered in rage, while Anytus, trying to preserve as much honour as he could, stammered: "He could have taken the lot! At least he's left us half!"[34]

In truth, though, Aristophanes had little need for Anytus to suggest Alcibiades as a target. Ever since his debut four years earlier, in 427, with *Banqueters,* he had been satirizing him. Here, in another play exploring how sophistic learning was fomenting tensions among the generations, an honest, old-school landowner invites members of his *phratry,* or kinship-group, to a banquet, at which his two sons, the conservative "Virtuous Boy" and the radical "Buggered Boy," stage a debate (a precursor of that between Rightful and Wrongful Reasoning in *Clouds*), during which the father blames the Buggered Boy's use of extravagant, newfangled vocabulary on his association with slick young prosecutors—such as Alcibiades.[35]

This is not the only place where Aristophanes suggests that Alcibiades was practising law in the 420s. In *Acharnians,* produced in 425, the Chorus (harping on once more about intergenerational discord) suggests that it would be fairer if old people were prosecuted by the old, while "the young can contend with that wide-arse-holed blabbermouth, the son of Cleinias."[36]

Once more, and tantalizingly, the veil is lifted for the briefest moment to reveal Alcibiades, confident and clever in his twenties, working the courtroom, dazzling some and alienating others with his stylish oratory. It should come as no surprise to find him here. Many an aspiring politician cut his teeth in the lawcourts—as a young man, Pericles had come to public notice through his prosecution of no less a figure than the great Cimon—and there is no reason to suppose that Alcibiades was any different. After all, the courts were a good training ground, an arena where, in front of a relatively small audience of up to five hundred jurors, and in a relatively controlled environment, it was possible to build a reputation and hone rhetorical skills that would prove invaluable for the altogether more daunting arena of the Public Assembly. Here, then, and before this audience, Alcibiades' voice must first have rung out in debate—a voice which was a gift to comic poets like Aristophanes.[37]

For Alcibiades suffered from a speech impediment, lamdacism, which meant that he mispronounced the r-sound as l. Whether this traulism was natural or affected, he made sure that it worked to his advantage, so much so that it was said to "suit his voice perfectly, making his speech both charming and compelling." But Alcibiades was not content to rely on his impediment and charm alone to make men sit up and take notice. Throughout his life he worked hard to ensure he found the right words for the circumstances, often pausing mid-speech until he found the perfect phrase—a habit which his enemies put down to his poor grasp of vocabulary, but which may equally well have been a device to make his audiences listen all the harder. And so his reputation grew, until he was recognized as a "man who spoke with extraordinary power," and more than any other politician of his day could fully grasp what needed to be said—and say it. Yet it is a salutary fact that, save for these brief hints in a fragment of Aristophanes, we would know nothing of Alcibiades' early forensic career.[38]

Despite his relative youth, however, Alcibiades was soon involved in other aspects of public life, too. As heir to a vast inheritance, he was obliged to contribute at least some of it to the public good. Athens operated a system called *leitourgia,* whereby, from the age of nineteen, wealthy citizens were selected annually to undertake legally compulsory "liturgies," funding a variety of civic enterprises from their own pockets. These could range from paying for (and often captaining) a trireme and its crew—as Cleinias II had done with such aplomb at Artemisium—to funding public dinners or serving as *choregus* (financing a chorus at a dramatic or musical festival). The cost of each varied widely, but, while none was cheap, all were prestigious, providing a superb opportunity to flaunt both wealth and munificence. A *choregus,* for example, acting as producer for a tragic chorus or for his tribe's performance of a *dithyramb* (an intricately choreographed, lavishly costumed hymn in honour of Dionysus) could not only delight an audience of perhaps some six thousand spectators in the Theatre of Dionysus, but, if successful, win a prestigious prize for doing so. Indeed it was as *choregus* that Pericles had first entered public life, bankrolling the great poet Aeschylus' tragic trilogy that included his stirring *Persians,* commemorating Athens' victory over the Persians at Salamis.[39]

Sweeping into the theatre in ostentatious purple robes, Alcibiades, too, fulfilled the role of *choregus,* and he attracted not just the admiration of men and women alike, but scandal. He was assigned the duty of producing a boys' dithyrambic chorus, which performed at the annual City Dionysia. A unique mix of solemn sacrifice, competition, imperial propaganda, music, dance, drama, and unrestrained partying, this early April festival, attended by audiences from across the Greek world, was an occasion when Athens and its leading citizens were most on show. How they conducted themselves would be observed, noted, and discussed for years to come. Which was why Alcibiades' behaviour was so scandalous.[40]

As with every other type of festival performance, the dithyrambs were competitive, and governed by strict rules. Only Athenians were allowed to perform, and *choregoi* could insist that members of rival choruses be ejected, if they could prove that their names had not been entered in the *phratry* lists.

According to one story—a calumny perhaps—it was this rule which provoked the scandal. It transports us to the theatre's wooden benches beneath the high Acropolis. As the fifty-strong company assembles, ready for its performance, one of Alcibiades' adversaries, Taureas, a wealthy member of an old Athenian family, unexpectedly comes forward from the crowd and formally questions the right of one of the boys to take part. Taureas is quite within his rights, and the rules state that such a challenge must not be questioned. But to leave it until the last moment, and to raise the issue in such full view, is surely provocative.[41]

Alcibiades is furious. He strides over to Taureas and the judges, and begins to remonstrate with them. When they refuse to back down, he reaches out. He seizes Taureas. And punches him. Hard. Then, as Taureas staggers back, he rains down blows on his opponent. Gasps of horrified indignation burst from the spectators in the audience, Athenians and foreigners alike.

They are aghast, and when the time comes for the performances, the atmosphere is charged. The audience applauds Taureas' chorus loudly and pointedly refuse to listen when Alcibiades' boys sing. And yet, when it's all over, the judges give the prize to Alcibiades. They are so terrified of the consequences of rebuffing him. Or so, at least, another enemy claims later in a law court to an audience fed on tales of wild Alcibiades' notorious misdemeanours.

For it is stories of his outrageous private life which dominate this period. In *Banqueters,* Aristophanes mentions a certain anonymous playboy born "when Phallenius was chief archon at Athens." There was no "Phallenius." The name was simply a play on "phallus"; and ancient commentators were in no doubt about whom this playboy was intended to represent: he could only be Alcibiades. Indeed, Alcibiades' private life really does seem to have been scandalous. But now it was women as much as men with whom he dallied. As one ancient commentator put it pithily: "As a boy, he enticed husbands from their wives; as a young man wives from husbands."[42]

On his return from the hardships of Potidaea, Alcibiades (despite the ongoing ennui of the war) was determined to live life to the full. In addition to ancestral estates in Attica worth a reputed hundred talents, he owned a large townhouse, of which he was inordinately proud, and set about decorating it in the latest style. To paint it, he chose the Samian artist Agatharchus, one of the pioneers of perspective, who was well-known, too, for his work in connection with the Theatre of Dionysus, where he created stunning scenic panels for performances of tragedies. But Agatharchus had no ambition to be a domestic painter-and-decorator and declined the invitation. Not that this deterred Alcibiades. He abducted the artist and locked him in his house. Only when its rooms and courtyard had been painted to his exacting satisfaction did he set Agatharchus free—graciously sending him on his way with a pretty speech and lavish gifts.[43]

It was a sign of Alcibiades' self-conscious modernity that he took such interest in the decor of his home. Most houses of the time were modest, single-storey structures, introspective buildings constructed around a courtyard with no outside windows. But by now a handful of larger, two-storey villas were appearing in Athens—elite residences, whose owners could entertain in style and wallow in the latest luxuries. Some began to lay floor-mosaics, and we know that Alcibiades fixed cloth hangings—perhaps around the courtyard's peristyle to provide welcome shade and flutter coolly in the scorching summer breeze. Furniture, too, was of the highest quality: couches for *symposia* with exquisitely carved wooden frames, occasionally inlaid with ivory, were draped with rugs in vivid colours and piled high with cushions; wall-cupboards groaned with chic pottery from ateliers in Athens' Ceramicus district; and as night fell, flames from finely detailed oil lamps cast warm shadows on the richly painted walls.[44]

When Spartan raids eventually abated, Alcibiades could begin developing his country estates. He had at least two: one near Acharnae on the northwest Attic plain at Pedion, which was relatively large, and another smaller estate east of Athens and Mount Hymettus at Erchia. His houses here were more utilitarian, with storage areas neatly packed with wheat and barley, lentils, millet, spices such as coriander, almonds, olives, honey, vinegar, and wine—while in other rooms women would card and spin the wool from Alcibiades' flocks, and walk back and forth in front of looms, as they wove clothing for their master and his household. Here, as in town, the work was carried out by a staff of well-trained slaves, but it was on his countryside estates that Alcibiades required his most specialized team. For it was here, most probably at Pedion, that he set up his stud farm, with its pasture lands and stables, exercise pens and race-track, a strictly regimented business calling not just for grooms, and stable-hands, and trainers, but chariot-technicians, and people to look after tack, not to mention jockeys and drivers. It was a massive enterprise, and one which almost certainly required a very thick-skinned and experienced manager.[45]

Alcibiades' pride in his properties knew no bounds. But, as usual, Socrates tried to bring him down to earth. Carved on a marble slab was displayed a map of the world as it was then known. Socrates took Alcibiades to see it and asked if he could point out Attica. He could. "And your estates and houses?" Alcibiades replied that they were not marked, to which Socrates exclaimed: "Exactly. They don't add up to even a small portion of the earth—and yet you hold them in such high regard?"[46]

Nothing daunted, in the Agora, while scruffy Socrates was buttonholing unsuspecting passers-by and subjecting them to a torrent of confusing questions, Alcibiades preened, peacock-like. His extensive wardrobe was the talk of Athens, and he was often seen, provocatively androgynous, surrounded by a coterie of his admirers, in a halo of exquisite perfume, wearing his distinctive shoes, ostentatiously trailing his expensive purple robes in the dust or yellow mud, careless even as he ruined them. The very way he walked—with his head tilted back at an affected angle—attracted comment. For Alcibiades knew well the value of self-publicity and the importance of what is now called "spin." It was said that he once bought a hunting dog for seven hundred drachmas—a vast sum, approaching the value of a pedigree horse. The creature had a particularly lovely tail, which one day Alcibiades lopped off. All Athens was outraged on the animal's behalf, and the gossip was of nothing else. But Alcibiades was delighted. "It's just what I wanted," he is reported to have said. "They won't have time to talk about anything worse that I might do."[47]

It was a shrewd remark, which betrayed a canny understanding of how best to manipulate not only gossipmongers, but potential voters. Already Alcibiades was carefully trying to craft his image as an amiable rogue—a privileged aristocrat, perhaps, but a man of the people, too, a golden boy who was more than happy to bestow some stardust on his followers. For, Alcibiades was nothing if not ambitious. And he was fuelled by a desire to win.

Witness his advice to a foreign admirer. As the economic hub of the Greek world, Athens attracted many settlers from other city-states, migrants, merchants, money men, for whom the port of Piraeus was a potential gold mine. Known as "metics" (literally, "home-changers"), some grew wealthy, others struggled to survive, and, while all enjoyed protection from the law, they held no political rights, could own no property unless especially entitled, were regularly enlisted in the army, and were subject to special taxes.

According to the story, one (anonymous) metic is so besotted with Alcibiades that he sells everything he owns and begs him to take it as a gift. Graciously, Alcibiades accepts and invites the man to dinner, after which he returns the money with instructions that the next day he must go down to the Agora, where the annual auction is being held for the right to collect public taxes. Even with such regulations as were in place, tax collectors could cajole and threaten, accept fat bribes, and generally rake in handsome profits. It was, therefore, a much coveted position. But whatever the regular collectors offer, Alcibiades tells the metic to bid a talent more. But he is frightened. He does not have that kind of money. It is only when Alcibiades' expression hardens, and he threatens chillingly to have him beaten if he fails to follow his instructions, that the metic agrees.[48]

The auction becomes heated. When it is over, and the metic has won the bid, his unsuccessful competitors crowd round him, threatening him, demanding to know how such a man as he could put up such a vast amount, clamouring for him to name his guarantor. As the man flounders, weak and embarrassed, from some way off a voice rings out. It is Alcibiades. "He is my friend. I am his guarantor." Intimidated, the tax collectors beg him to back down, and eventually he does—but not until after Alcibiades has insisted that the newly successful candidate pay the metic a talent as compensation.[49]

But the stage on which Alcibiades most desired to win was politics. Only his youth counted against him. To hold office, an Athenian must be at least thirty years old, so, once again, Alcibiades bent the rules. By now the ongoing cost of the war was taking its toll. At its outset, Pericles had believed that it would last no more than four or five years, and it was on this assumption that the Athenian treasury had calculated its war budget. After six years, however, there had been no let-up in the fighting. In fact, the theatre of conflict had expanded to include Sicily.[50]

Seduced not only by the persuasive words of Gorgias, the master rhetorician who led a delegation from Leontini, but by the prospect of further conquest, the Athenian Assembly had voted to send a task force west to try to liberate the island's Ionian Greek colonies from the growing threat of Syracuse. Reserves were in danger of running low, and as much money as possible needed to be wrung out of the allies.[51]

And so it was that, in 425, at the age of twenty-six or -seven, Alcibiades was appointed one of ten commissioners tasked with revising the annual tribute-lists of Athens' subject allies. Even if his appointment was in part a recognition of the work his father Cleinias had done before him, it was an acknowledgement of Alcibiades' extraordinary talents, too. For it must have involved the commissioners in travelling to each of the allied states, interviewing money men and politicians, and examining financial records, before settling on the new amounts that must be paid. Not only that: more than 225 small states, which had previously been exempt, were now called upon to make financial contributions, with the result that, by the end of the year, four hundred allies were now sending cash to Athens' coffers. The tribute had been increased by three hundred percent.[52]

The man behind these new demands on Athens' allies was a politician who had plagued Pericles with lawsuits in his final years and had risen swiftly to prominence in the wake of the elder statesman's death. Brash, swaggering, and crowd-pleasing, a man accused by his enemies of possessing a "cruel and violent nature," with a style of oratory which the conservative elite found vulgar, Cleon represented a new breed of politician who owed his wealth not to breeding but to industry. Like Anytus, he owned a tanning factory, which, in the eyes of the landed elite, made him nouveau riche, beyond the pale, an upstart and an interloper—though just thirty or so years earlier, in 459, Cleon's father, Cleaenetus, had enjoyed sufficient wealth to serve as a *choregus*. With the familiar old order under threat, establishment figures accused Cleon of aggressive showmanship, of hitching up his tunic so he could make flamboyant gestures as he spoke, of using unstatesmanlike, abusive language, of shouting down opponents in the Assembly.[53]

They were peeved, too, because, as he came increasingly to dominate political debate, Cleon openly demonstrated his disdain for Pericles's war strategy, and relatively swiftly succeeded in changing the rules of engagement. Whereas Pericles had argued for a policy of containment—withdrawing behind the city walls, allowing the Peloponnesians to ravage Attica while Athens dominated the sea lanes, and hoping that the Spartans would soon grow bored and sue for peace—Cleon advocated aggression. The war, he said, had reached stalemate. The Peloponnesians had not tired. The plague had sapped Athens of men and morale. And their finances were dwindling.

Again and again in the Assembly he proposed that the most direct route to victory was a show of total force. When a revolt on allied Lesbos was quashed in 427, Cleon thundered that Athens must slaughter every man on the island and sell its women and children into slavery. Only through such a show of strength could Athens keep her reputation and maintain her Empire. Under the spell of Cleon's oratory, the Athenians voted to support his resolution, and at once they sent a trireme east to carry out their orders. But the following morning, they awoke sobered and regretful. As concern spread through the Agora about what they had done. Some insisted that the Council convene another meeting of the Assembly. And now, on Pnyx Hill, cooler heads prevailed. A second vote was taken; the first was overturned; and, in panic, a further trireme was launched, its crew importuned with urgent instructions to row at full speed to reach Lesbos in time to stop the massacre. They did. Just. The commander of the first ship was about to read out the decree. Mass slaughter was averted, and instead the more lenient terms were promulgated. But still a thousand citizens were rounded up and killed.[54]

Cleon was undeterred. His can-do—must-do, at all costs and without moral qualms—philosophy had begun to seep into everyday political debate. And not just into politics. At the City Dionysia of 426, Aristophanes chose Cleon as the butt of his savage humour. In his *Babylonians,* in which the aftermath of Mytilene must have featured heavily, he portrayed him as a rabble-rousing firebrand, a tub-thumping demagogue, whose policies were undermining Athens and her Empire. Cleon responded with a lawsuit. It was Aristophanes, he charged, who had brought Athens into disrepute by ridiculing both its leading statesman and its democracy—and this at the City Dionysia, where foreigners were present.[55]

The central issue of the case was not just Aristophanes' supposed slander of Cleon, but the very nature of the democratic system itself, including *parrhesia:* the right of freedom of speech in law courts, the Assembly, and the theatre. If Cleon won, Athens would become a very different place. An anxious jury could clearly see what was at stake. They threw the case out of court.[56]

Aristophanes was jubilant, and set about tearing into Cleon even more vigorously, triumphantly pouring out his vitriol against him. At the next opportunity, the Lenaia festival of 425, a celebration of drama and Dionysus held in the chill winter months, he gloated over Cleon's defeat in his comedy, *Acharnians,* while twelve months later, in *Knights,* he likened his progressive enemies to "men who fish for eels: when the water's still, they catch nothing; only when they stir the mud can they succeed." In this comedy, Cleon—identified to the audience through his nickname, "The Dog"—is portrayed as a foreign slave, a Paphlagonian, who wants to subvert Athenian democracy. But his aims are thwarted by an unusual hero, a sausage-seller called Agoracritus. The meaning of this character's name is ambiguous—either "the quarreller in the Agora" or "the darling of the Agora." So is the character himself. Apparently divinely sent, he is inspired by Athene to play jokes on the Paphlagonian, defeats him and emerges victorious to the delight of all, declaring: "you would think I was a god." If the Paphlagonian represented Cleon, who was the sausage-seller? In Athens, as in many cultures, sausages were thought to resemble phalluses, and there was one man more than any other with the reputation of "selling his sausage" on the city streets, enchanting and provoking the Agora in equal measure, behaving as though he were divine. That man was Alcibiades, and it is likely that it was he, still hesitant yet already brilliant, whom Aristophanes was now setting up as a worthy opponent of the ambitious Cleon.[57]

Yet only months after *Knights* was performed, Cleon's reputation reached stratospheric heights. That April, Athens sent a fleet to Sicily to augment the forces already there, in an attempt to bring the campaign to a successful close. But in the seas off the southwest Peloponnese it ran into a storm. For one of its number, Demosthenes, this was a godsend. A canny former general, Demosthenes had learned from bitter experience of fighting in the mountains of Aetolia (where his hoplites had been routed by lightly armed guerrilla fighters) that conventional tactics needed to be rethought. Now he had "sought and gained permission to use the fleet as he saw fit for operations against the Peloponnesian coast." Initially the generals, eager to press on for Sicily, were reluctant to linger on their voyage. But then nature intervened. A sudden squall blew up and forced them to take shelter.[58]

Now, beached at Pylos in southwest Messenia, prevented from sailing by days of gales and high seas, and with the Athenians becoming bored and restless, Demosthenes persuaded his colleagues (for want of anything better to do) to let him build a fortress on the headland of Coryphasion, from which he could conduct raids and foment slave revolts. As grey surf smashed against the boulders far below, the walls took shape, and, by the time the rest of the fleet set sail, Demosthenes and a small garrison were safely ensconced on enemy soil.

Sparta responded, rapidly mobilizing an army and a fleet which occupied the Bay of Navarino south of Coryphasion, while a detachment of Spartan hoplites took up position on Sphacteria, the long narrow island which straddles the bay's mouth, and—after an unsuccessful effort to storm the Athenians' position—settled down for a long siege. But within days the Athenian fleet bound for Sicily returned, and gained mastery of Navarino Bay. At a stroke the tables were turned. The besieging hoplites on Sphacteria were now besieged. All that the Athenians need do (they thought) was bide their time and starve the Spartans into submission. But somehow the Spartans held out, and, with Autumn approaching, when choppy seas would make sailing hazardous, it seemed that the Athenians would not manage to maintain their blockade for much longer. Something needed to be done.

In the Athenian Assembly Cleon rose to his feet. Pointing mockingly at his archenemy, the old-school conservative general, Nicias, he announced that if Athens had real men as generals—if he, Cleon, had been in charge—the Pylos campaign would have succeeded long ago. If he were to sail to Pylos now, he could bring matters to a conclusion within the three weeks which remained before the weather broke. As the citizens bayed their approval, Nicias, thinking he was calling Cleon's bluff, retorted that he would willingly give up his post if the People really wanted to appoint Cleon general. The People really did. And so, somewhat surprisingly, did the aristocrats. For them, any outcome would be beneficial. Cleon might succeed, which would benefit all Athens, but failure would severely hamper his political career, which would benefit the elite. As for Cleon himself, a man who had never held command before, he calmly gathered a handpicked force of lightly armed troops, and with a squadron of triremes he raced down to Pylos.[59]

As they approached, they found Sphacteria ablaze. Whether started accidentally by the beleaguered Spartans or deliberately by the Athenians, fire was sweeping across the island, catching quickly in the desiccated undergrowth and sending sparks and wood-smoke high into the azure sky. Safe in their rocky clearings, the Spartans were untouched. But now, without the cover of dense undergrowth, they were exposed. The Athenians could see precisely how many they were. And where.

Working in close contact with Demosthenes, Cleon landed his archers, slingers, and javelin-throwers, together with a small number of hoplites before dawn. They caught the Spartans unprepared. Some were barely awake before their lives were taken. But, as the Athenian light troops ran to seize the hilltops, the surviving Spartans rallied. Drawn up in tight ranks they tried to fight a hoplite battle with the Athenians. But the Athenians simply taunted them, refusing to engage. Instead, a storm of arrows, stones and javelins rained mercilessly from the morning sky, while the din of shouting boomed remorselessly in the Spartans' muffled ears, and the stinging dust kicked up from the burnt wood made their eyes weep and blinded them.

At last the outcome was clear to everyone. Demosthenes and Cleon ordered a ceasefire and issued an ultimatum: surrender or die. Negotiators scuttled back and forth from the Spartans on the island to their superiors on land. In the end the word came back, "Do what you think best, but do nothing dishonourable." After the briefest of discussions, and for the first time in their history, the Spartans surrendered. One hundred and twenty elite warriors (together with 172 support troops) were put in chains and shipped back to Athens, while in the Agora their shields were proudly hung in the Painted Stoa with the triumphant inscription hammered into them: "the Athenians from the Spartans at Pylos."[60]

It was a turning point in the war. With such prestigious hostages in Athenian custody, Sparta's hands were tied. No more could she send raiding parties into Attica. No more could she effectively pursue hostilities. But this did not mean conflict with Sparta's Peloponnesian allies was at an end—and it was in this context that Cleon, with Alcibiades as one of his lieutenants, revised the tribute lists.

And still the war dragged on. The next year, 424, saw bad news from Sicily. The Athenian campaign had run out of steam. And worse. The brilliant Syracusan politician, Hermocrates, had somehow managed to convene a conference of the Greek states in Sicily, held in the southern city of Gela. Here, he argued that, no matter what their differences, it was wrong for Sicilians to invite Athenian soldiers onto the island's sacred soil. All Athens wanted was conquest, not liberation. Sicily belonged to the Sicilians. They must come to terms among themselves. They must send the Athenians back home. And so they did.[61]

Cleon was furious. Charging them with taking bribes, he dragged the unsuccessful generals through the lawcourts, causing two to be exiled and one to be fined. But internal squabbling was pointless. As long as Thebes and Megara were menacing her borders, Athens and Attica were still in danger of attack. In their offices just off the road which led west from the Agora, Athens' generals planned their next moves. They were ambitious. Demosthenes (rewarded for the victory at Pylos by being re-elected general) would sail round the Peloponnese into the Corinthian Gulf, from where, on an appointed day, he would launch an attack overland against Boeotia's western territories. At the same time, his colleague would invade Boeotia from the east. And to cap it all, while the Thebans found themselves caught in this pincer movement, democrats in several Boeotian cities would rise up and open their gates willingly to the victorious Athenians. If it worked, it could just end the war.[62]

As Demosthenes launched his fleet, his colleague, Hippocrates, mustered his own forces. The two men had worked well together in the past. Only months before, they had nearly managed to take Megara. Only the unforeseen arrival of the Spartan general Brasidas, *en route* for the far north of Greece, had thwarted them. It may be that Alcibiades served on this Megarian campaign under Hippocrates. Hippocrates, after all, was part of his extended family, the son of Pericles' brother, Ariphron, a blue-blooded Alcmaeonid with a fine equine name ("Horse-Strength"). But whether he campaigned at Megara or not, when the call-up lists were posted in the Agora for this new campaign, Alcibiades' name was on them. Unlike Socrates, however, he was not to be a hoplite. He was to ride for Athens in the cavalry.[63]

3

UNBOWED IN BATTLE

Eros, unbowed in battle! . . . No god can escape from you, or any man whose life lasts for a day . . . You hold the reins taut, force good men to do bad things.

Sophocles, *Antigone,* 781–792

THE CAMPAIGN AGAINST BOEOTIA, which saw Alcibiades and his young cavalry comrades clattering out in armour through the city gates of Athens, had been meticulously planned. Too meticulously, as it turned out, since, for it to succeed, not only must the timings of its tightly choreo-graphed manoeuvres be scrupulously observed, but strict secrecy must be kept at all times. As it was, though, loose tongues wagged and arrangements went awry. And what could have been a stunning victory ended in the hellish horror of a firestorm in Apollo's temple near the sea at Delium.[1]

It started with Demosthenes. Having sailed round the Peloponnese, he miscalculated the date and launched his attack prematurely. Meanwhile, to compound matters, the Athenians' plan was leaked to the Thebans. So, when Demosthenes and his army tried to put in to shore, they found the full force of the Boeotians drawn up against them—and, rather than fight a pitched battle, which they would undoubtedly have lost, they wisely decided to abort their mission. Which was what the fifth columnists in the Boeotian cities decided to do, too. When Theban troops, informed of potential insurrection, took up position in their public squares, the plotters quietly melted into the November night and forgot their passion for betrayal.

But none of this news reached Athens' general, Hippocrates. So, believing he would find Boeotia in a state of panic and confusion, he struck out northeast for enemy territory. The force he commanded was, by the standard of the day, immense—over seventeen thousand men. Citizens; metics; even non-resident foreigners from across the empire who happened to find themselves in Attica; hoplites; light-armed skirmishers; and cavalry: the almost endless column wound its way between Mount Parnes and Pentelicon, on past the wooded rise at Decelea, with Marathon and all its memories a few miles to the east, before at last descending through the broken fir-clad hills just north of Oropus, the most northeastern town of Attica, to a narrow plain which led down to the sea, a few miles inside Boeotia.[2]

Across the racing waters was Euboea, where, at the war's beginning, Athens' farmers shipped their livestock—sheep and cattle—safe from Spartan raiders, while on the plain itself, close to a sacred well, stood a squat Doric temple of Apollo, home to a fabled, gilded statue of the god. Around the temple sprawled a jumble of outbuildings, some of which had fallen into disrepair. According to tradition, the complex had been set up by the islanders of Delos, the god's birthplace, which was what now gave the sanctuary its name: Delium.[3]

As Alcibiades rode down towards the sea, he must have thrilled to the thought that now, at last, he was helping bring the war into Boeotia—for it was on Boeotian land that Cleinias, his father, had been killed at Coronea. And vengeance, the lust to get even, coursed through Alcibiades' blood. Now, though, he must perform the role assigned to him and the cavalry: to keep the plain secure while the foot-soldiers did their work; to harass any enemy contingents sent to investigate; to ensure the operation was not jeopardized. So as Alcibiades and his companions scoured the rolling hills, the army began the laborious job of building a stockade.

First they dug a trench around the sanctuary, heaping earth to form a low embankment. Into this they plunged sharpened stakes, and between them they piled everything that they could get their hands on—stones and bricks from nearby houses, vines from around the sanctuary, trees and shrubs—to form a rampart, while at strategic points they erected wooden towers. After two days it was complete. Just as at Pylos, so now at Delium, they had planted an Athenian outpost in enemy soil, a bridgehead from which further operations might be mounted. Phase one of the plan was a success. Which meant that now, with their mission accomplished, the vast bulk of the army could go home.

So, after enjoying a well-earned lunch, while Hippocrates and a small detachment stayed as a garrison at Delium, and the cavalry, including Alcibiades, saddled horses and prepared to ride back home, most of the hoplites and skirmishers packed up their belongings and set off on the road southwest, until they entered Attica. Here in a quiet valley the hoplites, tired from their labours, paused for a short while to enjoy the safety of their homeland, while their light-armed colleagues, more fleet of foot, pressed on for Athens.

And then: a message from Hippocrates. Against all expectations, he had learned that the entire Boeotian army was nearby. Almost immediately, Hippocrates was there himself. Hastily, the hoplites, armed and armoured, took up their formations, eight ranks deep. Hastily, such cavalry as had not been left on guard at the stockade cantered round to take up their positions at either end of the long line—among them Alcibiades. Hastily, Hippocrates rushed through the ranks, exhorting every man, reminding them of times they had defeated the Boeotians in years past. But he was only half-way down the line when, above them, there appeared the massed Boeotian troops. Silent. Silhouetted on the skyline. And the cool November breeze was gently ruffling their helmets' horsehair crests. Seven thousand hoplites; ten thousand lightly armed skirmishers; a thousand cavalry. And on their right wing, the Theban hoplites were drawn up a staggering twenty-five ranks deep.[4]

Now the Boeotians were chanting their war song and advancing down the hill, a terrifying, deafening wall of shields and sharpened spearheads. Now, too, the Athenians were lowering their helmets, and raising their own spears and shields, advancing up the slope to meet them. And then they clashed. But there was little they could do to stem the Theban phalanx's inexorable advance. Step by painful step, the Athenian left wing was forced to give ground, gradually backing down the slope. Meanwhile, against all odds, their right wing broke through the Boeotians' left—where the men of Thespiae, Tanagra, and Orchomenus were stationed—and in the tight space hacked them down. But then: confusion. In the *mêlée* no one could distinguish friend from foe. As spears sank home and sword-blades flashed, as many Athenians were cut down by their friends as by the enemy.

Then the thundering of hooves, and two squadrons of Boeotian horsemen, coming out of nowhere, bore down on the Athenian left wing. Terror. Chaos. Rippling, engulfing the whole army. The Athenians turned tail and fled. Over the rough ground they ran. Scattering in all directions. Some made for Mount Parnes; others, for friendly Oropus; still others, back to Delium. Without any plan. Anywhere, as long as they could dodge the killing. And everywhere Boeotian cavalry pursued them.

And it is now, in the panic of the rout, that again the mists part to reveal the young, heroic Alcibiades. As the fighting swirls around him, he is desperately trying to defend the fleeing infantry, urging on his horse, galloping across the maquis to impede the enemy, when, through the gathering twilight, he makes out two figures doggedly heading for the hills. One is the ex-general, Laches, who commanded the fleet in Sicily the year before. The other is Socrates. His *daimonion,* his inner voice, has directed him to take this path to safety, and, indeed, something about the philosopher's demeanour—calm, determined, imperturbable—has caused the Boeotians to keep their distance. So far. But that might change at any moment. Spurring his horse forward, Alcibiades thunders to his old friend's side, and, covering his retreat, remains there until, with nightfall, the Boeotians call off their pursuit. Arguably, Alcibiades has saved Socrates' life. The debt of honour that the philosopher once earned at Potidaea has been repaid.[5]

But for the Athenians the day that dawned with so much promise had ended in disaster. Just as at Coronea, twenty-four years earlier, a glorious incursion into Boeotian lands had been negated, when withdrawing troops allowed themselves to be first ambushed and then massacred. On this campaign to Delium, a thousand of the seven thousand hoplites who set out—14 percent—would lose their lives along with countless light troops and camp followers, and Hippocrates, their general. And although, with the next dawn, most of those who had escaped to Oropus and Delium were rescued by Athenian ships, the horror was not over.[6]

A few hundred men remained on Boeotian soil, a defiant garrison in the stockade around Apollo's temple. But they were trapped. The enemy had them surrounded. Moreover, they were forced to endure what for the Greeks was not just a gruesome but a sacrilegious sight. Flouting all accepted international tradition, the Boeotians had forbidden the Athenians to retrieve their dead. For seventeen long days, as winter took its grip on Delium, the corpses, stripped and naked, lay malodorous and bloating on the rain-soaked earth, while ambassadors from each camp argued legal niceties, and neither side backed down.[7]

At last, the Boeotians had had enough. Irked that the Athenians were occupying their land, feigning outrage that they were using holy water from Apollo's sacred well to drink and wash in, but mostly determined to send a message to the whole of Greece that they must be respected, they brought the siege to an abrupt, spectacular, and terrifying end.

The agricultural Boeotians had long been the butt of Athenian humour. Comedians dismissed them all as archetypal rustic simpletons. Now, though, their ingenuity belied the joke. Somewhere among their ranks was a technological genius. Following his specifications, the Boeotians sawed a tall tree trunk in half, lengthways, hollowed out the wood, plated the interior with iron, and rejoined the two halves with the iron tube jutting out some distance from the front. Next, beneath the tube's mouth, they hung a cauldron filled with lighted sulphur, coals, and pitch. Then they wheeled the whole contraption, mounted on carts, as close to the stockade as was safely possible, angled the muzzle high, and, pumping air with massive bellows through the barrel, stoked the flames. And from the iron tube there shot a well-aimed fireball. It was the world's first flamethrower, and its effect was devastating.[8]

The vines and planks that formed the stockade walls went up like kindling. The beleaguered Athenians panicked. They tried desperately to escape. But now the smoke was raining sling shot, javelins, and arrows. Some made it to the beach, where Athenian boats rescued them. Others—two hundred—surrendered to the enemy. Still others died. And the news was met in Athens with stunned horror.

Once more, the reality of war sank home. Once more, by some lucky accident, Alcibiades had come through unscathed. First it had been the cold and plague of Potidaea. Now the carnage and hellfire of Delium. And neither can have left him mentally unscathed. But somehow the routines of life must be observed. And in Athens, with its twists and turns, its festivals, its rituals, its holidays, its disappointments, its betrayals, its anticipations, and its fears—they were. As they were in private, too, by Alcibiades. For he had reached the age of thirty, when a young Athenian must take a wife.[9]

For most Athenians, indeed most Greeks, marriages were arranged. Jealous of their wealth, protective of their networks of connections, always with an eye to bolstering their power, as their daughters neared puberty, the heads of elite families scrutinized the up-and-coming sons of high society, shrewdly weighing each candidate's potential, taking soundings, calculating the advantages of matrimonial alliance. Often they did not look far. Many branches of the noblest family trees were so tightly intertwined that unravelling them can be virtually impossible.[10]

For any father looking for a son-in-law, Alcibiades—despite his reputation for philandering, extravagance, and violence—represented a good catch. His award for bravery at Potidaea, his panache at Delium, his early emergence into city life as one of the negotiators of the tribute lists, his energy and his charisma, his determination and his wealth: all these were most attractive. His premium was high.

Informal negotiations may have lasted many years, with political support discussed and potential dowries increased in the face of competition. But for Alcibiades, one family must have led the field: the family of the richest man in Greece; the family that Alcibiades' own mother, Deinomache, first married into; the family of Hipponicus—a man whose wealth was valued at two hundred talents. When he divorced Deinomache, Hipponicus remarried at least once, and around 436, when the tensions at far-off Epidamnus that would spark the war were first beginning to appear, he fathered a daughter, Hipparete ("Horse Virtue"). And it was over this young girl, now approaching fourteen years of age, a prize in her own way every bit as glorious as the *aristeia* won at Potidaea, that the bargaining and haggling were taking place.[11]

Despite Alcibiades' undoubted merits, an incident said to have occurred in his youthful past could have threatened to frustrate his chances. The story went as follows: as a young man—responding (so he claimed) to a dare—Alcibiades calmly walked up to Hipponicus and, quite unprovoked, punched him hard in the face. All Athens was awash with gossip. It was outrageous! Deplorable! So typical of the young upstart! But the next morning, Alcibiades rose early and strode through the yawning shadows of the city streets, the only sounds the bark of dogs, the bray of donkeys, cocks crowing, and the far-off doleful call of peacocks, once a diplomatic gift to an ambassador. Reaching Hipponicus' house, Alcibiades hammered loudly on the door, and, when he was admitted, apparently contrite, stripped off his tunic. Then, vulnerable and naked, he offered his body to the older man, telling him to beat him as savagely as he saw fit, in punishment for such disgraceful behaviour. At once Hipponicus forgot his anger and forgave him. Once more Alcibiades' charm and chutzpah won the day.[12]

Hipponicus' decision to wed his daughter, Hipparete, to Alcibiades may already have been made prior to Delium, for it is possible that Hipponicus fell in battle there. In Antiquity there were some who suggested it was Callias Hipponicou, his eldest son, who finalized the marriage. We have already caught a glimpse of Alcibiades in Callias' company, when Callias was entertaining the philosophers Protagoras and Hippias in the shaded courtyard of his chic urban house. But this was just one of many properties the family owned. Their deme of Alopece (which numbered Socrates among its members, too) was located outside the city walls, high on the bee-rich slopes of Mount Hymettus, a mere half-hour's walk from the Acropolis. From here, the family's tentacles spread wide, and their tight grip could be felt on many aspects of Athenian life, from politics to commerce to religion.[13]

Although they farmed rich tracts of land at Alopece, Hipponicus owed most of his monumental wealth to his control of a fabulous seam of silver, found two generations earlier at Laurium, in eastern Attica. Men had been mining here for nearly three thousand years, but it was in 483 that the extraordinary discovery of an abundant vein was made. Overnight it changed Athens' fortunes—it was this silver, pouring out of Laurium, that paid to build the fleet that smashed the Persians at Salamis, that, in the years which followed, made the Athenian economy the strongest in all Greece, and that (augmented by the tribute from her empire) kept the city buoyant in the first years of the war.[14]

Concessions for the silver mines were guarded jealously. Profits (Hipponicus earned six talents per annum) were astronomical. But they were won at an equally stratospheric human cost. At the height of production, a handful of wealthy families, jealously controlling operations, sent up to twenty thousand slaves (Hipponicus owned six hundred) to work in the most appalling and inhuman of conditions. Back-breaking, claustrophobic, stifling: the environment that these most wretched of all Attica's inhabitants endured, sweat drenching their exhausted bodies as they toiled in narrow, labyrinthine mineshafts, ensured their lives were bleak. And short. Penned by night into well-guarded prison camps, sent by day into the choking darkness, Laurium's workforce—men and women both—had more reason than most to resent their masters. Theirs was a grim gulag, a powder keg of sullen anger, primed for explosion.[15]

For Hipponicus and Callias, however, Laurium meant luxury. Which, being such pillars of the community, they were convinced that they deserved. For they could trace their descent not merely from Homeric heroes but from gods. And in particular from Hermes, the god of business deals and heralds. Which was appropriate, for, as it happened, the family boasted an ancestral priesthood of enormous sanctity and prestige: it filled the office of both Herald and Torch-Bearer at the Eleusinian Mysteries, a Panhellenic festival under Athens' tight control, one of the most profoundly religious events in the entire Greek world.

At the core of these Mysteries, held along the coast from Piraeus at Eleusis on the Bay of Salamis, were initiation rites that promised the soul's survival and rebirth after death. For it was here at Eleusis (so the Greeks believed) that the goddess Persephone, abducted to the Underworld by Hades, Lord of the Dead, had once returned to earth and the embrace of her mother, the grain-goddess Demeter. And just as Persephone could seem to die and be reborn, so, too, it was proclaimed, could mankind.[16]

In most Greek state religious festivals, offerings and prayers were made on behalf of not the individual but the community. The private beliefs of those involved were largely irrelevant. What mattered was the correct repetition of established ritual. But the Eleusinian Mysteries, although celebrated communally, were entirely personal. Alcibiades himself was an initiate. Surrounded by crowds of fellow neophytes, he, too, made sacrifices, washing piglets before slaughtering them as gifts for the goddess of the Underworld; undergoing the prescribed set of preliminary rites, the "Lesser Mysteries," held in March; then, eighteen months later, in September, partaking in the five days of the "Greater Mysteries."

These culminated in a daylong procession from the gates of Athens to the sanctuary at Eleusis, the drinking of *cyceon* (a psychoactive potion), the watching of a sacred drama, the revelation of the sacred objects, and the promise of eternal life. And such was their longing for life everlasting that

The road to Eleusis: the Sacred Way passes through Athens' Cerameicus Cemetery. (Photograph by the author.)

people flocked to Athens and Eleusis from across the Greek world—men and women, slave and free. Any Greek-speaker, pure from the stain of murder, could take part. For Alcibiades, the Eleusinian Mysteries would quite literally change his life.

Because the promise of the Mysteries was so intense, the priests who managed them were highly honoured. The most venerated of them all was the Hierophant, who revealed the sacred objects at the climax of the ritual, a role reserved for an ancient Eleusinian family. But almost as revered—and certainly as lucrative—was the office of Torch-Bearer. And this belonged to Hipponicus, inherited from his father, to be passed down to his son. In daily life, most priests were indistinguishable from their fellow citizens. Not so the Torch-Bearer. Alone in Athens, he was marked out, the wearer of elaborate long robes (designed, some said, by the playwright Aeschylus), his beard long and his flowing hair bound in a sacred headband. It was a costume which the Torch-Bearer wore even on the battlefield.[17]

Dressed in these sacred vestments, Hipponicus' father, Callias II, had fought the Persians at Marathon, and after the battle, so the slander-mongers said, they served him well. When the defeated enemy put to sea and tacked south towards Sunium, most of the Athenian hoplites ran for Athens to defend its shores from possible attack. But they left at Marathon a small contingent tasked with guarding not just the prisoners but much of the Persians' mobile treasury, abandoned in the haste of their escape. Among these guards was Callias II. As he patrolled the beach, his long robes flapping in the warm wind from the sea, it was said that a Persian saw him and, judging by his dress and his demeanour, thought him a king. So he raced across the sand and threw himself down on his face in front of him, before, begging his mercy, he took Callias II to a place where vast quantities of gold had been hastily buried in a trench. Whereupon Callias, "the most cruel and unlawful of all men," took the treasure for himself—and, to stop him telling others, butchered his informant on the spot. It was an unlikely tale, but one which stuck, and although, even in Alcibiades' day, comic poets could be assured of a cheap laugh by referring to Callias' family as the "trench-rich," the nickname was more likely to have derived from their mining interests than from foul play at Marathon.[18]

In fact, even before Marathon or the discovery of the silver seam at Laurium, the family's wealth was legendary. According to some they owed at least part of it to shady dealings in the time of Solon, but it was in the next generation that they truly burst onto the international Greek stage. In 564, Callias I, who had already won an equestrian race at Delphi, celebrated victory at the Olympic Games when his horse won the flat race and his chariot team came second. Perhaps it was to celebrate this triumph that he called his first-born son Hipponicus ("Horse-Victory"), a proud aristocratic name which would grace generations of his successors.[19]

But this was a turbulent time in Athens. Rich families were jockeying for power. When—after several abortive attempts—Peisistratus seized the reins, some, like the Alcmaeonids, were forced to flee. Not Callias. Despite having capitalized on Peisistratus' earlier misfortunes by snapping up his property at auction, and then "contriving every other type of aggressive action against him, too," Callias somehow survived. Perhaps his unconventionality worked in his favour—to avoid offending powerful rivals, he allowed his two daughters to choose their own husbands.[20]

Two generations later, the "trench-rich" Callias II, shared his grandfather's propensities. A three-time winner of the Olympic chariot race, he, too, liked not just horses but feisty women. When Cimon, son of Marathon's victorious general, Miltiades, was faced with a crippling fine, Callias II gladly paid it off—in return for the hand of Cimon's sister, Elpinice, in marriage. Tongues wagged. That Callias received no dowry was bad enough. But

Elpinice's reputation was scandalous. Intelligent and unconventional, she refused to toe the line in Athenian polite society. Rumours abounded about her relationship with Cimon. The two, it was alleged, were lovers. And had she not posed for Polygnotus' painting of the Trojan princess, Laodice, the loveliest of Priam's daughters? As for her behaviour in public, when Pericles prosecuted Cimon for bribery, did she not intervene in private to get him acquitted? And later, when Pericles crushed a rebellion on Samos, did she not have the nerve to point out to him that it was his policies which had caused the revolt in the first place? For a woman publicly to criticize a leading citizen took courage. And, ominously for Alcibiades, courage, cleverness, and unconventionality were qualities which Elpinice's granddaughter, Hipparete, his bride-to-be, possessed in abundance.[21]

Elpinice's husband, Callias II, like his grandfather Callias I before him, was equally nonconformist. The brother-in-law of Cimon, he was nevertheless close to Cimon's sworn enemy Pericles, so close that, according to tradition, he was sent by Pericles to Persia to conclude peace terms in 449. It was not the only time that he or members of his family would make the long trek east to the dusty plains of Susa and Ecbatana in the interests of diplomacy—or south to Sparta where Callias II was held in such high esteem that, when Alcibiades II renounced his Spartan *proxeny,* Callias II was the clear candidate to take it on. On his death, perhaps in 446, this *proxeny* passed (along with the office of Torch-Bearer and his enormous wealth) to his son, Hipponicus II. And when *he* died it came to Callias III, half-brother to Alcibiades. A man who spent a fortune on attending lectures given by the best known sophists. A man who, in the words of Xenophon (who knew him), "delighted in being praised no less by himself than by others." A man who would now be linked to Alcibiades by marriage.[22]

Even for the average family, an Athenian wedding was a most extravagant affair. For Callias and Alcibiades it offered the excuse for an almighty party. And a party made all the sweeter for Alcibiades because he had managed to extract a dowry of epic proportions from the family of his bride-to-be. For starters it included a down payment of ten talents—more than eighteen months' worth of mining revenues. Enough to buy sixty pedigree horses.[23]

As in most cultures, weddings were accompanied by tightly observed ceremonies. Traditionally, marriages took place in February, the month called in the Attic calendar "Gamelion"—quite literally, "marriage month." For Hipparete, the days leading up to her wedding were a flurry of activity, a welter of rituals to signify her passing out of childhood. Beloved dolls, balls, knucklebones, her clothing, even tambourines used as she danced in "maiden choruses" in honour of the gods: all were now put away or consecrated to the virgin Artemis, the goddess of wild nature, the protectress of the young, at whose lush sanctuary at Brauron, on the eastern coast of Attica, Hipparete had already spent a season with blue-blooded friends, dancing, racing, weaving yellow robes in rites of passage grooming her for womanhood.[24]

And now, on the eve of her wedding, she was presented with a pomegranate seed to eat, perhaps a symbol of the death of her virginity or an assurance that—just as the pomegranate tied Persephone to Hades' house—she would always have a place, should it be needed, in her childhood home. It was a promise she would soon have cause to remember.

As the sun rose on her wedding day, Hipparete's long lustrous hair was shorn and laid in offering to Artemis. Then, surrounded by the women of the household, some holding smoking torches, and accompanied by a young boy playing the *aulos,* she walked through the streets, veiled, her head lowered, in procession to a fountain, sacred to the Nymphs, themselves imagined as young girls on the cusp of marriage. With them the women took a special urn, which they now filled and carried home. And in the holy water Hipparete was bathed, a purifying ritual to mark her childhood's end. Then they anointed her in scented oils, dabbed perfume on her temples, garlanded her head, placed dainty sandals on her feet, and dressed her in exquisitely embroidered robes. Radiant and beautiful, she was as close to looking like a goddess as she would ever be. All she need do now was endure the seemingly never-ending wait until she was at last presented to her husband-to-be, Alcibiades.

For Alcibiades the process was much simpler. All that was expected of him was that he turn up at Callias' house with select members of his family (no doubt including Axiochus, the uncle with whom he first went whoring to Abydus), remember to bring along the requisite marriage gifts, and settle down to enjoy the fun.

It all began with sacrifices to the gods not just of marriage—Artemis and Aphrodite, the goddess Peitho (Persuasion), Zeus, and Hera—but of the family line, the "Tritopatores," embodiments of the bride's noble lineage, without which Alcibiades would never have considered marrying Hipparete. Not that Hipparete was present. During this and the feast that followed (families intermingling, but men and women strictly segregated), the bride was nowhere to be seen. It was only once the banqueting was over, with its raucous, bawdy wedding hymns, its plentiful libations, its impromptu speeches and its risqué jokes, when the room was hot with sticky, sweating bodies and the garlands were already threatening to wilt, that she was at last brought in.

Veiled, awkward, perhaps hesitant, she took her place among the womenfolk. The marriage was at hand. First the ostentatious presentation of the wedding gifts from Alcibiades to Callias. Then Hipparete was made to stand and brought before Alcibiades. This was the central moment of the ceremony. With anticipation ripe throughout the room, he took his bride's veil in both hands and raised it to reveal her face. Such was the strict seclusion in which girls were kept that it was probably the first time he had seen her. And with that action, that unveiling, they were married.

To cheers and celebration, they all poured out into the chill night. In the dark street by the door a wagon waited, decorated, twined with flowers. Up climbed Hipparete and Alcibiades, while in the driving seat sat the *parochus,* the "best man," perhaps Axiochus. A flick of the whip and the vehicle trundled off, with Callias and all the family and friends of both the bride and groom following on foot behind, the children crowned with myrtle laughing wildly as they ran. In time they reached their destination: Alcibiades' rich mansion, so extravagantly painted, with such luxurious hangings and sumptuous furniture. The wagon stopped and Alcibiades jumped down, sweeping Hipparete up in his arms and carrying her, as custom dictated, across the threshold.

Even now it was important that she avoid contact with the earth. Instead, she sat, a footstool at her feet, while she received the symbols of her new existence: pots and pans, a grill, a sieve, the house keys, emblems of her new domestic empire. This done, Hipparete ate a wedding banquet of her own, a sweet spread, rich with dates, and figs, and nuts, and honey cakes, redolent of fecundity to usher in her own fertility—before Alcibiades lifted her high and carried her off to his bedroom. And the *parochus* stood guard outside the door.

As the couple, a man of at least thirty and a barely pubescent girl, consummated their relationship, the house erupted in a frenzied carnival, pulsating music and wild dancing, drinking and carousing, singing, laughter, an incessant banging on the bedroom door, lewd suggestions and encouraging advice. And next morning: yet another procession from the house of Callias. At its head, a boy dressed all in white, a torch in his right hand. Behind him, young girls clutching baskets, and others loaded down with gifts. Exquisite pottery and clothing; necklaces and jewels; jars of cosmetics, perfumes, oils; rich robes and dresses; shoes—all of which Alcibiades, undoubtedly hung-over, received with pleasure.

What little is known of Hipparete and her fate does not imply an easy wedding night. Or that the long days, weeks, and months, and years that lay ahead got better. Even the best of marriages was seldom intimate. Xenophon, a young boy at the time of Alcibiades' society wedding, would later declare that there were few people a man would talk to less frequently than his own wife. For, other than enquiring after the smooth running of the household, there was so little about which he could converse with any interest. The age gap was one hurdle. The bride's lack of education or experience of life outside the cloisters of her family home was another. And what interest had Alcibiades in spinning or weaving or the religious festivals that only women were allowed to celebrate—or any of the tedium of her domestic life?[25]

For Alcibiades, a wife was the source of just two things: legitimate children and money. And he was determined that from the first would come the second. In the next few years Hipparete would bear Alcibiades a daughter (whose name has not been recorded) and at least one son, also called Alcibiades. Traditionally, the eldest son was named from his paternal grandfather. But if there was another, first-born son, a baby Cleinias, he did not live long, and he is never mentioned. More likely, in the naming of his heir, as in so much else, Alcibiades was happy to flout custom. His own name, after all, was so glorious.

It was in the matter of the baby boy that fissures would first open publicly in Alcibiades' relationship with his brother-in-law, Callias. Before the marriage, he would proclaim, the two had reached a gentleman's agreement: when Hipparete bore Alcibiades a son, Callias would pay him another ten talents. Such a "birth bonus" was unheard of, but this does not mean that it was *not* part of the initial bargain. Dowries usually represented 15 percent of the bride's family wealth. Alcibiades had received only 10 percent, which, in absolute terms, of course, was far from insignificant. But it was not what he might have originally expected. Perhaps there had been an agreement to stagger the payment, which was why the total amount received would now be greater than if the full figure had been paid at once. Whatever the reason, 20 percent of Callias' wealth was a significant amount, and twenty talents a most hefty sum. In fact, adding the two payments together, it was the largest dowry ever recorded in classical Athens. Perhaps, when it was first discussed, Callias had been distracted or assumed it was a joke and went along with it—only to be met now by an unequivocal demand: pay up or face the consequences. For Callias it would be a chilling moment. He had known Alcibiades so long, he must have seen the mask of charm slip previously as the limpid eyes glazed over in an icy stare. But then it had been directed towards others. Never towards Callias. Like the Gorgon's gaze, it petrified. And it would cause Callias to fear for his life.[26]

He would pay up. But he would make a public proclamation. In the event of his untimely death, he would leave everything he owned—his money, his house, his property, his mining interests, and his farms—not to his closest heirs but to the state. Only in this way, Callias would calculate, could he sleep safe at nights or walk the streets of Athens, free from the constant dread of Alcibiades' assassins lounging, loyal and unforgiving, in the shadows.

But he could not protect Hipparete. Any Athenian wife had to contend with myriad challenges. It was such a common superstition that too much domestic intimacy drained a husband of his *andreia*—his manhood and bravery—that six generations earlier, to ensure the procreation of new citizens, Solon had enshrined in law that a man must have intercourse with his wife at least three times a month. But there were just too many distractions! Sex was so easily available. From well-educated courtesans to backroom prostitutes turning cheap tricks in the brothels of the Cerameicus, to a sultry slave-girl with come-hither eyes, not to mention a good-looking boy, there was always someone other than his wife to turn the head of any married man. As a popular comedian a century later said: "It's hard for any wife to compete against a tart."[27]

For Hipparete, it would be impossible. Especially as Alcibiades did nothing to conceal his womanizing. At last, humiliated by his constant seductions, his incessant roistering with local whores and foreign courtesans, both free and slave, whom he even had the gall to "entertain" under his roof, his ham-fisted attempt to lure her into adultery with a paid proxy, so that she might be found equally unfaithful, Hipparete would slip out of his house and steal off home to Callias. And with Alcibiades doing nothing to woo her back, she would prove her mettle as the granddaughter of the indefatigable Elpinice and take a course of action, which few well-bred women would ever entertain, let alone set in motion: she would petition for divorce.[28]

Only now would Alcibiades appreciate just how potentially disastrous the situation was. If Hipparete was granted a divorce, the law demanded that he must return the dowry. And possibly the "birth bonus," too. Most, if not all of which he probably would have spent already. With financial ruin staring him in the face, there would be only one possible course of action open to him, and Alcibiades would take it. On the day of the hearing, he would sweep in, seize Hipparete, fling her across his shoulder, and carry her away, striding menacingly across the busy Agora, and back to his own house. Glaring. Daring anyone to intervene. And no one would.[29]

Confined, imprisoned, and alone, Hipparete would have little hope. A short time later, Alcibiades would set sail for Ephesus on business. When the news reached him that Hipparete was dead, it would come as an unutterable relief. With an icy smile, he might even recall the words of the poet Hipponax, himself from Ephesus: "A woman brings you pleasure only twice. The first time's on your wedding night; the second's at her funeral." Hipparete's death would be such a neat and satisfactory solution to Alcibiades' problems, especially as he would have the perfect alibi. No questions would be asked. Except, perhaps, by Callias. Whom, as events turned out, it would be most unwise to underestimate.[30]

But, for now, all this was in the future. Already, other challenges faced the newly married, would-be statesman. With the Delium debacle, the Peloponnesian War threatened to take a dangerous new turn. On the streets of Athens feelings were running high. It was not just the casualty figures—all the more significant, since the fighting force had been depleted by the plague. Or that the momentum gained at Pylos had appeared to stall. Or even the blow to Athens' kudos in the eyes of allied states.

Just a few weeks after the disaster at Delium, news reached the city that the Spartan commander, Brasidas, who had thwarted Athens' hopes of taking Megara a month or two before, had arrived in northern Greece at the head of a ragtag army made up not just of Peloponnesian mercenaries but Spartan Helot slaves. His mission was twofold: to foment revolt among Athens' regional allies, and cement relations with the oily Macedonian king, Perdiccas, whom the Athenians had found so unreliable prior to Potidaea.[31]

But even the beguiling Brasidas—despite his Spartan upbringing a man of wit and charm, a brilliantly accomplished strategist, as persuasive a diplomat as he was a ruthless general—even Brasidas found Perdiccas impossible. Especially since the Macedonian, despite his promises of help, was more interested in using him to bolster his own powerbase and expand his kingdom. And when, in the face of a hostile army, Perdiccas and his Macedonians simply melted into the night, leaving Brasidas to face the consequences on his own, the Spartan had had enough. Washing his hands of Perdiccas, he turned his mind to undermining Athens.[32]

Throughout the winter of 424/3, Brasidas worked tirelessly, until, one by one, inspired by his persuasive mix of blandishments and threats, he brought over to his side strategic city-states throughout Chalcidice, until on each of the three long promontories there was a Spartan stronghold. But his most glittering prize was Amphipolis, a relatively new Athenian colony founded only thirteen years earlier on the banks of the River Strymon.[33]

Athens' general in the region, Thucydides Olorou, was caught unprepared. By the time he reached the city, it had fallen. Only a panicked scrabble saved the nearby port of Eion. But it was too little to appease the Athenian Assembly. Fulminating at such gross ineptitude, Cleon easily persuaded the angry, nervous People to exile the hapless general. (Which allowed Thucydides, freed from the responsibilities of his command, to travel and observe, to question and reflect, and, in the end, to write his masterly, if slanted, history of the Peloponnesian War.)[34]

Cleon had good reason to be furious. What made Amphipolis so crucial was its location. As its original name, Ennea Hodoi ("Nineways"), suggested, it was a major transport and trading hub, where silver and gold came down from the Pangaion Hills to the northeast as well as timber from the wooded mountain slopes of Thrace. And Athens desperately needed all these raw materials, not least the timber, since, over generations, Attica and much of the accessible Greek mainland had been severely deforested, and to maintain the fleet in top condition demanded wood of the highest quality.[35]

So, flushed with his success at Pylos, Cleon led an army of his own up to Amphipolis, and there, in a squalid skirmish below the city walls, both he and Brasidas were killed. At a stroke the loudest voices advocating the continuation of the war were silenced. And a hush descended over Greece. For the first time in many a campaigning season, in parts of the war-torn land the truth of the old proverb could be appreciated: "In war sleepers are awakened by trumpets, in peace time by birds."[36]

Although Corinth, Boeotia, and others of her allies still had an appetite for war, in Sparta the high command's enthusiasm for continuing hostilities was growing lukewarm. Yes, the Spartans had the reputation for being the fiercest fighters in all Greece, but they went to war reluctantly. Almost a decade earlier, when strategies were being discussed, the more cautious had expressed concerns that hostilities would be drawn-out and costly. Now, with the defeat at Pylos and the death of Brasidas—not to mention the 120 prisoners of war being held as pawns in Athens—the majority of Sparta's board of five ephors were minded to discuss peace.[37]

So were many Athenians. Especially the older, more conservative politicians, who had seen their hero Pericles' policy of containment (in their opinion) recklessly and dangerously flouted by younger upstart firebrands such as Cleon, and who were (rightly) worried that the war had taken such a toll in terms of lives and treasure. And chief among these old-school statesmen was a man who would soon emerge as Alcibiades' chief enemy, the man who had inadvertently given Cleon the chance to shine at Pylos by handing him the generalship: Nicias Niceratou, the darling of the law of unintended consequences.[38]

Born around 470, Nicias was part of the Laurium mining cartel. Thanks to the thousand slaves he hired out to the state to work there, as well as to inherited wealth, he could play the gentleman, gathering around himself the great and good of Athens, promoting himself as a bulwark of the old establishment against the irresponsibilities of the feckless younger generation, letting it be known that if anyone deserved to inherit Pericles' mantle, it was he.

But Nicias was no Pericles. Where Pericles was a decisive general, Nicias owed victories to luck as much as skill. Where Pericles was an effulgent orator, his rolling phrases mesmerizing those who heard them, Nicias was hesitant and weak. And where Pericles, with his rational, enquiring mind, kept company with the greatest thinkers of his age, debating long-held certainties, questioning even the existence of the gods, the credulous and superstitious Nicias employed a private soothsayer, upon whose advice on business, politics, and personal decisions he came increasingly and cravenly to rely.[39]

What he lacked in charisma (and he lacked a lot), Nicias tried to make up for in his public benefactions. To enhance his reputation, he poured vast sums of money into those areas of life where politics and religion converged. The athletic games he financed were more opulent than any seen before. The dramas that he sponsored were more lavish. The statue of Athene that he set on the Acropolis, her robes and helmet plated in pure gold, was just one of many ostentatious offerings with which he wooed the city. But it was on Apollo's sacred island, Delos, that Nicias proclaimed his piety with most extravagance.[40]

In the dying years of the great plague, which had killed so many of his fellow citizens, Nicias ploughed a fortune into a stunningly theatrical ceremony designed to appease Apollo. For, as well as being the god of music, prophecy, and reason, Apollo was the god of healing—and disease. In the first book of the *Iliad*, we see him, angry at being disregarded by the Greeks, unleashing his arrows of pestilence against their army until men and animals fall dying, and the smoke from their pyres drills high into the air. But if he could inflict plague, Apollo could cure it, too. So, to persuade the god to forget whatever had provoked his anger against Athens and restore good health to the city, in 426, Nicias staged a religious ceremony of awe-inspiring grandeur.[41]

Its setting was the low-lying, sun-baked isle of Delos, a site of unusual significance. Here the goddess Leto, gripping a palm tree by the shores of a shallow lake, had given birth to Apollo. Here was the spiritual centre of the Ionian Greeks. And here, until 454, had been the site of Athens' imperial treasury. Bristling with offerings and statues, including twelve marble lions dedicated by the islanders of Naxos on a terrace overlooking the shallow lake beside which the god had once been born, Delos already boasted two temples built by the Athenians. Now, as they prepared to raise a third, Nicias led the Ionians in purifying the island. In night-time ceremonies, the remains of all who had been buried there were disinterred and removed to Rheneia, an island separated from Delos by a narrow channel. Meanwhile, it was solemnly proclaimed that no one might give birth or die—or keep a dog—on Delos.

But what would be remembered for centuries to come (and what later provoked Alcibiades to rival it) was the showmanship with which Nicias reorganized the Delia, the annual festival in honour of Apollo, his sister Artemis, and his mother Leto. Here, as an ancient hymn declared, "Ionians in long flowing robes assemble with their children and their modest wives" to watch athletics contests and sing hymns. In past years it had been characterized by a hugger-mugger exuberance, as worshippers rushed down to the seashore to greet each shipload of pilgrims as they arrived, urging them to perform their praise-songs even as they were disembarking, their garlands awry, their robes askew.[42]

For Nicias, dour, devout, and dutiful, this would not do at all. To achieve the gravitas that the festival (and he) deserved it must be done more properly. So, he choreographed a ceremonial of breathtaking theatricality. Instead of landing immediately at Delos, he and his chorus of worshippers put ashore with all their necessary effects (including sacrificial animals) on Rheneia, and, that night, Nicias' stage managers set to work. By sunrise, all was ready—a pontoon of boats, all gilded, painted, hung with gorgeous tapestries and garlanded with flowers, linked Rheneia to Delos.

As heat swelled and sunlight sparkled on the lapping waves, Nicias led a sumptuous procession, the worshippers all draped in dazzling robes, all chanting hymns and dancing in solemn, tight-drilled order. Then came the sacrifices and the banquets. And, when all was done, Nicias dedicated a life-sized bronze sculpture of a palm tree, a feat of wondrous craftsmanship, to stand close by an earlier colossal statue of Apollo, nine metres tall. Surely, now Apollo could not fail to favour Athens! Then Nicias went further. He bought a plot of land, a small estate, the annual revenue of which he entrusted to the islanders of Delos to pay not just for regular sacrifices but for their prayers to the gods for his personal salvation.

If only Nicias and Athens had possessed Apollo's powers of prophecy to foresee how it would all turn out. Just two years later, despite their dedications made on Delos, the god would not protect the desperate Athenians caught in the firestorm at his sanctuary at Delium; and a decade after that, thanks partly to the vengeful plots of Alcibiades, the prayers he paid the Delians to make for him would not save Nicias from pain, disgrace, and squalid death in Sicily.

For now, though, Nicias' display at Delos was a public statement of his god-fearing piety and old school, conservative values. Here was a man who simply had no time for the chic new morality of the younger generation, as he took every opportunity in public to make clear. And not least in his peace negotiations with the Spartans. Where sound sense demanded that Athenian opinion be united and all should enjoy some sense of ownership of whatever deal was made, Nicias imperiously excluded up-and-coming politicians, dangerously sidelining them from the process. And among those he thus offended was Alcibiades.[43]

Already for a long time Alcibiades had bitterly regretted that his grandfather had renounced the Spartan *proxeny*, the role of representing Spartan interests in Athens. Not least because that role had passed first to Hipponicus II and now to his son, Callias. If only Alcibiades could win it back! How central to the peace negotiations he would be! Thanks to ancestral ties, he already had powerful friends in Sparta, old comrades of his grandfather, whose friendship remained constant. Chief among them was the family, to whom he owed his name, with one of whom, Endius (the son of a Spartan Alcibiades), he was by now in ever closer contact. But try as they might, cajole or threaten, wheedle or suborn, neither he nor Endius could manage to convince the Spartan kings in whose gift the appointment lay. The *proxeny* remained elusive.[44]

But there were other ways for Alcibiades to woo the Spartans. While their shields glittered provocatively on the Painted Stoa, the Spartan prisoners from Pylos languished, kicking heels, weighed down by the humiliation of surrender. When peace came (as it surely must), and these warriors walked free, their gratitude and friendship could be useful. So, despite his lack of an official status, and acting purely on his own initiative, Alcibiades took it on himself to look after their welfare. His visits to them must have been extraordinary: the dazzling young aristocrat, pampered, perfumed, and luxuriant; the hardened Spartans with their killers' eyes, increasingly neurotic as they contemplated their disgrace, as they imagined the humiliation of their homecoming.[45]

Not only had they surrendered—the first surrender in all Sparta's history—the very manner of their defeat had been so unheroic. Not given any chance to fight at close quarters as hoplites must, they had been overwhelmed by the missiles of a mass of light-armed troops that struck down their comrades indiscriminately. In a quip, which Alcibiades would one day have bitter cause to recall, one of their number, asked if those who died at Pylos were *kalokagathoi* (beautiful and noble aristocrats), summed up the reality of facing a barrage of missiles with typically grim wit: "Spindles" (by which he meant arrows) "would be valuable indeed, if they could distinguish brave men from milksops." His remark was doubly damning: spindles were the tools of women, not of men—and in Sparta, the tools not even of free-born women but of Helot slaves.[46]

Arrows had always troubled Spartans. Almost as much as cowardice. Before Thermopylae two generations earlier, one Spartan tried to shrug off the fear that the Persians' arrows were so numerous that they would blot out the sun by joking: "Good! We'll fight them in the shade." For the Spartan prisoners from Pylos, such memories cannot but have rankled, especially since they could remember the fate of their two fellow countrymen who survived Thermopylae, one because he had been sent with a message to Thessaly, the other, suffering from ophthalmia, excused from fighting. For both, their shame at living while their comrades were all dead was too much to bear. One hanged himself; the other, at Plataea the next year, ran screaming like a madman at the enemy, deliberately seeking death.[47]

Although the bodies of the Spartan fallen were buried on the battlefield, it was said that, before their army marched to war, wives and mothers pointed to their loved-ones' shields proclaiming, "with it or on it"—come back carrying your shield or carried on it, dead. Don't be a coward. Don't throw away your shield. Do not surrender. But throughout the fifth century, the number of elite Spartan warriors had been declining. By the late 420s, fewer than two thousand remained. So, the 120 prisoners in Athens represented a significant proportion of Sparta's fighting force. When they returned from captivity, so Alcibiades clearly calculated, Sparta quite simply could not afford to give them the cold shoulder. A major shift in attitude would be required. And it would do no harm to Alcibiades to have these Spartans owe him favours.[48]

Equally, to exchange ideas with Spartans—however laconic their utterances might be—cannot have failed to stimulate a young Athenian aristocrat. Many among the rich and powerful had always viewed democracy with suspicion; the Assembly as a beast to be handled with extreme care; the People to be feared as well as courted. In the war's early years, when the Spartans were ravaging the plains of Attica, Pericles had done his best to muzzle public debate, lest popular sentiment overturn his rationally thought-out strategy. Even Cleon, the embodiment of the new demagoguery so despised by the conservatives, was aware of the perils of direct democracy, fretting that voters were seduced by a speech's beauty or persuasiveness regardless of the implications of its content, accusing them of being "enslaved to the pleasures of listening—more like the audience for a sophist's seminar than men debating the affairs of state."[49]

For some Athenians, democracy seemed unfair if not downright dangerous. Around this time, one went so far as to write and circulate a tract condemning the Athenian constitution for allowing the "worst type of person to enjoy better fortune than the best," characterizing the People as "corrupt, ill-educated, ignorant," and asserting that "everywhere in the world, the best people are opposed to democracy." Better by far, such anti-democrats contested, was how the Spartans organized affairs, with their *Ecclesia* (Assembly) of all the *Spartiates,* their five ephors (Overseers) and their *Gerousia* (Council of Elders) attended by seasoned warriors over sixty years of age—and by their two kings.[50]

To the disgruntled Athenian elite, the fact that every Spartan citizen could vote (albeit not by a show of hands in which each individual counted equally but by shouting, a system that quite literally allowed those with the loudest voices to carry the day)—that Sparta was therefore technically, in the narrow definition of the term, a democracy—was irrelevant. For while, in Athens, *demos* was simply another name for the impoverished majority, in Sparta, where there were relatively few citizens, all of them were landowners. In Athenian terms, then, they were *kalokagathoi,* not artisans, merchants, or urban poor. Moreover, the Spartans recognized the need for a well-defined social hierarchy, unlike in Athens, where "the People are no better dressed than slaves, and certainly no handsomer," and "a slave won't even make way for you in the road." Rich Athenians, then, thought Sparta a model society, and there were some who dared not just to voice their views in private but provocatively to dress like Spartans in public, "wearing their hair long, eating meagrely, not bathing." The Athenians had a word for such behaviour: laconizing. And Aristophanes knew precisely who was at the heart of this pro-Spartan movement: Socrates and his aristocratic disciples.[51]

If they were to wield political power in Athens, however, even Socrates' most avid students (current and former) must reconcile their elitist views with their city's democratic constitution. Even Alcibiades. In 422, at the age of thirty, he could not just marry—he could be appointed by lot to hold office. Still more importantly, thirty was the minimum age at which an enterprising, popular young politician could be elected general. Which, for a man, who had been awarded the *andreia,* the prize for his valour at Potidaea ten years earlier, was a not unreasonable ambition.[52]

First, though, he must make his mark on the Assembly. Previously, he had carved a niche as a beautiful object of adoration, or caused men to wonder at his bravery in battle. Now, Alcibiades must prove himself as a persuasive orator, a man of strategy, a politician of great vision. Yet he seemed curiously reticent. According to one anecdote, even his first appearance in the Assembly was characterized by awkward buffoonery: as he was walking through his local district of Scambonidae, Alcibiades heard a sudden roar and loud applause from the direction of Pnyx Hill. Curious, he stopped a passer-by and asked what was going on. "They're holding a public subscription," he was told. "The citizens are being invited to contribute money to the war effort." At once Alcibiades rushed up to the Pnyx, leaped onto the Speakers' Platform and generously offered a donation of his own. The crowd cheered. The handsome Alcibiades grinned delightedly and raised his arms to acknowledge their applause. And in that moment a quail, which he had been carrying beneath his robes, escaped and fluttered off. A quail? Why was he carrying a quail? Because birds such as quails were traditional courtship gifts, and Alcibiades (in this anecdote surely in his twenties, still unmarried) was on his way to meet a lover. The Assembly shrieked with delight. Men started to chase the flapping bird. Shouts of encouragement. Loud hoots of laughter. The meeting degenerating into farcical confusion. Until one man caught the bird and swaggered back triumphantly to present it to the grateful Alcibiades. The man was a ship's helmsman, his name, Antiochus. And from that moment onwards, he was Alcibiades' close friend—until years later, when Antiochus would ruin him.[53]

Whether it took place or not, the anecdote reveals much about the nature of the Athenian Assembly. Sometimes mocking, sometimes rowdy, sometimes belligerent, although seasoned politicians such as Pericles and Cleon could admonish it, condemning its fickleness and censuring its lack of strategy, for a young man still not fully confident in his oratory, the Assembly was an institution to be feared. With its multitudes of disparate attendees packed onto the hill—more than five thousand people each with his own opinions, more than five thousand voices, five thousand throats potentially to bay in disapproval—it resembled nothing so much as the Hydra, the mythical monster, whose regenerating heads the hero Heracles was ordered to destroy, a demonic hybrid, the stuff of nightmares. And Alcibiades may well have been terrified.[54]

Another anecdote suggests that it was Socrates who helped him overcome his fear. The story tells of Alcibiades, tongue-tied and nervous, confessing his anxieties to his mentor. The two are walking in the bustling Agora beneath the slopes of the Acropolis, where men are going about their trade. As they pass a cobbler's stall, Socrates points to an artisan as he hammers nails into a shoe. "Are you afraid of him?" he asks. "No," replies Alcibiades. They bump into the town crier. "Or of him?" "No, not of him." And then they see a tent-maker sewing up his leather strips. "Or him?" "Not him, either." "But isn't Athens made up of men just like them?" asks Socrates. "If you don't fear them individually, don't fear them in the Assembly!"[55]

If true, the story is revealing. Later, it was said that Alcibiades proclaimed himself more in awe of Socrates' abilities as a speaker than of Pericles'. However, Socrates' skill was that of a fine swordsman, stabbing at his rivals individually, with deadly pointed questions, slicing through their arguments with the razor sharp blade of his own intellect. But conversing with one person, or even with a handful, was, in reality, nothing like addressing the Assembly. In the bear pit that was Pnyx Hill, when he mounted the Speakers' Platform, an orator must be not just assured and confident but utterly mesmeric. His words must grip his listeners; his arguments, must move them and inspire; his voice, his gestures, his entire delivery must fire their hearts and minds. He must resemble the finest actors in the Theatre of Dionysus, as they moved their audience to tears or laughter. Yet, unlike those actors, the orator could hide behind no mask. He must assume responsibility for the words he spoke. And what he said could impact markedly on real lives and result in death.[56]

No wonder, then, if Alcibiades was hesitant. But once on the Pnyx, once standing there, the focus of the People's concentration, once breathing in their energy and hearing their applause, once he knew that he could move them, mould them, hold them with their fears and their ambitions in the palm of his outstretched hand, confident of when to speak and when a pregnant silence was as devastating as the most well-chosen words, Alcibiades, with his trademark traulism, played to his strengths. And what strengths those were. He had not just enjoyed the basic grounding in rhetoric, which was part of every young Athenian's education, but he had grown up in the house of the silver-voiced Pericles and the honey-tongued Aspasia; with Callias, he had attended lectures by the revolutionary orator Gorgias of Leontini; he had heard the fulminating speeches of Cleon and his fellow politicians in the popular Assembly; he had honed his own skills in forensic debate in the lawcourts. By the time he first stood on the Speaker's Platform, Alcibiades must already have been versed in almost every trick of the trade.[57]

In time—indeed, in a very short time—he would become one of Athens' leading orators, ready to assume the mantle of Cleon as Athens' leading demagogue. Two generations later, another captivating rhetorician would recall him as the greatest speaker of his age, while one polymath wrote of how, more than any of his contemporaries, he knew exactly what to say in any situation. In his lifetime, too, he was applauded. Even the comic poets admired his brilliance. At first it was his political adversaries who most recognized his abilities; in time the whole of Athens regarded them with awe.[58]

So, now, articulate, persuasive, privileged, and wealthy, radiant in his reputation for bravery in battle, Alcibiades launched his political career. That he was capable of great things was undeniable. But as Plutarch would reflect: "In the same way as, thanks to its fertility, the soil of Egypt, they say, can produce 'many beneficial drugs growing next to poisons,' so Alcibiades possessed one of those exceptional characters with huge potential for both good and evil." For the Athenians, it only remained to see which aspect of that character would now come to the fore.[59]

And yet, almost the very moment that Alcibiades, by temperament a man of action, came of age to hold high office, Nicias' negotiations with the

Spartans bore fruit. At the Assembly held in the Theatre of Dionysus in March 421, days after the dramatic festival had finished, and just a few weeks shy of ten years since the Peloponnesians launched their first attack on Attica, the terms of the peace treaty were ratified. Animals were sacrificed, libations poured, and delegates from both sides exchanged solemn oaths. Among the seventeen Spartan representatives were the two kings, Pleistoanax and Agis; among the Athenians a slew of generals, men like Laches and Demosthenes and the strutting Lamachus—whose triple-crested helmet was the target of many jokes by Aristophanes—and the self-satisfied, self-righteous Nicias.[60]

From him, both in Athens and beyond, the treaty would be known as the Peace of Nicias. For he more than anyone had engineered it. But the People yearned for it, as well. The past ten years had been debilitating. Losses of citizens from plague and war, losses of livelihood from raids on farmsteads, losses of prestige and self-belief from harsh defeats and careless oversights had all combined to make the city weary. Only months earlier they had learned of a Spartan threat to tighten the noose round Athens by building a fortress in Attic territory—more bluster than real danger, since the Athenians still held a powerful weapon of their own, the Spartan prisoners; but nonetheless, a stark reminder of Athens' potential vulnerability.[61]

The terms of the peace treaty were simple. Effectively, it restored the *status quo* which had existed in the years before the war. Cities such as Amphipolis, which Sparta had seized from Athens, were to be returned. Likewise, Spartan territories such as Pylos, which Athens was now occupying. And any ongoing sieges must be lifted. The majority in Athens seemed not to care that, at a stroke, the treaty not only undid any gains the city might have made in the last decade, but rendered their great sacrifice of life quite meaningless. It was enough to have neutralized Sparta as an enemy. And not just neutralized her: gained her as an ally. For already some of Sparta's confederates, including two of its strongest, Thebes and Corinth, were refusing to accept the treaty's terms, and in the weeks that followed, it became increasingly clear that they still wanted war. Feeling suddenly isolated, the Spartans scrabbled to shore up their relationship with Athens. The same teams of negotiators met to thrash out terms, and soon with the swearing of oaths the treaty was ratified. As its first line proclaimed: "The Spartans shall be allies of the Athenians for fifty years."[62]

A generation earlier, Cimon had imagined Athens and Sparta as two yoked horses pulling the chariot of Greece to victory, and with the two great powers united the future should have been rosy. Surely not even the Thebans would dare oppose them now. And certainly not Argos, the powerful pretender, which saw itself as the rightful leader of the Peloponnesians, and whose own treaty with Sparta had just run out. With good governance and luck it might just be that Pericles' war aims had been achieved: that the Greek world was divided up in such a way as to let Sparta seem to dominate the land as Athens ruled the waves, while at the same time undermining Sparta's authority at the head of a united Peloponnesian League.[63]

But the high and mighty Nicias' refusal to involve the younger generation in his peace deal was already causing dangerous political splits. At the same time, his—and the Spartans'—inability to bring the other warring states on board exposed real tensions. Meanwhile, both the Athenians and Spartans were encountering problems of their own in honouring the terms of their agreement. And, as if that were not enough, in Athens there was one man who was viscerally opposed to any talk of peace. Alcibiades was having none of it.[64]

4
STIRRING THE HORNETS' NEST

> The best portent of all is when you fight for your own country!
> Why be afraid of war and battle?
>
> Homer, *Iliad,* 12.243–244

ALCIBIADES WAS NOT THE ONLY MAN determined that the Peace of Nicias should fail. Almost as soon as it was signed, the treaty started to unravel. Not only were the problems of implementing many of its clauses manifold, there were simply too many parties opposed to it. That Sparta's allies, Corinth and Boeotia, should refuse to come on board was inevitable: Boeotia, which shared a common border with Attica, recalled all too vividly how, a generation earlier, Athens had tried to annex it, while Corinth, being, like Athens, a major maritime trading power, was never going to concede control of the sea to her greatest rival, especially in the light of Athens' relatively recent treatment of Corinthian interests at Corcyra and Potidaea. Their response now was instructive. The Corinthians refused all overtures from Athens, while the Boeotians made the most tenuous of treaties: a temporary truce, whose terms must be re-ratified every ten days, a peace rooted in hostility and mutual suspicion.[1]

But it was the response of discontented individuals that was most threatening. While Nicias, the Spartan king Pleistoanax, and those who had spearheaded peace negotiations basked in the glory of their achievements, others—more hard-headed pragmatists—scrambled to shore up old friendships and forge new alliances in anticipation of what they were certain would be a new outbreak of hostilities. For, as it would later be grimly observed, to most Greeks "an alliance does not mean peace but merely a change of war."[2]

As each jostled to achieve a strong position in advance of that new war, the prize they all sought was Argos, for an alliance with this proud and ancient city would, they believed, be key to victory. The capital of the Argolid, Argos lay a little inland at the head of a great bay ringed by mountains in the northeast of the Peloponnese. Legend told that it was from this bay that Agamemnon had once sailed for Aulis to join up with the allied Greeks before attacking Troy; from here a mighty expedition had once marched to Thebes to take part in a war between the sons of Oedipus; and it was to Argos that the hero Perseus had once returned, clutching Medusa's severed head, which he buried deep beneath the market place, a talisman to keep his city safe. Temples were everywhere. On the conical hill, around which Argos clustered, there were shrines of Athene and Apollo, and at a distance of some five miles to the northeast, the richly terraced sanctuary of Hera was one of the most holy sites in Greece.[3]

Lying, as it did, between Corinth and Sparta, Argos was of great strategic importance. For generations it had entertained ambitions to dominate the Peloponnese, but invariably they had been thwarted. In the past it had fought bitter frontier wars with Sparta, which had chipped away at its holdings to the south. In one encounter, fought in 546 over rocky Thyrea, rather than engage with their full armies, each side left behind three hundred warriors to battle to the death. Whichever city could boast even one man surviving on the battlefield would be entitled to claim victory. Two Argives survived, and hurried home triumphantly to tell their news. But, thinking him already dead, they had left one Spartan badly wounded on the battlefield. With the Argives gone, he staggered to his nearby camp and rasped out the news of Sparta's triumph. Then, ashamed to have survived while all his comrades perished, he committed suicide. It was named the Battle of the Champions and, shortly afterwards, following a more conventional encounter, the Spartans annexed the land.[4]

Just over fifty years later, in 494, another brutal clash between the cities shook the entire Greek world. The two armies faced each other, but for long days neither attacked. Then, one morning, when the Argives were busy with their breakfast, out of the blue the Spartans overran their camp. Those men of Argos who survived ran in panic for the safety of the sacred grove at Sepeia, but even here the Spartans showed no mercy. First they tried to coax the Argives into giving themselves up, pretending that they had been ransomed. But any who stumbled out from the thick undergrowth was butchered. When the remaining Argives found out what was happening, they refused to move. So the Spartans set the sacred grove on fire and burned them alive.[5]

For most of the fifth century, however, the two cities were at peace, and Argos used the opportunity to consolidate its power, overrunning neighbouring towns and villages such as Tiryns and Mycenae, once homes of Homeric kings, and growing quietly prosperous. However, by 420, not only had its treaty with the Spartans run out, but, more worryingly, the old enemy had suddenly and unexpectedly allied itself to the other most powerful city on the Greek mainland, Athens. Caught between them, where did that leave Argos? Unless it acted quickly, it was in danger of finding itself overrun, a pawn in a bigger power game. Which frightened Corinth, too. If Argos joined forces with Sparta and Athens, Corinth would be vulnerable indeed. For months, ambassadors criss-crossed the Peloponnese, desperately trying to redraw the diplomatic map. While Argos and Corinth agreed terms and set out to woo neighbouring cities such as Mantinea and more distant city-states such as Elis into joining a Peloponnesian alliance of their own, Sparta demonstrated her displeasure by marching north into Arcadia and annexing a few (albeit minor) towns on the border of the Argolid.[6]

But, despite these minor victories, Sparta's cachet with her erstwhile allies was at an all-time low. This riled many of her citizens. They hatched plans both to bring the Boeotians and Corinthians back into the fold and to induce Argos, too, to join the Peloponnesian League as Sparta's ally. But negotiations were spectacularly botched. Sparta refused to give in to demands to return contested towns and territory (including Thyrea), and in Argos the only outcome was that ever wilder suspicions circulated against all concerned.[7]

At the same time, relations between Sparta and Athens were threatening to sour. Through no fault of her own, Sparta was unable to comply with all the terms of the peace treaty. For one thing, she failed to restore Amphipolis, whose citizens simply refused to return to the Athenian fold, especially when they learned of the treatment meted out to their near-neighbour, the rebellious Scione, whose male citizens Athens slaughtered, and whose women and children she enslaved. Sparta's failure to restore Amphipolis prompted the Athenians in turn to refuse to give back Pylos. Which caused the Spartans, desperately looking for a bargaining chip, to try to persuade the Boeotians to return the Athenian frontier fort of Panactum. Which the Boeotians agreed to do only if the Spartans made a separate alliance with them. Which was forbidden by the terms of the Peace of Nicias. But which the Spartans did anyway to ensure the return of Panactum. Which the Boeotians dismantled before they abandoned it. Which further upset the Athenians, who were already sufficiently upset, not least because they had released in good faith the Spartan prisoners captured at Pylos and could no longer use them as a bargaining chip.[8]

Which was when Alcibiades decided that conditions were ripe to take matters into his own hands. For some time he had been leading a staunch opposition against his arch-enemy, the condescending Nicias, in the Assembly, fulminating against the older politician's dithering inadequacy and dangerously pro-Spartan sentiments, pointing out how, five years earlier at Pylos, Nicias had failed to strike the killer blow and capture the Spartan hoplites stranded on Sphacteria, something Cleon managed to achieve in a matter of mere weeks; how, recently, Nicias had failed to stop his friends, the Spartans, breaking the peace terms by making a separate alliance with Boeotia; how, generally, Nicias did all he could to appease Sparta while nervously, unpatriotically blocking overtures of friendship from any other state; how Nicias, in brief, was a Spartan lackey who thought nothing of selling Athens short.[9]

Now, with emotions running high, Alcibiades sent a personal message to his influential contacts in Argos, inviting them to come to Athens to discuss forming an alliance, and to bring their friends from Elis and Mantinea with them. It was a clever move; its timing, perfect. Not only were the more militant Athenians irked by Nicias' prevarications, they had been forced to look on impotently as ambassadors from Sparta, Corinth, Thebes, and Argos, as well as many other interested states, visited one another's councils and assemblies, forming plans and discussing possible alliances. For months the expectation had been growing that at any moment Argos might side with Sparta and that a powerful new confederacy—a united Peloponnese plus Megara and Boeotia—would rise up to threaten Athens.[10]

Meanwhile, such were the international uncertainties that in Argos tensions had been rising, too, and with them an increasing paranoia that Sparta and Boeotia were on the verge of allying with Athens to attack the Argives. Already a delegation had been sent from Argos south to Sparta in an attempt to shore up relations—something Alcibiades knew he must prevent at all costs.[11]

What, then, did he offer the Argives? Undoubtedly he pointed out that it was much more natural for democratic Argos to ally with democratic Athens than with oligarchic Sparta; that Sparta, with her history of land-grabs, was an unreliable bedfellow for the Argives; that, with Athens' military aid, Argos had a realistic prospect of achieving her long-held goal of overtaking Sparta to become the dominant force in the Peloponnese. Whatever the incentives Alcibiades put forward, the Argives were intrigued. There was no harm in keeping options open. So, they sent instructions to their delegates in Sparta to play for time and make no promises. And they accepted Alcibiades' invitation to talks.[12]

But, like Nicias and his conservatives, the Spartans, too, were desperate to preserve the peace, and at the same time as the Argive envoys came to Athens to negotiate, a Spartan delegation turned up, too, keen to address both the Council and the Assembly. Whoever appointed the Spartan representatives had chosen well. Among them was Alcibiades' old family friend, Endius. This put Alcibiades in an awkward situation. Traditionally, the relationship of *xenia*, guest-friendship, which Alcibiades and Endius enjoyed, meant that each should not just offer the other hospitality, but do all he could to help the other's interests. Now, though, if he did what he considered best for Athens (not to mention worst for Nicias), Alcibiades would have no option but to speak out against Endius and jeopardize their long-held family friendship. And, according to Thucydides, this is precisely what he did. In style.[13]

Thucydides' account is as follows. The Spartan delegation arrives with an agenda: to discourage an alliance between Athens and Argos; to request that Athens return Pylos; and to reassure the Athenians that Sparta's alliance with Boeotia is not directed against them. At a meeting of the Council, the ambassadors lay out their case convincingly, assuring their audience that they possess full powers to reach an agreement on these and all other disputed questions. Alcibiades is not a little anxious. The Council has received the Spartans warmly. Consensus is in the air. The next day the delegates are due to speak in the Assembly, and, if the People likewise warm to them, it will scupper any hope of an alliance with the Argives.

So that evening, wishing to drive a wedge between Nicias and the Spartans, and to show them to be unreliable, Alcibiades meets with the Spartan envoys and gives them his word that he will personally ensure that Athens returns Pylos—if they make no mention of the full negotiating powers, with which they have been invested. (Plutarch provides extra colour. He adds that Alcibiades warns the Spartans that the rowdy Assembly is nothing like the staid, polite Council, and that the People will make mincemeat of them if they know that they possess full powers.)

Come the morning, then, the Spartans step onto the Speaker's Platform, where almost the first question they are asked (by Alcibiades himself, says Plutarch) concerns the nature of their negotiating powers. When they now claim that these are limited, the Assembly, stoked by Alcibiades, erupts in fury. Surely just yesterday they said they had full powers! How can the Athenians trust a word they say! The Spartans are ejected, the Argive delegates brought in, but an earthquake causes the Assembly to be adjourned before any decision can be reached.

The story of the wily Alcibiades stealing a march so easily on Nicias and the gullible Spartan envoys makes for an entertaining anecdote. But it is unlikely to be true. Why would the delegates trust the untried Alcibiades rather than the elder statesman Nicias, with whom they had already negotiated peace terms so successfully? Why would they so blatantly contradict what they had said the day before? And as for the proud Endius—having been so roundly duped and publicly humiliated, surely he would think his *xenia* with Alcibiades so compromised that he would never speak to him again! And yet he did. Their friendship was unbroken.[14]

It is not impossible that Thucydides' main source for this episode was Alcibiades himself. The details of his private conversation with the Spartans, the recital of his emotions, the exposition of his motivations: all suggest that—perhaps at the Olympic Games that year, or later in Thrace, reminiscing over wine as the sun sank low across the northern sea, when it

The Pnyx: until the end of the fifth century BC, the Speaker's Platform was situated in the area towards the left. (Photograph by the author.)

mattered little whom he offended—it was Alcibiades who spun Thucydides a yarn so seemingly convincing that Thucydides believed it.[15]

It is more likely that the truth is dramatically more mundane, but politically no less impressive. The Spartans may well have convinced the Council of their good intentions. But for Alcibiades this was not enough. Whether or not there was a secret meeting, when the delegates appeared in the Assembly next day, Alcibiades most likely grilled them, demanding to know exactly what they meant by their "full powers." Did the Spartans have the power to restore Potidaea, for example? Surely not. Or to prevent their Corinthian allies from attacking other Athenian-held cities in the north? Again, surely not. Or to annul their treaty with the Boeotians, which the Athenians found so threatening? As he listed grievance after grievance, addressing the broader picture, illustrating, case by case, the shakiness of the foundations of the peace, he would have exposed the limits of the Spartan envoys' powers. They could agree to anything they liked, but unless they could put words into action, their promises were worthless. It was an argument based on *realpolitik*. Perhaps in the past Sparta might have had sufficient clout to ensure her allies toed the line, but with her reputation at an all time low, she was in no position to make promises.[16]

Somehow, next day, when the Assembly was reconvened, Nicias managed to persuade the People not to act too hastily but, rather, let him lead a delegation of his own to Sparta to discuss such issues as Amphipolis and the Spartans' treaty with Boeotia. But he came back empty handed. Sparta's powers were limited, indeed.[17]

So, no doubt enjoying more than a little *schadenfreude* at Nicias' expense, Alcibiades once more introduced his Argive friends to the Assembly. This time there was no earthquake. This time there was nothing Nicias could do to intervene. After a show of hands the People's will was clear. They granted Alcibiades his treaty and alliance with the Argives. And not just with the Argives—with the cities of Elis and Mantinea, too, both erstwhile Spartan allies. It heralded a new alignment between Athens and much of the northern Peloponnese, and it was meant to last a hundred years. Only the Corinthians, despite being allies, too, of Argos, refused to come fully on board, though neither they nor the Spartans made much fuss.[18]

It was a major coup, and Alcibiades was triumphant. Still only thirty-two years old, he had redrawn the map of international Greek politics and offered Athens the promise of a greater influence in Peloponnesian affairs than it had ever hoped for. The members of the new alliance were not slow to flex their muscles. At that year's Olympic Games, Elis (the city responsible for the Festival's administration) seized the opportunity spectacularly to humiliate its once-feared enemy, Sparta. Claiming that the Spartans had invaded Elean territory in contravention of the Olympic truce, the governing body of the Games barred them from taking part. It was a highly provocative move. As the Festival approached, there were many who expected the Spartans to turn up in force and compel the Eleans to let them compete. Together with a contingent of Athenian cavalry, two thousand troops from Argos and Mantinea poured into Elis to help secure her border.[19]

In the end, the Spartan army stayed away. But at least one of their citizens slipped through the net to attend the Games in a purely private capacity. Lichas was a venerable and (for a Spartan) oddly clubbable man, with ties to far-off Libya and Samos, a man renowned for his splendid hospitality to guests who came to Sparta for the Gymnopaediae Festival, where young men danced war dances without weapons. Not only that, he was Sparta's *proxenos* in Argos, and, as such, a member of the negotiation team which had failed to secure an alliance between the cities. So, perhaps it was partly to regain some sense of his self-worth that Lichas tried to circumvent the current ban on Spartans competing in the Games. At any rate, he somehow managed to persuade the committee to allow his chariot and team to race under the colours of Boeotia. It may be that the authorities felt that, given the odds that he would not win, there would be no harm done. But Lichas' chariot did win. And when he calmly walked out into the hippodrome to place a garland on the winning charioteer's head, the spectators were furious. They demanded retribution. So there and then the judges seized Lichas and beat him with rods, the punishment for a cheating competitor.[20]

Lichas may not have been the only man beaten at these Olympics. A late author records that Alcibiades, too, was once flogged at the Games for the crime of hubris, because he boasted that his city was the best in all of Greece. If true, he is perhaps more likely—eager and enthusiastic, as he was, and not yet sufficiently assured of his own place in international politics—to have made the boast at these Games than at any other. Besides, it may be that the judges chose to beat him in a bid to make reparation to Lichas and the Spartans. Whatever the truth, the chariot race made a profound impact on Alcibiades. When he returned to Olympia for the next Games, he would make sure that he won it.[21]

For now, though, politics were paramount. At the close of the Games, there was a frenzy of activity as delegates and competitors packed up their kit. Most headed home. But not Alcibiades. Nor the most skilled negotiators from Argos, Elis, and Mantinea. Instead they made straight for Corinth, where they hoped to notch up another triumph by persuading this richest and most elegant of cities to join their alliance with Athens. No sooner had they arrived than a Spartan delegation turned up, too, and tried to thwart them. That the negotiations were long drawn out suggests that the Corinthians were wavering. The end came, as it had at the Athenian Assembly just months before, with an earthquake, a sign the gods had had enough. So with the approach of winter, everyone went home.[22]

For Alcibiades, though, there was much still to look forward to. His star was blazing bright, and in the aftermath of Nicias' humiliation in the

Assembly he had been elected one of Athens' generals. It was arguably the highest accolade imaginable, especially for one so young and relatively inexperienced. But in a society without formal military training schools, where generals were invariably chosen from the aristocracy, where leadership was learned through experience of war, where commanders fought in the front ranks, and personal courage was an imperative, Alcibiades' lineage, not to mention his outstanding service record and especially the award for bravery that he had won on his very first campaign, stood him in good stead. Besides, his charisma, panache, and confidence were such that men would willingly entrust themselves to him. It was both a sign of Athens' trust in him and an enormous opportunity. For as a general, especially on campaign, Alcibiades could wield almost limitless power. Whereas in the Assembly, a politician could be challenged, shouted down, or ignored, on the battlefield his word was law. And successful generals, popular with their troops, could capitalize on their soldiers' loyalty when they returned home, too. Almost all the most successful statesmen of past generations had led Athens to military victory.[23]

But the challenges which faced a general were legion. He must be equally adept at leading hoplites in pitched battle on the plains of Greece and commanding fleets of triremes as they smashed their way through enemy formations in the hostile waters of the open sea. He must know how to ambush and besiege, how to gather military intelligence and use it to his best advantage, how to capitalize on victory, and how to recover from defeat. He must be a good judge of topography. He must determine when it was more prudent to retreat than offer battle. He must gauge when to be lenient, while being conscious that, at times, he must be merciless. He must be far-sighted and a clear communicator. And he must be brave. The attrition rate for generals was high. Over the course of the Peloponnesian War, twenty-two Athenian generals (around 12 percent of their total number) were killed in battle. Not only that. Often immediately after a battle, and certainly at the end of their year's command, each general must face a board of enquiry, where the penalties for those found guilty of having led a botched campaign were serious indeed. Some were fined. Some exiled. Some even put to death.[24]

In Athens, the generals' headquarters, where Alcibiades was now based, stood on a street leading west from the Agora close to the Council hall, a lawcourt, and a range of other civic buildings clustering on either side of the magnificent new stoa of Zeus Eleutherios, with its proud panoply of shields belonging to Athenians who died in battle. It was here that strategies were planned, logistics calculated, call-up lists prepared. It was a place of power and formidable prestige. For some appointed to a generalship, its allure was irresistible. Whenever he held the post, the dully self-important, pale-faced Nicias would ostentatiously spend every daylight hour cooped up in the headquarters building, basking in his brilliance, instructing his private secretary to tell anyone who asked that he simply had no time for other meetings or appointments, let alone for public entertainments or private dinner parties.[25]

No wonder that the energetic Alcibiades relished the chance to get as far away from the war office as possible and put his new military and political strategies to the test. At the heart of his policy was a radical new reinterpretation of the Ephebic Oath, which committed young men to increase and enhance the lands of Athens, and which called as witness Athens' wheat and barley, vines and olive trees and figs. Previously these had been understood to mean crops cultivated within the boundaries of Attica and Athens' empire. Not so, said Alcibiades. Rather, combining sophistry with patriotism, he argued that what the oath really signified was that Athens' boundaries embraced wherever in the world these crops and fruit trees grew. And that meant the entire habitable earth.[26]

Moreover, he was determined that his vision of a global Athenian empire should be achieved at as little cost as possible to Athens. So, in early summer 419, he took a small detachment of Athenian hoplites and a company of archers and sailed south for Argos. Here he mustered an Argive army, hoplites and light troops, and with them he marched first to nearby Mantinea, another staunchly allied city, where he swelled his force still further. And now he set his plans in motion. With his huge mass of militia and their sprawling wagon train, Alcibiades advanced through the plains and mountain passes of Arcadia, close to the borderlands of Sparta, intimidating and cajoling, binding villages and townships tight into a new alliance with Athens.[27]

Alarmed, the Spartans mobilized their army, every fighting man, and marched north towards their frontier under their young king, Agis. Still relatively inexperienced as a general, Agis had been on the Spartan throne for some eight years, but he had yet to win a major victory. Back in 426, his first invasion of Attica was halted because, it was claimed, of bad omens; his second, a year later, was cut short when the Athenians took Pylos, and Agis was compelled to dash back home. So this was his first real opportunity to prove himself, and it seemed he had the full force of the Spartan war machine behind him. But before they crossed the border, the priests—as they did at the onset of any expedition—made sacrifice, plunging their hands into the steaming entrails to examine them for omens. And what they saw dismayed them. The enterprise was doomed to failure. The army must turn back. Perhaps it had always simply been a hollow threat, a show of strength, as Sparta went through the motions, loath to let Alcibiades and his allies flaunt themselves so close to Laconia without response. But the aborted attack can have done little for Spartan morale.[28]

Meanwhile, Alcibiades and the joint force under his command reached the allied city state of Elis. Here he augmented his army with fresh troops, before doubling back northeast for the city of Patrae, where he convinced the inhabitants to throw in their lot with the Athenians and their allies. And more. Employing an irresistible mix of menace and diplomacy, he persuaded them to emulate Athens by building long walls between their city and the sea. During the discussions, when one of Patrae's citizens objected, saying that Athens was swallowing them whole, Alcibiades beamed his charming smile and replied: "Maybe. But it will be bit by bit—and starting with the feet. The Spartans would swallow you head first in one gulp!"[29]

The significance of Athens' occupation of Patrae cannot have been lost on anyone. Sited on the southern shores of the Gulf of Corinth, the city was of huge strategic importance: the Athenians already had a naval base on the north coast at Naupactus, and, with Patrae secure, it looked increasingly possible that they could control all shipping in and out of the Corinthian Gulf. And if they did that, they could effectively block off Corinth from the west, cutting its vital trade routes not just with the west of Greece but with Sicily and southern Italy as well. It only remained to take and fortify the low-lying sandy spit of Rhium, a little to the north of Patrae, where the Gulf was at its narrowest, a mere mile and a half in width, and a blockade could be secure.[30]

But when Alcibiades set out to capture it, he discovered, drawn up near the sea, where the waves were ribboning the shore in a hissing effervescence of white surf, a mass of hoplites, grim men from Sicyon and Corinth and other towns and cities on the Gulf, who had everything to lose if Rhium fell. Already Alcibiades had achieved so much in one campaign. He did not want to throw it away now. A good general chooses his battles, and to fight now was not in Athens' interests. So Alcibiades allowed discretion to prevail and the Corinthians to keep their hold on Rhium.

After all, if calculations went to plan, the Corinthians would soon find that, while Alcibiades was occupying Patrae, in the northeast of the Peloponnese, his Argive allies were similarly seizing Epidaurus. Now less famous than the local theatre at the sanctuary of Asclepius which bears its name, the town of Epidaurus clustered on a small peninsula in an idyllic bay on the Saronic Gulf, embraced by wooded mountains. For generations it had resisted its southern neighbour, Argos, and now it formed an eastern buffer zone between the Argives and Corinthians. Occupy Epidaurus, then, and Alcibiades and his allies would not just gain a useful harbour on the west of the Saronic Gulf. They could harass Corinth with greater ease.[31]

Concocting the pretext of a religious slight, the Argives twice descended on the land of Epidaurus, and twice failed in their purpose. And yet again the Spartans under Agis marched north to their frontier. And again, with the omens unfavourable, their army was disbanded. When news of the stalemate came to Alcibiades, he made all haste to Argos with a thousand hoplites. But by now the momentum had stalled. And, besides, the autumn rains were coming, and no one had the belly for continued fighting. So Alcibiades returned to Athens, his campaigns a qualified success.[32]

But that winter the Spartans braved the stormy seas, and themselves sailed to Epidaurus, where they established a protective garrison. To the Argives this constituted an act of extreme aggression. And it was not just the Spartans who were to blame. The Athenians, they protested, were equally at fault—they should not have let the Spartan ships sail in their waters. Amid a welter of acrimony, Alcibiades caused a motion to be passed in the Assembly that a clause be added to the pillar on which were inscribed the terms of the Peace of Nicias. It read: "The Spartans have not abided by their oaths."[33]

Soon, in retaliation for Sparta's meddling at Epidaurus, and no doubt backed by Alcibiades, raiding parties were fanning out from Pylos, falling on the Spartan farms and smallholdings of Messenia, while at the same time guerrilla fighting between Argos and Epidaurus intensified. And the winter passed uneasily. In Athens, Alcibiades' enemies accused him of jeopardizing the peace treaty with Sparta; in Argos his friends complained that Athenian support was unreliable; in Corinth and her allied cities real fears were expressed that military inaction would see them outmanoeuvred. Having stirred the hornets' nest without achieving his aims of establishing permanent Athenian positions on Corinth's east and western flanks, it was perhaps not unsurprising that, despite his real successes of the year before, Alcibiades failed to be re-elected general.[34]

Yet his interest in Argos, and his conviction that the city was key to Athenian military policy, remained undulled. With the coming of the fighting season the next year, 418, it became all too clear that Sparta thought so, too. In her Ecclesia, wily strategists had been warning for some time that their natural inclination for non-intervention was in danger of allowing the Athenians to outmanoeuvre them. It was time to seize the initiative.[35]

By midsummer, reports began to filter into Athens that an army of unprecedented size was mustering. The Spartans were readying to march on Argos with their full strength of hoplite warriors, augmented by vast regiments of trusted Helot fighters. And the forces of Corinth and Boeotia were also on the move. What were the Athenians to do? Opinions were divided between hawks and doves. Some urged caution: to get dragged into such a conflict was to risk rekindling all-out war. Others pointed out that Argos was an ally, and that Athens was obliged to help her. At last, a vote was taken. To send two generals with a task force of a thousand hoplites and three hundred cavalry in support of Argos. And accompanying them as special envoy should be Alcibiades. Faced with the Spartan show of naked force, the tide of Athenian opinion was turning once more in his favour.[36]

But when they got to Argos, they were met by an unexpected—and unpleasant—surprise. Far from being on the brink of a great battle, the Argives had made a treaty with the Spartans; the hostile armies had gone home; and the Athenians were no longer welcome. For Alcibiades this represented a potentially humiliating blow. And the more he discovered about what had happened, the more bizarre it seemed.[37]

Learning that the armies of not just the Boeotians and Corinthians but many other cities, such as Sicyon and Megara, were assembling to the north, the Argives had decided to cut off the Spartans as they marched to join them. But, although they intercepted Sparta's army in Arcadia late one afternoon, at sunrise the next morning they awoke to find that it had given them the slip. Now desperate, the Argives had marched back to secure the passes from Nemea, north of their city, the route they were sure that the enemy must take. Then more bad news. Against all expectations, the Spartans had crossed the mountains further south. Closer to Argos. To the Argive army's rear. Panicking, the Argives turned around and hurried for their city. But as they did so, Sparta's allies poured through the northern passes behind them. Cut off from the safety of Argos, and surrounded by what Thucydides hailed as the "finest Greek army which had ever been assembled," the Argives faced annihilation.[38]

But as the heat broiled the plain, and the glitter from the many tens of thousands of well-polished breastplates rippled in the summer sunlight, two men rode out from the Argive line. One was a general, the other, Sparta's *proxenos* at Argos. Hastily, they convened a meeting with Agis, Sparta's king. And with no authority vested in any of them, they concluded a peace treaty. As the news spread through the army, soldiers were stood down, their regiments dispersed, and by nightfall the plain was deserted. Then came the recriminations. Never mind that their soldiers would most likely have been slaughtered, the Argives turned with fury on their general, who managed to escape death only by clinging to an altar.[39]

Nonetheless, Argos was clearly divided. And in shock. The reception the Athenians received was hostile. But Alcibiades was convinced that he could turn things around. With the support of soldiers from Elis and Mantinea, who had been ready to fight for Argos and were still billeted in the city, he succeeded in gaining permission to address the democratic Argive assembly. So, handsome, eloquent, and self-assured, he laid his case before them. It was a *tour de force*.[40]

The peace treaty, he argued, was unconstitutional, ratified by Spartan lackeys without the citizens of Argos granting their consent—or their loyal allies, either. And now, since that was so, and since the enemy had disbanded and the Athenians had come to lend support, there was no better time to pursue the war, to reclaim Arcadia, to expunge the humiliation of such a craven climb-down. While a significant proportion of the Argive oligarchs reacted to the speech in stony silence, the mass of the assembly applauded Alcibiades and voted to do as he suggested.[41]

Fired by the words of Alcibiades, the allies marched into Arcadia, first liberating hostages imprisoned in the mountain stronghold of Orchomenus, before sweeping south to rendezvous at Mantinea with the reinvigorated Argive army. From here their plan was to capture the city of Tegea near the border with Laconia and, perhaps, to take the war to Sparta.[42]

But the Spartans were on their guard. They, too, had been aggrieved by the events at Argos. For Agis to have shrunk from fighting when the odds were on his side was shameful. His war record was hardly glowing, and this new peace deal with Argos had merely dented Sparta's reputation further. Indeed, they thought that Agis' generalship and judgement were so questionable that, from now on, ten advisers would accompany him on campaigns. He had one last chance to prove himself. He must win a victory. Determined to restore his reputation, and aware that failure would leave Sparta mortally exposed, Agis marched north to Mantinea with the largest army ever mustered by the Spartans.[43]

The first that the Athenians knew of it, the Spartans were already past Tegea and burning crops and houses just a few miles south of where they and their Argive allies were encamped at Mantinea. Swiftly they took up a strong position, assembling in their ranks on a steep slope from where they could look out across the broad, flat, fertile plain, towards the distant mountains—from where, too, they could see the Spartan troops advancing, grimly silent, coming ever closer. And the skirling of the *auloi* keeping them in step. A wall of shields, each painted with an inverted "V," the capital Greek letter, Lambda, signifying the *Lacedaimonioi,* the "Spartan People": a bristling of lowered spears; a blood-red surge of scarlet cloaks and tunics; a blaze of polished helmets surging up the slope towards them. The distance closing. Now just a javelin's throw away. In moments the two sides would clash. But then, quite unexpectedly, the Spartans sounded the retreat. Agis' nerve had broken, or perhaps good counsel had prevailed. And the Spartans were gone.[44]

Triumphantly the Athenians and their allies marched down to the plain, where the next day the whole ritual played out again. But this time they were not so lucky. Despite some grotesque bungling on Agis' part, whose consequences were averted only when his generals refused to follow orders, the Spartans broke through the allied lines, stabbing, slicing, hacking. Only Agis' ineptitude allowed the bulk of the Athenians to flee, though they left their dead and dying on the battlefield—among them Laches, whom Alcibiades had once protected on the retreat from Delium. Most of the Argives, too, made it to safety, but the Mantineans suffered badly.[45]

In a single day, so many fortunes were reversed. At a stroke, Sparta's recently dulled kudos was revitalized, her mystique as a fighting force reanimated, the glory of her king, the hapless Agis, burnished to such brightness that, on his jubilant return, he was hailed as a conquering hero. In Athens, there were no such celebrations. In this one battle the allies could—and maybe should—have crushed Sparta so emphatically that she was neutralized for years to come. Instead, it was Athens that had come out badly, and although she made a show of helping in the war with Epidaurus, it was becoming all too clear that certainties were shifting, and there were those in Argos who were questioning precisely where their loyalties lay.

In his role as special envoy, Alcibiades will probably have witnessed the defeat at Mantinea. But, even if he only heard of it at second hand, it did not diminish his resolve. In his mind, and rightly, the importance of preserving the Athenian alliance with Argos was as great as ever. Repeatedly he visited his contacts there, to reassure them, bolster their resolve, and boost their influence. But that autumn, while Alcibiades was in Argos, a Spartan delegation turned up, led by the Argive *proxenos* in Sparta, Lichas—the man who had been whipped at the Olympic Games two years before. He was, he warned, merely an advance guard. The entire Spartan army was encamped just forty miles away at Tegea, where they were awaiting news of the outcome of his talks. If Argos were to vote for peace, the army would disband and return home. If, on the other hand, Argos opted to continue hostilities . . . [46]

Desperately, Alcibiades described the benefits to Argos in maintaining its alliance with Athens. Coolly, Lichas laid out the opposite scenario, the consequence of non-cooperation with the Spartans. And although discussions seemed to stretch interminably, it became increasingly clear how they would end. By now, the pro-Spartan movement was no longer afraid to speak out. Indeed, there were those who positively yearned for a more Spartan style of government—hard-headed young aristocrats, members of the elite regiment of hoplites, which formed the backbone of the Argive army, a regiment which (it was rumoured) the Spartans had deliberately let slip at Mantinea, so they would do their work thereafter.

When Alcibiades at last sailed home to Athens to debrief the Assembly, his news brought little comfort: the Argives had suspended their democracy; an aristocratic oligarchy was in power; and it had sworn a fifty-year peace treaty and alliance with the Spartans. Soon afterwards, a message even came from Argos instructing the Athenians to give up their campaign against Epidaurus. The Athenians had little option but to agree. At a stroke, one of the most vital planks in Alcibiades' war strategy had been removed. It could have dealt a major blow to his career. Instead, he managed to present his role so positively—while he was in command, and Athens and her allies were following his policies, Sparta had been on the back foot; once he was out of office, Argos and much of the nascent Arcadian Alliance had been lost—that the next spring (417) he was again elected general.[47]

This predilection for appointing generals for a year and then discarding them, this flip-flopping over foreign strategy and war aims, this inconsistency was one of the main weaknesses of Athenian democracy. Somehow, Pericles had managed to ensure he was elected to the generalship year after year, which allowed him to see through a long-term policy. But since his death, the political landscape of Athens had changed drastically: the balance of power was more precarious; the passion of the People to hire and fire at will much keener; and the need for generals to win quick victories, and so trumpet their immediate success, meant that it was impossible to plan a long drawn-out campaign.

But still Alcibiades kept his eye on the prize that was Argos. There, opinion was irreconcilably split. The oligarchs assiduously cultivated their relationship with Sparta; the democrats yearned to be reunited in alliance with the Athenians. As time went on, the leaders of those democrats, meeting first in secret, then more blatantly in public, regained much of their lost confidence. By now the stark realities of the new regime were sinking in, as it became increasingly clear that, having lost the independence it had cherished for so long, Argos was nothing but a puppet state of Sparta. So a plot was hatched. And in the early days of July, the democrats staged a coup.[48]

Its timing was perfect, planned carefully to coincide with the beginning of the Spartan Gymnopaediae Festival, one of the most solemn ceremonies in their calendar, when many an Argive oligarch had travelled down to Sparta as a diplomatic guest. On the appointed morning, the democrats attacked. For hours, fierce fighting ebbed and flowed through the lanes and streets and squares of Argos, but, by nightfall, the democrats were in control. When they heard the news, the Spartans rushed to arms; but, after more measured consideration, they aborted their attempt to get the city back. Nonetheless, the threat of military action still hung in the air. And the Argives turned once more to Athens.[49]

It was the moment Alcibiades was waiting for—perhaps a moment he had even helped to engineer. And he lost no time in executing his response. Sailing south to Argos, he addressed the still jubilant assembly. Athens would be delighted to renew the alliance, he assured them—and so that the Athenian navy could protect the Argives, while her merchantmen could keep them well supplied in case of siege, he would personally supervise the process of turning Argos, like Athens itself, into the equivalent of an island fortress. So, just as two years before at Patrae, the citizens began a hurried building programme: to construct two parallel, high-battlemented walls, around a mile in length, to link their city to the sea. Such was the urgency with which the work was undertaken that the entire population, men and women, slaves and free, took part in the construction. And such was Alcibiades' determination that it be done well that he shipped in specialists from Athens—stone masons and carpenters—to help complete the walls more quickly. He was the hero of the hour, the darling of the Argives. But the project was doomed to disaster.[50]

That autumn, when an attack was least expected, the Spartans, led by Agis, marched into the Argolid. With them were their allies, including the now-oligarchic Mantinea, which had recently gone over to them, too. But if they hoped that a fifth column might open the city gates to them, or that the Argive democrats, cowed by such a terrifying display of military might, would meekly surrender, they were disappointed. The city remained secure. But with the walls still uncompleted, it was a simple—if symbolic—task to pull them down. As the Spartans marched back home for winter, they made a detour to the long-contested border town of Hysiae and glutted their revenge by sacking it and massacring its men. They had every cause to feel disgruntled. For a few brief months, the Spartans had achieved their grand ambition of dominating the vast bulk of the Peloponnese. Now, thanks to Alcibiades, that dream had been rudely shattered.[51]

Soon, Alcibiades gave his clearest signal yet that he intended to ensure that Athens' grip on Argos was unshakeable. In the first balmy days of summer, his generalship extended for another year, he sailed into the city's harbour with a fleet of twenty triremes. With him he brought a list. It contained three hundred names: three hundred Argive citizens, leading oligarchs, whose loyalty was suspect. Swiftly they were rounded up, dragged from the streets, abducted from their homes, and bundled into the ships. And then they were dispersed to nearby islands to languish as hostages under Athenian guard, a guarantee that Argos' commitment to her alliance would not waver.[52]

But it was not only Argos that was the focus of Alcibiades' attention. Although there is no mention in the sources, it is almost certain that at this time, too, he was courting Athens' other subject states and allies, entertaining their great and good, whenever they visited his city for international festivals such as the Great Dionysia or the Panathenaic Games, perhaps even sailing east to Ionia and the islands to press the flesh, and strengthen his personal support there. For, increasingly, he was constructing a network of alliances and loyalties, a nexus of powerful people, seduced by his charisma and impressed by his determination, men he could rely on to support his deep-seated conviction not only that the Peace of Nicias was built on sand, but that war with Sparta was inevitable. Indeed, desirable.[53]

All this put him even more at odds with the conservative doves. To them, Alcibiades' policy of backing Argos and attempting to create an Arcadian Alliance was irresponsibly provocative. It had even caused the death of two Athenian generals, not to mention a fair number of hoplites, when the army was dragged into fighting against its so-called Spartan allies at the defeat of Mantinea. Yet despite it all, the Peace of Nicias was holding—though only just. Somehow Sparta, still desperate to avoid open conflict, had turned a blind eye to Athens' aggressive involvement with Argos and her Arcadian allies, while in Athens there were those, especially within the older generation, for whom a renewed war with Sparta was anathema. Better by far, they thought, to allay the Spartans' fears by keeping out of the Peloponnese and concentrating on reclaiming those cities in the north which had fallen in the war—cities such as Amphipolis, which still refused to return to the fold.[54]

Indeed, the Athenians had failed to make much headway in the north at all. Not that their treatment of Scione, at the tip of the peninsula on which Potidaea stood, can have elicited much goodwill. Since the massacre of that city's male population and the enslavement of its womenfolk and children, the situation in the region had been volatile, not least because of the erratic behaviour of the Macedonian king, Perdiccas, whose loyalty had been so unpredictable in the past. Even now, as Alcibiades was consolidating his grip on Argos, the Athenians had been waging a campaign against Amphipolis in a desperate attempt to win the city back. But thanks to Perdiccas, who had promised his support, but, as so often, in the end neglected to appear, the operation was a failure.[55]

That its general was the condescending Nicias did not go unremarked by Alcibiades' supporters. Or by those of Nicias. Indeed, the gulf between the two men and their opposing policies was becoming ever wider, even threatening to undermine the stability of the Athenian democracy. A consistent foreign policy was hard enough to maintain at the best of times. But now two of Athens' leading generals and politicians were advocating completely antithetical strategies, each energetically pursuing his own aims, one to the detriment of the other, and neither was prepared to compromise. It was impossible to see how the situation could not but end in disaster.

5

COURTING THE HYDRA

In politics, it's hard to please everyone.

Solon, frag. 7 (West)

WINTER SET IN, and on the hard-packed earth of Athens' streets, in her jostling Agora, in the claustrophobia of the packed Pnyx, emotions swirled as entrenched opinions hardened and rifts already fracturing society gaped wider. And the cause of many of these rifts was Alcibiades. With his anti-Spartan policies threatening to tear apart the Peace of Nicias, an increasing number of his opponents viewed him not just with suspicion but with downright fear. Among them was Archestratus, a man who had been friendly with the sons of Pericles. He summed up the mood of many when he remarked: "Athens has no room for more than one Alcibiades." Indeed, there were some who would go further. Athens, they would argue, had no room for Alcibiades at all.[1]

So, nervous of the future, should the situation carry on unchecked, they resorted to a mechanism that, for more than a century, had ensured the smooth running of their democracy, a mechanism that had curbed the ambitions of several assertive egos in the past, and the only real mechanism legally available by which Alcibiades' enemies might seriously thwart him. Early in 416, they passed a motion in the Assembly for a vote of ostracism.[2]

In the pressurized world of Athenian democracy, where wealthy politicians jostled for the greatest power and influence, the primary purpose of ostracism was to stop anyone from becoming so unassailable that he could suspend the constitution and enthrone himself as tyrant. Its secondary purpose, however, was just as significant: to enable the People, at a stroke, to break a stalemate—to resolve a political impasse by banishing the leader of one faction for ten years, thus allowing his rivals to pursue their policies relatively unimpeded.

Back in the mid-fifth century, Pericles had twice benefited from votes to ostracize his enemies, when first Cimon, then Thucydides Melesiou were expelled. But Pericles' friends and family had not been immune. In the 480s, both Megacles IV and Pericles' own father, Xanthippus, were ostracized, while later his music teacher, the *éminence grise* Damon—a man suspected by his enemies of persuading Pericles to pander too much to the People—was exiled, too. And, of course, there had been Alcibiades' grandfather. In fact, the list of those ostracized read like an Athenian *Who's Who*: every victim (except Damon) a member of a leading family, his expulsion as much a mark of honour as a stigma.[3]

The events of recent months and years had not just exposed the extent of Alcibiades' ambitions. They made it clear that two distinct and diametrically opposed policies were being set out for the Athenians to follow: the peace initiative of Nicias, and the warmongering of Alcibiades. As long as both men remained in Athens with a significant body of the voting populace behind them, the city would be dangerously split, vacillating between two mutually exclusive strategies. It did not take a genius to see that such a situation contained the potential for disaster. So, on that chilly January day in 416, when the motion was put forward on Pnyx Hill that an ostracism vote be taken, the citizens of Athens, muffled against the winter weather, raised their hands in world-weary agreement. The time for prevarication was over. What they wanted was clear policy. Either Nicias or Alcibiades must go.[4]

In democratic Athens, there were no political parties. Yes, there were many people, who would follow their favourite statesman wherever he might lead them—especially if he had already shown his luck and judgement on a military campaign. And there were those, too, who could be relied on to turn up and vote in exchange for favours or in fear of threats. But the great majority owed no allegiances. Whenever the Assembly was convened—on average up to forty times a year—they would troop up from their homes, or shops, or workrooms (sometimes so unwillingly that they had to be herded forcibly through the streets), to watch the politicians posture on the platform, to listen to the arguments, and cast their votes as the inclination took them on the day. High principles, recalcitrance, self-interest: the motives which inspired them were myriad. But a good speech by a man whom they respected could work wonders.[5]

In 416, Nicias and Alcibiades were not the only ambitious politicians. Two other men, both members of the younger generation of up-and-coming aspirants, were among the frontrunners of those jostling for power.[6]

One was Phaeax. Born of an old aristocratic family, Phaeax was charming and urbane, a natural diplomat. Indeed, he had already served on a number of sensitive missions, most notably—some seven years earlier, in 422—to South Italy and Sicily. For, despite the failure of their recent campaigns in the region, Athens had not abandoned her ambitions of conquest. Especially as her old enemy, Syracuse, was so quickly growing in power. The last offensive had been thwarted at Gela by the Syracusan Hermocrates, when he persuaded the cities of Sicily to make a pact against the Athenians. Now, for Athens to have any hope of success, that pact must be dissolved. Phaeax and his colleagues enjoyed some success, winning the friendship of such Sicilian Greek cities as wealthy Acragas, Camarina, and Catane. However, on balance there was still too much hostility towards Athens to attempt another military expedition. And besides—at the time—people simply did not have the stomach for another war. But none of this was Phaeax's fault and, as his cachet grew, other diplomatic missions quickly followed, to Thessaly, and Thesprotia, Molossia, and Macedonia. No wonder Alcibiades considered him a rival. Though not in all respects. Despite his urbanity, persuasiveness, and wit in private, in the Assembly, Phaeax was a poor, stumbling orator, the victim of many jokes, "the best of conversationalists, the most impossible of speakers" as the comic poet Eupolis described him. Still, he managed to wield influence, and there were those who saw him, too, as a candidate for ostracism.[7]

And then there was Hyperbolus. One of the new breed of Athenian politicians, Hyperbolus owed his wealth to commerce. He owned a lamp-making factory. And if this were not enough to alienate him from old-school conservatives, he saw himself as the natural successor to Cleon, strutting on the Speaker's Platform as if he owned it. He was, they said, so thoroughly common, always quibbling, with such an acid tongue! Even before Cleon's death he had been warlike, serving as a trireme captain, stoking the fires of Athenian ambitions in the west, so mad for conquest that he even wanted to make war on Carthage, the greatest maritime power in the western Mediterranean. And now that he saw Alcibiades making such considerable headway, turning his eyes, too, towards the west—now that he saw so many of his own natural constituents fawning over Alcibiades instead—Hyperbolus was aggrieved.[8]

It was Hyperbolus who proposed the ostracism. And two months later, the vote on whom to exile would be held: sixty days, in which those most at risk must try to shore up their support, vilify their rivals, and do everything they could to win sufficient popularity to avoid being banished; sixty days, in which friends and confederates toured the demes, reminding voters of old favours, painting rosy pictures of the future should their man remain in Athens, making grim predictions for their safety should they be seen to vote for the wrong candidate; sixty days, in which the course of public policy might be decided, and which must have rushed by in a flash.[9]

And then the day itself. Sunrise, and the Agora was transformed, its centre, where the Athenians would congregate, fenced off. Leading into the enclosure were ten entrances, one for each tribe, with huge voting urns placed by each gateway. Initially in dribs and drabs, then in a steady flow, the citizens arrived. Some clutched the fragment of broken pottery, the *ostracon,* on which they had already scratched the name of the man they wished to exile. Others collected already-inscribed potsherds from partisans of those they wished to stay. Still others (with less foresight but more independence) collected blank *ostraca* from public officers and incised them there and then. There were even some, the illiterate, who, trusting in their honesty, asked total strangers to write the name on their behalf.[10]

People still remembered one time this happened, in 482, when an ill-educated countryman approached someone nearby the enclosure gate, held out his ostracon, and asked him to inscribe on it the name, "Aristeides." "Why Aristeides?" the other enquired. "Because I'm sick of hearing everyone going on about him being so just!" At which Aristeides wrote his own name, gave it back to the citizen, and contributed to the votes which exiled him that year.[11]

By mid-morning, the hubbub was tumultuous. For a few tense hours, the Agora was the crucible of Athenian political life. And what a stage it was: the broad earth dotted with plane trees; to the west, a row of public buildings bathed golden in the morning sun; to the north, the Painted Stoa, shops, a spacious courtroom; more shops and private houses to the east; while, to the south, behind another courthouse and a gleaming stoa and fountain-house, the Acropolis, with its bloom of statues, shrines and temples, rose sheer and dark against the dazzling sky. The compound was now packed with many thousands. Six thousand was the figure needed for the ostracism to be valid, the whole procedure scrutinized with care by the city's ten most senior officials. At last, maybe at an appointed time or simply when sufficient votes were cast, the magistrates declared the ballot closed. The urns were emptied, the potsherds counted, and the result announced. And the candidate chosen to be ostracized that year? Hyperbolus! Somehow his whole strategy had backfired spectacularly, and within ten days the man who set the vote in motion must pack his bags and leave the city for ten years—to sail, in fact, to Samos, where he grew rich as a businessman supplying Athens and her fleet.[12]

How could this possibly have been? When it seemed so certain that one of the two big beasts of Athenian politics, Nicias and Alcibiades—or even the powerful if unpersuasive Phaeax—would be exiled, how was it that the axe had fallen on Hyperbolus, a man so confident in his powerbase that he proposed the ostracism in the first place? It may have been a quirk of numbers. After all, there is nothing to suggest that the policies of Alcibiades, Hyperbolus, or Phaeax were so very different from one another. And if personality was then added to the mix, there were sufficient men in Athens who clearly loathed Hyperbolus. And so, perhaps, the vote was fair.[13]

Even at the time, the truth was hard to tell. Now it is impossible. In one sense, however, the truth is irrelevant. Because, in the spring of 416, what mattered more was how the vote was greeted in the streets. Many had welcomed the ostracism as a chance to clear the air, to resolve the tensions which the ongoing policy divisions between Nicias and Alcibiades exposed, to cleanse the stables of the partisanship and hostility which were mounting every day, transforming Athens into a heaving rats' nest of increasingly ugly suspicion. Now, though, those suspicions turned their focus on the ostracism process itself. Rumours scuttled through the city. It was a stitch-up. A conspiracy. A perversion of the democratic process. Phaeax and Alcibiades— or even Nicias and Alcibiades, the scandalmongers somewhat implausibly proclaimed—had made a back-room deal. They had formed an unholy alliance to preserve their skins. They had persuaded their supporters to present a united front against their common enemy, Hyperbolus.[14]

That a conspiracy between Nicias and Alcibiades could be seriously credited was a sign of how febrile Athenian politics had become. If anything, personal hostility between the two men was growing. And now that the partisans of the ostracized Hyberbolus, in their opinion so cruelly used, had entered the fray, accusing their enemies of undemocratic practices, the atmosphere, whether on the Pnyx or in the Agora or down on the quayside at Piraeus, was becoming ugly indeed. And at the same time, the warmongers were growing more determined.

Which was why, at the age of thirty-six, having just escaped the vote of ostracism, and building on his military and diplomatic successes of the previous four years, in 416, Alcibiades made his boldest bid yet to position himself as one of the most powerful players in the entire Greek world. By now he was easily at home in the bear-pit of the Assembly, and, cheered on by his partisan supporters, he continued to pursue an aggressive foreign policy, joining his voice to those of others advocating strengthening Athenian control over not only the entire Aegean but the wider Mediterranean as well.

For, although Athens ruled the waves, one island still managed to resist being sucked into her empire: Melos, rugged and volcanic, with hot sulphurous springs, the furthest southwest of the Cyclades. Its inhabitants had, for centuries, exploited rich natural resources such as obsidian and gypsum, and fished the seas for tuna. But this was not what attracted the Athenians' attention. Rather, they were irked that Melos (which Athenians such as Thucydides claimed was a Spartan colony) had refused to join the Delian League against Persia, was not part of Athens' empire, and remained defiantly neutral in the recent war. In theory, at least. In 427, it had not just allowed a Spartan fleet to use its harbour, but made contributions to the Spartan war effort. So, the next year, Athens had tried to conquer it. With a fleet of sixty triremes and two thousand hoplites, the Athenians descended on the island, but, despite causing damage to its fields and rural industry, they could not force the Melians to surrender.[15]

Clearly, then, Melos was unfinished business, a thorn in Athens' side, and—being so strategically positioned—a potential weak spot to be exploited by her enemies. To Alcibiades, however, the chance to defeat Melos represented so much more than just an opportunity to strike a blow against Sparta. It was a golden opportunity to embarrass his domestic rivals, too. For, the general who had failed so badly in his mission to take Melos ten years earlier was none other than the self-congratulating Nicias. And since he had backed the policy of annexing the island so enthusiastically a decade earlier, there was little realistically that Nicias could say now to resist it. The motion passed unopposed, and, within weeks, an allied force was sailing south to Melos. Its mission: to take the island at all costs—by diplomacy if possible, but, if not, through siege and blockade to starve the inhabitants into submission and use whatever force seemed necessary. It was only a matter of time, it seemed, before Athens' allies could boast yet another member.[16]

Not that Alcibiades would take part in the campaign. Having survived the ostracism, and with affairs in Argos settled, aggression trained on Melos, and little else politically to occupy him, he could now afford to concentrate on boosting his personal kudos. Throughout his adult life, he had played a conspicuous role in Athenian public life, acting as *choregus* for dithyrambs and dramas, and performing such other liturgies as were required of him. But for some years now, his ambition had been burning to win glory on the international stage, too—at the Panhellenic Games, where his ancestors' fame had shone supreme as they raced their chariots to victory.[17]

Already his own chariots had competed and won crowns at Delphi and Nemea—and at the Panathenaic Games, too, part of a larger festival established over a century-and-a-half before and celebrated every four years in honour of the city's patron goddess, Athene. An exuberant jamboree—a melange of processions, banquets, music, sacrifices, equestrian events, athletics, a male beauty contest, and a boat race—the Panathenaic Festival was celebrated in late August to mark Athene's birthday. At its heart was a parade for Athens' citizens and metics, men and women, young and old, which snaked through the city from the Sacred Gate across the Agora and up onto the Acropolis, where, in the searing summer sun, a hundred oxen were ritually sacrificed and a sacred robe presented to an ancient statue of the goddess hewn from olive wood.[18]

But it was to contests that most time was given, and the greatest contest of them all was the chariot race. Situated near the sea close to the old port of Phalerum, the hippodrome was some four hundred feet in length, a deadly circuit of packed earth, the site of one of the most thrilling spectacles in the ancient world: teams of four horses, perfectly matched, impeccably trained, pounding the earth in a swift blur of hooves; sleek racing-chariots, low to the ground, built for speed, not safety, their well-greased wheels jouncing across the hard-packed earth; the charioteers, clad in long linen robes tightly belted with cross-straps, canny and ruthless professional drivers, instinctively knowing when to draw the reins taut for the corner, to lean back, to whip on their horses for maximum speed.[19]

And in 418, in the lull between the defeat at Mantinea and his ongoing negotiations at Argos, Alcibiades had entered a team in the chariot race and won. His prize: 140 amphorae of olive oil, pressed from trees consecrated to Athene in a sacred grove near the Academy, each vessel resplendent with an image of the goddess standing proud between two columns, helmeted and armoured, a spear gripped in her raised right hand.[20]

Despite their pomp and pageantry, and despite attracting competitors from the length and breadth of the Greek world, the Panathenaic Games had never quite achieved Peisistratus' ambition of rivalling the circuit of international athletic festivals held at Nemea, Corinth, Delphi, and Olympia. All four were exceedingly prestigious, but the most prestigious were the Olympics. Traditionally founded in 776, these were the earliest of all the contests, part of a quadrennial festival in honour of Olympian Zeus. An exclusively male event, the Olympics comprised a heady mix of sacrifice and banquet, contests and processions, five days of ritual and rivalry straddling the night of the first August full moon.[21]

The footrace, the most ancient of Olympic events, may have been the most preeminent, but in terms of kudos, ostentation, and panache, not to mention sheer display of wealth, nothing could beat the chariot race. Hence the scandal in 420, when Lichas wormed his way into taking part and winning, despite the temporary ban on any Spartan entering the competition. Hence, too, in 416, Alcibiades' determination to use the race to bring himself before the eyes of Greece in a way no man had ever done before, nor would again in years to come. A determination that he realized with theatrical aplomb.[22]

That August, with dazzling self-confidence, magnetic poise, and an unerring instinct for self-promotion, Alcibiades entered into the Olympic Games not one but seven chariots for the four-horse chariot race. Which meant that he brought with him no fewer than twenty-eight horses. Indeed, he probably brought more, reserves should any become lame or injured. It was both a shameless flaunting of extraordinary wealth and a naked statement of pure power—the acknowledged power of Athens and, more pointedly, the power to which Alcibiades aspired himself.[23]

Ten years before, Delos had echoed to pageantry and drama as Nicias transformed the Ionians' Festival of Apollo, when he led his chorus, singing, dancing, garlanded, across the pontoon bridge from Rheneia, before purifying the island and laying the foundation stone for a new temple. Now at Olympia, where not just athletes and spectators but the richest and most powerful politicians of their day were gathered for the Games, in an extravaganza stage-managed to perfection, Alcibiades would eclipse his rival's reputation and blazon his own name before the whole Greek world.

The years of glad-handing, of charming the key players of Ionia with his wit and wiles, of drinking long into the night with the richest and most powerful of all Athens' allies, sketching his seductive vision of the future, outlining plans in which they all could share, in which they could accumulate both riches and prestige: now all of this was flowering to fulfilment. And here, at the ninety-first Olympic Games, there were many who were clamouring to help him.

Before the festival was even fully underway, the many thousands flocking to Olympia were greeted by a most impressive sight: an exquisite silken tent, a pavilion shimmering with gauzy hangings and adorned with gorgeous tapestries; on its floors, rich carpets; soft pillows strewn on intricately carved and tight-sprung bed frames; low tables stacked with precious vessels crafted in silver and gold. It was a gift to Alcibiades from his friends at Ephesus, part residence, part reception room, a lavish headquarters, twice the size of that of Athens' official delegation, from which he could direct his well-planned charm offensive.[24]

Clustering strategically nearby were other tents, perhaps less opulent but resplendent nonetheless, each with its entourage of slaves and lackeys, the temporary homes of wealthy landowners or the flamboyant nouveaux riches from Athens, and the islands, and Ionia. They formed a stark contrast with the bulk of bivouacs which crowded round the sanctuary: ramshackle huts, torn canvases, unsteady lean-tos, home to the many thousands who had swarmed to see the Games, their clothing already rank with sweat, while, with so little running water and no sanitation, the sweltering air reeked fouler with their stench.

It was on the second day of the Olympics that the chariot race was run, part of the funeral games held in memory of the legendary hero, Pelops. Preceded by the horse race, it was the second fixture of the day. And, because of its danger, the most nail-biting. Already the hippodrome was packed with people, flanking three sides of the oval race track four *stades* (around 750 yards) in length, with a tight turning corner at both ends. Earlier that morning the chariot teams had taken part in a parade, the well-groomed horses led at walking pace around the hippodrome for the spectators to size up and admire. Now, though, for the race itself they were manoeuvred, snorting, straining, whinnying, into the starting gate, a newly-introduced V-shaped mechanism which allowed for a staggered start. And then the switch was thrown. A bronze eagle shot up high above the altar by the apex, the series of gates opened, and the chariots shot out onto the race track. They ran six laps, some drivers trading speed for safety, others deliberately hanging back, while others still, misjudging crucial distances, crashed in a confusion of thrashing hooves and splintered chariots. Swerving the carnage, those still in the running urged their horses on, the thunder of hooves drowned out by the shouts of the spectators, until at last they turned the bend for the last time and galloped down the homestretch, every muscle straining for the finish.[25]

The result this year was breathtaking, if unsurprising. As Alcibiades watched the chariots shoot past the post, he felt enormous satisfaction: first, second, third—they all belonged to him. It was a cause of great rejoicing, a well-earned pretext for an orgy of self-aggrandizement. When his grandfather, Megacles IV, won the chariot race at Delphi, he commissioned the preeminent praise singer Pindar to commemorate his victory in verse. When

Alcibiades returned to Athens, garlanded in his Olympic triumphs, he recruited the tragic poet Euripides to write his victory ode:

It is of you I sing, you, son of Cleinias!
Victory is wonderful. But the most wonderful of all, won by no
   other Greek,
is to run home with the winning chariot, the second, too, and
   then the third,
to walk unwearied, crowned with Zeus' olive leaves,
to hear your name proclaimed loud by the herald.

And not just that. Alcibiades commissioned two paintings from the celebrated artist, Aglaophon of Thasos. Both were allegorical. The first showed two winsome goddesses, the incarnations of the Games at Delphi and Olympia, crowning Alcibiades with victor's garlands. The second showed another beguiling goddess, the embodiment of the Nemean Games, "more beautiful than any woman alive," sitting enthroned, with Alcibiades on her knee, her pale arms thrown around his neck. When, in the winter following his victory, the paintings were exhibited, all Athens crowded around to see them.[26]

However, that lay in the future. Now, at Olympia, Alcibiades would celebrate his victory in style. On the evening following the chariot race, it was traditional for wealthy private citizens to host mouthwatering banquets, lavish entertainments for fellow countrymen and honoured guests. But this year was different. This year one man, Alcibiades, took it upon himself to host the entire undertaking and provide food and drink to all the many thousands who had flocked here for the festival—the entire crowd of spectators, citizens of the entire Greek world, who had seen his chariots race home in triumph only hours before.

Alcibiades could well afford such largesse. Especially since not all of it came from his own pocket. To ingratiate themselves with the rising star of Athens, proclaim their loyalty, and provide for celebrations which they were certain would be his, the men of Chios had not just brought shiploads of fine fodder for his horses, they—and the citizens of Cyzicus—arrived with herds of sleek, fat cattle to be first sacrificed then roasted for the feast, while, not to be outdone, the islanders of Lesbos had shipped countless amphorae of the wine for which they were renowned.[27]

As for Alcibiades, he furnished the gold and silver tableware, the bowls and dishes, jugs and pitchers from which the food and drink was served. They were, however, not strictly his. They were "borrowed" from the treasuries of Athens. Not that Alcibiades was at any pains to let this fact be known. Indeed, later, when the same vessels were being used for an official state banquet, there were those who recognized them and assumed that Alcibiades had kindly lent his private tableware to Athens for the occasion.[28]

But it was not just Alcibiades' wealth—whether personal or borrowed—that was on show at the Olympic Games. The entire sanctuary glittered with riches from across the Greek world. Within the marble temple of Zeus, completed forty years before, was a statue of the seated god, the work of Pericles' friend, Pheidias. Like his statue of Athene in the Parthenon, it was faced in ivory and gold, a work of art so fabulous that later pilgrims would proclaim that it would be the greatest of misfortunes to die never having seen it.[29]

This was not the only breathtaking artwork. Everywhere there were bronze and marble sculptures of victorious athletes whose cities embraced the entirety of the Greek-speaking city states from the wealthy eastern cities of Ionia to the western colonies of Sicily and Southern Italy. And on a low rise to the north, overlooking the grave mound of Pelops, there shone in the late sun a row of treasuries, squat strongholds built to look like temples, crammed with precious offerings, ostentatious gifts to the gods placed here in this sanctuary in permanent safekeeping—albeit with the proviso that, in times of trouble, they could be borrowed back and melted down if their cities desperately needed them. Most were set up by Dorians, men ethnically linked to Sparta—from Sicyon in the Peloponnese, Cyrene in North Africa, and from Selinus, Gela, and Syracuse in Sicily. To see the riches glinting through the open doors was to taste the potential of their cities' wealth. For an Athenian like Alcibiades, for whom only recently Sicily had seemed a prize ripe for the plucking, these tokens of the island's riches must have been most beguiling.[30]

Buoyed by his successes at Olympia, the cheers of spectators and delighted banqueters still ringing in his ears, Alcibiades returned to Athens riding the golden glow of popularity and, perhaps, too, entertaining the

The row of treasuries perches above the Temple of Hera at Olympia. (Photograph by the author.)

vision of potentially lucrative campaigns. Once home, official celebrations of his victories continued. Like other Olympic champions, he was awarded signal honours: special seating in the theatre; free meals for life in the Prytaneum; and a gift of 500 drachmas—small change to Alcibiades, but useful nonetheless. And then, of course, there were the celebrations surrounding not just the first performance of Euripides' victory ode, but the unveiling of the paintings by Aglaophon, all of which were designed specifically to keep him at the focus of the public eye, and the memory of his victories alive.[31]

But if Alcibiades expected that his Olympic triumphs would win the praise and gratitude of his fellow citizens en masse, he was in for a bitter disappointment. If anything, his performance at the Games, the pinnacle of his career to date, had served only to expose still more the deep cracks in the fabric of Athenian society.

The first signs of dissent came from a private individual, a man who had considered Alcibiades a friend and who consequently placed his trust in him.

Months earlier, Teisias heard rumours of a superb racing chariot and team of horses owned by the city of Argos. The more Teisias learned, the more he wished to own and race it himself. Since Alcibiades was an expert in such matters and held such influence among the Argives, Teisias asked him to investigate. If it were as good as it was said to be, Alcibiades must negotiate its purchase on his behalf.[32]

Now Teisias alleged that Alcibiades had reneged on their agreement. His claim was that, having examined the chariot and horses, Alcibiades did indeed broker their purchase, but instead of then passing them to Teisias, he kept them, entered them at Olympia, and told Teisias that there was nothing his erstwhile friend could do about it. The situation was aggravating enough, but that the showdown between the two men happened at the official registration held at Elis before the Games began was downright humiliating. According to a speech made in a later lawsuit, Teisias (presented somewhat unbelievably as a man of modest means, whose one desire was to win victory on behalf of Athens and his family) appeared at the ceremony as the chariot and team's owner, intending to register them. But thanks to his influence with the Olympic committee, Alcibiades succeeded in refuting Teisias' claims, and it was in Alcibiades' name that the chariot competed.[33]

The truth is difficult to unravel. Was it a gentleman's agreement gone wrong? Did Teisias fail to pay Alcibiades the agreed amount in time? Or, having seen the team's potential, did Alcibiades deliberately break the trust placed in him and keep it for himself? And would any of this have mattered, had not this very team won first prize—the only prize that was awarded? Such was Teisias' anger that he would undoubtedly have brought the case to court the following year had events not intervened. Even as it was, though, the controversy quickly took on almost legendary status—to such as extent that Teisias quickly earned the nickname, "Diomedes," a reference to the mythological Thracian king whose mares were stolen by the hero Heracles. In the absence of a speedy trial, resentments festered. Indeed, they grew so bitter that, nearly twenty years later, Alcibiades' son was indicted for the offence and faced a fine of five talents, though the verdict, and whether he was forced to pay, is not recorded.[34]

But it was on the political scene in Athens that Alcibiades' Olympic showmanship made the greatest impact—an impact which, arguably, would change the course of history. His swagger at the Games was a gift to his enemies. To them, it was clear evidence (if evidence were needed) of his true anti-democratic character, his naked ambition to usurp the leadership of Athens, to rule the People not as "first citizen," as Pericles had done, but as a tyrant—like Peisistratus more than a century before; or, worse, like the hateful Hippias, whose rule had degenerated into violence before he was ignominiously expelled.[35]

And what greater proof was needed than the silken tent, in which Alcibiades had held court throughout the Games? Not only was its sheer size and magnificence completely inappropriate for a private citizen of democratic Athens, it begged comparison with another infamous tent—the tent of the Persian Great King Khashayarsha, whom the Greeks called Xerxes. For had this despot not travelled with a luxurious pavilion of his own, his residence and command centre, as he cut a swathe of suffering through Greece, before descending upon Athens to burn and pillage and enslave? Had not the victorious Greeks discovered his tent, abandoned on the battlefield at Plataea, still with its embroidered draperies intact, still furnished with its gold and silver couches, its tables set with gold and silver vessels for a feast—like the gold and silver vessels purloined by Alcibiades from Athens' vaults? Indeed, had not the servants of the Great King's general cooked a sumptuous meal for the victorious Greek commanders to enjoy—as Alcibiades had caused his chefs to cook to a victory banquet at Olympia? And was the Great King's tent not brought to Athens and displayed before the People for their derision and contempt—before Pericles cunningly appropriated its design for his brave new Odeon, its roof supported by the masts of Persian ships defeated in the sea battle at Salamis, the symbol of brutal despotism tamed for a democratic concert hall? Surely, by behaving like some Persian pasha, flaunting his eastern tent at the Olympic Games in front of the entire Greek world, Alcibiades was sending a signal that, if things went his way, the days of the Athenian democracy were numbered![36]

Whether real or manufactured, the outrage against Alcibiades grew. For his enemies, the fact that the foreign policies he espoused were already bearing fruit cannot but have rubbed salt into their wounds. That autumn, the siege of Melos, which had lasted many months, was brought to an abrupt end when, throwing themselves on the Athenians' mercy, the citizens surrendered. But mercy was not forthcoming. Angered that the Melians had dared to resist so long, and determined to make an example of them, the generals—acting in accordance with the will of the Assembly—slaughtered all the men of military age and sold the women and children into slavery. (Not that the Athenians were strangers to such brutal measures. It was, after all, a mere five years since they had inflicted the same penalty when they captured Scione in the Chalcidice.)[37]

One of the chief proponents urging this punishment on Melos, this signal to other island states that to resist was not just futile but suicidal, was Alcibiades. It was a policy from which he benefited personally. The surviving islanders were rounded up and shipped, traumatized, to Athens, where a slave auction was held. Among the lots on offer, Alcibiades' eye fell on a particularly lovely Melian girl. He bought her and took her home to be his concubine; and, when he later learned that he had fathered a son by her, he arranged to pay for the boy's upkeep, although by then he, Alcibiades, was far from Athens.[38]

In advocating this treatment of the Melians, not to mention his alleged trickery of Teisias in the matter of the chariot team and the strutting vanity of his performance at Olympia, Alcibiades had travelled far from the values of his old friend, Socrates. The rift that may have set in after the performance of Aristophanes' *Clouds* some seven years before had driven a wedge between the two men. Certainly, the philosopher's chief apologist, his student Plato, tried famously to argue that, by early 416, their paths had long since diverged.[39]

Painting a wistful picture of the lull before the storm which was about to break around Alcibiades' and Athens' ears, Plato's *Symposium* imagined Socrates at the house of the handsome young tragic poet, Agathon, for a party celebrating his victory at the dramatic festival of the Lenaea. The scenario for this, the last time that Alcibiades and Socrates are imagined meeting, is almost achingly nostalgic. Agathon's dining room is filled with good-natured friends—among them Aristophanes, the awkwardness engendered by his treatment of Socrates in *Clouds* long since forgotten.[40]

Most symposia were riotous affairs, the scene of drinking games and laughter, where pretty slave-girls laid aside their *aulos*-flutes to pander to the male guests' carnal needs, and patriotic songs were bawled out late into the night. The lyrics of such songs as survive are telling, for many of them hark back to the first days of democracy, when Hippias was overthrown and the

Athenian People liberated, lyrics that served to reinforce their hatred of potential tyrants:

I'll wreathe my sword in myrtle leaves
like Harmodius and Aristogeiton,
when they slew the tyrant
and set Athens and its people free!

Harmodius, you are not dead!
You live still in the Islands of the Blest,
home to Achilles, swift of foot,
and Tydeus' son, Diomedes.

But Agathon's guests have chosen not to sing or to carouse. Instead, they will indulge in philosophical debate. Their subject is Eros—at its most basic, sexual attraction; at its most spiritual, the force which animates pure reason and causes souls to strive for what is good. Each of the banqueters has expounded his own theory, and Socrates has just finished speaking, when a loud hammering is heard on the street door. "It sounded," writes Plato, "like a party of revellers—there was even the sound of a flute girl."[41]

Almost immediately, a voice is heard, shouting noisily and drunkenly. It is Alcibiades, demanding to see Agathon and congratulate him on his victory. Then the door bursts open. And there is Alcibiades, his head crowned with a garland of violets, ivy leaves, and ribbons, swaying in magnificent inebriation in the flute girl's supple arms as his friends, too, try to support him. The garland, he declares, is for Agathon! Will the diners let him in and drink with him? To a man they say they will. Clumsily Alcibiades takes off his garland while others remove his shoes, and it is only when he is reclining that he realizes who it is that he has positioned himself beside: Socrates. Lustily, Alcibiades seizes a half-gallon wine cooler and drinks down its contents before, persuaded by his fellow symposiasts, he launches into an encomium of his old friend.[42]

Elegant, well-structured, and peppered with quotations from not just Homer's *Odyssey* and *Iliad* but even Aristophanes' *Clouds*, his speech is far from what might be expected from a drunkard. In it, Alcibiades unwittingly picks up many of the themes that Socrates himself has explored earlier, and in doing so he reveals that the philosopher is, in fact, the living embodiment of the spiritual Eros. Like Eros, Socrates is weather-beaten, shoeless, able to endure hardship; he is not beautiful himself, but desires beauty and perfection; he seeks beautiful companions to help him produce spiritual children; he yearns for knowledge; he initiates his followers into his mysteries to help them on their path towards the discovery of absolute eternal beauty.[43]

But, in bringing Alcibiades to the symposium, Plato is doing more than using him as a literary mechanism. He deliberately has the dissolute young politician distance himself from the philosopher's moderating influence. Socrates, says Plato's Alcibiades, is the only man who can make him feel ashamed. When they are together, Alcibiades moderates his behaviour, but, as soon as he is on his own, he succumbs to the blandishments of the crowd. Only in Socrates' presence can he admit his imperfections to himself, but he deliberately stops his ears and neglects his true interests in favour of his political career. Do otherwise, he says, "and I would keep on sitting next to him till I grew old."[44]

It is not by chance that Plato sets this most striking of encounters at Agathon's victory party of early 416. Or that he offers us so vivid an image of the charismatic Alcibiades, louche and good-looking, in the company of a disreputable flute girl, his head garlanded with violets, a flower which—ever since the praise-poet Pindar's famous evocation of Athens as "shining, violet-crowned, the delight of poets, protectress of Greece"—had been so closely connected to his city. Yet even as he bursts into the room, Alcibiades is an enigma. Yearning for philosophy, he lives a life of dissolution. Drunk, his speech in praise of Socrates is clear-eyed and articulate. Uninvited, he has come from nowhere, and when the symposium is over he has disappeared.[45]

But it is for his rejection of Socrates, his admission of his inability to follow in his master's path, that Plato has chosen this moment above all others to present us with Alcibiades and to let us hear his credo. It is as if, conjured up by this disparate collection of Athenians all united in their talk of Eros, the symbol on his shield, he hovers on the threshold of the dining room, the uninvited guest—like Eris, "Strife," appearing at the wedding feast of Peleus and Thetis before she reveals the golden apple that will provoke the Trojan War and end the age of heroes. It is as if the greatness of Athens, too, is hanging in the balance, and by having Alcibiades so roundly (if regretfully) reject his master, Plato absolves Socrates from the catastrophes which are so imminent.[46]

For, as the seasons turned, and the year of Agathon's symposium—with its spring ostracism, Alcibiades' summer Olympic victory, and the autumn massacre at Melos—slid into winter, seeds were sown that would soon blossom to disaster. In the bitter months of early 415, when the days were at their shortest, grim men came to Athens where, at the People's invitation, they stalked onto the Speaker's Platform and poured out their woes. They were Sicilians from cities at the island's two extremities: the Ionian foundation of Leontini in the east; the native Sicilian Segesta in the west. Both had grievances with hostile neighbours. Both said they had justice on their side. Both begged Athens to intervene to help them. And both had a powerful advocate. Standing foursquare beside them in the pale winter sunlight, feeding the city's appetite for new campaigns, was Alcibiades. Laying out the case for Athens' intervention. And a new expedition to Sicily.[47]

6

BETWEEN SCYLLA AND CHARYBDIS

> Destruction lies in wait for you, your ship, and your companions,
> if you attack [Sicily]. And, if you do escape, you will return home
> only after many years, with all your comrades dead, and in a ship
> belonging to another.

Homer, *Odyssey*, 11.112–115

SICILY. The island had occupied the thoughts of Athens for well over a decade now. Ever since the charismatic Gorgias delivered his bewitching speech to woo the People on behalf of Leontini twelve years earlier, its lure had been almost irresistible. Twice the Athenians had put to sea, determined to bolster Sicilian opposition to the city that was fast becoming the most powerful force in the Greek west: the Corinthian colony of Syracuse, land-locked Leontini's aggressive seaboard neighbour. Twice they had been thwarted: the first time in 424, when Syracuse's dazzling spokesman, Hermocrates, rallied the Sicilian Greek city states at the Congress of Gela to unite against what he claimed was Athenian imperial aggression; the second in 422, when Phaeax and his colleagues failed in their charm offensive to secure the coastal cities of the east. Both times the failure had been not military but diplomatic. But now that Athens had such a persuasive orator in Alcibiades, might it not be time to try again? Especially as the Athenians were bound by treaties to help not just Greek-founded Leontini in the island's east but the native Sicilian city of Segesta in the west as well, both of which were now requesting aid.[1]

Leontini's gripe was quite simply that Syracuse had annexed both her city and her land, driving out her democrats, and shamelessly courting her wealthy oligarchs. Segesta's complaint, too, involved a neighbour. A long-term quarrel with Selinus, the powerful harbour city to the south, founded two centuries before by colonists from Megara, had recently blown up again, thanks to a border dispute and a spat over marriage rights.[2]

As they addressed the Assembly, the ambassadors brought forth so many arguments to coax and to cajole, to persuade the People to support them. For Syracuse to dominate the island would be bad enough; but once Sicily was dominated by the Syracusans (who were colonists of Corinth), it was likely—no, certain—to support the Peloponnesians in any future war with Athens. Better to nip such a threat in the bud. Better to do what Alcibiades had already begun to do in the Peloponnese (albeit with mixed success), when he supported Argos, formed the Arcadian League, and launched pre-emptive strikes, which took the war to the enemy at relatively little risk to Athens. Attacks on Selinus and Syracuse would strike a blow against their mother-cities, Megara and Corinth, both of which were under the control of oligarchs and arch-enemies of Athens. And, what was even more alluring, Athens would not be faced with any costs—Segesta was so rich that she would fund the war.[3]

They were compelling arguments, pitched perfectly to persuade both the more farsighted among Athens' citizens and younger hotheads impatient for adventure, eager to prove themselves in battle. In an Assembly buzzing with anticipation, it was voted to send delegates to Sicily both to gauge the situation at Selinus for themselves and to discover at first hand whether the Segestan coffers really were as full as the ambassadors claimed. When the delegates returned, they were in bullish mood. They had dined lavishly at banquets served on gold and silver plate; they had inspected the glittering treasury in Aphrodite's cliff-top temple at Segestan Eryx; they had even been taken on a tour of a new temple currently being built in pure Greek style at Segesta itself, a sure sign—if one were still needed—of the city's economic confidence. In short, they reported, money would be no problem. To underline their point, they invited the Segestan ambassadors to join them on the Platform, announcing that they had brought with them two tons of unminted silver (the equivalent of sixty talents, enough to pay the crew of sixty triremes for one month) and assuring the Athenians there was much more where that came from. If the Assembly gave the expedition its consent, all that remained to be done was appoint a general, equip the fleet, and sail to Sicily. And this time, there was every likelihood of military success.[4]

It must have seemed almost too good to be true. In a mood of high excitement, the votes were taken, the commanders chosen, the rules of engagement laid down. These were so vague as to be all-encompassing: to send sixty ships to help Segesta against Selinus, to support Leontini against Syracuse, and generally to "conduct themselves in Sicily in whatever way seemed most in Athens' interests." Although the initial proposal called for only one general (Alcibiades), the number was soon increased to three: Alcibiades, of course, who had promoted the expedition with such gusto from the start; the parsimonious Lamachus, a seasoned military commander with a number of successful overseas campaigns under his belt; and Nicias— Nicias, the middle-aged mining mogul, who had so willingly resigned his military command when Cleon offered to dash down to Pylos and defeat the Spartans; Nicias, the architect of peace, the most reluctant of his city's soldiers; Nicias, who may well have been the *proxenos* of Syracuse; Nicias, the sworn enemy of Alcibiades.[5]

Why Nicias? Perhaps the factions in the Assembly were still so evenly balanced that it was inevitable that, if Alcibiades was chosen, Nicias would be, too. Or perhaps the Athenians hoped that he would be a "wise head," a voice of reason, if ever Alcibiades' ambition encouraged him to take incautious risks. Perhaps there were those seduced by the magic of his name— since Nicias and *nike* ("victory") sounded similar, just as the name Lamachus seemed redolent of *mache* ("battle"). Or maybe, with the debacle of the previous year's ostracism fresh in everybody's minds, they were only too happy to be rid of both the leaders of the factions splitting Athens, to send them abroad, so that the city might enjoy some peace and quiet.

Whatever the reason, Nicias was none too happy. He wanted nothing to do with the Sicilian adventure, and four days later, at the next meeting of the Assembly called to discuss logistics, he did his best to pour cold water on the whole endeavour. In a blistering speech, he not only condemned the undertaking as foolhardy, but laid into its chief architect, Alcibiades.

Recognizing the fragility of the peace that he himself had brokered, Nicias begged the Athenians to reconsider. The expedition, he warned, would deprive the city of many of its fighting men and leave Athens vulnerable to attack—especially, he added with his trademark pessimism, if it suffered a defeat. Much better not to sail at all, or, if they did, to make a short, sharp show of strength and then come home again. For, even if Syracuse did grow in power, it was unlikely to wish ever to become embroiled in a war on mainland Greece.[6]

Nicias had already taken a sideways swipe at Alcibiades for undermining the peace treaty, but now (according to Thucydides) he laid into him in an excoriating attack, in which his frustrations spilled out in a flood of vitriol. Without actually mentioning his name, Nicias fulminated against "someone here in the Assembly, who is feeling smug about being appointed general, who has encouraged you to make this expedition entirely for his own selfish ends." This person's prime motivation was, he sneered, to use the war to turn a private profit, to help defray the costs of his race horses. This person was, he thundered, "too young for such a high command"; the enterprise was not "the kind of thing to be resolved or executed by a young man in a hurry."[7]

Finally, having whipped himself into a lather of righteous indignation, Nicias launched a spittle-sputtering invective against the whole younger generation who, he jeered, were chasing unreal dreams. The wiser, older voters must not let Alcibiades' supporters browbeat them. Rather, Nicias concluded (somewhat improbably dragging in the Hippocratic oath), they should behave like true physicians, acting only for the good, refusing to do anything to harm their city.[8]

The Assembly erupted into cheers, and jeers, and catcalls as speaker followed speaker, some few supporting Nicias, but most in favour of the expedition. At last, with passions boiling, Alcibiades himself swept up onto the Platform. His speech was brilliant. He began by addressing his detractors head on. His horses and his prowess at the Olympic Games were nothing to be ashamed of—indeed, his victory was Athens' victory, and the city could bathe in his success and brilliance. For brilliant he was and, if the People did not accept this now, then they most surely would once he was dead! His private life was his own. He should be judged on his record in the civic sphere, on the splendour of his public generosity, on his strategy of shifting the theatre of war away from Attica, on his diplomatic successes in both Argos and Arcadia. Nor should his age be held against him—in a gracious gesture of conciliation, a striking demonstration of political maturity, he declared his full support of Nicias as fellow general, arguing that his own energy matched with Nicias' reputation for good fortune made for a winning combination.[9]

Next he turned to Sicily, and a wide-ranging analysis both of the island's strengths and weaknesses and of its native populations' willingness to help Athens in her struggle against Syracuse. Athens, he urged, owed her allies support. And, besides, it made sound military sense to launch preemptive strikes. "You don't just wait to be attacked before defending yourself—you do all you can beforehand to prevent yourself from being attacked in the first place." To maintain her empire, Athens could not afford simply to sit back and do nothing; even to hold on to what she now possessed, she must work tirelessly to enlarge her frontiers. Athens, he declared, owed her success to the restless energy of all her citizens. Peace and inactivity would only lead to downfall. The dynamic younger generation was as crucial as the old. "So do not be swayed by Nicias' *laissez-faire* policy or his pitting the young against the old . . . Do all you can to take this city forward, understanding that without each other youth and seniority cannot achieve anything." As in the past, so now, only through unity could they achieve success.[10]

It was a statesmanlike performance, and one that caught the imagination of the People. But Nicias—the blinkered Nicias, who yearned only to spend his twilight years in peace and quiet—tried one last time to put them off. And in doing so, sowed the seeds of failure and tragedy. Taking to the Platform one last time, he painted a bleak picture of the problems which the expedition faced, the great wealth and number of the cities that would oppose them, the huge size of their fighting force. The campaign would be long and hard. To have any hope of success, its numbers must be scaled up to include more ships, hoplites, archers, slingsmen, not to mention shiploads of supplies of wheat and barley, and a platoon of bakers to turn it into bread. Only a mighty military presence could ensure success. And, having emphasised the sheer scale of the costs and dangers, Nicias reached his conclusion: if you disagree, then—please—relieve me of my generalship and appoint someone else.[11]

For Nicias, to give up his command was an outcome devoutly to be wished. But it was not to be. Far from being deterred by his assessment, the People thrilled to the challenge. How could such a massive expedition possibly fail? The prospect of certain victory galvanized both young and old. They pushed Nicias to put a figure on how many ships and hoplites he required. Confused, and without thinking, he blurted out "a hundred triremes, and at least five thousand hoplites—but . . . but I must consult my colleagues!" Exultantly, the People voted his proposals through, poured down from Pnyx Hill, and began making preparations. So, thanks to Nicias and his ineptitude, the stakes were raised abruptly to unanticipated heights, and a strategic task force swelled into an invading horde.[12]

All Athens was in a frenzy. As Aristophanes so vividly described it: "a mob of soldiery; quarrels over trireme captains; pay doled out; Athene's figureheads being gilded; crowded stoas; measurements of grain; wineskins; oar leathers; buying big oil jars; garlic; olives; nets of onions; wreaths of flowers; sardines and flute girls; black eyes; oars being planed down in the dockyards; thongs being fitted, leathers stretched; and a din of flutes and fifes and penny whistles tapping out the time." Meanwhile the excitement grew. In gymnasia at the Lyceum or the grove of Academus, in seedy bars beside the Cerameicus, in noisy barbershops close to the seafront at Piraeus, it fuelled almost every conversation. And in the Agora, beneath the budding plane trees, old men with walking sticks were drawing maps in the sand—maps of Sicily and southern Italy, maps of the seas and harbours, maps of the coastline south to Africa. In eager conversations, their ambitions multiplied: from adding Sicily with all its wealth and its potential to Athens' abundant empire, to pushing further—south, even to Carthage; west, to Spain—until they became lords of the entire Mediterranean. It was such a heady vision.[13]

But in private there were some, such as Socrates, who had grave doubts, while many powerful politicians remained vehemently opposed both to the expedition and its chief architect, Alcibiades. Thwarted in the Assembly, they tried to make their voices heard in other ways. One of their chief weapons was religion. And superstition. Some claimed that during the debate on Sicily, the sound of women's lamentations had been heard, drifting on the spring breeze as they celebrated annual rites for the death of the vegetation god, Adonis. These howls of grief, they said, were a bad omen. Alcibiades' response was swift. To quash concerns and soothe the credulous, he not only paraded a succession of compliant soothsayers before the People but instructed passages to be read aloud from ancient books of oracles, all confidently foretelling victory.[14]

Then, overnight, in early June: disaster.[15]

The sacrilege was probably discovered first by women hurrying to fountain-houses before dawn, before the men of Athens were awake, surprised as their sandaled feet crunched fragments of smashed marble. But by the time the cocks were crowing and the sun was rising over Mount Hymettus, flooding the Attic plain with light, its dazzling reflection gleaming on the metal statues high on the Acropolis, the news was already spider-webbing through the city, householders staggering stunned and dazed onto the streets.

The sight that met them was profoundly troubling, an unholy wreckage striking at the very safety of both Athens and her forthcoming expedition. For, throughout the city, statues had been systematically disfigured and defaced. But not just any statues. Whoever was behind it had chosen their targets carefully: the so-called Herms—squared pillars topped with the head of the god Hermes, and furnished, halfway up, with genitalia and an exuberant, erect phallus. Many stood prominently outside public buildings, temples, stoas, and gymnasia; others at street corners, or by the doors of private houses; still others in the Agora, where a cluster in the northwest corner, close to the sacred Oath Stone, included three that had been dedicated sixty years before by Cimon following a famous victory. Each of these three bore triumphal inscriptions, summed up concisely on the central Herm:

> The Athenians dedicated this in recognition of their generals,
>   acknowledging the benefits they have bestowed and the great
>   work they have done.
> Whoever looks on this in future time will be filled with greater
>   courage to fight with greater resolution for the common good.

Most Herms, however, held no military message. Instead, it was believed that they protected the buildings outside which they stood, apotropaics standing sentinel to ward off evil. For Hermes, god of businessmen and heralds, was also the god of guard dogs, a thief who nonetheless kept safe the homes of all who honoured him, a trickster god, who yet could be relied on to keep watch. But he had other attributes as well. As messenger of Zeus, Hermes acted as a conduit between heaven and earth, conveying visions (true and false) to those he lulled to sleep with his enchanted herald's wand. He was the god of magic, too, and necromancy. He was the god who conveyed the souls of the dead down to the Underworld. And he was the god of travellers.[16]

For a city whose sons were soon to set out on a long and dangerous journey, and which was relying on her men to fight with resolution while the gods protected those at home, this act of mutilation struck at the very core of her well-being. Perhaps the rational philosophers could shrug it off, but they formed a tiny fraction of the population. Most Athenians—like Nicias, indeed—were deeply superstitious, and for them it was not just that the heads and genitals of lifeless statues had been broken; the magic force-field that kept buildings safe and radiated out to form a nexus, linking Herm

Its head and genitalia no longer intact, a Herm keeps watch below the Temple of Nemesis at Rhamnus. (Photograph by the author.)

to Herm, to shield the city had been smashed apart, an act of vandalism with profound religious significance. And not just religious significance, as it soon turned out. Political significance, as well.

At once, people began to speculate. Who was responsible? What were their motives? In the absence of evidence theories multiplied. Some suspected foreign *agents provocateurs,* Corinthians, trying to prevent an Athenian attack on their colony of Syracuse. Others, however, laid the blame much closer to home. It was not unusual, they said, for privileged young men when drunk to go on the rampage, committing acts of mischief, and even defacing religious monuments. Surely this is what had happened here. If so, however, it was a prank, which had gone too far. But perhaps it was not a prank at all. Perhaps it was a calculated act of political insurrection aimed at undermining the very fabric of the democratic state.[17]

The city was already in great turmoil. The previous year's ostracism had failed to deliver the decisive outcome for which so many hoped; Nicias' recent speech in the Assembly had merely helped fuel tensions between old and young; and there were still many bitterly opposed both to the expedition and to its instigator, Alcibiades. Rumours began to circulate that well-organized groups of young men had been seen meeting by moonlight in the Theatre of Dionysus before fanning through the city to wreak havoc. Tongues wagged. Fingers pointed. But no one could discover the truth. Which was remarkable. Not only the sheer scale of the operation, but the fact that no one seemingly saw or heard the wreckage taking place meant that it must have been meticulously planned. Perhaps foreign agents *were* involved. Or perhaps the perpetrators *were* Athenians. Perhaps they were misguided souls who believed in sympathetic magic, who thought that by attacking the power of Hermes they were attacking the leading Syracusan, Hermocrates, who had thwarted them nine years before at the Congress of Gela, and whose name meant precisely "the power of Hermes." Or could it have been a bizarre attack on Alcibiades, who had regularly been satirized by Aristophanes under the phallic names Phallenius and Triphalles ("Thrice-Phallused"), a curious attempt to diminish his rampant political power? Or perhaps the perpetrators were rich men opposed to the Sicilian adventure, disgruntled because the People had passed a motion imposing a special wealth tax to fund the expedition. Or perhaps they were friends of Nicias—not that Nicias himself would have sanctioned such a boldly impious undertaking, but, if it had been intended to stop the fleet from sailing, it chimed completely with his views—indeed, a few months later, two of his brothers were accused of taking part. Yet at no time does it ever seem to have been mooted that the war on Sicily should be aborted or postponed.[18]

So, who did it? With no obvious suspects in sight, the Assembly and Council held daily meetings to discuss what was fast becoming a crisis. A special Commission of Enquiry was set up, with the offer of not just immunity from prosecution but rewards to any who came forward with information leading to a prosecution—information about not just the mutilation of the Herms but any other irreligious act that might have been committed in the city. And at once the floodgates opened. At a stroke, anyone wishing to make accusations of the most malicious kind against his enemies had effectively been granted *carte blanche*. And Alcibiades' enemies jumped at the opportunity.[19]

Completely ignoring what should have been blatantly obvious—that Alcibiades was the last person in Athens who would wish to jeopardize the success of an expedition he himself had masterminded—they let it be known to anyone prepared to listen that they believed him to be responsible. After all, it was just the sort of thing that a young man as wild and irresponsible as Alcibiades would do. As irreligious, too. Which was why, when further accusations were levelled against Alcibiades citing other instances of impious behaviour in his private life, there were many who believed them, too.

Just days before the fleet was due to sail, indeed, even as the triremes were undergoing their final sea trials, at a packed and tense Assembly one of Alcibiades' opponents rose to his feet. His name was Pythonicus, which, translated, can mean both "Apollo's Victory" and "The Prophetic One," and it was perhaps because of this that his associates had picked him as their spokesman. Now, pointing at Alcibiades, he launched his tirade. The expedition, he foretold, was fraught with danger. And why? Not because Alcibiades had been among those who defaced the Herms. Rather, Pythonicus took advantage of the febrile atmosphere now gripping Athens to accuse him of another and potentially more dangerous impiety. Alcibiades and his associates, he claimed, had profaned the venerated Mysteries of Eleusis, mimicking their rites in a private house. In front of a slave. Who was uninitiated.[20]

In the current climate of social, political, and religious turmoil, this was a bombshell. The Eleusinian Mysteries were among the most sacred of all Athenian religious institutions, a ceremony that epitomized everything that was good and holy, a sacrament that lent stability to the state. By offhandedly mimicking their central rites before the uninitiated, Alcibiades' enemies suggested, he was not just displaying his scorn for the gods, but actively undermining the very fabric of the Athenian democracy.[21]

Amid rising indignation, Alcibiades tried to refute the charges. But there was little he could do. The presidents of the Assembly ordered all who were uninitiated to depart, while the slave in question, a young man called Andromachus, was summoned and interrogated. As Alcibiades listened, his horror mounting by the minute, Andromachus spun his tale in vividly convincing detail. He identified the house where the profanation had occurred. He named some of those responsible. He accused Alcibiades of having taken the role of High Priest, while his host played the Torch-Bearer and another friend, the Herald. And he listed two more slaves who had been present. As the evidence mounted, it seemed increasingly impossible that it could not be true.[22]

The Mysteries had been satirized before, most notably (for us) by Aristophanes in *Clouds*; the same comic poet would feel safe to burlesque them again eleven years later in his *Frogs*; while Alcibiades' friend Critias, himself a tragedian, went so far as to stage a scene showing an initiation ceremony into a mystery religion, which made free use of vocabulary and phrases lifted from the Eleusinian Mysteries. But in the current climate, the implications of the accusation were potentially devastating. Especially in light of everything else that was alleged of Alcibiades.[23]

As if in a nightmare, all his past extravagances rose to haunt him, not least the playfully ambiguous motif on his shield showing Eros wielding a thunderbolt, which suddenly seemed hideously crass—in Greek mythology and religious iconography, only Zeus (and occasionally Athene) was granted the thunderbolt as weapon, and to award it to the god of Lust could be construed as blasphemous. And then there was the ever-present curse on Alcibiades' maternal family, the Alcmaeonids, a curse so useful to his enemies, which could be dredged up whenever anyone should wish to undermine him.[24]

To make things worse, two dramas recently performed in the Theatre of Dionysus had quite inadvertently prepared the ground in which such accusations against Alcibiades could flourish. Not only had the comic poet Eupolis staged *Baptae* ("The Dippers"), in which he envisaged a group of effeminate young men, including almost certainly Alcibiades, introducing a new mystery religion into Athens, complete with its initiation rites (a production which, some rumourmongers later claimed, led to his drowning at the hands of Alcibiades), but Euripides had staged his devastating *Trojan Trilogy* whose third play, *Trojan Women,* contained dire warnings of the implications of embarking on a voyage in the company of impious men. Sea voyages were hazardous enough, but knowingly to embark on a ship with an ungodly man was to invite disaster.[25]

Now in the Assembly, as they listened to Andromachus being led in painstaking detail through his statement, the audience of initiates recognized much that they themselves had experienced in the Great Hall of the Mysteries at Eleusis. And consequently it did not take much effort to assume that the accusations were true. But were they? Had Alcibiades and his friends really profaned the Mysteries? Or was there something else going on that his prosecutors had cleverly latched on to, to let them whip up not just religious indignation but envy and class hatred against him?

The setting, in which the profanation was alleged to have occurred, was a meeting of an exclusive club (*hetaereia,* literally "companionship group"). There were several such clubs in Athens, each with a maximum of around twenty-five members drawn from the richest and most powerful families. Their main function was to provide a political and business network, members of which could be relied on for the most part to support each other. But there was a distinct social element attached as well, which often involved heavy drinking and riotous partying. And because things might be said or done at meetings, which no one wanted to become public knowledge, new members were required to swear solemn oaths to bind them in close brotherhood. Given that the most solemn ceremony in which any of them had participated was that of the Eleusinian Mysteries, it was perhaps unsurprising that there were many similarities between these and the clubs' initiation rites.[26]

It was unsurprising, too, that non-members took delight in spreading scabrous rumours about what went on at meetings, from which they would forever be excluded. One even claimed that, to test the extent of his fellow club members' resolve, Alcibiades had placed a fake corpse in a darkened room and showed it to his friends, begging them to help him cover up the murder. No matter if the episode were true or not, his enemies used it and other pieces of malicious tittle-tattle to reinforce the notion that Alcibiades considered himself to be above the law. And from there it did not take much to argue that he considered himself to be above the constitution, too, that what he really wanted was to do away with the democracy and install himself as tyrant, an autocratic ruler like Peisistratus and Hippias a hundred years before. Especially as in Greek minds sacrilege and tyranny went hand in hand.[27]

There was so much evidence his enemies could draw on. There was the extravagance of his flamboyant lifestyle, how he poured vast fortunes into race horses and chariots, how he flaunted his position at Olympia, how he held court there as if he were some eastern potentate lounging in his perfumed silken tent. There was his recent speech to the Assembly, in which he proclaimed his preeminent excellence, setting himself above the common people, while suggesting that his brilliance at Olympia was Athens' brilliance, that he was Athens' champion, that the two were indivisible. And there were the rumours of his pact with Nicias or Phaeax to pervert the constitution and the course of democratic justice in the ostracism vote.[28]

In his speech encouraging the People to sail out to Sicily, Alcibiades had argued that he should be judged not by the peccadilloes of his private life but by his public works. Now, though, his enemies were doing their best to prove that what he did in public mirrored what he did in private, and that, in both spheres, he was manipulating personal alliances to provide unfair advantages. Thanks to the constant drip of rumour, he was increasingly suspected of having played a role in the very public desecration of the Herms. Now he was being accused directly of participation in a very private parody of the Eleusinian Mysteries. On the first charge there was no proof; as far as the second went, any similarities between his club's initiation rites and those at Eleusis were probably purely circumstantial; but all this was irrelevant. And Alcibiades knew it.

He knew, too, that quite simply he had been outplayed. To sail to Sicily without the situation being resolved would be dangerous in the extreme. In his absence from Athens, his enemies would have a field day, inventing new accusations, uncovering new witnesses, producing newly trumped-up plots. It was crucial to quash the charges immediately. Once and for all.

As Andromachus was led down from the Speaker's Platform, Alcibiades bounded up to speak. He categorically denied everything. He pleaded with the People, if they wished, to put him on trial now. Without delay. Not just on this charge, but on any other that they wished. If they found him guilty, they could execute him. If not, they must clear his name, and let him sail to Sicily free from all suspicion.[29]

But before the People could agree, his rivals got onto their feet to argue equally impassionedly that to try him now would mean postponing the sailing of the expedition, which, given its readiness, must be avoided at all costs. Rather, they should let Alcibiades go as planned. He could always be put on trial when he came back. It was such a clever move, and its timing was impeccable. Much of Alcibiades' support in the Assembly came from the younger fighting men of Athens, and with both Alcibiades and the army far removed in Sicily, it would be considerably easier for his enemies to persuade the remaining voters, the older generation, who were already sceptical of his ambitions, to have him recalled to face a hostile jury. And with the People eager for their Sicilian adventure to begin, there was nothing Alcibiades could do. "So," as Thucydides so concisely put it, "it was agreed that he should sail."[30]

And so it was that very shortly afterwards, even before the dawn broke on a fine midsummer's day, almost everyone in Athens surged down to the quayside at Piraeus, a chattering, excited throng of men and women, citizens and foreigners, pouring down the broad, straight road, the Long Walls towering high on either side. Skirting Piraeus' grid-planned streets, with its deserted agora, its theatres, and its two small harbours, Zea and Munychia, they soon spilled out onto the sea front, until, with much good-humoured elbowing and jostling, they found a space where they could stand and see the view.[31]

It was breathtaking. A hundred triremes, their newly gilded figureheads glinting radiant in the rising sun, lay lazy in the flat calm waters of the harbour. For now, their masts and sails were stowed away, and with their streamlined forms, hulls caulked just recently with tarry pitch and crimson-stained with ruddle, huge staring eyes fresh-painted on their bows, they looked like beautiful sea creatures, hybrid dolphins with long oar-feathered wings. Each of their owners had expended huge amounts of money in their unacknowledged competition to create not just the fastest and most deadly but the loveliest, most graceful ship, each crewed by the finest oarsmen they could find. Already the supplies for the first leg of the voyage were on board, and it was time for the hoplites to embark. Long lingering hugs with loved ones by the harbour wall, last pieces of advice, eyes glittering with tears—and then the young men were aboard and lining the narrow decks as they looked back to shore.

And then the braying of a trumpet call, and a hush descended on the many thousands gathered there. It was time for the prayers that would precede departure. Normally each ship would make its own prayers separately. But not today. In a tightly stage-managed ceremony, a herald led the huge assembly, as together in unison they repeated the sacred words. Then on the triremes wine was ladled into gold and silver cups (no doubt the same state vessels that Alcibiades had used for his Olympic banquet less than a year earlier), and, as the singing of the customary hymn resounded round the mighty harbour, libations were poured into the clear sea, dark streams of wine in offering to Poseidon for a safe voyage.

And with that, the rowers bent over their oars, the helmsmen swung the ships' prows round towards the open sea, and the long column of triremes nosed out into the open waters. As they left the harbour, they may have passed to starboard the tomb of Themistocles, the father of Athens' navy, who had led the Greeks to victory at Salamis, but whom the People had condemned; who had fled for his life to Persia, but on whose death the People had repented and requested that his body be returned for burial; whom Alcibiades cannot but have had in mind, when he spoke a few weeks earlier of men, whose brilliance the People recognized only when they were dead. Then, when all were out at sea, they drew up abreast in a long line, and, as the trumpet sounded once again, the triremes raced each other out as far as the island of Aegina.[32]

For Alcibiades, the voyage south and round the pale blue mountains of the Peloponnese must have felt liberating. On his flagship trireme, a ship he had provided at his own expense, he had caused a section of the deck to be removed so that a hammock might be strung, in which he could relax and watch the world float by—and feel the freedom of the warm sea breeze, as it seared his face and burnt away the stifling hothouse memories of the Assembly. Yet, even as he sailed to new adventures, the memory of Themistocles' fate cannot but have given him pause. Like Themistocles before him, he was leaving Athens to his enemies. Who knew what mischief they might stir up in his absence? It would not have been surprising if Alcibiades was even now weighing his options.[33]

The ships made good speed, and soon they were tacking north to Corcyra, where they met up with the merchantmen, as well as a number of other triremes, which had sailed here directly from Chios and the islands of the east Aegean. And then, divided into three huge squadrons, each commanded by one of Athens' generals, the fleet struck out for Italy. And almost immediately they ran into problems. Greek sailors seldom, if ever, spent the night at sea, preferring to put out at dawn, before dropping anchor by late afternoon in congenial harbours, or dragging their ships ashore on friendly beaches. Now, the Athenians were relying on being welcomed on their voyage by the cities of South Italy, with which they enjoyed good relations. But they soon found that the reality was very different, as city after city refused not only to open their gates, but even to trade with them. Two even denied them anchorage and drinking water.[34]

The problem was the sheer size of the expeditionary force: 134 triremes, two smaller Rhodian warships, over 5,000 hoplites, 480 archers, 700 slingers, and 30 horses. Not to mention thirty lumbering merchant ships, carrying not just grain, but bakers, builders, and carpenters—all of whose skills would be essential in the event of a long siege—as well as a hundred smaller transport vessels requisitioned by the state. And, as if this were not enough, the expedition had attracted an unofficial merchant fleet, ships of all sizes and degrees of seaworthiness, a floating marketplace of private businessmen and traders confident of growing rich on the back of Athens' military success. Thanks to both Nicias' pessimism in the Assembly and the ensuing optimism that had gripped the city at the thought of conquest, what had initially been conceived as an efficient task force of just sixty ships had turned into a lumbering armada.[35]

Not unsurprisingly, many of the cities of South Italy and Sicily were now deeply suspicious of the Athenians' intentions. Had they really come simply to assist their allies in Segesta and Leontini as they claimed? Or was their intention to subdue the entire region and add it to their empire? Certainly, the sheer scale of the operation seemed to suggest the latter. Coasting around the yawning Gulf of Tarentum, its lush, well-watered coastal plains studded with increasingly unfriendly cities, Alcibiades cannot but have experienced a growing frustration that his original concept for the expedition had been dangerously jeopardized by Nicias, as well as a determination to impose his own strategy on the campaign as soon as possible.

At last, the fleet reached the westernmost tip of Calabria. And its goal came into view: Sicily, her pale blue jagged mountains stretching far off in the haze, like the Peloponnese seen from Athens. As they sailed on north, still hugging the Italian coast, the waters narrowed, until, by the time they came to Rhegium, they could make out not just corrugated tree-lined hills, but the houses and temples of Messana just across the strait. Here was the channel whose turbulent waters, so the Greeks believed, were guarded by Scylla and Charybdis, monstrous forces which had once all but destroyed the ships of the hero Odysseus. The Athenians had high hopes that for them, at least, these seas would be more welcoming. But at Rhegium, again they were shunned. Despite close ties with Leontini, the nervous Rhegines closed their gates, denying all access, and refusing to commit to helping Athens, until the rest of the Greek cities of South Italy agreed on a common policy, so that, with their ships drawn up along the narrow shore, the Athenians were forced to camp out in a precinct sacred to the goddess Artemis.[36]

Which was where they heard the bad news from Segesta. Trusting that city's promise of financial aid, the Athenians had sent three triremes to collect the money needed to pay the next month's wages. But instead of returning with sixty talents as agreed, the three ships' captains now brought only thirty. And not just that. They revealed that the delegates from Athens who had visited Segesta in the spring had been duped. What they thought were valuable treasuries in Aphrodite's temple at Eryx turned out, in fact, to be cheap gewgaws. The costly plate, on which their hosts had served them sumptuous feasts, had been borrowed from other cities and carried furtively around from house to house as the occasion demanded. No further work had been done on the temple at Segesta. And its treasury was empty. The soldiery were furious. If Alcibiades saw parallels with his own behaviour at Olympia the year before, when he passed off the state gold and silver as his own, he was not about to mention it. Only Nicias professed to be unsurprised.[37]

Faced with a growing list of problems, the three Athenian generals held a council of war, at which it quickly became all too obvious that they possessed no common strategy. Predictably, Nicias was in favour of doing as little as possible. For him, the best scenario was to sail with the whole fleet to Selinus, and by diplomacy or force effect a reconciliation between that city and Segesta. Then—unless they could find an easy way of helping Leontini—they should sail along the coast of Sicily in a show of strength. And then they should go back home.[38]

Lamachus had another idea entirely. Viewing the situation with the clear eye of a military tactician, he came straight to the point. The real enemy was not Selinus. It was ambitious Syracuse, a shining beacon for any city wishing to stand up to Athens. It needed to be neutralized. A sudden assault on Syracuse, when its generals were least expecting it; a victory beneath her walls; swift occupation of her outlying suburbs—achieve these things, ride the momentum, and Athens would gain both wealth and allies. And now was the time to do it. When the Syracusans least expected it.[39]

Cannily, however, Alcibiades proposed a third strategy, which, typically for him, involved both diplomacy and persuasion: negotiators should be sent to every town and city on the island, not only to encourage them to forswear whatever friendship they might have with Syracuse but to gauge how much goodwill there was for Athens. The greater the support, the easier it would be to keep the army well supplied. With most of the island on their side, the Athenians would be able either to compel Selinus and Syracuse to negotiate, or to defeat them in battle. And the first and most important city to win over was the closest—Messana, across the straits from Rhegium, so crucial to controlling the Sicilian seas, a city which Laches had been at pains to take for Athens in the previous military expedition eleven years before.[40]

It was a measured plan, one which took account of recent history. After all, Athens' last foray into Sicily had been thwarted at the Congress of Gela, precisely because Hermocrates had managed to convince the islanders to fear what he painted as the Athenians' aggressively imperial ambitions. Unless the Sicilians were brought onside this time, and early in the process, the same could very well happen again. The cool reception, which had met the fleet in Italy, was evidence enough of how suspicious people were of Athens' motives. To launch an immediate attack on Syracuse would merely compound their fears, and threaten to jeopardize the entire operation.

Given the personalities involved, it must have been a heated meeting. But in the end, Nicias was out-voted (a result that even he must have expected); Lamachus threw in his hand with Alcibiades; and Alcibiades boarded his flagship trireme to be rowed across the straits to Messana on the first leg of his diplomatic offensive. But despite his charismatic charm, and no doubt to his considerable surprise, his attempts to woo the people of Messana enjoyed only limited success. Like the Rhegines, they refused either to enter an alliance with the Athenians or to let their troops into the city, offering merely to set up a temporary market outside the walls, where they could buy provisions.[41]

Alcibiades cannot but have been disappointed. Based partly on pure optimism, his strategy had foundered at the first hurdle. Nonetheless, he refused to be disheartened. Leaving Nicias at Rhegium, he and Lamachus sailed south with sixty triremes to the Sicilian town of Naxos. Founded by Euboeans more than three hundred years earlier on a headland by a bay ringed with knobbly mountains at the mouth of the River Acesines, Naxos had long been an ally of Athens.[42]

Here at last Alcibiades and his troops received the welcome they so craved. With their triremes safely drawn up on the sandy beach, the ships' crews could wander through the city streets, some visiting the altar of Apollo (where athletes from across all Sicily sacrificed before they set out for the Great Games at Olympia and Delphi, Corinth and Nemea), most spending money in the agora and drinking in the local bars. Here many were no doubt regaled with tales of the hundred-headed giant Typhon, the enemy of Zeus, said to be imprisoned nearby deep beneath the earth, weighed down by a tall mountain—Etna, from deep within whose caves (the poet Pindar sang) erupted "pure, sacred flames, which no man might come near. Rivers of burning vapour pour out by day, while in the dark of night, with clattering thunder, searing fire hurls rocks down to the glassy sea . . . a miracle to watch, a miracle to hear of." A later Athenian playwright, Carcinus, knew another story: that Etna's flames first flared in sympathy for Demeter, when her daughter Persephone was taken from her. The fires of Etna, then, were proof, should proof be needed, not just of the punishment in store for any who thought they could disregard the authority of the gods, but of the power of Demeter, the great earth-goddess of the Eleusinian Mysteries.[43]

Even closer to Mount Etna was Naxos' own colony, Catane (modern Catania), just over thirty miles to the south, and it was here that Alcibiades and Lamachus sailed next. But once more their hopes of a warm welcome were thwarted. Many in the city were well disposed to their southern neighbour,

Syracuse, and viewed Athens with suspicion. And so Catane's gates were barred. It was a worrying development. For Alcibiades' plans to be successful, he needed to win over as many Sicilian cities as he could. He was relying on the island's Ionian population to support him. But even they seemed resistant to his cause.[44]

Rather than press the case too strongly, the Athenians continued sailing south, and the next day they reached Syracuse. It was a bewitching city. At the north of a huge shallow bay, the so-called Great Harbour, with a long low promontory to the south, and steep cliffs beetling to the west, it incorporated a low island, Ortygia, linked by bridges to the mainland, on which shone a proud array of beautifully appointed villas and tall, glittering temples. To the pediment of one, the Temple of Athene, a bronze shield was affixed, which blazed beneath the sun, a beacon for sailors far out at sea. Close by there was even an enchanting pool, the Fountain of Arethusa, whose fresh waters were said to flow beneath the seas directly from the Peloponnese, a link with the city's spiritual motherland. Ortygia was the home of the elite. Here, two generations earlier, the tyrant Gelon had his palace, and now the leading democratic politicians—Hermocrates among them—lived here, too. Meanwhile on the mainland, below the deep stone quarries, the prosperous agora boasted businesses as booming as any in Athens or Piraeus, its merchants trading goods unloaded in their two fine harbours not just from Greece and Asia Minor, but from Italy, and Spain, and Southern France. And even, ultimately, from Carthage.[45]

But it was not the city's history or architecture that fascinated Alcibiades. Rather, it was its defences. Leaving the main body of his fleet at sea, he boldly sailed with ten triremes into the Great Harbour, ostentatiously coming close enough to shore for his herald to make a proclamation. The Athenians, he boomed, had come with one purpose: to help their flesh and blood, the people of Leontini, who had been unlawfully driven from their city by the Syracusans. Any Leontinian now in Syracuse should leave immediately and join the cause![46]

If he hoped by taunting them to provoke the Syracusans to launch their fleet and attack his small flotilla of ten ships, only for the other fifty to swoop in and win a famous victory, Alcibiades was disappointed. He was unopposed. But he did make the most of his opportunity. With the Syracusans watching impotently from the shore, he sailed slowly back and forward, leisurely noting the defences, examining the ship-sheds where the triremes were kept safe, parading his own cool condescension to his enemy. And then, with his nine ships following in his wake, he sailed serenely out to sea and, joining the remainder of his fleet, struck north. Back to Catane.

For Catane irritated Alcibiades. He was determined not to let the city get the better of him. Although the citizens still refused to let the army in, he managed to persuade them to allow him to address their popular assembly, and put forward Athens' case. So, at a meeting in the theatre, with Lamachus at his side, Alcibiades, the consummate performer, launched into his speech. The benches were packed. Almost everyone who opposed upsetting Syracuse was present, determined to out-argue Alcibiades, focussed on his every word, insistent that Catane would not be moved. Which was precisely what Alcibiades had counted on. For, as his beguiling words rolled off his tongue, he knew that elsewhere in the city friends were at work, stealthily helping to dismantle a shoddily-made gate, welcoming the Athenians inside. Even as he spoke, there were whispers in the theatre as the news spilt out: Athenian soldiers were calmly strolling through the agora! Catane was in Athens' hands! It was a veritable coup, achieved only thanks to the swagger and panache of Alcibiades.[47]

However, it set a dangerous example. Few cities in the future would be so trusting. But perhaps that would not matter. With the pro-Syracusans sensibly abandoning Catane, and the rest of her citizens voting to embrace Athens' cause, Alcibiades and Lamachus summoned Nicias to join them with the rest of the fleet. Suddenly, things seemed to be coming together. Not only did they have a base in Sicily, but news came that the southern port of Camarina was offering an alliance, too. And that Syracuse was rattled. Indeed, that it had launched its triremes. With no time to lose, the Athenians put out to sea, and steered quickly south. But once more they found no sign of any fleet at Syracuse, and when Alcibiades reached Camarina he was rebuffed. When they saw his triremes lolling on their beach, the people of that lovely town were rattled, and had second thoughts.[48]

So Alcibiades turned around and sailed back to Catane to consider what the expedition's leaders should do next. But he found a new ship in the harbour, the *Salaminia,* one of Athens' two state triremes. A ship invariably sent out on official business. And he soon discovered what that business was.[49]

Back in Athens, the atmosphere, already fraught when the expedition sailed, had descended into outright hysteria. In the public imagination, the two sacrilegious acts—the mutilation of the Herms and the alleged profanation of the Eleusinian Mysteries—had become inextricably linked, and populist demagogues had easily constructed a convincing case that both were evidence of an oligarchic plot to overthrow the democratic constitution. Meanwhile, emboldened by offers of immunity from prosecution for those providing evidence, a growing number of people had come forward to point the finger of blame against their enemies. The state jails were filling up, and many an aristocrat chose voluntary exile rather than risk the consequences of what seemed to be fast turning into a revolution. But one man, a member of Callias' family, the Ceryces, found another solution. Implicated in the smashing of the Herms, this vile creature, Andocides, turned state's evidence and denounced not just himself but a large number of his friends and family. He saved his own skin, but many of those he accused were rounded up and executed.[50]

With the wind now fully in their sails, Alcibiades' personal and political enemies—probably including his erstwhile friend and brother-in-law, the Eleusinian priest Callias—kept up their attacks, producing witness after witness of his involvement in other profanations of the Mysteries. Riding the wave of unreason sweeping through the city, they repeated their baseless accusations that Alcibiades' ambition was to become tyrant. To back up their arguments, they cited evidence from their dimly recalled past, perhaps even causing extracts from the *Histories* of Herodotus to be read out in public, reminding the People of the bad old days of Hippias and warning them once more of the Alcmaeonid curse.[51]

Still the hysteria mounted. When rumours swept the city that a Spartan army had been spotted marching north, it was immediately assumed to have been summoned by Alcibiades; fearing attack, the Athenian militia slept fully armed in the sanctuary of Theseus, ready to do battle at a moment's notice. Despite its being a false alarm, suspicions grew. And spread. In Argos, they accused Alcibiades' friends, too, of plotting an oligarchic revolution. Surely, they said, the three hundred aristocratic prisoners, whom Alcibiades had seized as hostages, and distributed on nearby islands, must be involved. So they had them all recalled and executed.[52]

But what of Alcibiades? With his enemies in Athens baying for blood, there was no way that he could be allowed to exercise such power in Sicily. No! For, as everybody knew, the gods would never let an army win that had selected as its leader an enemy of religion! So, with more circumstantial evidence being discovered by the day, and the whiff of pious indignation heavy in the air, one of Cimon's sons impeached him on two charges: of smashing the Herms and profaning the Mysteries. And Athens' legal system swung into action. There was only one course open now: Alcibiades and his associates must be recalled and tried. Which was why the *Salaminia* was anchored at Catane. Its crew came with the strictest orders. To avoid disturbance in the army or revolt among the Argive and Mantinean allies, they were not to arrest Alcibiades. Rather they were to reason with him and persuade him to return home willingly. In his own ship.[53]

So, with Nicias scarcely able to suppress his satisfaction, the two triremes, the *Salaminia* and Alcibiades' flagship, backed out of harbour and set off north. Their route took them to democratic Thurii, the grid-planned city founded almost thirty years before, a good place for a stop-over to take on supplies and catch up with old friends. And for the *Salaminia*'s crew to enjoy some well-earned rest and recreation.

But in the morning, when they should have put to sea, Alcibiades and his friends were nowhere to be seen. Not being in custody, they, too, had gone ashore at Thurii. But they had not come back. At first the *Salaminians* were unconcerned, but as the hours went by they became anxious. Search parties scoured the streets and hammered on the doors of likely houses. But try as they might, they could find no sign of their quarry. Alcibiades had disappeared.[54]

7

SLEEPING WITH THE ENEMY

Yes, I follow Ares, Lord of War, but I'm also well-versed in the Muses'
gift—desire.

Archilochus, frag. 1

ONLY A FEW WEEKS LATER, Alcibiades was scarcely recognizable.
Gone was the calculatedly chic, lazily handsome, sumptuously dressed, well
coiffed, perfumed Athenian dandy. In his place, a tough-looking thug, his
hair and beard growing longer by the day, his upper lip close-shaved, the
reek of onions and garlic on his breath, and just one woollen blanket for
his clothing. It was not that, to elude capture, he had disguised himself as
a tramp. Far from it. Instead, to escape his enemies in Athens, he had found
asylum in the city state which had for centuries been Athens' bitterest enemy.
He had become a Spartan.[1]

How had he possibly achieved this? The prosaic answer is that, at Thurii,
he and his companions had gone ashore, no doubt announcing that they
were visiting important friends, no doubt implying (correctly) that to fail
to do so would be to cause offence or raise suspicions, and no doubt arguing, too, that, until they were officially under arrest, they were free to
come and go as they pleased. Shoreside, they must have acted quickly. And
to an already well-formed plan. Perhaps Alcibiades had already managed to

communicate with his confederates in Thurii. For, with all the precision of a clandestine undercover operation, in the short hours of the night, he and his co-accused associates managed to board another ship and set sail east towards the rising sun. To have remained in Thurii for any time was surely far too dangerous. Not only might they be discovered; if the Athenians were forewarned, their ship might subsequently be intercepted as it sailed for Greece.

Even in Antiquity no one could agree what happened next. Some said that Alcibiades went first to Argos—or to Thebes—though neither of these destinations makes much sense, either geographically or politically. Instead, Alcibiades and his fellow renegades almost certainly sailed with all haste to Cyllene, the westernmost tip of the northern Peloponnese, from where they made the short journey overland to Elis. This was, of course, the city that controlled the Olympic Games, where Alcibiades had shone so brightly scarcely twelve months earlier. The city, too, whose government he had persuaded to join an alliance with Argos five years before. The city that, despite its long-held animosity towards the Spartans, had failed to support her Arcadian and Argive allies at Mantinea, thwarting Alcibiades' hopes of victory and, with them, the best chance of dealing Sparta a death blow.[2]

It is unlikely that the presence of the fugitives in Elis was public knowledge, though tradition tells of at least one man who recognized Alcibiades and taunted him with the question: "Can't you trust your own country?" Alcibiades' response was bitter: "In most things, yes. But when it comes to my life, I wouldn't trust my own mother not to make a mistake and pick up a black pebble instead of a white one, when she casts her vote." But somehow they stopped word getting out, and so they stayed there for long weeks, holed up behind the high walls of some trusted mansion, as messages were sent across the mountains south to Sparta. Until, at last, word came that the Spartans would allow them in.[3]

Which again raises the question: how had Alcibiades possibly achieved this? After all, for years, he had been not just the most vociferous opponent of the Peace of Nicias, but the architect of the Arcadian League, which came within a hair's breadth of crushing Sparta—and, most recently, of Athens' expedition against pro-Spartan Syracuse. It must have taken all Alcibiades' negotiating powers. Doubtless he had useful lobbyists. One may have been King Agis, whose father, Archidamus, had once been a close personal friend of Pericles. Almost certainly, another was his family *xenos,* Endius (whose help in the period that followed suggests either that Alcibiades' trickery of him in the Athenian Assembly was a fiction, or that he was extraordinarily forgiving). Doubtless, too, the 120 Spartan prisoners of war, whom he had taken such pains to help after their defeat on Sphacteria, were also well disposed—immediately upon their shameful homecoming they had all been disenfranchised, but such was the shortage of true Spartan citizens that, after only a short time, they were rehabilitated, and their rights restored. And it may well be that there still existed some residual goodwill towards Alcibiades, whose family their kings had once entrusted with the role of *proxenos* to represent the city's interests in Athens.[4]

However, there was a powerful faction, too, that was strongly opposed to letting such a dangerous enemy into Sparta. And these men Alcibiades set out to pacify by offering to act as both agent and advisor in what everybody knew must be the imminent renewal of the war with Athens. Indeed, he claimed, even before leaving Sicily, he had begun working on Sparta's behalf to thwart Athenian ambitions on the island. For some time (so he said), he had been cultivating friends in Messana. Just before the *Salaminia* arrived (so he maintained), these friends were on the brink of turning their city over to the Athenians. But before he sailed home (so he alleged), he had sent a message to the pro-Syracusan party in Messana, thanks to which the plot had been revealed and his erstwhile allies, rounded up and killed. If this were true, Alcibiades had struck Athens a major blow. Certainly, events of the next winter would seem to back him up. When the Athenians again tried to bring Messana onside, they were once more unsuccessful. The trouble was—as Alcibiades must have realized—unless the Spartans took the trouble to investigate, there was no way to prove his part in any of it.[5]

But the Spartans were prepared to give him the benefit of the doubt. And some time in late summer, perhaps at night with Spartan guides, almost certainly overland, Alcibiades and his band of fellow travellers, reassured by a solemn offer of immunity, rode out from Elis and across the hard Arcadian massif until they reached Laconia and the broad, verdant valley of the River Eurotas—clear waters lapping reedy banks, well-cultivated fields, with low hills to the east, while, to the west, the towering vertebrae of Mount Taygetus stretched south towards the sea.[6]

As he rode further towards the cluster of scattered villages which constituted Sparta, Alcibiades was determined more than ever to do all he could
to destroy those men back home who, in their turn, had sought to destroy
him. After all, he had already heard the verdict they had passed. Since he
set out for Sicily, the flames of outrage had been stoked the more as accuser
followed accuser—some from hatred, others simply to deflect suspicion
from themselves—in the witch hunt to condemn Alcibiades. Even members of the Alcmaeonids, his maternal family, had incriminated him in the
profanation of the Mysteries, implicating Axiochus, his uncle, too. Now,
when the *Salaminians* returned without him, the Athenians had met in the
Assembly. For them, the fact that he had run away was sufficient proof of
guilt. So they condemned him *in absentia* to death. And without Alcibiades, the sinful, godless traitor, there to kill in person, his enemies vented
their baying fury in almost every other way conceivable.[7]

In an indulgent gesture of pure melodrama, all the country's clerics—not
only the Eleusinian officials, but every priest and every priestess of every
sanctuary in Athens—paraded solemnly at sunset onto the Acropolis.
Among them was Callias, Torchbearer at the Mysteries, the man who once
was Alcibiades' companion, who had been so delighted when his sister married Alcibiades, whose friendship slowly turned to hatred when Alcibiades
extorted money from him and when his sister died, and who announced to
the Assembly that he feared for his own life. Now, as the representative of
Athens' piety, Callias could savour his revenge. As the sun sank red over
Mount Aegaleos, the clerics turned towards the west, where the Greeks believed the savage death-gods had their home, and, ritually shaking out their
purple robes to rid them of pollution, they intoned blood-chilling curses
on the heads of Alcibiades and his confederates. Only one priestess refused
to be involved: Theano, the priestess of Aglaurus, responsible for overseeing
the swearing of the Ephebic Oath, whose terms had so inspired Alcibiades.
Protesting that prayers, not curses, were her remit, she declined to condemn
her protégé.[8]

Meanwhile, Alcibiades' enemies used the full powers of the state to attack the impious renegades *in absentia*. Undoubtedly, Alcibiades and his associates had sailed to Sicily with strong-boxes full of their own portable
wealth, and perhaps they somehow managed to take them on their flight
from Thurii as well. They must certainly have sent urgent messages to friends

in Athens requesting that they secure and hide as many of their possessions as they could. For they knew that, if the People could not have their skins, they would have their property.

Still, it must have come as an unwelcome blow when the fugitives discovered the details of what had happened: a decree passed in the Assembly; their houses, their estates, and their belongings confiscated and offered at public sale to the highest bidder. (The auction raised 100 talents.) Then inscriptions set up, which recorded every item—from Thracian slaves and cooking pots to prizes from the Panathenaic Games, from tracts of land to Alcibiades' fabled wardrobe of gorgeous wild silk robes—all recorded for posterity, a tangible memorial to the luxury of the offenders' lifestyle, sure evidence of the kind of men these were, who scorned the state's most sacred values. Once more, Alcibiades' private lifestyle had been turned into a public issue. At the auction and on the stone inscriptions, his dirty linen was quite literally displayed. And it did not stop there. On the Acropolis, a further inscription, a "stele of disgrace," listed all those implicated in the double scandal of the mutilation of the Herms and the sacrilege against the Mysteries. And a sentence of death was passed on all those named, with the reward of a talent to whoever succeeded in killing any one of them. Which only enflamed Alcibiades' ire the more. As he turned his back on Athens and his persecutors, he was heard to growl: "I'll show them I'm alive!"[9]

Now, then, as he rode deeper into Sparta's heartland, Alcibiades was weighing how best to present his case and harm his enemies. In some ways, he must have felt that he was coming home. After all, he bore a Spartan name. He had been wet-nursed by a Spartan woman. His friends—his mentor, Socrates—had all preferred the possibilities of the Spartan oligarchic constitution to the louche democracy of Athens. But he must tread carefully. There were so many hierarchies to which he must appeal.

The Spartan constitution was nothing if not complex and bizarre, the brainchild (it was said) of a shadowy figure from the distant past, Lycurgus. It ensured that Sparta was presided over by not one but two hereditary kings. Each was the head of an ancient family (the Agiads and Eurypontids), both of which traced their lineage back to twin great-grandsons of Heracles. The kings' role was both military and religious: during any campaign one led the army out to war, while the other remained in place at home, or—if both were required to fight—they commanded separate forces. But supreme executive power lay not in their hands, but with five political ministers, ephors, who were elected annually to govern Sparta, holding supreme executive power in all matters concerning peace and war.[10]

The kings were also members of a thirty-strong committee of preeminent elders, the *Gerousia,* which acted not only in an advisory capacity, but as a pre-deliberative body and, with the addition of the ephors, as Sparta's supreme court. But these were not the only organs of state. There was also the *Ecclesia,* an assembly of all Spartan citizens, which had the power to ratify or reject many important decisions, and whose vote was generally carried not on a show of hands (as in Athens) but by shouting: the motion which gained the loudest acclaim won the day.[11]

To qualify as a citizen and a member of the *Ecclesia,* a Spartan must undergo a long, arduous education, responsibility for which (unlike in Athens) lay with the state. At the age of seven, boys were taken from their families and enrolled in the *Agoge,* a highly regulated boot camp, where they learned at first hand the arts of killing and survival, honing their bodies to endure extremes of heat and cold, at times living off the land, making themselves "animal in nature," arguably sloughing off humanity to become tough, murderous machines, vying to be selected (at the age of eighteen or nineteen) for membership of the elite *Crypteia,* a ruthless liquidation squad, tasked with policing Sparta's Helot slaves.[12]

For it was ironically their need to protect themselves from their own slaves that drove the Spartans to endure harsh lives of self-inflicted hardship. The Helots were the aboriginal inhabitants of the territories of Laconia and Messenia over which the Spartans ruled. But as her power increased, rather than extend the benefits of Spartan citizenship to her new subjects (as Athens did when she annexed Attic towns such as Eleusis), Sparta enslaved them. Although she let them live in their own villages, she forced the Helots to work the land for their new masters, and imposed her will with a rod of iron. Not unsurprisingly, this led to festering resentments, which, given that the Helots dramatically outnumbered their Spartan overlords, was potentially very dangerous indeed. On more than one occasion slave revolts threatened to topple the Spartans' dominance—which was why Sparta annually declared war on her Helots, thus officially sanctioning the *Crypteia* to assassinate any whom they deemed to be too independent. Yet, such was their own dependence on the Helots that the Spartans invariably had to utilize them when they went to war, taking them on campaign not just as servants and camp-followers, but as fighting troops. Indeed, when Brasidas marched to Amphipolis in 424, his Spartan army was composed entirely of Helots.[13]

For most Athenians, then, Sparta seemed a topsy-turvy world, a weird, distorted mirror image of their own way of life. While Athenians thrived on doing business, Spartans were forbidden from all commerce, relying instead on both the Helots and another class, the relatively free *Perioikoi* ("those who live all around"), to farm, manufacture, trade, and generally keep the country and its economy afloat. While Athenians relished the joys of domesticity, eagerly seeking out the choicest delicacies in the Agora, Spartans proudly renounced luxury and indulgence, eating notoriously basic meals in military-style messes, sharing their possessions and denying their own desires and jealousies to achieve what was best for the state. Sometimes a Spartan husband even shared his wife, if he thought that another man was capable of fathering a stronger son than he could. Which to an Athenian was shocking. Indeed, while Athenians kept their wives and daughters under the strictest watch at home, Spartan women enjoyed some independence. They could inherit and own land and property. And, as mothers and future mothers of warriors, while not leading a military lifestyle themselves, they were educated to a relatively advanced standard, while in public they not only underwent a rigorous athletic training, but danced at Sparta's state religious festivals, where their dark eyes and shapely ankles earned the praise of poets and onlookers alike. Unsurprisingly, at least one of these Spartan women would attract the gaze of Alcibiades.[14]

For now, though, his thoughts were all on making the best impression. And not long after his arrival, in a meeting of the *Ecclesia,* he got his chance. He used it not only to ingratiate himself with Sparta, but to attack his Athenian enemies both at home and in Sicily. For, by now, the long fraught summer had at last drawn to an end, and in Sicily both sides were using the dead winter months to regroup and garner what support they could from potential allies. While Nicias and the Athenians were sending envoys to the Carthaginians and the Etruscans, Hermocrates had prevailed upon the Syracusans to seek help from the Peloponnese. Already his delegates had enjoyed considerable success in Corinth, and now they had arrived in Sparta to put their case here, too. But, as usual, the Spartans were loath to become involved in a foreign war. They would certainly provide all moral support imaginable; but sending troops was not for them.[15]

It was now that Alcibiades made his move. Invited by his Spartan sponsors to address the *Ecclesia,* he stood up to deliver one of the most important speeches of his life. In style and content, this must be very different from the self-congratulatory speech he had delivered just that spring in the Athenian Assembly, where he painted himself as Athens' champion. Moreover, he must tread a careful path, presenting himself as a man who, despite betraying his city, could still be trusted by the Peloponnesians; who, despite having done all he could to harm Spartan interests in the past, nonetheless was quite logically now helping them; who, despite everything around him changing, remained constant to his own beliefs and values.[16]

Structuring his arguments with the utmost care, he laid out his case and offered his advice. He began by addressing his own situation, his family's *proxeny,* his generosity towards the Spartan prisoners of war, his deep disappointment at being excluded from the negotiations leading to the Peace of Nicias. He even argued (somewhat disingenuously) that by discussing terms with his personal enemies in Athens, Sparta had forced him into helping Argos and the Arcadians to attack her interests.

Next he defended his role in the Athenian democracy, where (he claimed) he had acted at all times constitutionally, as a moderating force, trying to unite the People, while others divided them. Not, he stressed, that he thought highly of the democratic system, despite its having provided Athens with fifty years and more of prosperity and growth. In an extraordinary attack, he argued: "We men of reason have always recognized democracy for what it is, and more than anyone I have good cause to fault it. But then there's nothing new that can be said about what is so clearly an acknowledged folly!"[17]

Having nailed his political colours so spectacularly to the mast (or, at least, the colours which would help him win this argument), and warming to his theme, Alcibiades proceeded to seduce the Spartans further by letting them into a state secret (or, at least, appearing to do so). The conquest of Sicily, he proclaimed, was just the start of the Athenians' ambitions. From there they would move on to annex not just Italy but the Carthaginian Empire, before, their army swollen with foreign mercenaries from as far away as Spain, and their fleet greatly engorged, thanks to new ships built in Italy, they turned their sights back on the Peloponnese, blockading it by sea, attacking it by land, until it surrendered. For Athens' ambitions were no less than to rule the entire Hellenic world.[18]

Perhaps this really was the dream held in Athens by a few idealistic zealots, but it is unlikely ever really to have been part of the objective of the Sicilian campaign. Especially not in Alcibiades' original conception of a small task force going to the aid of Leontini and Segesta. But the truth was unimportant. What mattered was that Alcibiades was sowing the seeds of worry in the Spartans' minds. Which allowed him to push home his first piece of strategic advice: it was important to nip Athenian ambitions in the bud by preventing the fall of Syracuse. And to do this, it was necessary to send troops. Not necessarily Spartan troops. But a Peloponnesian army led by a true Spartan general who would instil discipline and increase morale.[19]

Significantly, just as he had in Athens, Alcibiades was advocating a policy which would take the war as far as possible from the city whose cause he now espoused, minimizing the risks to its citizens, while helping maximize potential successes. In doing so, he was throwing his weight behind the Syracusan and Corinthian ambassadors, who had already addressed the *Ecclesia,* and supporting a motion that had already been put before the Spartans, albeit one on they had not yet agreed.[20]

His second piece of advice was one with which the Spartans were similarly familiar. Just before the Peace of Nicias, they had been seriously considering establishing permanent military outposts in Attica, similar to the Athenians' stronghold in their own territory at Pylos. Now, with the Syracusans urging Sparta to assist them by renewing her war with Athens (which they hoped would cause the Athenians to leave Sicily, or at least send no more troops there), Alcibiades suggested that they revisit that idea. But, instead of creating a ring of fortlets, he advised that they establish only one, which would be carefully sited to inflict the greatest damage to Athens at the smallest cost to Sparta. Its location should be Decelea, a village on the south slopes of Mount Parnes, just fifteen miles north of Athens. It was a place with which the Spartans were familiar. According to mythology, when Theseus made off with the Spartan Helen, it was the Deceleans who showed her brothers where he had hidden her—as a result of which, in historical times the Spartans not only showered the Deceleans with special honours

The unfinished temple at Segesta, Sicily, redolent of empty promises. (Photograph by the author.)

but deliberately spared their land from depredation during the Peloponnesian War.[21]

Of even greater significance was Decelea's geographical position. Not only was it ideally sited for raids within Attica, it lay on the route overland from Athens to Euboea, where Attic farmers had shipped their cattle to protect them from the Peloponnesians during the last war. Moreover, and of potentially even greater significance, it was close enough to the silver mines at Laurium both to allow the Spartan garrison to interfere with the mines' workings, and to provide a refuge for any slaves who managed to escape the harsh conditions there. Without Laurium, Athens' wealth would decline, her infrastructure would become more stretched, her allies would cease to hold her in such awe (and would so be more reluctant to pay their annual tributes), and her economy would go into a downward spiral.[22]

What Alcibiades neglected to add, of course, was that each of his suggestions would also inflict maximum harm on two of his bitterest personal enemies: military harm on Nicias in Sicily; and economic harm on both Nicias and Callias at Laurium. He did refer to these men, however, and to men like them, in his clever peroration. Returning to the theme, with which he had begun (his patriotism, or, rather, his perceived lack of it), he wove a smart, sophisticated argument. At its heart was the idea of friendship and enmity, and the accepted Greek morality of helping friends and harming enemies. His enemies, he argued, were not the Spartans, who were simply doing the best they could for their own country, but those in Athens who had "forced their friends [by which Alcibiades clearly meant himself] to become their enemies." With such men in control, Athens was Athens no longer. "I do not think I am attacking a homeland that belongs to me; rather I'm doing all I can to reclaim a homeland I no longer have. The man, who truly loves his city, does not allow himself to lose it unfairly, and not fight to get it back; no, he yearns for it so much that he'll do everything he can to get it back." Then, with a final throw of his gambler's dice, Alcibiades vowed that "if I harmed you badly as an enemy, I can do you great good as a friend," reminded his audience of his two suggestions, and sat down.[23]

How he was received was crucial to his future wellbeing. There was nothing controversial in his advice—indeed, much of it the Spartans had already thought of for themselves. Rather it was his sophistic self-defence on the charge of treachery that might irritate his no-nonsense, honest hosts. And no doubt this did cause some Spartan eyebrows to be raised. But it convinced those of his audience who mattered—the majority of the *Gerousia*, and King Agis (who now found himself in the ascendant, since the policies of his colleague, Pleistoanax, a champion of the Peace of Nicias, were so clearly unravelling). Particularly convincing was the picture Alcibiades painted of Athenian ambitions. And especially, in the words of Thucydides (possibly based on an interview with Alcibiades himself), "since they took into account the fact that they had heard it from the man who best knew the reality of the situation."[24]

Not that they followed his advice to the letter. Instead of sending a true Spartan to Syracuse (which could conceivably be seen as breaking the terms of the Peace of Nicias), they sent Gylippus, a so-called *mothax*—a man who, despite being of dubious parentage, had nonetheless been sponsored by a citizen and brought up in the *Agoge*. In fact, Gylippus was the son of a true Spartan, but his father had been tarnished by the scandal in which King Pleistoanax was said to have been bribed by Pericles and, as a result, sent into exile. In Thurii. Which meant that, through his father, Gylippus must have already enjoyed enviable connections with many of the most influential families in southern Italy and Sicily.[25]

As for Alcibiades' advice to fortify Decelea, the Spartans at first were hesitant. Deeply religious, they were loath to be the first to break the oaths that they had sworn to seal the Peace of Nicias. Indeed, during the recent war, they had been extremely nervous, knowing that it was they and their allies who had broken the terms of an earlier treaty, and fearing divine punishment as a consequence. So, for now, they bided their time.[26]

Spring came, carpeting the slopes of Mount Taygetus in a riot of flowers; then summer, and its baking August heat, which broke some evenings in explosive storms, crackling and rattling around the mountains, illuminating the scarred valleys with blinding sheets of lightning. Sparta's religious festivals came and went as well: the early summer Hyacinthia, a celebration of the death and rebirth of the hero Hyacinthus, held at Amyclae, one of Sparta's spiritual hubs, a few miles south of main cluster of villages, where a colossal throne, topped by a statue of Apollo, towering forty-five feet high, presided over three days of parades and contests, banquets, and sacrifices; the Gymnopaediae, where men (and perhaps women), divided into age groups, performed "unarmed dances" in the summer heat; the Carneia, fertility rites sacred to Apollo, held in the dying days of August, where a ram was sacrificed to ward off plague. Now, as Spartan as the Spartans, Alcibiades most likely attended all of them, taking every chance he could to rub shoulders with the power brokers or watch as gaily painted, flower-strewn carriages conveyed the Spartan girls and women to and from the sanctuaries.[27]

However, as a foreigner, albeit a distinguished guest, Alcibiades was barred from taking part in many aspects of Spartan life. He was probably billeted (perhaps at the house of his *xenos,* Endius) in the relatively chic village of Pitane, where the Agiads lived. Unlike other Greek cities, which felt the need for protective ramparts, Sparta possessed no walled urban area. Rather, it was made up of four villages, all clustering around the low hillock, which constituted the acropolis, with Pitane to the northwest and Limnae, home of the Eurypontid dynasty, to the northeast. From any of them, it was a short walk to the agora, with not just the offices of the ephors and *Gerousia,* but the Persian Stoa, paid for from the spoils of the Persian Wars, and famous because, in place of columns, its roof was supported by statues of defeated Persian generals. Nearby, there were other reminders of Sparta's glorious past: the tomb of the hero, Orestes, whose bones (they claimed) had been unearthed and brought to Sparta more than a century before; the memorial to Leonidas, the hero of Thermopylae, the tomb said to house his repatriated remains topped with a marble statue and accompanied by an inscription naming each of the Spartan hoplites who had died with him in glorious battle. Everywhere were shrines and sanctuaries—not least the Brazen House, a temple to Athene Polias on the acropolis, whose interior walls were clad in sheets of bronze and decorated with bronze reliefs showing the deeds of Heracles. And east, past the marshy sanctuary of Upright Artemis, across the clear-flowing Eurotas, high in the wooded hills above Therapne, the sanctuary of the Heavenly Twins, the Dioscuri, sat proudly, close to a low pyramid, the tomb of the Homeric hero Menelaus, the shrine of his bride, the lovely Helen.[28]

With time on his hands, Alcibiades no doubt hunted in these fragrant hills, and on Taygetus, and galloped with the kings and their royal retinue across the valley, down to the sea at Gytheum. For, where horses were concerned, the aristocracy of every nation (regardless of its politics) spoke a common language. One particularly ardent horse-lover was Cynisca, half-sister of King Agis. Like all Spartan women, Cynisca enjoyed far greater freedom than her Athenian sisters, and she used hers not just to ride but to breed fast racing horses. For the twenty-five-year-old princess, the dashing Alcibiades, fresh from his stunning victory in the Olympic chariot race, must have been irresistible, exciting, and exotic, a man from whom she could learn much.[29]

But it was not Cynisca who excited Alcibiades. Rather, it was her sister-in-law, King Agis' wife, Timaea. Although Alcibiades was ineligible for membership of any of the messes at which Spartans ate their evening meals, he still could be invited as a guest to the royal mess where the two kings dined together—and, more importantly, he could be offered hospitality in private homes. So, perhaps it was at Agis' house, or at a festival, that Alcibiades first met Timaea. And the spirit of adventure consumed him. Her hair close-cropped like every other married Spartan woman, Timaea was young, tall, and beautiful. The challenge of seducing a Spartan queen seemed suddenly irresistible. Not only for its own sake. Or for the thrill of bedding one of his hosts' wives. Or even for the satisfaction of getting back at her husband, King Agis, who had smashed his plans of conquest at the Battle of Mantinea. But because, should she become pregnant with a son, the chances were that Alcibiades' descendants would rule Sparta. Of course, the risks were enormous. But in his personal life, risk did not seem to worry Alcibiades. Besides, Sparta had very fluid adultery laws, and it was not uncommon for husbands to allow younger, fitter men to father children by their wives for the sake of the public good. So, what could there possibly be to lose? As for Timaea, used only to gruff, unpolished, and laconic Spartan men, the scintillating Alcibiades with his urbane charm, his sharp wit, his confident persuasiveness, not to mention his seductive good looks, must have been beguiling in the extreme, and the attention that he paid her, irresistible.[30]

As luck would have it, when, by 413, the Athenians had broken the terms of the Peace of Nicias so flagrantly that the Spartans could renew the war with easy consciences, it was Timaea's husband, King Agis, who, as the winter winds began to blow, was chosen to lead the task force north to Attica and follow Alcibiades' advice by occupying the stronghold of Decelea.[31]

It was to prove one of the most brilliant moves of the entire war. Everything that Alcibiades predicted came to pass. With a year-round Spartan presence just a few menacing hours from their city walls, the Athenians found their freedoms severely restricted. No one knew where the next Spartan raid might hit. Nor was it like the annual incursions into Attica, which the Peloponnesians had made at the start of the first phase of the war back in the late 430s and early 420s. Then the countryfolk knew that, when the raids were over (and none lasted more than forty days), they could return to their homes and farmsteads, even if these might have sustained damage. Now they must either abandon their rural livelihoods completely, crowd into Athens, and endure the cramped conditions, which in the past had proved such fertile breeding-ground for plague, or brave it out at home, never knowing, from one day to the next, when their houses might be torched or when they themselves might face the sharp edge of a Spartan sword.[32]

And the slaves at Laurium did indeed desert in droves. From the time that Agis first put out the word that they would receive asylum until the ending of the war, more than twenty thousand managed to escape their labour camps and steal through the mountain glens to safety. For the Athenian economy, it was a massive blow. For slave owners such as Callias, it was catastrophic. Already a spendthrift, with every slave who made it out to Decelea, he saw his once-enviable wealth dwindle and disappear.[33]

And it drained Nicias' coffers, too. Not that he was now in much of a position to worry about his wealth. Under his poor generalship, the Athenian expedition to Sicily had gone from bad to worse. Lamachus had been killed in battle. Now suffering from kidney stones (thanks to which he was, no doubt, on a heavy regimen of opium), and terrified of returning home to Athens with his army empty-handed, Nicias begged the Athenians either to relieve him of his command or to send out a second expedition equal in size to the first. Just as at the start of the campaign, the overly optimistic Assembly chose the second course. A botched attempt to lay siege to Syracuse led to the Athenians themselves being besieged by land and sea. Poorly maintained, their triremes rotted, and, in August 413, when they tried to fight their way out of the Great Harbour, they were defeated. A last, sad attempt to march overland to safety ended in disaster, when the Syracusans, led brilliantly by Gylippus, overtook the dispirited Athenians, slaughtered many, rounded up the rest, and incarcerated them in the stone quarries of Syracuse, where they died in their thousands, their swollen corpses lying unburied in the late summer sun. As for Nicias himself, although Gylippus wanted to bring him back to Sparta to stand trial (how Alcibiades would have relished that!), he and his fellow general Demosthenes were executed by the triumphant Syracusans. Albeit at a distance, Alcibiades could savour the sweetness of revenge.[34]

By the time he heard of Nicias' death, however, Alcibiades' own circumstances were once more changing. Visits to Timaea in the moonless Spartan night were in themselves distracting, and the discovery that she was pregnant was enticing. But for a restless conniver such as Alcibiades, there was more to life than sex and fatherhood. And in Sparta there were new strategic possibilities and potential new alliances. The Persians were showing an interest in entering the war. On Sparta's side.[35]

Despite the defeat of their two expeditions against Greece, for over sixty years the Persians had continued to maintain a strong interest in the affairs of their troublesome western neighbours. The assassination of the Great King Khashayarsha in a palace coup in 465 had ushered in the reign of Artaxšaça (Artaxerxes) I, whose policy towards the Greeks was much more nuanced than his predecessors. It was he who may have signed the Peace of Callias with the Athenians in 449, and the years that followed saw ambassadors from the Greek states trekking east along the Royal Road, the scrupulously maintained, tightly guarded highway that linked the Persian provincial capital of Sardis in Lydia to the royal seat at Susa, while Persian officials travelled west on diplomatic missions to Athens and Sparta. For the Persians, the goal was to achieve through statecraft what they had failed to achieve through warfare: to repossess the Greek cities of coastal Asia Minor, while neutralizing the threat posed by a potentially united mainland Greece. For the warring Greeks it was quite simply to win a wealthy backer, who would help bankroll their campaigns against each other.[36]

Already in the earlier phase of the war, the Athenians and Spartans had both done their best to woo the Great King. In 426, Aristophanes could use such negotiations to guarantee a hearty, if wry, laugh by bringing on stage a character dressed as a gibbering Persian envoy, while criticizing Athenian diplomats for spending too long on a mission of their own to Persia, where they "endured" the most lavish hospitality: travelling in curtained coaches, drinking sweet wine, banqueting on entire oxen and exotic birds. At the same time, the Athenians had been doing all they could to intercept diplomatic missions between Persian and Sparta, too. To their delight, they discovered one message which, translated, read: "Concerning the Spartans, the Great King cannot understand their terms. They have sent many representatives, but no two people say the same thing." But when, on the back of this, Athens sent its own legation to Persia in 425, it was thwarted. It had reached only as far as Ephesus when it learned that Artaxšaça was dead. For a time, Persia was in turmoil, and, when Dārayavahuš (Darius) II at last succeeded in imposing his control, he had little time for Greece. However, all this changed in Autumn 413. In Sparta's favour.[37]

Ever eager to meddle in foreign affairs, a year or so before, the Athenians had thrown their support behind a young Persian rebel, Humarga (known to the Greeks as Amorges). For Dārayavahuš, this was nothing short of an act of the most unforgivable treachery—after all, the Athenians and Persians were meant to be at peace—and, when he heard of their disaster in Sicily, the Great King thought the moment had come to teach upstart Athens a lesson while at the same time dealing his rival, Humarga, a deadly blow. To achieve which, he resolved to enlist the help of Sparta. And to enlist the help of Sparta, he turned to his two western provincial governors, Farnavaz (Pharnabazus) II and Chithrafarna (Tissaphernes).[38]

Being so vast and sprawling, the Persian Empire relied on a tightly organized and thoroughly efficient administrative hierarchy. While, for the most part, the Great King held court in the imperial heartland, progressing with the seasons between the sumptuous royal cities of Susa and Persepolis, Ecbatana and Babylon, accompanied at all times by his harem, his eunuchs, and his bloated entourage—a bustling cloud of scribes and bodyguards and magi priests—he entrusted the administration of his provinces to satraps (viceroys). As the Great King's representatives, these satraps ruled from their own residences, miniature versions of the royal palaces. As long as their territories remained at peace, paid taxes to central coffers, supplied troops on demand, and generally contributed to the empire's good, the satraps enjoyed a fair degree of autonomy. Indeed, rather than impose Persian structures on all elements of provincial life, it was generally considered wiser, for the sake of stability, to adapt, where appropriate, to local conditions, and to involve members of the native populations in administrative life.[39]

Many of the satraps held long family associations not only with the Persian royal household but with the regions over which they governed. Thus, Chithrafarna was the great-grandson of one of the tight-knit group of noblemen who had staged the palace coup that placed Dārayavahuš I on the throne in 522, as a result of which he was entrusted with the government of much of the western empire, including the entire coast of Asia Minor. It was this man's son (Chithrafarna's grandfather) who had led the crack regiment, the so-called Immortals, when Khashayarsha invaded Greece in 480, and the family retained its prominent position in the years that followed. Thus, in the wake of Artaxšaça's death in 424, when revolts spread and much of Persia's empire was in meltdown, the new Great King, Dārayavahuš II, did not think twice before appointing Chithrafarna as the man to crush the rebellion in his western provinces.[40]

At the head of a vast army, Chithrafarna defeated the traitorous satrap, Pišišyaothna (Pissuthnes), and brought Lydia back into the fold. But he did not quash the rebellion entirely—Pišišyaothna's son, Humarga, was still at large, and it was he that the Great King wanted to enlist the Spartans to help crush. Nonetheless, thanks to his energetic loyalty, Chithrafarna found himself confirmed in place as satrap of Lydia, and, for the past two years (since 415), he had been ruling from his palatial headquarters at Sardis, the golden city that had once been home to the Lydian King, Croesus.[41]

An equally new appointment was the satrap of Hellespontine Phrygia, the territory bordering Chithrafarna's to the north—though here the succession had been peaceful. Farnavaz, too, was a member of an ancient Persian family. Indeed, related in blood to the Great King himself, he was but the latest in a dynasty that had loyally served successive rulers since the days of Korush (Cyrus) the Great. For eighty years, since his great-grandfather Artavazda (Artabazus) was rewarded with the province for the part he played in Khashayarsha's invasion of Greece, the family had occupied the provincial palace at Dascyleum by the shores of a shallow lake, well stocked with fish and chattering with wildfowl, close to the Sea of Marmara and the Greek city of Cyzicus.[42]

It was possibly in early 413 that Parnaka (Pharnaces), Farnavaz's father, died, and the dashing young Persian was installed in his place, a man, who, like his noble contemporaries, had been educated to ride, shoot arrows, and speak the Truth. For the Persians were devout followers of the prophet Zoroaster, worshipping Ahura Mazda, the Wise Lord, god of light and truth, whose enemy, Angra Mainyu, was the Lie. And for rulers such as Farnavaz and Chithrafarna, this meant not only leading lives of righteousness, but ruling their people with equity and justice.[43]

But it did not ensure that Farnavaz and Chithrafarna liked each other. In fact, the two men were vicious rivals. From the moment that they found themselves in office, each regarded his neighbour with profound suspicion, as they contended for the Great King's favour, desperate to be seen as his most loyal and able servant. So, when Dārayavahuš let it be known that no time must be lost before Humarga and his Athenian allies were brought to heel, each satrap eagerly, yet independently, did all he could to be the one to cement a Spartan alliance.[44]

For Chithrafarna, the situation seemed especially urgent. He was already smarting because the Great King had chastised him for not levying the expected taxes from his province. Deferentially, he blamed the Athenians for destabilizing Lydia with their support for the renegade, Humarga. But he could see how high the stakes had just become. To keep the King's regard, he must defeat Humarga and neutralize the Athenians. And above all, he must make certain that it was he, not Farnavaz, who gained the credit.[45]

Soon envoys from both satraps were making their respective journeys up the Eurotas valley, past the deep snow-shrouded slopes of Mount Taygetus from Gytheum to Sparta. Here, they found not just each other, but a veritable flock of diplomats already shivering in Spartan guest rooms—among them delegates from Chios and Erythrae, cities which (along with neighbouring Lesbos) were eager to exploit the opportunities that Athens' defeat in Sicily afforded to break away from Athens' empire. In Sparta, of course, they had a willing intermediary. Alcibiades had strong connections with both cities—and especially with Chios, which had proved its friendship so spectacularly at the last Olympic Games, providing fodder for his horses and cattle for his feasts. Now, quite unashamedly, he was stoking the flames of their discontent, promising that he would mediate with Sparta to help them throw off the shackles of Athenian rule, selling out the city of his birth to win their loyalty.[46]

In fact, the Chians and Erythraeans had already been negotiating with Chithrafarna, too, and together they put forward a persuasive case. So, however, did Farnavaz's delegation. It also contained emissaries from Greek cities, including one from Cyzicus, another of Alcibiades' sponsors at the 416 Olympic Games. If anything, their argument was even more compelling than that of Chithrafarna. Their suggestion was that Sparta and the Peloponnesians send a fleet and army to prise control of the Hellespont away from the Athenians. If successful, they would deal their enemy a mortal blow, for, to feed her citizens, Athens relied heavily on imports of wheat, especially from the Black Sea. Each year, in the late summer, long convoys of laden grain ships lumbered west from the Crimea and the northern Black Sea coast, down through the Bosporus, and into the Propontis, the Sea of Marmara, before clearing the racing narrows of the Hellespont, heaving out into the Aegean and crawling on past hazy islands on the home strait for the busy wharves and warehouses of Piraeus. To maintain the grain supply, Athens must keep the sea lanes open, but two stages on the voyage were particularly vulnerable: the pinch-points of the Bosporus and the Hellespont. At its narrowest, the Hellespont is less than three quarters of a mile across. To control these waters, as Farnavaz was now suggesting, was to control the fate of Athens.[47]

In Sparta, opinion was divided. While some favoured throwing their weight behind Farnavaz's plans for a blockade, Alcibiades argued passionately in favour of supporting Chithrafarna. In doing so, he was acting entirely in character. Just as in the war council at Rhegium, Alcibiades had advocated taking the longer view—ensuring that potential allies were onside before launching an attack on Syracuse—so now, he promoted the benefits of fomenting rebellion among Athens' allies on the Asiatic coast, chipping away at the foundations of her empire, striking at her economy. Already, thanks to his advice, the revenue from the silver mines at Laurium was being diminished. Starve her of the annual tribute-tax from her Aegean subjects, too, and Athens would be seriously impoverished. Soon it would make little difference whether the grain fleet sailed or not. The Athenians would quite simply be unable to afford to pay for it.[48]

Behind Alcibiades was his old friend and family *xenos,* Endius. And, at this crucial moment, Endius' support was particularly valuable, for this year Endius had been elected ephor, one of the five most powerful men in Sparta. His friendship with Alcibiades can have done him little harm. After all, significant parts of Sparta's foreign policy had been shaped (or encouraged) by Alcibiades in the year or so before, and his suggestions regarding Syracuse and Decelea had already borne rich fruit. So it was little wonder that (much to the chagrin of Farnavaz's envoys) the two men managed to persuade the Spartans to back Chithrafarna and pursue the Ionian option. It was little wonder, either, once the situation in Chios had been checked on, and it became apparent that it was precisely as the delegates had said, that both Alcibiades and Endius would be sent out with the fleet to help supervise affairs in theatre.[49]

However, up in Decelea, Sparta's new outpost north of Athens, King Agis had other ideas. From his icy fastness on the chill slopes of Mount Parnes, he had been conducting diplomacy of his own. Already he was hopeful that, thanks to his agency, nearby Euboea would revolt from Athens. Meanwhile, ambassadors had come to him from Lesbos, too, offering to hand over their island to the Spartans. As spring came to Greece, Agis slipped south to Corinth to attend a meeting of the council of the Peloponnesian allies. Here, he argued vehemently that their ambitions should not be confined to Ionia. Yes, they should sail to Chios, and accomplish all they could there. But then they should sail on to Lesbos. And to the Hellespont as well. And, while the Athenians were still reeling from their Sicilian debacle, they should press home their advantage in every way they could.[50]

It was good advice, but the allies were slow to follow it. The Corinthians, especially, were dilatory. Their minds were focussed rather on the Isthmian Games, the international religious and athletic festival held every two years in late spring at the Sanctuary of Poseidon on the southern shores of the narrow Isthmus of Corinth—in Pindar's vivid image, the "bridge across the restless sea." So, they did little more than drag their triremes east over the *diolcus*—the paved trackway, almost four miles long, which had been laid across the Isthmus two hundred years before to allow the transport of ships overland between the Gulf of Corinth to the west and the Saronic Gulf to the east. And when the Games *were* held, and the Athenians attended them, they maintained such lax security that the Athenians, already suspicious of the Chians' loyalty, easily discovered their intentions. When the Peloponnesian ships at last set sail, Athens' (albeit much depleted) fleet was waiting for them. They disabled some and chased the rest ashore at the beaches of Cape Spiraeum, where they mounted a blockade.[51]

When the news reached Sparta, it was met with gloom. Ever the pessimists when it came to overseas adventures, many Spartans easily convinced themselves that this first defeat was simply a foretaste of what was to come. Much better, they argued, to abort their plans entirely! Once more it was up to Alcibiades to stiffen their resolve.[52]

He had every reason to do so. From a military point of view, Sparta was already experiencing a revolution. In the first stage of the war, the Athenians could rely comfortably on their superiority at sea. But since their disastrous campaign to Sicily, where they had lost most of their ships, not to mention many of their most experienced crewmen, this superiority could no longer be assured. Not only did Peloponnesian states such as Corinth possess strong fleets, the Spartans were already building a navy of their own.

Down in the dockyards of Gytheum, the first of their triremes had already completed successful sea-trials. And although sailing was not in Spartan blood, Alcibiades the Athenian was on hand with valuable advice. Not just that—once they had the knack of it, with Persian gold from Chithrafarna, they could construct and crew an almost limitless navy, while the Athenians, increasingly insolvent, would struggle even to maintain the fleet they had. To throw away a chance like this would be pure folly.

However, there were personal reasons, too, why Alcibiades was keen to leave for pastures new. Quite recently, Timaea, Queen of Sparta, had given birth to a baby boy. But although it had been given the royal name, Leotychidas, the women of the household were already whispering scandalous news: that, in private, as she dandled the infant on her knee or clasped him to her breast, Timaea murmured something else entirely. She called her newborn "Alcibiades." Far off in Decelea, too, Timaea's husband, Agis, was entertaining doubts. He remembered how his residence in Sparta had been shaken by an earthquake more than ten months previously, while he was sleeping with his wife; how he had run out of his house in terror; how he had not had sexual relations with her since. The ghastly truth dawned on him: he was not the baby's father. He had been cuckolded. By Alcibiades. The man whom he had entertained, whose cause he had supported, whom he considered a friend. And, although there was nothing in Spartan law forbidding adultery, for a proud Spartan king, it was intolerable. Now every mention of his newborn son, every congratulation sent by foreign allies, only served to fuel his growing hatred of the Athenian interloper.[53]

So, Alcibiades got to work. First he approached Endius and murmured into his receptive ear that it really would be in his old friend's interest if (with Alcibiades' assistance) it was he, rather than Agis, who effected the revolt of Athens' subjects in Ionia and brought about a treaty between Persia and Sparta. Then, through the now-pliant Endius, Alcibiades convened a full meeting of the ephors and advanced fresh arguments: act quickly, and the Spartans could still enjoy the element of surprise; sail now, and they could get to Chios before the islanders heard news of the Peloponnesian fleet's defeat; only let Alcibiades set foot in Ionia, and he would so convince his influential friends there of Sparta's eagerness, and Athens' weakness, that their cities would come flocking to join his cause. Fired by Alcibiades' passion, the ephors voted by a majority to follow his advice.[54]

Hasty orders, swift preparations, a perfunctory last farewell (perhaps) to a tearful, anxious Queen Timaea, a quick chuck under the chin for the baby Leotychidas, and three men—Alcibiades, Endius, and Chalcideus, the Spartan chosen to command the fleet—galloped down the long, straight road between fields of toiling Helots and budding apple orchards, olive groves, and clumps of walnut trees, down past the Sanctuary of Apollo Hyacinthus at Amyclae, down to the Laconic Gulf and Gytheum, where, at anchor in the limpid harbour, five triremes were awaiting them. It needed only a moment for the libations to be poured, the prayers to be made, the hymn for sailing to be sung. And with the almost certain blessing of the Dioscuri, Sparta's twin gods of the waves, the ships' anchor stones were cut free, oars splashed, and the tiny squadron slipped out towards the open sea. Its destination: Asia.

8

IN A PARADISE GARDEN

Now you're in Lydia, feted foremost . . . as, when the sun has set, the white-rose-fingered moon eclipses all the stars.

Sappho, frag. 96

SURPRISE WAS EVERYTHING. As they bowled on east, Alcibiades and the Spartan fleet seized every vessel that they came across—from labouring merchantman to tiny bobbing fishing boats—to stop their crews from blabbing that the ships were on their way.[1]

When they touched land in Ionia on the western shores of Asia Minor, envoys from the nearby island of Chios hurried to meet the Spartans. Wealthy businessmen and merchants, many were already known to Alcibiades. And many shared his bleak view of democracy. Which was unsurprising. Like their rich Athenian counterparts, they lamented the degree of power wielded by the People. For, although by no means a fully fledged democracy, the Chian Council included not just landed aristocrats but successful commoners as well, men who had benefited from the island's renaissance in the wake of the Ionian Revolt some eighty years before, who grew rich from the boom in Chios' prosperity as part of Athens' empire— not least because of its privileged status. Unlike most of Athens' subject states, Chios was exempt from paying tribute. Instead, it willingly allowed the Athenians to use its powerful fleet as they saw fit. But although the island was populous and thriving, many of its people were increasingly unhappy. Chian ships and men had taken part in Athens' doomed Sicilian adventure. Lives and money had been lost. With Athens' star no longer at its zenith, there was an increasing feeling that the time had come to cut free.[2]

Encouraged by the Chian envoys, the Spartans at once put to sea for Chios itself, only now releasing their flotilla of captured boats and ships, their crews turned loose to beetle back to their home ports with news that events had taken an intriguing turn. At Chios, the arrival of the five Spartan triremes was met with incredulity. As citizens rushed to the quayside to view this unexpected sight—a Spartan navy!—Alcibiades was hurried to the Council Chamber. With him was the Spartan admiral, Chalcideus, and together they spun their tale. Omitting the inconvenient detail that it had been first defeated and then blockaded at Spiraeum by the Athenians, they announced that the Peloponnesian fleet, too, was on its way. The Spartans' easy voyage here to Chios was proof (if proof were needed) that the Athenians no longer ruled the waves. The tide had turned. The old order was coming to an end.[3]

It was music to the Chian Council's ears. Overturning two generations of tradition, they declared independence from Athens' empire. And, when across the straits the citizens of mainland Erythrae heard the news, they followed suit. Soon, three of Sparta's triremes were scudding round the headland to Clazomenae, the hometown of Pericles' great friend, the philosopher Anaxagoras. On board was almost surely the persuasive Alcibiades: no sooner had they reached the city on its tiny island a stone's throw from the shore, with its pellucid, shallow waters the haunt of swans and seabirds, than the Spartans brought it, too, into their net. It was all going so swimmingly. Keep up the momentum, and the war would be over before it had even restarted![4]

But Athens was not prepared simply to let events take their course. Despite still reeling from the Sicilian disaster, and aware of her deepening economic crisis, when the Assembly heard the grim news from the east, it responded with swift resolution. Nineteen years before, at the beginning of the war, Pericles had insisted that a special reserve of 1,000 talents be set aside for use only in extreme emergency. The time had come to use it. Chios was a not just a vital ally. Until now it had been reliable as well. If it had so readily rebelled, what of those who were less trustworthy? There were many in Athens who recalled the dark days of 440, when, aided by the Persians, the revolt of Samos had severely threatened the empire's stability. The danger now facing them was even greater. It must not be allowed to spread. So, with an overwhelming show of hands, the People voted to send out the navy.[5]

Scurried preparations. Hasty precautions. The officers of seven Chian triremes, serving in the blockade at Spiraeum, taken into custody. Their slave crews liberated, rowing now for Athens. Then the speedy embarkation and the thump of oars as eight sleek warships shot out from Piraeus and scudded with all haste towards the firestorm.[6]

For both sides, time was of the essence. Even as the small Athenian fleet was straining to make landfall, Alcibiades and Chalcideus sailed south for Teos, a well-appointed city on the southern shores of the Erythraean peninsula, whose hills stretched sun-baked between Chios and the Gulf of Smyrna. Take Teos and they would secure the territory they already had. As the Athenians, too, knew well. With both squadrons racing hard to reach the city, it was the Athenians who first pulled into harbour. Their admiral hurried ashore and pleaded with the Teans to stay loyal. For a little while, it seemed they would. And then the combined fleets of the Spartans and the Chians swung into view, outnumbering the Athenian ships three-to-one. For the first time, Alcibiades faced fighting his fellow citizens. But as his triremes scudded ever closer towards Teos harbour, the white foam hissing round their deadly rams, the Athenian ships put out to sea and, rather than attack, turned tail and rowed with all speed south for Samos. It must have been a moment of pure exhilaration. The first phase in the new campaign was over. The Athenians were routed! And with their warships fleeing, Teos and key swathes of Ionia were already in Spartan hands. Alcibiades' strategy was working perfectly. It was time to begin the next stage in his plan.[7]

If the Athenians were expecting him to pursue them into Samos, they were wrong. Alcibiades' sights were on another prize: Miletus, on the mainland further south, a city known to him since adolescence, where he had old friends and good contacts, a trading hub, a busy port. The city where his grandfather had lived out his years of exile. The city of Aspasia. The jewel in Ionia's crown. With Miletus in his hands, Samos and that other wealthy city, Ephesus, would be sandwiched north and south between Spartan-held territories. Surely, they would not hold out for long. It was a strategy that he had tried (albeit unsuccessfully) to implement against Corinth eight years earlier. This time it must surely succeed.[8]

Again, a sense of urgency drove Alcibiades. It was his fervent wish to secure Miletus for the Spartans before Athenian reinforcements could arrive. Besides, the other Peloponnesians, too, were sending him fresh ships, and he wanted to prove he had no need of them. With just five Spartan triremes and the Chian fleet, he, Alcibiades, could achieve miracles! Undoubtedly his contacts in Miletus were awaiting him. There had been ample time since Alcibiades set out from Sparta to apprise his allies of his plans. So, the Athenians at Samos were caught off balance. As the Spartan ships swept round the headland of Mycale and down across the great bay to Miletus, they were unopposed. By the time Athens' fleet was scrambled, the city was already in Spartan hands.

It was a signal triumph. And the Persian satrap Chithrafarna made sure he was on hand to share in it. As the Athenian triremes skulked nervously off the rocky islet of nearby Ladē, Chithrafarna, with his courtiers, jangled jubilantly into Miletus for the first of a series of high level talks with his new Spartan allies. But it was Alcibiades who most took the satrap's fancy. Ever adaptable, always knowing perfectly how best to beguile and captivate, Alcibiades from the start set out to charm Chithrafarna. Here, in Ionia, the liberating victor, he no longer needed to subject himself to Spartan rigours. It was, after all, as the sparkling hedonist that the Milesians best knew Alcibiades. To appear otherwise have would been simply to confuse them! And it must have been such an almighty relief to wash again, to enjoy fine delicacies, to wallow unashamedly in sensuous luxury. For Chithrafarna, himself not just a hardened soldier and a seasoned diplomat, but a man acutely sensitive to worldly pleasures, Alcibiades must have seemed sent by Ahura Mazda to be his soul mate, his brother, his friend.[9]

For the Persian, too, all seemed to be turning out so well. Within a short while, he was negotiating a treaty with the Spartans. And on such unbelievably generous terms! Yes, he agreed to help them in their war with Athens, but, in return, he extracted a clause recognizing the Great King's possession of "all the lands that he now holds and that his ancestors once held." And, given that the Great King's ancestors once held the Greek cities of not just

Asia Minor, but (albeit briefly) much of mainland Greece, this would surely make Dārayavahuš a very happy man indeed.[10]

But while Alcibiades, Chithrafarna, and the Spartans were congratulating themselves in Miletus, the kaleidoscope, as so often happens, skewed unexpectedly, and the pattern broke. Fresh fleets arrived from Athens and, within a matter of a few weeks, not only regained Teos, but fomented a popular uprising in Samos which drove out the aristocrats and established a radical new form of popular government, excluding all landowners from power. Meanwhile, in mainland Greece, the Peloponnesian fleet broke out from Spiraeum and headed east, under the command of a new Spartan admiral-in-chief, Astyochus. With him he brought new orders, evidence that the power struggle in Sparta had not abated. They stated that the Spartan fleet was now to pursue not Alcibiades' strategy, but King Agis' initial plan: to move on, secure Lesbos, and then sail north to take the Hellespont. But almost at once momentum stalled. On Lesbos, initial successes were followed by defeat. The Peloponnesians sailed to the safety of Chios, but the Athenians, scenting victory, pursued them. Soon, news filtered south to Alcibiades in Miletus that not only had Clazomenae been retaken, but the Athenians had defeated the Chians in a series of savage battles, overrun the island, and were even now blockading the city by both land and sea.[11]

And before he could react, in Miletus Alcibiades, too, was under siege. Spartan inaction had emboldened the Athenian fleet at Ladē. When they launched an attack on the coast a few miles south, Chalcideus raced to the scene with a few hastily assembled troops. But in the fighting he was killed, and his men were defeated. Then, with the dog days of summer drawing to an end, and with them the sailing season, the stakes were suddenly and unexpectedly raised with the arrival of a new Athenian fleet commanded by the energetic Phrynichus. For many years, this wily Athenian had been a personal enemy of Alcibiades. And now, from his forty-eight ships, he was disgorging three-and-a-half thousand men, including fifteen hundred Argives, onto the shores around Miletus, and hunkering down for a long siege. Once more, a fast response was crucial. In the Milesian war rooms, experienced tacticians met to thrash out a plan—and among them were Alcibiades and Chithrafarna.[12]

In truth, they had few options. The best response was the most obvious. So they threw the city gates wide open and poured out from Miletus, a ragtag force of citizen militia, tough fighters from the Peloponnese, and Persian mercenaries and cavalry. Spurring their horses on towards the enemy, Alcibiades and Chithrafarna galloped side by side, the white dust billowing behind them. Soon, it was all confusion. On the right wing, the Milesians clashed with Argive hoplites in a shoving welter of unbridled slaughter, shield pressing hard on shield, as spears shattered and flashing sword-blades dripped with blood—until, at last, the Argives turned and ran, abandoning three hundred of their dead and dying on the baking plain. But on the left, as Alcibiades and Chithrafarna tried in vain to rally them, the Peloponnesians fell back; their phalanx collapsed; and, in disarray, with the Athenians pursuing them, they and the Persians—and the victorious Milesians, afraid of being cut off—raced back inside the safety of the walls, defeated.[13]

Prospects seemed grim. But, as darkness enfolded the city at sunset, word came of a miracle. A Spartan relief fleet was nearby—fifty-five triremes not only from the Peloponnese (led by a Spartan officer, Therimenes) but from Sicily as well (commanded by the Syracusan hero, Hermocrates, one of the staunchest enemies of Athens). They had been bound for Miletus, but when they heard about the fighting there, they changed course and headed south until they knew what best to do. It was imperative that they be contacted with all speed and brought urgently to help. So, brooking no argument, and with no time to lose, Alcibiades saddled his horse, and under cover of the deepening night slipped out from the beleaguered city to ride the nearly twenty miles along the ghostly tracks between tree-studded hills down to the beach at Teichiusa, where the fleet was drawn up for the night.

It was a dangerous gamble. With the price of a talent on his head, Alcibiades was a valuable catch, and there was many an Athenian for whom his capture would be life-changing. But luck and daring goaded Alcibiades—or perhaps he thought it safer to risk the darkling road than to be taken when the city fell—and, before dawn, he had reached the fleet. A swift debrief, and an impassioned plea that "if they did not wish to sacrifice Ionia and the Cause, they must sail now to stop the siege," and the ships were back at sea, tacking round the headland for Miletus. When the Athenian general, Phrynichus, heard of their approach, he gave the order to strike camp, embark, and sail post-haste for Samos. Discretion, not valour, was the order of the day: if his fleet were destroyed now, the fall of Athens would soon follow. So, as his ships vanished in the morning mists, the Peloponnesian fleet rounded the western cape and sailed with all speed into Miletus' military port. On deck was Alcibiades. His midnight ride had won the day.[14]

But there was still much to be done, and a debt to be repaid to Chithrafarna. The Persian pretender Humarga, ally of Athens, was holed up in Iasus, a city on a rocky promontory just round the bulging cape from Teichiusa and some twenty miles by sea south east of Miletus. With the Athenian fleet beating a retreat to Samos, it was unlikely that Humarga had yet heard of how events had just unfolded at Miletus. And if that were the case . . . [15]

So, next morning, the Peloponnesian fleet, together with the Chian ships, which had also been blockaded at Miletus, again put out to sea, and soon they were racing south towards Iasus. No flags were raised, no signs to say whose ships they were. And unopposed, they glided in to the clear harbour. Humarga and his men thought that they were Athenians. But then they learned their error. Fierce fighting in the agora and up the narrow lanes, which led to the acropolis, and soon it was all over. Boiling with pent-up frustration, the army sacked the city, delighting in its wealth. Meanwhile, to Chithrafarna's trembling joy, they captured Humarga alive, a fine prize to present to the Great King, a token of the satrap's loyal efficiency, an inducement for royal gratitude on a lavish scale. As Humarga's defeated mercenaries gladly exchanged one loyalty for another, Chithrafarna garrisoned what was left of Iasus and, together with Alcibiades, returned to the welcome comforts of Miletus.[16]

Soldiers, sailors, and commanders: all had good cause for rejoicing. In the Ionian city that night, the generals celebrated victory: the Spartan, Therimenes; the Sicilian, Hermocrates; the Persian, Chithrafarna; and the Athenian, Alcibiades. Nothing could have thrown the strangeness of the times into sharper focus than this curious gathering of unlikely bedfellows, representatives of cities, many of which had been at war for generations, toasting, among other things, their navy's victory over Athens, whose fleet was, until recently, the envy of the world. The other ranks, too, had reason to make merry. The booty from Iasus was significant, and, besides, in gratitude for work well done, Chithrafarna seized the moment, opened his coffers, and distributed the wages that he had promised through his emissaries to Sparta. But with Humarga taken and his satrapy secure, the wheeling, dealing Persian tried to drive a bargain. Henceforth, he said, he could pay only half of the agreed amount. Hermocrates protested. A better deal was struck. But it left a sour taste and eroded trust.[17]

It was not the only discordant note to mar the harmony of the past few months' successes. Swashbuckling, flamboyant, and triumphant, the smouldering Alcibiades attracted not just applause but jealousy, and there were those who muttered in the Spartan camp that he was unreliable, deceitful, treacherous. His ally, Chalcideus, had been killed in action, his *xenos*, Endius, was no longer ephor, and, in this city of the senses, surrounded by Ionian friends, it is unlikely that he tried hard to keep up the stoic lifestyle with which he had beguiled the Spartans. Still, he must have sensed the danger.[18]

When Chithrafarna departed from Miletus, Alcibiades went with him. First, they sailed across the gulf and took the road a few miles north to the city of Magnesia on the Meander, with its fruitful plains and rolling foothills. Then, further inland to Sardis, the provincial capital, with its ceremonial royal court perched high atop a steep hill ringed by strong walls; below it were more residential palaces; a second wall; and, spilling down towards the River Pactolus, a third walled zone with private houses, shops, and workshops. On three sides: jagged mountains. On the fourth: fine pastureland. And, far off in the winter haze, a chain of eerie tumuli, grave-mounds of ancient Lydian kings, stood out pale blue above the placid waters of Lake Gyges.[19]

Undoubtedly, Alcibiades amused Chithrafarna with wild tales of his ancestor, Alcmaeon I, how he had tricked Lydia's King Croesus, as he stumbled from the treasury weighed down with gold and gold dust. Perhaps he told him, too, how, writing in his *Histories,* Herodotus had recently embellished the tale of Croesus, imagining him meeting the Athenian lawgiver, Solon, and learning almost too late the truth of the Greek maxim: "Count no man happy till he's dead." For fortunes can be overturned and dashed to pieces in the blinking of an eye. As Alcibiades was now experiencing for himself. He was already safe at Chithrafarna's side, basking in the glow of his new friendship, when news arrived that stopped him in his tracks. The admiral, Astyochus, had received fresh, urgent orders. From Sparta and King Agis. To put Alcibiades to death.[20]

As at Athens, so, too, in Sparta: when Alcibiades was on hand to charm, dazzle, seduce with the sheer force of his magnetic personality, he could convince even many of his harshest critics of his indispensability. Once he was gone, however, his magic evaporated with him. It was like remembering excesses from a riotous symposium in the stark light of the next day's dawn.

Sardis: satrapal seat of Chithrapharna and site of the Paradise of Alcibiades. (Photograph by the author.)

Not just sober reconsiderations and hardheaded reappraisals. But a desire to distance oneself as far as possible from the withering evidence of decadence and dissolution.[21]

Undoubtedly, one of the main instigators of Sparta's new hostility was Agis. His motives were not just personal (his wife's adultery) but intensely political, too. For much of his early reign, Agis had been sidelined, condemned for his attempts at diplomatic settlements, patronized for his poor military skills. Even now, he was at Decelea only because Alcibiades had persuaded Sparta's ephors to send him there. Yes, he was achieving much. But last winter, when the Spartans were debating which strategy to back—the one

Agis favoured (to accept Farnavaz's support and secure the Hellespont) or Alcibiades' preferred option (to win over Ionia)—they had supported Alcibiades. And since then, what talk there was in Sparta had been dominated by accounts of Alcibiades' brilliance, as if he were singlehandedly responsible for every victory. Which rankled. And not just with Agis. With many of the other strutting Spartan and Ionian egos, too. So, they had gone to the ephors with accusations, undermining Alcibiades, questioning his motives, and, when the seeds of doubt had sprouted, demanding he be killed. Yet Alcibiades still had loyal friends in Sparta, among them Queen Timaea, and they smuggled out the message, which snaked its way across the sea and inland to the satrap's palace. Alcibiades was forewarned.[22]

By now, though, he was already sloughing off his ties with Sparta and immersing himself wholeheartedly in Persian life. It is possible he took a crash course in the Persians' language. Certainly, he embraced their lifestyle, tying his hair up in a bun, curling his well-oiled beard (a symbol of machismo in the Persian court), dousing himself in the perfumes for which Sardis was so famous, and dressing not just in sumptuous robes and beautifully fringed tunics of linen, wool, and mohair (deep-dyed in vibrant reds and vivid yellows, and adorned with ornaments in glittering gold foil), but in those other garments so associated by Athenians with decadent, eastern effeminacy: trousers.[23]

Unquestionably, too, sitting beside Chithrapharna, in a special place of honour, as his "tablemate," bejewelled and with a characteristic Persian signet ring hanging from a golden chain around his neck or wrist, he enjoyed the legendary hospitality of the satrap's court: banquets held in dining rooms hung with close-woven tapestries and strewn with the softest carpets, while, in the torchlight, concubines plucked harps and sang soft, soothing songs in eastern cadences as, languidly, still others danced; the sweet red wines of Sardis; mezés of fragrant stews and flatbreads, followed by the sweetest of desserts; and, on Chithrafarna's birthday, the greatest feast of all, perhaps a mouth-watering indulgence of roast oxen, horses, asses, camels, cooked whole in huge ovens, and carved before the guests. This was a day of lavish present-giving. But not to Chithrafarna. *From* him. In Persia, the powerful bound their subjects to them through their largesse, and a painstakingly judged hierarchy of gift-exchange proclaimed the recipient's place in the tight social order.[24]

If feasting was part of the performative display of power, so, too, to Alcibiades' delight, were horses and horse racing. Like the Great King, Persian satraps kept well-stocked stud farms. One boasted 800 stallions and 16,000 mares, while, from across the empire, the best animals were sent each year to the royal capitals—360 from Cilicia alone, one for each day of the Persian year—some to provide cavalry mounts, others to draw the Great King's chariot, still others (some hand-picked from the celebrated herd of 160,000 white horses which roamed the Nisaean plain) to be sacrificed to the sun and waters, or in memory of the Empire's founding father, Korush.[25]

In the hunt, too, Chithrafarna enjoyed Alcibiades' company. Unlike on mainland Greece, where hunters journeyed far into the mountains and maquis, in Persia, the animals were brought down to the huntsmen. In sprawling game parks, beaters (sometimes members of the Persian military) drove captured animals into fenced-off compounds where, mounted on sleek horses, the satrap and his guests, huge mastiffs by their sides, waited tensely for the beasts' arrival. Like much of Persian court life, it was theatrical in the extreme, watched over by an audience of courtiers and concubines. The skill lay in the killing, a ritual slaughter, in which the satrap took centre stage, proclaiming his (and, through him, the Great King's) power to tame the unbridled forces of chaos and the wild. His was the privilege of the first spear throw, and to pre-empt him was to risk wrath and demotion. For Alcibiades, this stylized replication of the chase must have seemed very much at odds with his past experience in the scrublands of Attica and the foothills of Sparta's Mount Taygetus, yet to ride at the satrap's side was a sign of honour and companionship. And that was what mattered.[26]

In truth, Alcibiades was learning fast, blending so perfectly with his new surroundings that they quickly seemed his natural habitat. This adaptability was part of his undoubted genius. In dynamic Athens, he had been thrusting and provocative; in self-denying Sparta, tight-lipped and austere; in courtly Persia, reverential, suave, urbane. "He had the knack," wrote the insightful Plutarch half a millennium later, "of taking on and embracing the habits and lifestyle of other men, transforming more completely than a chameleon. This is a creature, which they say can change into any colour except one: white. Yet Alcibiades was able to blend in with good and bad alike, and there was nothing he could not impersonate or become expert in. It was not so much that he could easily slip from one way of living to another, or that he completely changed his character, but that when he perceived that his behaviour would offend those with whom he happened to be keeping company, he quickly assumed a persona which might be pleasing to them."[27]

Yet there was still much to learn. And more surreal for Alcibiades even than the Persian hunt—and yet no less important—were the hours he spent with Chithrafarna in his garden. As provincial representatives of the Great King, satraps were obliged to mirror imperial court life, so that its values might percolate into every corner of the land. And gardens—parks or "paradises"—were a key constituent of this life, another sign of the Great King's power to tame and structure nature, to impose order in an otherwise chaotic world. To stock this miniature, if idealized, kingdom, teams of gardeners transported trees, and shrubs, and vines from every corner of the Persian realm, carefully transplanting them, solicitously tending them, expertly irrigating them to create formal landscapes of breathtaking beauty. Geometry and symmetry were paramount, and a clever use of sightlines meant that, strolling through the paradise, new vistas opened unexpectedly, revealing now a throne, now a pillared pavilion at the end of a long avenue. Some satraps, kings, and princes themselves gardened, and Chithrafarna had spent a fortune on his paradise and orchards with their bubbling streams and meadows, "laying them out lovingly and with the utmost artistry with plants and all that is conducive to luxury and the peaceful contemplation of fine things."[28]

As a special honour to his new-found friend, in whose company he spent so many happy hours here, Chithrafarna renamed his garden "The Paradise of Alcibiades." It was a charming gesture. But it committed the wily Chithrafarna to nothing. In the past few generations, important Greeks who came over to the Persians had been lavishly rewarded. Even those whose families had done the Persians most harm. When he captured the son of Miltiades (who later led the Athenians to victory at Marathon), instead of harming him, Dārayavahuš I presented him with a house, a wife, and rich gifts. When the Spartan King Demaratus was ousted from the throne and fled to Persia, the Great King awarded him three cities to rule over. And when Themistocles, the victor of Salamis, was chased from Greece, rejected by his native Athens and vilified by Sparta, he was welcomed with open arms, appointed governor of Magnesia on the Meander and allowed to use the revenue from no fewer than five cities to pay for his food and wine, his bedding, and his clothing. Indeed, so honoured was he, that a life-sized statue of him took pride of place in Magnesia's broad agora. But these men had committed themselves to Persia. Alcibiades had not. His loyalties were still untested; the Spartans, Persia's allies, had placed him on their death list; and, despite his amiable companionship, he had yet to convince Chithrafarna of his political and military worth. Yet, the time was fast approaching when he must.[29]

While Alcibiades and Chithrafarna were enjoying the finer things of life at Sardis, back on the coast, hostilities had not abated. Despite high seas and driving winds, the Spartan and Athenian fleets, desperate to gain ground, or to retain it, had braved the lashing winter waves, sometimes blown dangerously off course to founder on hidden reefs and rocks, each trying to intercept the other as they raged up and down the coast. At last, the Spartans raised the siege of Chios, but when Astyochus refused to help the islanders, the Chian slaves revolted from their masters and brought back the Athenians. At home in Sparta, Astyochus was denounced as a traitor, and a commission of enquiry was sent out to investigate. One of its number was the venerable Lichas, the man who had been whipped for competing at the Olympic Games eight years before.[30]

The Spartans faced other problems, too. Not least in their negotiations with Chithrafarna. They had already insisted on rewording the draft treaty, removing the clause which had blithely conceded so much Greek territory to the Persians, promising instead that "the Spartans and their allies will *not make war against or harm* any land or city that now belongs to the Great King or once belonged to his ancestors." Now, at a meeting with Chithrafarna, summoned hastily to the coast, Lichas railed against the new terms, too. Neither treaty was acceptable. Sparta, which had fought so hard in the first phase of the war to present herself as the liberator of the Greeks, could not condone effectively conceding many of the islands and much of mainland Greece to Persian influence, in effect passing them from one imperial master to another. For Chithrafarna, this was intolerable. The Spartans had always been unreliable negotiators, and to have to tell the Great King that the treaty's terms had changed again was not just embarrassing but undermining of his authority. Infuriated, Chithrafarna stormed out of the negotiations and swept back to Magnesia. And to Alcibiades.[31]

For by now, in early 411, with winter drawing to a close and the traditional campaigning season ready to begin, the two men had moved back closer to the theatre of war. But with not only Athens now, but Sparta, too, having passed a death sentence on him, Alcibiades took considerable pains to keep some distance from the combatants, while at the same time offering Chithafarna counsel, which would benefit not just the Persians but himself. His greatest fear was that the Spartans would bring the fighting to a swift conclusion, become the dominant force in Greece and, as part of their post-bellum settlement, demand his return or execution. It was in his interests to prolong the war as long as possible.

So, in private with Chithrafarna, after dinner, or in strolls in the gardens at Magnesia, where the spring anemones would soon carpet the rich hillsides, Alcibiades murmured his advice: rather than let the Spartans deal a knock-out blow, the Persian should be more sparing in his support, since the longer the war dragged on, the weaker each of the Greek sides would gradually become, and a weak Greece was in Persia's best interests. If Alcibiades but knew it, this was what many in Athens feared the most. And, indeed, what the Athenians were even now being counselled to avoid by Alcibiades' *bête noire,* the acerbic-tongued, politically savvy comedian, Aristophanes. In his *Lysistrata,* staged in 411, he allegorized the war as a battle between the sexes, arguing that only when Athens and Sparta learned how to live in harmony would Greece be strong. Addressing the fighters on both sides, his central character, Lysistrata, questioned:

> You all, who share one country and one history, one family, all of
> you, all Greeks, all worshipping as one, competing all as one in
> the Olympic Games, with all of your achievements, Delphi and
> Thermopylae, art, architecture, literature, this special, wonderful,
> so fragile glory that is Greece—our enemies [the Persians] are
> arming themselves even as we speak, and what do you do?
> Slaughter Greek men! Sack Greek cities![32]

But in the scented gardens of Magnesia, such a war of attrition, aimed against both sides, offered Alcibiades his best hope of making something of his situation, and perhaps even winning back his city. So he pressed his arguments still further. The Persians had offered to support the Spartans with their own Phoenician navy. Much better, though, to string them along, pretend that the Phoenician ships were on their way, sap the morale of Sparta's trireme-crews, as they waited for reinforcements that would never come. And to sap morale still further, Alcibiades suggested that Chithrafarna make payments to the Peloponnesian fleet well in arrears and piecemeal. There were good reasons, he declared, why Athens paid its oarsmen only half the wages that the Persians were paying the Spartans: give them too much, and sailors would spend it on debauchery; pay them promptly, remove their incentive to remain in service, and they were likely to desert, when the going got tough. But with the generals and leading men, he advised Chithrafarna to do the opposite: to bribe them lavishly—their greed for more would keep them loyal.[33]

And besides, he continued, perhaps the Persians should not be helping Sparta anyway. Perhaps they should be helping the Athenians. For, if Athens, a predominantly naval power, should win the war, she would do Persia no harm. She presented no real danger. Indeed, since signing the Peace of Callias, the two empires had existed side by side in harmony for nearly forty years. But Sparta was another proposition entirely. Like Persia, Sparta's strength lay in her land army, and if she became the dominant power in Greece, she could potentially pose a far greater threat to Persia than Athens' navy ever had. Besides, from the start, the Spartans had presented the war as struggle for liberation, a fight for the freedom of Greek cities from the evils of Athens' empire. Did Chithrafarna really think that they would meekly hand Greek Ionia over to the Persians when the war was over? Better to preserve the status quo. The asymmetric nature of the war meant that there could be no winner. Let Athens still dominate the sea, and Sparta, the land. And, if either side seemed to be winning, then Chithrafarna must support the other. But keep them fighting. Wear them out. That way, the Persians could reduce Athenian power and rid their own land of the Spartans, who already showed signs of encroaching seriously on their territory.

Much of this advice chimed with Chithrafarna's own thinking. Despite the Spartans' initial successes in Ionia, won mainly thanks to speed and surprise, the Athenians had responded swiftly and successfully. Moreover, the arrival of fresh fleets from the Peloponnese and Syracuse meant that Chithrafarna's expenditure was now far greater than he had anticipated. Hence his enthusiasm for cutting sailors' pay. Besides, with the Spartans' repeated rejection of the wording of the treaty, the Persians were beginning to lose patience. Perhaps it was indeed more politic at least to seem to lessen his support for Sparta, and to consider backing the Athenians, if only to demonstrate to Sparta the consequences of not playing by Persia's rules.[34]

Chithrafarna's problem was that it was not in his power to change imperial policy. Only the Great King could do that. But by chance, in the spring of 411, Dārayavahuš II was visiting his western provinces. Like his predecessors, constantly on the move, he had every reason to see and be seen by his subjects in lands that had so recently been convulsed by Humarga's revolt, and his progress along the Royal Road to Sardis was a meticulously staged demonstration of his undisputed power. Riding in his golden chariot pulled by snow-white horses, accompanied by his thousand bodyguards, and travelling with a monumental train of curtained carriages containing the royal family and concubines, a snaking caravan of servants and attendants, a creaking convoy of bright-painted wagons—some laden down with precious jewellery, furniture, and clothing, others with huge jars of water from the River Choaspes near Susa, the only water that the King allowed himself to drink—his arrival at the provincial capital must have impressed even the flamboyant Alcibiades. Here was showmanship on a scale of which even the most ambitious of Athenians could only dream.[35]

The pomp surrounding the King's person was extraordinary. While outside, the Great King's feet could never touch the ground. Instead, when he descended from his chariot by means of a golden footstool, expensive rugs were spread over the earth for him to tread on as he made his way inside the palace. Once installed there, access to his presence was jealously protected. But among those granted audience was Alcibiades. Once more, every detail was calculated not just to impress his subjects but to distance the Great King, to demonstrate his special status and supremacy. On a dais beneath a baldachin—four golden pillars supporting a purple canopy, into whose tasselled border were woven lions and the winged symbol of Ahura Mazda—Dārayavahuš sat crowned and godlike on a golden throne between two incense burners. Dark-eyed, hook-nosed, long-bearded, his soft-shod feet resting on his golden footstool, he wore robes shimmering with gold thread and picked out with jewels. In his right hand he held the sceptre. In his left a lotus flower. And behind him, motionless, the officers of his Immortal Guard, their long spears held erect.[36]

Although Chithrafarna's audiences, too, were richly choreographed and formal, they paled before the King's. For a Greek like Alcibiades, the closest he had come to such a show of power was seeing the colossal statue of the seated Zeus in his temple at Olympia. But Zeus was a god. Dārayavahuš was a man. Even the protocol for greeting the Great King was awarded by Greeks only to the gods. The act of *proskynesis* was demanded of anyone granted a royal audience. It was demanded, too, of Alcibiades. So, as he approached the throne, he knelt down, bowed low, and touched the earth with his forehead, before kissing his right hand and stretching out his arm towards the Great King in an act of ritual obeisance.[37]

Then Alcibiades proposed to Dārayavahuš the strategy he had discussed with Chithrafarna. And Dārayavahuš accepted it. So says Thucydides, and this may well be the account which the historian heard from Alcibiades, and it may well be that Alcibiades believed it. Yet it is equally likely that Chithrafarna held his own private meetings with the Great King, where his own advice was more nuanced. Yes, the Persians should play a longer game, especially since the outcome of the war remained unknowable and the Spartans seemed inconstant. But the goal must remain the repossession of Ionia, and only with a Spartan victory could this ever be achieved. For the moment, there was no harm in using Alcibiades, in allowing him to think he had the Great King's ear, in letting him play out his plan until the Persians could evaluate the situation and gain a better picture of how things would fall out. After all, Alcibiades was in a unique position to know how best to negotiate with both Athenians and Spartans. And if, in the end, he found himself on the wrong side, so be it.[38]

Back in Magnesia once more, Alcibiades was allowed to play the potentate. It was he who received envoys from Chios and the other rebel cities, requesting money to aid them in their fight with Athens. It was he, too, who sent them imperiously away, rebuking them for their impudence, telling them that the Persians were already risking their lives to defend them, and that it was unreasonable to expect them to risk their money, too—especially since the Chians were so rich.[39]

But it was other envoys whose arrival most pleased Alcibiades. They came from Samos. From the island's leading citizens acting both on their own behalf and as conduits for a powerful clique of the Athenian commanders there. They had heard (as Chithrafarna no doubt hoped they would) of Alcibiades' great influence with Persia's satrap. And they wanted him to use it now on their behalf. Even if this meant forgiving Alcibiades, absolving him of all the charges laid against him, and recalling him to Athens.[40]

The Samians and Athenians each had different motives, but both were driven by money. The Samian elite bore most of the costs of fighting. But the democracy, not they, held all the power, and this they found exasperating in the extreme. Better by far, the wealthy felt, to stage a coup and direct the progress of the war themselves. Meanwhile, in Athens, too, the democratic government was in financial difficulties. It was fast running out of money. Not only was Athens largely cut off from its silver mines at Laurium, her empire, until now a reliable source of revenue, was haemorrhaging badly. Only recently, news had come that Rhodes had gone over to the Spartans, pouring no fewer than thirty-two talents into the Peloponnesian war effort. If Athens were to enjoy any hope at all of defeating Sparta, she desperately needed rich backers. The richest they could think of were the Persians. And the obvious man to help liaise with them was Alcibiades.[41]

For Alcibiades, the approach was not entirely unexpected. There were many Athenians who were still on his side, who regretted the treatment he had received at the hands of his enemies and the People, and who would be delighted for him to return. And through private correspondence, Alcibiades had already been in contact with his friends in the Athenian fleet overwintering on Samos, letting it be known that (magnanimously) he would be more than happy not only to be reconciled with Athens but to ensure the Persians' support—if Athens suspended the fickle democracy that had condemned him and established an oligarchic government in its place. A government well-disposed to Alcibiades. Only when he felt confident that his enemies at home were neutered and his safety was assured could he possibly consider coming back.[42]

When the emissaries, star-struck, returned to Samos, they shared the outcome of their meeting with the Athenian army. Not unsurprisingly, the rank and file greeted the proposal unenthusiastically. But when they were reminded that Athens' dire financial state meant that, very soon, they probably would not be paid, whereas the Great King's coffers were overflowing, their opposition melted, and, while some were still not happy, they agreed to let the proposition be considered. Faced with the stark choice, monetary gain trumped political principles. Better to hold their noses now, do what must be done, and revisit the debate on constitutional niceties when their situation had improved.[43]

Besides, could not Athens' woes be traced back almost to the very day when she forced Alcibiades into exile? Until then, everything had gone so well. Brought up on a diet of triumphalist speeches, which played up their city's victories and airbrushed out defeats such as Delium and Coroneia, the soldiery had long been encouraged to view their history as an inevitable progress towards ultimate supremacy. And so it seemed to be. From Marathon through the Persian Wars and the growth of Athens' empire to the victories in the first part of the current war and Alcibiades' formation of the anti-Spartan Arcadian League during the Peace of Nicias, victory (they now recalled) had seemed to follow victory. And the Sicilian Expedition, brainchild of Alcibiades, would have expanded Athens' empire all the more, had Alcibiades not been removed from post. Look what had happened then! They needed no speeches to remind them of such recent history. First the failure of the expedition, and the loss of lives and ships. Then the Spartan occupation of the fort at Deceleia, and the loss of revenue from Laurium. And now the loss of allies, too. Their big mistake had been to rid themselves of Alcibiades! Get him back, and surely with him Good Fortune would return.[44]

Only one of the generals made his disagreement known: Alcibiades' old enemy, Phrynichus. The man who, thanks to Alcibiades' arrival with the Peloponnesian fleet, had been forced to lift the siege of Miletus the previous autumn. In an impassioned speech, he argued his case: there was no way that the Great King would favour the Athenians over Sparta, when the Persians had already suffered so much at Athens' hands; there was no way, either, that Athens' democratic allies would remain on side, if the city were transformed into an oligarchy; and, as for Alcibiades, there was no way that he genuinely preferred the prospect of oligarchy to democracy, when all that he was really interested in was himself.[45]

But no one wanted to heed Phrynichus. Not when the prospect of Chithrafarna's money was at stake. So, they chose one of their number,

Pisander, to lead a delegation back to Athens. He was a clever choice. A towering bear of a man, he was wealthy and well-known in the past for airing democratic views in the Assembly. Not only that, he had served on the commission that had investigated the profanation of the Mysteries and led to Alcibiades' downfall. What better man to argue for the prodigal's return?[46]

So, braving the grey winter waves, Pisander and a small group of fellow envoys boarded a trireme and pushed off from Samos harbour. Their destination: Athens. Their mission: to unpick the democratic constitution and do what no one could have imagined in their wildest dreams even a few months earlier. Engineer the rehabilitation and recall of Alcibiades.[47]

9

TRADING PLACES

What is each man's opinion of Alcibiades? The city's suffering pangs as bad as childbirth! . . . It longs for him, but at the same time hates him too. But on balance it must have him!

Aristophanes, *Frogs,* 1423–1425

"THE MAN WHO LOVES HIS CITY," as Alcibiades had once declared in Sparta, may yearn "for it so much that he'll do everything he can to get it back," but, in truth, he must have known that nothing would be plain sailing. The Athenian Assembly, as he had learned to his cost, was both unpredictable and vengeful. If it blamed Alcibiades for the recent loss of so many lives on Sicily, and the ongoing rebellion of its Ionian allies, there was every likelihood that it would never welcome him back. Meanwhile, closer by on Samos, opinion remained dangerously divided. Friendly voices may have carried the day, but there were still those who were passionately opposed to having anything to do with Alcibiades. Chief among them was his bitter enemy, the Athenian general Phrynichus.[1]

As recorded in Thucydides' contemporary account, the story of how Phrynichus tried to undermine Alcibiades raises more questions than it answers. It goes like this: frightened for his own safety, if Alcibiades should be recalled, Phrynichus sent a secret message to Astyochus, the Spartan general.

In it, he gave chapter and verse of Alcibiades' recent dealings with the Athenians, revealing that Alcibiades was doing his best to undermine the Spartan cause and win Chithrafarna's support for Athens. But, instead of acting against Alcibiades, Astyochus took the letter to Magnesia, where he not only showed it to Alcibiades and Chithrafarna but, "so it was said," agreed to become a paid agent of the satrap.[2]

The sequel, also recorded by Thucydides, is equally perplexing: Alcibiades immediately sent a letter to the Samian authorities and the Athenian generals on the island who supported him, revealing Phrynichus' treachery and demanding his execution. But Phrynichus found out and again wrote to Astyochus. The contents of this new communiqué were dynamite. After rebuking the Spartan for leaking his first letter, he not only offered to help him capture Samos but gave a detailed account of the island's defences, outlining the best strategy for taking it. But once more Astyochus took the letter to Magnesia. Meanwhile, however, Phrynichus had second thoughts. Regretting his treachery, he warned the Samians that the Spartans were about to attack, and hurriedly set about building fortifications. So, when the inevitable letter came from Alcibiades accusing Phrynichus of betraying Samos to the Spartans, no one believed it. Instead, many suspected that Alcibiades was using inside intelligence of an imminent Spartan attack to smear Phrynichus' good name, as a result of which Phrynichus' own reputation was considerably enhanced.

Taken at face value, the episode makes little sense. Elsewhere, Thucydides describes Phrynichus as both "a man of good sense" and a general who did everything he could to prevent the destruction of the Athenian ships at Miletus. Now we are required to believe that he was not just as opportunistic and double-dealing as Alcibiades, prepared to betray both Samos and the fleet from private hatred, but a vacillating coward, a fool who persisted in communicating with Astyochus despite knowing that the Spartan would turn his letters over to Alcibiades and Chithrafarna. We are required, too, to see the Spartan Astyochus as a venal traitor who uncharacteristically failed to capitalize on a golden opportunity to win a famous victory against Athens, preferring instead to throw in his lot with Alcibiades and take the satrap's shilling. And we are required to suppose that Chithrafarna was so far under his friend Alcibiades' spell, and that the Great King, too, was so utterly convinced by the Athenian's persuasive arguments, that the Persians had by now truly abandoned their policy of supporting Sparta, being instead so genuinely committed either to backing Athens or to preserving the *status quo* that they preferred to expose Phrynichus rather than deal their age-old enemy a crushing blow. We are required, in fact, to see all the major players in the game as treacherous and injudicious dupes except for one man: Alcibiades.[3]

Which suggests that the truth was rather different, that, once again, Thucydides accepted a version of the facts that showed Alcibiades in the best possible light, and his enemies in the worst—that what has been preserved as history is, in fact, Alcibiades' own spin. While subsequent events serve to reinforce this suspicion, the truth is harder to discern. It is not impossible that, in sending his letters, Phrynichus was deliberately trying to lure Astyochus into a trap. Indeed, the speed with which he oversaw the fortification of Samos ("faster than it would have otherwise been built," writes Thucydides), suggests that Phrynichus was deliberately trying to bring matters quickly to a head—or at least to demonstrate his own energy as an Athenian patriot. A swift victory over the Spartan fleet, he may have reasoned, could turn the tide of war in Athens' favour and thus negate the need to enlist Chithrafarna's aid, let alone to recall Alcibiades. That Astyochus failed to take the bait simply proves the Spartan's canniness.[4]

As for Thucydides' perplexing interpretation of Phrynichus' motives, and the allegation that Astyochus sold his soul to Chithrafarna—these sit uncomfortably in his narrative. But they make perfect sense if they came from Alcibiades. Ensconced in his palatial quarters at Magnesia, granting audience to some, rebuffing others, it was entirely in Alcibiades' interests to sow seeds of distrust and peddle disinformation that would blacken or bring down his enemies. Phrynichus was the one man who spoke out in Samos against Alcibiades' return. How convenient if he were now made to appear suspect, a mole in the Athenian camp willing to betray the army to the enemy, a turncoat in the mould of Alcibiades, ready to forsake his country out of personal hatred.

And as for Astyochus, from whom could Thucydides have learned of his alleged arrangement with Chithrafarna if not from Alcibiades? Although Astyochus enjoyed fractious relationships with many of his Spartan officers, there is no suggestion that any of them were aware of the charge or made subsequent use of it against him. How much more likely that, unable to carry out his orders and bring about Alcibiades' death, Astyochus was trying to undermine Alcibiades' relationship with Chithrafarna by revealing the extent of the promises he had made to the Athenians on Samos—something of which the satrap was previously unaware? How much more likely, too, that Alcibiades, irked by this, should try in turn to ruin the Spartan's reputation? Whatever the truth, the episode suggests that, with the stalling of the war, a mood of extreme tetchiness engulfed Ionia, that suspicion was rife not just between the warring sides, but within allied camps as well, and that at or near the heart of this suspicion lurked Alcibiades.[5]

The game was most certainly afoot. And, while Alcibiades was doing his best to slander his enemies and work his magic with Chithrafarna, emphasizing the advantages of helping Athens, while arguing that the Spartans' rejection of the terms of the peace treaty proved beyond doubt their unreliability as allies, events in Athens were turning out entirely as he had hoped.

In fact, the Athenians were already prepared to entertain ideas about a change of constitution. More than a year earlier, in 413, they had appointed ten *probouloi,* high-ranking officials drawn from the great and good, whose role in part superseded that of the Council. Entrusted not only with setting the Athenian economy back on a relatively even keel but with steering a safe, focussed, and consistent course through the uncharted and emotionally turbulent waters that threatened to engulf the city in the wake of the Sicilian debacle, theirs was an unenviable task. That they had been appointed at all was evidence of a deepening distrust in the democracy which had unthinkingly squandered so many lives and so much treasure on the unwarranted campaign to Sicily. And it was also a precedent.[6]

So, when the hulking Pisander and his fellow envoys mounted the Speakers' Platform on the chilly Pnyx, they found the Assembly not entirely averse to the suggestion that the democracy be suspended and an oligarchy set up in its place. Of course, it helped that many of the poorer citizens were absent (a relatively large number were serving on campaign as oarsmen in the fleet, overwintering on Samos, the very island from which the envoys had just sailed), while a good proportion of the landowners and merchants still in Athens relished the idea of power being in the hands of the rich. Not only that. Many quite rightly questioned whether, with her finances so perilously low, Athens could still afford to make the payments on which the democratic government depended for everything from Council membership to jury service to waste collection and disposal. Better, they said, to use state monies for the upkeep of materiel and fighting men, and turn the administration of the city over to those who did not need paying at all. It all made sound fiscal sense. Which did not mean that there were not vociferous opponents. Especially to the proposal that Alcibiades should be pardoned and reinstated as an Athenian citizen. Among them were Alcibiades' personal adversaries. Not surprisingly, the most impassioned arguments came from Callias and his fellow Eleusinian priests, the men who had so passionately cursed Alcibiades as they shook out their purple robes on the Acropolis less than four years earlier, who had offered prayers of thanks that they would never see their enemy alive again.[7]

As the priests wailed theatrically, calling on the gods never to permit Alcibiades' return, trying to whip up an emotional storm of whistling and cat-calls, Pisander calmly asked each of the dissenters in turn: "Given that the Peloponnesians have as many ships at sea as we do, with a greater number of allied cities, and the Great King and Chithrafarna on their side to provide money (while we Athenians have none), what hope is there of saving Athens, unless someone brings the Great King over to our side?" Put like that, there was just one answer: there *was* no hope. The only solution was to use Alcibiades to enlist the help of the Great King. And the only way that either man would agree to have dealings with Athens was if it became an oligarchy. Better to bow to pressure now and survive than be stubborn and defeated. They could always reintroduce democracy when the danger was over, and they had refilled their coffers.

So pragmatism triumphed over religious (and political) scruples, the Eleusinian priests were silenced, and the motion to suspend the democracy was passed. Plans were laid to draw up a new constitution, and, although for now the Council and Assembly met as usual, they did so in a climate of heightened fear. For, in truth, Athens had never really regained an even keel since the scandal of the Herms and the Eleusinian Mysteries, followed so closely by the slaughter of her sons in Sicily. And now, with tensions growing once more, neighbour distrusted neighbour, and friend suspected friend. Many, who spoke out vehemently against the proposed oligarchy one day, were found brutally murdered the next, their bodies dumped unceremoniously in the streets for all to see. The long-held, long-cherished custom of *parrhesia,* freedom of speech, was now remembered as an odd, quixotic luxury. And, as the carapace of totalitarianism hardened, the People increasingly began to acquiesce, meekly falling in with what the oligarchic leaders wanted.[8]

Meanwhile, thanks to some judicious words from Pisander, blaming Phrynichus for the loss of Iasus and the defeat of Athens' ally Humarga, a trireme was sent post-haste to Samos to strip Alcibiades' enemy of his command. A quick tour of the city's political clubs, a few well-chosen words of encouragement to those most likely to become leading lights of any new oligarchic constitution, and Pisander and ten colleagues were soon bustling back east with a renewed sense of optimism that, in a matter of mere days, thanks to Alcibiades, they would be outlining their needs to Chithrafarna, and the satrap would be underwriting them. It was all turning out so wonderfully well![9]

Sailing into the wide Gulf of Miletus, the Athenians made the short journey inland, following the course of the River Meander until they reached Magnesia. Here they were welcomed into the satrapal palace with every respect due powerful ambassadors, and at the appointed time shown into the audience chamber for the first of a series of summit meetings. Like all dealings with the Persian high command, the conclave was formal in the extreme, a study in procedure calculated to leave no one in any doubt where the true power lay—with the Persian Court and its representative, Chithrafarna, seated, delicately coiffed and richly robed, on his lavishly-carved throne, his well-shod feet resting on his golden footstool. And close to him, no doubt enjoying the moment, was Alcibiades. It was he who would conduct negotiations, a Greek treating with Greeks, albeit as a mouthpiece for the Persians.[10]

The first meeting went relatively smoothly, as Alcibiades set out the essence of Chithrafarna's terms. For anyone following the Persians' recent negotiations with the Spartans, they were entirely predictable: the Athenians must surrender to Persia the whole of Ionia as well as the Aegean islands closest to the coast. It was a sign of Athens' desperation that her ambassadors were willing to agree. Not only did such a concession fly in the face of everything the city had stood for since her intervention in the Ionian Revolt three generations earlier, but to give up Ephesus, and Samos, and Lesbos, and the rest would mean giving up much of her Empire, not to mention

Magnesia on the Meander, where Alcibiades received Chian and Athenian envoys. (Photograph by the author.)

the annual tax revenues accrued from these subjects and allied states. Still, for the moment, at least, it seemed worth it.

Over the course of two lengthy meetings, both sides thrashed out the details. Then, at the third, Alcibiades introduced a final clause. The Athenians must "allow the Great King to build ships, and sail wherever he wished along his coast with whatever fleet he liked." It was only now that the enormity of the situation truly sank in. Athens had long prided herself on being mistress of the sea. For nearly forty years, her ability to keep Persia's Phoenician fleet out of the Aegean had guaranteed the safety of mainland Greece from seaborne attack. It made little difference whether a democracy or oligarchy governed Athens—how could the ambassadors possibly convince their fellow citizens that such a deal made sense? No matter what persuasive arguments he had prepared, or what sophistic reasoning he now employed, not even Alcibiades could reassure the delegates. The meeting ended in acrimony. For the Athenians there was only one person to blame: Alcibiades. He had deceived them! He had led them on! He never did want a deal! Boiling with humiliation, Pisander and his colleagues stalked off for Samos.[11]

Once more, Thucydides' account is baffling. According to him, from the very start, Chithrafarna was opposed to an alliance with the Athenians. Alcibiades knew this. So—to conceal the fact that he had brought the Athenians to Magnesia under false pretences, and that he actually possessed little influence with the satrap—he deliberately ramped up the Persians' demands so high that the Athenians walked away, thus allowing him to blame them for the failure of the negotiations. The truth was undoubtedly more simple. For the Persians, the bottom line was that they wanted to control Ionia and the sea around it, since this would provide their empire with a natural western border. This had been at the core of the treaties they had tried to sign with Sparta, even if they had also introduced ambiguous wording, which could be interpreted as staking a claim to parts of mainland Greece as well. In the end, it did not really matter to the Persians which Greek state ensured that these demands were met. So, having failed to secure a treaty with Sparta, Chithrafarna pragmatically tried to reach an agreement on the same terms with Athens instead. Indeed, for the Persians, the policy of playing Athens and Sparta off against each other, of supporting one and then the other, which Alcibiades was so proud of having persuaded them to follow, had no real aim other than to discover which side might best accommodate their ambitions to annex Ionia and the nearby islands. Once it was clear that their best hopes lay with Sparta, they abandoned any pretence of aiding Athens.[12]

But for Alcibiades it was crucial that the Athenians should not know this. For him to have any hope of triumphing over his enemies in Athens, of beating the system, of returning home, the darling of his people, it was essential that they still believed not only that that the Persians could be persuaded to support them, but that he was the man who had the Persians' ear. Once more, it is likely that Thucydides' account, with its insights into the key players' motivations, comes directly from Alcibiades; and, once more, it is misleading.[13]

In truth, the breakdown of the talks was a significant setback for Alcibiades. Through Pisander he had learned that, as requested, his friends in Athens had succeeded in paving the way for an oligarchy in the expectation that Alcibiades in turn would furnish Persian aid. But now, despite what he might argue, Alcibiades had been unable to secure his side of the arrangement. His gamble had failed. And, to make matters worse, no sooner did the Athenian delegation leave Magnesia than Chithrafarna reopened his negotiations with the Spartans, summoned their generals to a meeting on the Meander Plain, paid their troops handsomely, and at last concluded a peace treaty which was acceptable to both sides. Despite the bravest face that he could put on it, for Alcibiades it marked a signal failure, perhaps the lowest point yet in his dramatically fluctuating life.[14]

The Athenian Empire was in a turmoil too. No sooner had Pisander left Magnesia than he was feverishly stirring up dissent. In Samos, he advised the island's leading lights to have nothing whatever to do with Alcibiades and encouraged them to form an oligarchic government. Then he and his colleagues fanned out across the Aegean, single-mindedly doing everything possible to overthrow the democratic constitutions of as many members of the Empire as they could, replacing them with their own wealthy friends.[15]

Back in Athens, Pisander surrounded himself with many of the city's richest and most powerful intellectuals, members of the clubs that he had toured on his last visit. Although all were in favour of an oligarchy, their political outlooks were by no means uniform. They ranged from relative moderates such as Theramenes, the son of Hagnon (the man who had founded Amphipolis some twenty-six years earlier), to extremists such as the cerebral yet devastatingly brilliant orator Antiphon, and (now that there was no longer any threat of Alcibiades' return) Phrynichus, the general who had been so opposed to Alcibiades on Samos, and still harboured simmering resentments.[16]

In the preceding weeks, they had already prepared their ground, creating an atmosphere of terror and uncertainty in the streets of Athens. Believing that they would soon be welcoming Alcibiades back home to join an oligarchy, a group of passionate young zealots had sought to win his favour by killing a number of his political rivals. And if Alcibiades was no longer expected to join the new regime, it made little difference: what mattered was that, thanks to the suspicion that now haunted Athens, no one was prepared to stick his neck out and oppose those bent on overthrowing the democracy and seizing power. So, when the coup came, all went smoothly. Its leading members, now identified as "the Four Hundred," occupied the Council Chamber, invested themselves with the trappings of government and, while promising that at some time in the future they would consult with the Assembly (now notionally restricted to the five thousand richest citizens), began to consider how best to end the war.[17]

Meanwhile, on Samos, tensions boiled over into violence. Here, too, the oligarchs had embarked on a campaign to undermine the democracy and terrorize the citizens. Among their many victims was Hyperbolus, the populist politician ostracized in 416, who since then had been enjoying a comfortable living selling supplies to the Athenian army on Samos. Soon matters came to a head. A handful of leading Athenians, democrats to the core, who were stationed on the island, were determined to resist. To keep their intentions hidden, they moved through the camp unobtrusively, glad-handing soldiery and oarsmen, garnering support and whispering their plans. So, when the time came for the oligarchs to stage their coup, the democratic opposition was prepared. The Athenian democrats poured out, attacked the ringleaders, slaughtered some, and caused the rest to flee. In the face of heavy odds, Samos remained a democracy.[18]

Because events were moving so quickly, no one on Samos had yet heard of the oligarchic coup in Athens. So they sent one of the state warships, *Paralus*, to convey the happy news that the island's democracy had been preserved. But when it reached Piraeus, *Paralus* was impounded, and its staunchly democratic, all-Athenian crew reassigned to other duties. All, that is, except one man. Somehow, he slipped the net and stole back to Samos with chilling (if exaggerated) news of the atrocities being perpetrated throughout Athens. Army and fleet exploded into uproar. Voices demanded immediate action: to sail home at once and restore the democracy. But wiser heads prevailed. To leave Samos now would be to leave Ionia open to the enemy. Better to sit it out. If democracy had died in Athens, it was alive and well on Samos. With the Athenian army. Which no longer served its oligarchic city, but itself. For it alone upheld its city's values. Unwittingly, the soldiery found themselves echoing Alcibiades' sophistic arguments in

Sparta: in resisting Athens, they were not attacking their homeland; rather, they were doing all in their power to reclaim it.[19]

Uniting their men and encouraging a reasoned response were two brilliant tacticians: Thrasybulus, a trireme captain, and a hoplite called Thrasyllus. Both had been among those leading the resistance to the Samian oligarchs. Now they played a vital role again, binding even the most hotheaded to observe due moderation by requiring every man to swear a solemn oath to uphold democracy and resist both the "Four Hundred" oligarchs back home and their Spartan and Persian enemies on the coasts and islands of Ionia nearby. Now they were on their own. But they still could win. They still had ships and men, and they could get supplies and money. And more. They could even win over the Persian Great King. For, as the only legitimate government of Athens (albeit in exile), they could grant immunity from prosecution, and recall Alcibiades![20]

So, at last, in the spring of 411, in the Assembly of the People's Army, Thrasybulus stood up and made the speech, for which so many had been hoping for so long. In it, he proposed that Alcibiades be awarded amnesty from every accusation laid against him; that he should be invited home, if not to Athens, where none of them now belonged, at least to the bosom of the Athenian People, and to the command of its armed forces on Samos. His arguments fell on fertile soil. Suddenly, the fate of Alcibiades, unjustly accused by his enemies, seemed to chime with the fate of the Athenian patriots, unjustly divorced from their city by the overweening oligarchs. The cause that both were fighting for was one! (No matter that Alcibiades had so recently been such an enthusiastic advocate of oligarchy.) So, when the vote came, there was little wonder that it fell resoundingly in favour of the motion.[21]

Within hours, Thrasybulus had put to sea for the short voyage to the mainland and the flat road inland to Magnesia and the court of Chithrafarna. How the satrap reacted when he heard of Alcibiades' recall is not recorded. Possibly he felt no small relief that his troublesome, if entertaining guest was leaving him, even if it did now set them squarely on opposing sides. Yet the studied protocol, with which he saw off Alcibiades, was almost certainly sufficient to convince Thrasybulus that the two men were still friends. Especially since Thrasybulus so needed to believe in that friendship.[22]

As for Alcibiades, Thrasybulus' appearance was a godsend. With the treaty signed between Persia and Sparta, he had no real role left with Chithrafarna, and, although he was assured of the satrap's protection, the life of a Persian courtier, with its sanitized hunting and interminable strolls through gardens, hardly suited a man whose ambition trumped even his love of luxury. And yet, the Athenian People to whom he was returning were so different from those whom he had left just four years earlier. Then they had been wealthy, confident, anticipating victory not just in Sicily but across the Mediterranean. Now they were impoverished, their allies and subject cities abandoning them by the week, their Spartan enemies bankrolled by Persia and supported not just by armies from the Peloponnese, but by ships from as far away as Syracuse. Thanks (in part) to Alcibiades, a Spartan army was dug in on Attic soil. And now thuggish oligarchs held power in Athens—thanks (again, in part) to him and his insistence that he could not return as long as the city was being ruled by a democracy. Which made it doubly ironic that he, an exile, should be rehabilitated by an exiled, and rampantly democratic, army.

Still, if he were not only to survive but thrive, Alcibiades must put the best spin on his situation. And as he entered the Assembly of the People's Army, he did precisely that. Having hastily trimmed his beard to a length more acceptable in an Athenian, scrubbed off any kohl still lingering around his eyes, and exchanged his Persian robes for a Greek tunic, he stepped onto the platform, basking in the deafening cheers of the assembled soldiery. Despite his wanderings, these were his people, men whose moods and fears and aspirations he understood so well. And he knew exactly how to play them. He knew, too, that the democratic army was not his only audience, that his speech would be reported far and wide. So he pitched it not just at the sea of faces turned expectantly towards him beneath the Samian spring sun, but at the oligarchs back home in Athens, and the Spartans and the Persians across the dancing waters in Miletus and Magnesia.[23]

First he spoke of his own exile, detailing his sad suffering (so underserved!) since his enemies first conspired to drive him out of Athens, justifying his flight to Sparta (what else could he possibly have done?), and explaining how he saw the current situation, before warming to a tantalizing, glittering account of the months he had just spent with Chithrafarna. He emphasized their friendship. He waxed lyrical about the trust and influence he had established with the satrap. And he painted an extravagant (if entirely bogus) picture of what the army could expect now that they had him back. Chithrafarna, he assured them, had promised him his full support! Whatever money the satrap had, he would donate to the Athenians—anything they needed, anything at all, even if it meant he had to pawn his silver couch! Not only that, he had pledged to bring in the Phoenician fleet to fight alongside Athens' navy! All that Chithrafarna needed in return was for the Athenians to welcome the return of Alcibiades! If they did that, he could truly trust their judgement!

Much of his speech was total fantasy. But Alcibiades understood the power of propaganda. The Spartans, when they learned of it, would question the extent of the Persians' reliability; the Athenian oligarchs and his own enemies at home would fear his power; and the army in Samos would be inspired with a new confidence to go out to fight and win.[24]

For, in truth, the situation was bleaker than at almost any stage so far. In the past few weeks and months, the Spartans had begun to implement the second phase of the strategy that they had honed the year before: to seize the Hellespont and Bosporus, and so prevent the grain convoys from the Black Sea from reaching Athens. Already the strategy was working. Dangerously well. Earlier that spring, a small force of Spartans (probably including some Milesian diplomats) had struck north from Miletus and journeyed overland, undetected by the Athenians, to the Hellespont.[25]

Their immediate goal was the city of Abydus. It was here the adolescent Alcibiades had once been educated in the arts of love. But rather more important to the Spartans was its situation: dominated by a low acropolis at a sharp bend in the Hellespont, where the already narrow channel was especially pinched, and the waters boiled with greater turbulence, the city's harbour was so well protected that it was the safest anchorage on the Hellespont's Asiatic shores. Moreover it was a colony of Miletus. It was the perfect springboard for the new campaign. And without a fight, and willingly, it capitulated. To the Spartans—and their new ally, the Persian governor of this northwest province, the satrap Farnavaz. At last, after so many months of watching his rival Chithrafarna playing politics in Ionia, the energetic Farnavaz scented action.

Just two days later, another Hellespontine city, Lampsacus, capitulated to Farnavaz and Sparta, too. The Athenians scrambled to recapture it and quickly shored up their own position in the town of Sestus on the southern shores of the Chersonese opposite Spartan-held Abydus. But already other cards were falling. A short while later, news came from Byzantium, the city that controlled the crucial access to the Bosporus and Black Sea. It, too, was offering to come over to the Spartans. And there seemed nothing the Athenians could do. Their weakness was exposed when ten Peloponnesian ships managed to sail up the Hellespont, across the placid waters of the Sea of Marmara, and on east to Byzantium, where their admiral oversaw the city's revolt from Athens. By now it was clear to everyone: the war had entered a new phase; the theatre had expanded north and east; and unless Alcibiades and the Athenians acted with all speed, the vital lifeline to the Black Sea's grain fields would be cut off.[26]

Which was why Alcibiades needed to achieve three things: to convince the still-vacillating soldiery on Samos that, faced with such an existential threat, it was really not a good idea to sail back to Athens and confront the Four Hundred; to do all he could to maintain the illusion that he had the undying support of Chithrafarna; and (in the glaring absence of this support) to scrabble together enough money to pay his men—especially as Farnavaz was making it well known that he was a much more dependable paymaster than Chithrafarna ever was, and that he would give good money to any who came over to the Spartans' side.

His first goal Alcibiades achieved at once. Not afraid to go against the democratic army's wishes, he assured them that it would be suicidal to for them to return home to confront the oligarchs just now, when the Spartans and Persians would take advantage of their absence not just to overrun Ionia but to seize the Hellespont and Bosporus, thereby achieving a victory whose terms would probably involve the removal of any prospect of Athenian democracy for years to come. It was a mark of the respect in which the army held him, and their yearning for strong leadership, that both now and a little later, when further disturbing news arrived from Athens, they allowed themselves to be persuaded. "It was," remarks Thucydides somewhat icily, "the first time he really helped his city, and it was no small thing . . . No other man would have been able to persuade the crowd, but he prevented them from sailing."[27]

Indeed, such was the passion with which the army welcomed him, their belief in his strategy, and their trust in his leadership, that they immediately elected him one of their generals. So it was in this new official role that Alcibiades set off at once—back to Magnesia and the court of Chithrafarna. Not that he can have entertained much hope that he could miraculously persuade the satrap to tear up his treaty with the Spartans and cause the Great King to support Athens. Rather, his faith was in appearances, that, with his speech at Samos ringing in their ears, the Spartans would interpret his visit to Magnesia as further proof that Chithrafarna was indeed preparing to switch sides—that it would rile them.[28]

As expected, Alcibiades made no progress in persuading Chithrafarna to support the Athenians (if he even tried at all). But as an exercise in counter-information to undermine the enemy's morale, it was a triumph. And not the only one. Already the Spartans were growing wary of both Chithrafarna and their own general Astyochus, suspecting them of double dealing. Thanks to reports, possibly deliberately spun by Alcibiades, that had been trickling out of Magnesia for some time now, they believed that Astyochus, abrasive and unpopular at the best of times, was in the pocket of the Persian, while the satrap was pursuing the policy (advocated by Alcibiades) of helping (and thereby weakening) both sides. In an assembly of the army at Miletus their anger erupted, as anger often does, over the issue of wages: Chithrafarna, they shouted, was paying them neither in full nor on time, and it was all Astyochus' fault![29]

The crews of the triremes that had sailed to Sparta's aid from Syracuse and Thurii were particularly furious. Tempers rose. Another officer, Dorieus of Rhodes, a three-time Olympic victor in the brutal pancration contest, spoke out against Astyochus. Astyochus, in fury, raised his stick to smite him, and the soldiery surged forward, a yelling mob, their rage exploding into bloodlust as they raced to seize Astyochus, who turned and ran to a nearby altar, clinging onto it in terror. Only their piety prevented them from dragging him away and killing him. At the same time, the Milesians themselves attacked the fort built by Chithrafarna near the city and expelled the Persian garrison. The mood in the Peloponnesian high command was ugly. Lichas, the grand old man of Spartan politics, more used to the hoplite's heroic code of conduct than to temperamental outbursts of a trireme's crew, was appalled at such breaches in protocol, and, when the time came for Astyochus to return to Sparta at the end of his period of command, he made sure that he sailed accompanied by a delegation of detractors, determined to bring the admiral to account.[30]

Alcibiades' strategy of causing the greatest mayhem with the greatest ease was paying off beautifully. When he returned from Magnesia to Samos, there was much with which he could congratulate himself. But there still remained the problem of the Phoenician ships. In his speech to the army on Samos, he had made such an issue of being able to co-opt the Persian fleet to Athens' cause. Of course, it was an empty promise, but, back then, that hardly seemed to matter as long as it achieved its desired effect: a warm welcome for the returning exile. Now, though, the situation was more pressing. Now, so Alcibiades had heard, Chithrafarna was about to sail south to Aspendus, a little inland from the mouth of the River Eurymedon, where the Persian fleet was stationed. And with him he was taking Lichas. When they returned, they would be bringing the fleet, 147 warships, with them. And, if those ships really did fall in on the Spartan side, then the Athenians—and, more specifically, Alcibiades himself—would be in trouble.[31]

So with a squadron of just thirteen triremes and a somewhat watered-down promise either to bring the Phoenician ships over to the Athenian side or at least prevent them from joining the Spartans, he put out from Samos—first south, then east towards Aspendus. Each morning, as he watched the dawn break over the sharp-silhouetted mountains, each evening, as the sun burned its trail of fading gold across the sea, each day, as he lay fretting in his hammock, he must have wondered how on earth he could pluck even the most tenuous success from what cannot but have seemed a well-nigh impossible situation. And yet the next time he was heard of, bowling back along the coast from the Eurymedon to Samos, he had achieved his goal. At least in part. The Phoenician fleet was reassigned. No longer was it set to join the Spartans. The threat was over.[32]

Even in Antiquity, it was unclear exactly what had happened. Some thought that, when he reached Aspendus and saw the size of the Phoenician fleet, Chithrafarna changed his mind—it simply was not big enough for the task in hand—and so he aborted his mission. Others believed that the satrap never had any intention of bringing the Phoenician ships to the aid of the Spartans. They explained his fruitless voyage by saying that he was merely stringing the Peloponnesians along in furtherance of his policy of wearing down both sides, while Alcibiades, knowing this, sailed after him merely to confuse and confound the enemy into questioning where the satrap's loyalties lay. Or even that Chithrafarna had summoned the Phoenician fleet to the Eurymedon simply to disband it.[33]

Caught up as they were in their own internecine war, none of the Greeks took the trouble to step back to view the larger picture. If they had, they would have found out that, before arriving at Aspendus, or perhaps when he was there, Chithrafarna received orders of his own. From the Great King. Uprisings in Egypt and Arabia were threatening Phoenicia. The fleet was needed there. Without delay. Saving an imperial province took priority over helping Sparta. Perhaps, given the sensitivity of the security situation, Chithrafarna failed to give Lichas and the Spartans a satisfactory reason for why the ships took off elsewhere. Perhaps Lichas failed to communicate it to the Spartan high command—he died on, or shortly after, his voyage back to Miletus. Or perhaps the Spartans, believing that the world revolved around them, and already (thanks to Alcibiades) suspecting the satrap's trustworthiness, simply did not believe him.[34]

For Alcibiades, of course, the disappearance of the threat that the Persian fleet presented was a stroke of incredible luck. Once more he had emerged unscathed from a painfully tight spot. Indeed, the fact that Chithrafarna failed to provide the Spartans with the promised ships played into his hands perfectly—as their suspicions about the Persian's motivations showed. So it was with renewed confidence that everything was going his way that Alcibiades made his leisurely return. Now he could afford to focus on the third of his concerns: raising funds to pay his soldiery and enable the army, cut off from supplies from home, to continue the war effort. So, on his way, he stopped not just at Cos to sack the city of Meropis, but at Phaselis, Caunus, and Halicarnassus to extract money from their wary citizens, before sailing into Samos with his ships weighed down with welcome booty. And before the assembly of the army, he boasted that, thanks to him, Chithrafarna was now even more well-disposed to the Athenians than before.[35]

But even in Alcibiades' brief absence, events had been moving at a pace. Two especially significant developments must have dominated the briefings he received as soon as he was back on Samian soil. The first concerned Athens, where (just as in so many fields of action at this time) Alcibiades had succeeded in wielding influence even from afar. Before sailing south, he had sent envoys to announce back home that he, too, was vehemently opposed to the Four Hundred oligarchs. The People, he said, must hold out and present a united front. He had every confidence that he could effect a reconciliation between them and the army on Samos, and defeat the Spartans. The irony of Alcibiades—a man who had so recently refused to countenance returning home unless under an oligarchy, and who had been so passionately accused just four years earlier of wanting to install himself as tyrant—now stepping forward as the leading champion of democratic Athens cannot have been lost on many. But, for the moment, his views chimed in total harmony with the prevailing opinion on the street. And they galvanized the citizenry to action.[36]

In fact, even among the Four Hundred, there had been growing disquiet about the course on which the oligarchy appeared increasingly to be set. It was not just that some of the most extreme hardliners, unhappy to share power even with their colleagues, were so clearly striving for supreme command. Moderates such as Theramenes were troubled by the schism between the government in Athens and the army in Samos, especially since the charismatic Alcibiades was now establishing such a power base of his own with the Athenians in the east. They were worried, too, that the more radical among them were more than capable of negotiating a surrender to the Spartans on terms that would be unacceptable to the majority—and that, if this happened, it could lead to civil war.[37]

Already, King Agis had advanced as far as Athens' walls in the expectation that the gates would be opened, only to find himself opposed—despite the power of the Four Hundred—by a determined phalanx of Athenian cavalry, hoplites, archers, and light-armed skirmishers, who drove him back to Decelea. So it was likely that, even if a peace treaty were signed, Athens would be ungovernable without the use of overwhelming force. Not only that—the army currently on Samos would sail back home to try to liberate the city. Better, it was thought, for the regime to end even if the fiscal policies that they had put in place must not. Better that the government be placed into the hands of the Five Thousand, the wealthier segment of the populace made up of merchants, businessmen, and landowners, a limited democracy, but one which (unlike the Four Hundred) would be constrained by checks and balances.[38]

The moderates were inspired by the message of support from Alcibiades. But motivating them still more was a sudden flurry of building work down at the main port of Piraeus, a strengthening of fortifications at the harbour mouth in such a way that they could be held by just a small force. To Theramenes and the moderates, it suggested only one thing: that the oligarchic extremists meant to seize the entrance to Piraeus and allow the Spartan navy in. The fact that forty-two enemy triremes were already massing down near Gytheum, no doubt for a voyage north, simply increased their fears. And when a diplomatic mission, charged with discussing terms, returned from Sparta, passions boiled over.[39]

As he was leaving the Council Chamber, one of its number was attacked in the Agora and bled to death where he collapsed. The crowd which formed around the dying man had no need to be told of his identity. He was Phrynichus—the enemy of Alcibiades; the general who had so lately been recalled from Samos; the suspected turncoat who had conducted bizarre correspondence with the Spartan admiral. What deals had he and his cronies concluded in Sparta? Had they betrayed their city?[40]

By now, the Spartan fleet was drawing nearer. From its new anchorage at Epidaurus, it made a sortie, sailing around Aegina within full view of Athens—surely the prelude to its bid to take Piraeus. The oligarchic moderates and their more democratic allies could afford to wait no longer. The hoplites assigned to reinforce the harbour walls bundled their overseer into custody. Immediately word shot up to Athens and the Council Chamber. Mayhem. The hardliners accused Theramenes and his followers of treachery. Together, the Four Hundred rushed down to the sea. On both sides tempers boiled. Bloodshed was only just avoided. Theramenes voiced his support for the rebellious hoplites. And amid the noisy chanting of slogans, the crowd rushed to the new walls and helped dismantle them.[41]

For the Four Hundred it was the beginning of the end. The situation was compounded first when the Spartan fleet sailed unopposed past the mouth of Piraeus harbour on its way to Euboea, and then when a force of thirty-six Athenian triremes was defeated as it tried to defend that island. But when Euboea—whose pastures were a vital source of Athens' food supplies—capitulated to the Spartans (a disaster that, according to Thucydides, the Athenians ranked higher than even the Sicilian debacle), Athens' citizens panicked. They poured en masse onto the Pnyx, the trampled earth still warm in the September heat, and voted to overthrow the Four Hundred. In its place, they established the more inclusive regime of the Five Thousand, though the true number of those who now attended the Assembly (essentially anyone who could afford to pay for his own armour) may well have been somewhat larger.[42]

While hard-line oligarchs fled for their lives, even their memory was reviled by their now-jubilant successors. Especially harsh treatment was accorded to the enemies of Alcibiades. The poet Sophocles laid charges against Pisander *in absentia,* but an even more outré fate befell the murdered Phrynichus. One of the first acts of the new Assembly was to pass a decree bringing him to trial posthumously. When he was found guilty, his bones were exhumed and ceremonially removed from Attica. As if that were not enough, his property was confiscated, his house destroyed, and a bronze *stele* was set up to proclaim his crimes.[43]

It was probably no coincidence that the man who proposed the decree that damned the memory of Phrynichus was an old associate of Alcibiades. Critias had been his friend since boyhood. As adolescents, they had both been ardent followers of Socrates, turning up together to hear him debate with Gorgias. As adults, both had been implicated in the mutilation of the Herms, although after anxious weeks spent in the city's squalid jailhouse, Critias was exonerated of involvement and set free. Indeed, until now, the deeply intellectual, profoundly aristocratic pro-Spartan Critias had steered clear of politics, preferring instead to turn his hand to literature, pouring out not just a torrent of elegiac poetry but well-crafted (if controversial) dramas. In them, he questioned the existence of the gods: when human beings began to sin in secret, one suggested, "some clever man invented fear of gods in order to sow terror in the hearts of wicked men . . . And so he came up with religion."[44]

Now, though, in the joyful aftermath of the Four Hundred's demise, Critias at last felt ready to engage in politics. Formed primarily from the hoplite class, the new Assembly of the Five Thousand was eager to normalize relations with the fleet in Samos. One clear way to achieve this was to confirm in post the generals whom the fleet had appointed the previous winter. Who, of course, included Alcibiades. But for Critias and other leading politicians, this was not enough. For them, it was important to draw a line under the events of the previous four years and start afresh. So it was crucial that they should both grant an absolute pardon and officially recall those exiled in the febrile aftermath of the destruction of the Herms and the desecration of the Mysteries.[45]

In later years, some said it was Theramenes who proposed the motion for the exile's exculpation. But Critias was adamant that he was the bill's author. Indeed, to celebrate his role, he dashed off an elegiac poem, which he addressed to Alcibiades, declaring:

> I it was proposed the resolution for your homecoming before the
>   full Assembly,
> and thanks to me they wrote it into law. Now my tongue seals the
>   deed![46]

For Alcibiades, back on Samos, it was delicious news. Yet, any celebrations were short lived. The second development of which Alcibiades learned on his return to the island was much less welcome. For some time, the Spartans had been tired of dancing attendance on Chithrafarna's every whim. The non-appearance of the Phoenician fleet had been the final straw. So Mindarus, their newly arrived commander, announced a change of plan. From now on, the Spartans would throw in their lot with Farnavaz, the satrap of Hellespontine Phrygia. He had already proved himself to be a good paymaster and reliable ally to the small Spartan force which occupied Abydus. He certainly could not be worse than Chithrafarna! The season, too, was ripe. Within weeks, the convoys of grain ships were due to pass through the Hellespont *en route* from the Black Sea to Athens. Intercept them, and Mindarus would strike his enemy a deadly blow.

So, in a brilliantly executed operation, while the Athenians were occupied in besieging Eresus on the west coast of Lesbos, Mindarus had led his ships in a bold dash north, passing undetected to the east of the island, sailing, even as the light was fading, past the coast near Troy, where the grave-mound of Achilles squatted dark on the horizon, before reaching the mouth of the Hellespont. The Athenian ships at Sestus had scattered in terror, but, when their main fleet arrived soon after, they had regrouped and, although still numerically inferior, defeated Sparta's triremes, where the swirling waters of the Hellespont narrowed at Cynossema. It was the first real naval engagement of this new phase of the war, and news of the victory was met with huge relief at Athens.[47]

But the threat remained. The grain ships were on their way. It was essential that the Hellespont be kept open. Swift messages were sent out, summoning as many Athenian ships as could be safely spared from other duties to sail at once to Sestus. When he heard the pressing news, Alcibiades at once launched eighteen triremes from their base at Samos, and, slicing through the rolling swell, he raced towards the Hellespont. He knew that time was of the essence. In their urgent desire to control the straits, both the Athenians and Spartans would seize whatever chance they could to lure the other side to battle. He might already be too late.[48]

10

RULING THE WAVES

In war, each side makes plans to destroy the other, but only rarely do they know how these plans will turn out.

Xenophon, *How to be a Good Cavalry Commander*, 9.8

CACOPHONY. The thump of oars as they smacked into the sea—a hundred and seventy long blades for each trireme, dipping and rising with the hiss of foam in unison. The groan of timber as the slender ships, their black hulls caulked in pine pitch, straining to the very limit, shot through the racing waves. The throaty rasping of the trumpets. The muffled chanting of the oarsmen—*Rhuppapai! Rhuppapai! Rhuppapai!*—as they bent and pulled like sweating, rank automata, increasing their momentum up from thirty strokes to forty strokes a minute and above, until they were careering at a speed of ten knots, straight for the side of an enemy vessel. Their aim: to crash into it. Deliberately. With their bronze-clad ram to punch a hole into its hull beneath the water, not so that it would sink (their design meant that triremes rarely, if ever, sank) but so that, waterlogged, wallowing, and heavy, it became unmanoeuvrable, its sailors a sitting target, their only hope of safety to jump overboard and swim for land, hoping that the men lined up along the shoreline were their friends, not vengeful enemies.[1]

It was for this moment that the trireme was devised, and its crew was trained to peak performance. Protected by a screen to fend off javelins and arrows, their backs to the prow and the direction of travel, not even those on the topmost of the ship's three rows of benches had much inkling how the battle was progressing. Those below them had no idea at all. Instead, they must put their trust in their captain and helmsman, blindly obeying orders, trying to shut out the stench and fear, bracing themselves for the impact as they smashed into the enemy, aware that, at any moment, a hostile trireme's ram could rip through their own hull: fifty tons of cruel destruction, exploding in sharp splinters and a churning rush of sea.

The trireme was a prototype torpedo, a streamlined weapon painstakingly designed to inflict the deadliest damage. One hundred and twenty feet in length, twenty feet wide, and with a draft of just over three feet, it was an artful construction of well-chosen timber—oak and pine, fir and ash, mulberry and elm, each chosen for its strength or flexibility, all cut, and trimmed, and planed, and hammered into place with wooden dowels, the whole construction bound together with huge girding cables stretched taut from stern to prow, to give structural integrity and stop the ship from warping. It was an elegant vessel. Its sternpost, below which the helmsman stood, curved back upon itself like a graceful, fanning tail, while, beneath a

Sleek and deadly, the *Olympias,* a modern replica of a trireme, undergoes sea trials. (George Atsametakis/Alamy Stock Photo.)

golden figurehead, the prow was decorated with two eyes carved from thin sheets of marble, their irises picked out in bright red ochre. And jutting from the hull: the rowing frame, the outrigger, which enabled the levels of the rowing benches to be staggered, one below the other, allowing the employment of the three banks of oars from which the ship was named. To an onlooker, it brought to mind a gorgeous hybrid creature, part dolphin and part bird, its dipping, rising oars like beating wings as it skimmed the water. But its beak was deadly, a three-pronged ram, a bronze sheath, which protruded, greedy, from the prow below the waterline, hungry for hostile blood.

A naval battle called for nerves of steel, strict discipline, experience, split-second timing—and good weather. A three-foot wave could swamp a trireme, rendering it useless. So most encounters took place in calm waters near the shore. Here, the manoeuvres so beloved by admirals and trireme captains could be exploited to the full. At their core was the imperative to ram the enemy ship broadsides, a tactic that involved not only slamming into it at full speed, but—immediately after impact—backing oars, and breaking free as fast as possible before becoming fatally entangled with the stricken ship. To facilitate this, every rower must pull as one or else oars would foul, rhythms would be lost, and the floundering vessel would soon find that it was easy prey. In open waters, fleets would try to outflank one another or smash through enemy formations and quickly arc around to attack them from the rear.

But in the narrow straits and fast-flowing currents of the Hellespont, tactics such as these could not be used. Instead, ships' captains must employ these unfamiliar conditions to their best advantage: thanks to the speed at which the water flowed, an extra three knots could be added to the velocity of an attack, if made downstream. But the swirling eddies were treacherous, and hidden rocks were lethal. An encounter in these straits was unpredictable. Yet for the Athenians, desperate to keep supply lines open, failure to engage the enemy was not an option.

Early one morning, at the beginning of November 411, fourteen Spartan triremes on course for their naval base at Abydus prepared to sail into the Hellespont. When they heard the news, Thrasybulus and Thrasyllus, the Athenian generals at Sestus, immediately launched twenty triremes of their own and bore down on the approaching squadron. For the Spartans' captain, Dorieus, to fight would have been suicidal. Instead, he beached his ships at Rhoeteum, near the grave-mound of the hero, Ajax, where purple hyacinths flowered in spring, and waited for the Athenians to attack.[2]

But instead, Thrasybulus and Thrasyllus backed water, and Dorieus pushed out from land to continue on his voyage upstream. However, he had not gone far before the Athenians were back, in full force, with a fleet of seventy-four ships. Again the Spartans sought the safety of the shore. This time at Dardanus. But now, despite the local Spartan garrison running to their sailors' aid, the Athenians felt confident of victory. Steering their triremes as close to shore as possible, some shot off volleys of arrows from the decks, while others, armed for a land battle, waded through the waters under hostile fire and engaged the enemy.

But by now the Spartan admiral Mindarus had learned of the engagement. Fresh from making sacrifice to ancestral ghosts at nearby Troy, he sailed south from Abydus with the entire Spartan fleet: eighty-four triremes, which, together with the fourteen ships of Dorieus, seriously outnumbered the Athenians. At the same time, the Persian satrap, Farnavaz, mobilized his army and marched on Dardanus. Suddenly the tables had been dangerously turned. Those Athenians on land splashed back to their ships, and the triremes wheeled east to face the enemy.[3]

For a moment, both sides maintained position, their vessels well spaced, dead in the water, their oarsmen mentally preparing for the clash to come. And then the trumpets sounded, and the orders to advance. As the vessels picked up speed, up on the narrow decks the well-trained archers launched their first salvos, while a knot of hoplites waited for the moment they might leap onto a stricken enemy trireme and slice a swathe of blood through the rowing benches.[4]

The stakes could not have been higher. Defeat the Athenians, destroy their fleet, and the Spartans would win the war. For, without her ships, Athens was nothing. Without their grain supply, her citizens would starve. Only a few years earlier, it would have been so easy for an experienced Athenian crew to outmanoeuvre any Spartan ship. But the best oarsmen had died in Sicily. These rowers in the Hellespont had been together only a few years, in which time they had won just a single victory. The Spartans, on the other hand, had made great progress as a naval power. And they had with them Syracusans, old sea dogs who had trounced Athens' navy in their own Great Harbour and caused it the greatest ignominy it had ever known.[5]

As helmsmen watched for the right moment, calculating the best angle for a fatal ramming, keeping one eye open for an unforeseen attack, triremes danced their intricate manoeuvres all the way from Dardanus to Sestus. The afternoon wore on. Dogfights became desperate. But neither side was making any inroad.

And then, at last, the unexpected. Even as the light began to fail, eighteen ships hove into view. Approaching upstream. Past Rhoeteum. With no way to distinguish them, neither side knew whose ships they were. But both renewed their efforts. This fresh squadron could turn the battle! Ploughing their hissing furrows through the roiling waves, the whites of their marble eyes glaring in the gathering gloom, the water dripping from their threshing oars, the triremes came ever closer. Still no clue of their identity. And then a purple flag was hoisted, and they knew. Alcibiades was sailing to the aid of the Athenians.[6]

The Spartan ships wheeled round and fled. Against a strong headwind they rowed with all speed for Abydus. But their ships were so spread out that many could not make it. With the waters increasingly storm-tossed, captains were forced to beach their ships and use their hulls as barricades against the oncoming Athenians. Fierce fighting raged along the shore. And then the Persians swung into action, racing to the aid of their Spartan allies. In the thick of the mêlée, Farnavaz himself was seen in the descending twilight—tall, bearded, even now distinguished by his elegance—spurring on his horse, splashing out into the turbid waters as far as he could go, slashing with his sword, keeping the Athenians from the Spartan ships.[7]

Night brought an end to operations. Alcibiades had tipped the balance. The Athenians had won. Triumphantly they sailed to Sestus, knowing that, with winter setting in, there would be no more fighting. The Hellespont was safe. And Athens was secure. For now.[8]

But it was no time for inaction. Despite their victory, the Athenians were in serious difficulties. Quite simply, there was no longer any money in the treasury to pay the soldiery. Added to which, although the Hellespont was now the main focus of the war, Ionia and the other areas of empire on which Athens relied for revenue were far from secure. Moreover, Attica itself was under threat on all sides. For now, though, raising cash and keeping sea lanes open must take precedence. So, while Alcibiades remained in Sestus to guard the Hellespont and oversee the strengthening of Athens' naval base, his colleagues toured the north Aegean, cultivating friends, such as the newly installed King Archelaus of Macedon, and pillaging enemies, to negotiate, extort, or simply steal as much money as they could lay their hands on.[9]

They were still absent when news reached Alcibiades that Chithrafarna had come north for an important summit with his colleague, Farnavaz. With the Athenians still convinced that Alcibiades and Chithrafarna were good friends—indeed, remembering that Alcibiades had reassured them only months before that he was on better terms than ever with the Persian satrap—this seemed a golden opportunity. Surely Alcibiades needed only one short meeting with his friend to persuade him, and their financial troubles would be ended. Knowing his rivalry with Farnavaz, Chithrafarna must be longing for an opportunity to do him down by helping the Athenians.[10]

Alcibiades, of course, knew otherwise. But there was nothing he could do. So, his bluff well and truly called, but dressing to impress, he decked out a trireme, assembled an imposing retinue, scraped together a dazzling array of gifts, and set out to see the satrap. The location of their meeting may have been Dascyleum, where Farnavaz's luxurious palace lolled on a low hill by the shores of a teeming lake just south of the Sea of Marmara. Its setting was lush, delightful, loud with birdsong; its population drawn from every corner of the Persian Empire; its bold architecture influenced by that of Greece; its shrines and temples fragrant with rich offerings to the gods of Persia and Babylon, Greece, Lydia, and Phrygia; its most venerated rituals presided over by the long-robed magi.[11]

If Alcibiades found their meeting awkward, Chithrafarna was doubly embarrassed. Officially, the Persians supported Sparta and were at war with Athens, yet Chithrafarna had sworn friendship with the Athenian Alcibiades. He had received Athenian ambassadors for negotiations at his palace in Magnesia. He had been accused of following Alcibiades' advice of wearing down both sides, while truly helping neither. He had failed to pay the Spartan soldiery in full on time. And questions were still being asked why, during his visit to Aspendus, the Phoenician fleet had been stood down. Aware that all this was undermining his standing in the eyes of both his allies and the Great King, Chithrafarna could not afford to be wrong-footed again now, especially when the intricacies of any private conversation he might have with Alcibiades might be overheard, reported (or misrepresented) to his rival, Farnavaz, and from him find their way unerringly to the Imperial Court.

So—to avoid any doubt—no sooner had Alcibiades come into Chithrafarna's presence than the Persian ordered his bodyguard to seize him and arrest him. As they bustled him away through the long, dark corridors, Alcibiades cannot but have wondered if they were leading him to execution. What better way for Chithrafarna to prove his loyalty to the Great King, to show his full commitment to the Persians' policy, than to hand Alcibiades over to the Spartans? It was no secret that there was an order out to kill him. For almost a year, Chithrafarna had been shielding him. Had that protection come to an abrupt and fatal end?[12]

Yet, rather than be faced with the assassin's knife, Alcibiades was taken outside, bundled, chained, into a wagon, and transported under armed guard across well-watered plains and grassy pastureland by the banks of tumbling streams. A hundred and fifty miles. A journey of long days and sleepless nights. A journey south, to Sardis, where he had been feted so extravagantly just a year before. What happened there is mired in mystery. But less than a month later, Alcibiades was galloping beneath the stars along the white road west towards Clazomenae, and a boat, which took him round the louring headland and across the sea to Lesbos.[13]

The story that he wove was tortuous: that Chithrafarna was reluctant to arrest him; that it was all for show; and that, in Sardis, the satrap, prostrated with shame and abject with apologies, had allowed him to escape. Perhaps that was the truth. It certainly served Alcibiades well. And undermined Chithrafarna. Perhaps Alcibiades did possess some nugget of salacious information, with which he could blackmail the satrap. Or perhaps he simply escaped. But by now, even on Lesbos, where he stayed to overwinter, any hope that Alcibiades could bring Chithrafarna over to the Athenian side had vanished.[14]

Winter, with its high seas and its icy winds blowing down from Thrace, was a time for sailors to hunker down in front of crackling fires, make any repairs necessary to ships, and plan for the future. For both Athenians and Spartans, it was becoming clearer by the day that control of the Hellespont and Bosporus was crucial to the outcome of the war. Crucial, too, for the Athenians were the preservation of the fleet and the continued accumulation of sufficient cash to pay the troops.

As a result, when the generals at Sestus heard that Mindarus was preparing to attack them, they were worried. More than half of their ships, and many of their men, were out of port on fundraising missions. Those that remained, outnumbered more than two to one, were dangerously exposed. It seemed they had just one option: to evacuate Sestus, make contact with the rest of the Athenian fleet, and once more engage the Spartans in a sea battle.

So, even before the onset of the settled days of spring, 410, Alcibiades was summoned north from Lesbos to join the fleet at Cardia on the north coast of the Thracian Chersonese—a city outside the Hellespont and less open to attack. Among those joining him were his staunch allies, Thrasybulus and Theramenes, the leader of the opposition to the Four Hundred oligarchs the previous summer.[15]

But when, at last, the ships were gathered, news came that the Athenians had been duped. The Spartan admiral, Mindarus, had sailed not to Sestus, but east to Cyzicus. Surrounded by salt marshes on a promontory leading to a hilly wooded isthmus, this island city on the southern shores of the Sea of Marmara had briefly rebelled from Athens only months earlier before returning to the fold. Its capture now would mark the start of Sparta's expansion east towards Byzantium, and enable Persia to regain part of her north coast. So, as Mindarus sailed from the west, Farnavaz had brought his army overland from Dascyleum, just thirty miles to the south. And together they had taken Cyzicus. At any time this would have been a blow. At the start of the campaigning season, it seemed the direst omen for the year ahead. The Athenians must respond. They must win back the city.[16]

So, while Alcibiades hastened overland to Sestus, the fleet sailed out to the southern tip of the Chersonese and waited for the night. Then, in the darkness, their oars muffled, their crews silent, the pitch-black triremes nosed into the Hellespont. Thirty-eight miles they had to row, straining against the current—determined to evade the lookouts at Abydus and the other Spartan strongholds strung out along the southern shore—but at last, after Sestus, where they picked up Alcibiades and the forces he had mustered there, the narrow channel widened, and they emerged into the Sea of Marmara. A final call on their dying reserves of energy, and, as day broke overcast and drizzling, the oarsmen brought their ships to safety on the island of Proconnesus, where, exhausted, they made landfall and settled down to sleep, secure in the knowledge that they had managed to elude the Spartans. For not only had they not been seen from shore, they had seized all the small boats they had encountered and made them sail with them. And, when they reached Proconnesus, they issued a grim warning: anyone caught trying to cross the sea to Cyzicus with news would be put to death.[17]

A day of rest, and before the next dawn they were wakened early. The weather had turned ugly. Thick cloud and driving rain made the sea rough and choppy. Normally, it would not have been a day for sailing. But for the Athenians, it was perfect. Struggling to be heard, his words snatched away by the lashing wind, Alcibiades addressed the rank and file: to win now was essential; the Spartans could rely on the Great King for money and support; the Athenians had no one but themselves; so they must fight at sea; and they must fight on land; and they must scale the very city walls; and they must be victorious![18]

With these brave words ringing in their ears, the oarsmen and marines filed onto the triremes, and soon they were pitching across the open sea towards the southern shore. The generals had formulated an audacious plan. While half the ships headed for the lee of a low promontory north of Cyzicus, where they disembarked a crack force of hoplites, Alcibiades, with forty triremes, curved round towards the city's western harbour. Visibility was so dreadful that, even if the Spartan watchmen were not huddling inside their huts for shelter from the icy rain, there was little danger of being seen.[19]

Then, as the Athenian ships drew near the harbour, the sun broke through the clouds. It was such perfect timing. The Spartans saw them. Thinking that they had become detached from the main fleet in bad weather, Mindarus at once gave the order to embark, and soon eighty Spartan ships were pursuing Alcibiades out into open water. The trap was sprung. When they saw what was happening, Theramenes and Thrasybulus shot out with their ships from behind the headland, one south, the other west, to join Alcibiades in encircling the Spartans.

But they were too late! When Mindarus realized what was happening, he slewed his ships around and pressed with all haste for the shoreline, where Farnavaz and his Persians were encamped. Close behind was Alcibiades, ramming some stragglers, seizing others, until all the ships were crowded in the shallow waters. The Spartans leapt out and tried frantically to draw their triremes up onto the narrow beach while, from Athenian ships, amid a dark deluge of arrows, grappling hooks arced through the air. When they connected with a Spartan stern, Athens' oarsmen strained to drag the enemy ship out to sea. Meanwhile, Alcibiades and his marines dropped from their triremes into the chill sea, advancing up towards the beach, where a line of Spartan hoplites stood, the Persians beside them.

Heavily outnumbered, they would have been overwhelmed, had Thrasybulus not sailed to the rescue, leading his own marines against the Spartan flank and—for a moment—drawing their fire. But, faced with the Persians and Spartans, even with these new reinforcements, the Athenians could not last long. And then, the moment they had hoped for: the trumpet calls proclaiming that not just Theramenes and his marines, but the hoplites who had earlier been disembarked on the headland had arrived and were engaging, too. Squeezed between two desperate Athenian detachments, Mindarus urged his men to superhuman feats of daring and advanced on Alcibiades, who was threatening his left flank. The fighting was savage. Desperate. Interminable. Until a sword flash, an eruption of blood, and Mindarus fell, choking his life out on the scrubby beach. When they saw it, the Spartans suddenly lost heart. They turned and ran, with the Athenians close on their heels, until Farnavaz and his cavalry prevented the pursuers from going further.

It was already clear, though, that the enemy was broken. So clear, indeed, that the Athenians could saunter back to the seashore, where the lapping waves were streaked with blood, and calmly sail back to spend the night relaxing on nearby Proconnesus. They knew what they would find next morning. And they did: the gates of Cyzicus wide open; no Persian or Spartan left; and on the beach a chaotic clutter of abandoned triremes. Only the Spartans' Syracusan allies had thought to deprive the victors of their ships. That night, they had stolen back, filled the wet hulls with inflammable material, and torched them.[20]

As for the rest, the Athenians took great satisfaction in sawing off the prows, with their figureheads and rams, to keep in their headquarters buildings as welcome souvenirs, while—as was also customary—to commemorate their victories at land and sea, they set up trophies, tree stumps adorned with armour captured from the enemy and installed at the very place where the battle had turned to their advantage. (In Greek, *trepein* or *tropein* means "to turn.") They took great satisfaction, too, in stripping the city of its fantastic wealth, which would guarantee them pay for months to come. But perhaps their greatest satisfaction came when an Athenian patrol intercepted a communiqué to Sparta from the Spartan camp. It was laconic in the extreme. Just eleven words long, it read: "Ships lost. Mindarus dead. Men starving. Don't know what to do."[21]

That last detail was so delicious. At a stroke, in one engagement, the Athenians seemed to have turned the tide, to have reasserted their control. The mood back in the city was one of jubilation: lavish sacrifices on the Acropolis and at the city's other temples; celebrations long into the night. At Sparta, on the other hand, the mood was grim. Before long, their negotiators were riding north across the isthmus into Attica to sue for peace. Leading them was Endius, hoping, no doubt, that this time he would be more successful than he had been ten years earlier, when, before a packed Assembly, his *xenos,* Alcibiades, exposed the weakness of Sparta's negotiating stance.[22]

Now, in a short but punchy speech, Endius set out the Spartans' terms: an immediate end to fighting; a prisoner exchange; the abandoning of occupied positions in each other's homelands (the Athenian fort at Pylos in Messenia, which had never been returned; the Spartan fort at Decelea); and, as far as other territories were concerned, an acceptance of the situation as it currently stood. War, he continued, was in no one's interests, but least of all in the Athenians'. Thanks to their agreement with the Great King, the Spartans had no financial worries; the Athenians, on the other hand, were economically hard-pressed. And besides, if her fleet were seriously defeated only once, Athens' grain supply from the Black Sea would be cut off. Better to end the suffering on both sides now, before the situation became any worse.[23]

Less than a year before, Athenian ambassadors, albeit creatures of the Four Hundred, had done everything they could to end the war. Since then, despite their recent victories, little had really changed. Dejected by defeat in Sicily, worn down by the defections of her subject states, increasingly hemmed in on all sides by her enemies, politically unstable, and in financial meltdown—surely Athens would accept the Spartans' terms. Especially since they were delivered by Endius, *xenos* and ally of Alcibiades, the hero of the hour. For although Athens owed her recent victories chiefly to the brilliance of Thrasybulus, it was (as ever) Alcibiades who stole the limelight. It was he who was lauded as the conquering hero. But, if such were the Spartans' calculations, they were badly flawed. The Athenians' backs were to the wall, yes, but this merely made them all the more determined. Besides, since the overthrow of the Four Hundred and the return of Alcibiades, the war seemed to be taking a new turn. Now was not the time to throw away everything they had been fighting for.[24]

Many Athenians, not least those members of the still-ruling Five Thousand with oligarchic leanings, were ready to embrace the Spartans' terms. Still more, however, patriotic democrats, adamant that temporary setbacks should not mean surrendering the fruits of a century of sacrifice, found them entirely unacceptable. Not only would they mean abandoning vast swathes of territory in Ionia and the Aegean islands, they would enable Sparta to retain and strengthen the key cities of Byzantium on the Bosporus and Abydus on the Hellespont, from which to threaten Athens' grain supply, should war flare up again.[25]

Why trust Sparta anyway? Even by negotiating with Athens, the Spartans were flouting the terms of their peace treaty with the Great King. And, as for that treaty, the Spartans had shown themselves more than willing, when it suited them, to concede Athens' Ionian territories to the Persians. No, the Spartans could not be trusted; the terms that they were offering were flawed; and they must be rejected. Besides, even if the Five Thousand were to accept them, the fleet had already shown (when it was based on Samos) that it would not meekly go along with anything it considered unacceptable. So, Endius and his colleagues returned to Sparta empty-handed.[26]

A few months later, in a well-ordered, peaceful transition, the rule of the Five Thousand came to an end, and the return of democracy to Athens was underpinned by solemn oaths made by each citizen never again to allow the constitution to be overthrown. Indeed, the character of this new democracy was, if possible, more radical than anything before. Not only were citizens once more paid to hold the offices they were assigned by lot, but now the very poor were granted a daily allowance, a handout to ensure they did not starve. An awareness of the need for reconciliation with the fleet in the Hellespont played an important part in the reaffirmation of the city's democratic character. But the bullish atmosphere in Athens had much to do with it as well. Whether grounded in reality or built on wishful thinking, a new spirit of optimism gripped the city. It was time to regroup and renew.[27]

Legal specialists were tasked with editing and publishing the ancient law codes of Draco and Solon that underpinned Athenian society and justice, while, on the Acropolis, building work—begun when the Peace of Nicias was signed but subsequently abandoned—was resumed on the Temple of Athene Polias ("Athene Who Protects the City"), a sprawling complex incorporating a number of smaller sanctuaries and housing the holiest of all the city's statues of Athene. At the same time, around the jewel-like Temple of Athene Nike ("Athene of Victory"), a balustrade was built, adorned with exquisite sculptures of winged victories leading bulls to sacrifice. The message could not have been clearer. After years of political and spiritual upheaval, which had seen the desecration of the city's Herms, the scandal of the Mysteries, a reign of terror, and the imposition of an oligarchy, democracy had been restored and, with it, those traditional values of religion and law which for a hundred years had made the city great.[28]

But still, to survive and fight (and pay not just her office bearers but now her urban poor), Athens and her navy needed money, while, well-funded but with their fleet destroyed, the Spartans needed ships. And so there was effectively a stalemate. For the rest of 410 and much of 409, in both mainland Gytheum and the Troad's dockyards of Antandrus, Spartan carpenters sawed, shaped, and planed, then hammered into place the wooden planks which formed the shells of warships. Still other shipwrights lowered in the sturdy ribs and fitted outriggers; others looped and tightened the thick girding cables, 300 feet in length, 250 pounds in weight, while women wove linen into sails, blacksmiths cast rams, great bales of rope—papyrus, hemp, and linen—arrived on quaysides for the rigging before, at last, the air thick with the heavy scent of pitch, the hulls were caulked, and the triremes made seaworthy.[29]

Meanwhile, the Athenians were busy, too. When it came to raising cash, Alcibiades knew what must be done. His experience in his twenties serving on the commission to reassess the tribute list had taught him much, and—despite the profligacy of his private life—he could be shrewd in his handling of the public purse. Among his first actions, after stripping Cyzicus of all its wealth, was to sail with Theramenes east along the northern shores of the Sea of Marmara, putting in at two cities, Perinthus and Selymbria, to extort money on the way, before reaching friendly Chrysopolis ("The Golden City") on the southern shores of the Bosporus, opposite Byzantium.[30]

His reasons for choosing Chrysopolis for his eastern base were twofold. First, with Byzantium in Spartan hands, Athens must increase her presence in the area if the vital Bosporus were not to fall to the enemy. Second, and equally important, controlling both the channel and Chrysopolis would enable the Athenians to make money. For, as well as fortifying the city, Alcibiades, the canny tax collector, established a customs house and imposed a 10 percent tariff on any merchant shipping sailing through the Bosporus.[31]

Not that Alcibiades himself remained in Chrysopolis. Arch-strategist and compelling negotiator as he was, he well appreciated the necessity of bringing on side as many interested parties as he could. Although many of his movements for this year of 409 are not recorded, there are good reasons to suppose that he was not just actively bolstering relationships with Greek cities on the northern shoreline of the Hellespont and Sea of Marmara but pursuing alliances with the leaders of the powerful northern kingdoms which extended far inland—kingdoms of immense wealth and even more immense potential, kingdoms that had already shown their willingness to support Athens in the past, the kingdoms of Thrace. Here was a potential ally almost as rich as Persia. If Alcibiades could bring Thrace into the war—even if he could persuade the Thracians only to help fund the Athenian war effort—it would significantly bolster the chance of victory. It may be that he already had Thracian connections he could draw on. But even without these, his personal charisma and persuasive tongue were powerful weapons in his charm offensive to entice the local Thracian warlords.[32]

From now on, Alcibiades moved tirelessly across those vaguely demarcated hinterlands, where the territories of Greek colonies leached into Thrace. Deals were sealed and promises sworn, personal relationships forged, and oaths of loyalty extracted. Soon he could boast not just a considerable Thracian army, bound to him personally in allegiance, with which he could augment the land forces of Athens, but a chain of strongholds and fortified farmhouses threading the northern Hellespont, personal gifts from Thracian princelings seduced by his charisma, and eager to exploit the influence he promised on the Athenian stage.[33]

Meanwhile, despite the lull in fighting, all was not peaceful. A series of reports—some bleak, some encouraging—reached the Hellespont. Thanks to a storm, and the incompetence of their general, Anytus (whose tableware the youthful Alcibiades had once so spectacularly purloined), the Athenians had lost their valuable forward base at Pylos; elsewhere, Nisaea, the port of Megara, which they had held for fifteen years, was back in enemy hands; her erstwhile ally off the northwest coast of Greece, Corcyra, had declared neutrality; and the agriculturally vital island of Euboea was entirely lost.[34]

On the other hand, the Spartans had suffered a considerable setback, too: she could no longer draw on the support of Sicily. The island was experiencing problems of its own. Still determined to destroy Selinus, Segesta, that faithless city, which had helped lure Athens into her ill-fated expedition, had sought another ally: Carthage. And now, bent on conquest, the Carthaginians were ravaging the south of Sicily. So, the Syracusans could no longer lend their fleet to Sparta—it was desperately required at home.[35]

And then: more news. Thrasyllus, with a squadron of Athenian ships, had sailed out from Piraeus. Although his ultimate goal was the Hellespont, he had been tasked with conducting a mission to Ionia *en route,* where he was not only to accumulate as much booty as he could, but to bring as many rebel cities back into the fold as possible. But he was singularly unsuccessful. Although he managed to take Colophon, perched on a hillside high above the Gulf of Smyrna, when he struck inland to Lydia to raid and pillage, his army was attacked and scattered. Already he had lost momentum. Which was fatal, since he had not yet even tried to tackle his main goal of reclaiming the wealthy trading port of Ephesus. A two pronged attack, which in theory should have led to victory, met fierce resistance not just from the Ephesians, but from the Persian army, led with great energy by Chithrafarna. Four hundred of Thrasyllus' one thousand hoplites were cut down as the Athenians turned tail, clambered into their triremes, and fled north to Lesbos.[36]

Here they encountered the Syracusan fleet as it raced back home to face the Carthaginians. A brief sea battle saw Thrasyllus' ships victorious. He took four Syracusan vessels with their crews, whom he sent back to Piraeus. They were imprisoned—in an act of well-judged retribution—in the local stone quarries. (Unlike the Athenian prisoners at Syracuse, however, they managed to dig their way to freedom and escaped to Decelea.) On board one of the four ships, Thrasyllus found Alcibiades' cousin. Alone of all the rest, Thrasyllus set him free.[37]

When they reached the Hellespont, now in the grip of winter, Thrasyllus and his men received a frosty welcome. The veterans of the victories at Cyzicus, Abydus, and the other battles of the year before were far from happy about having to associate with losers. For the generals, the black mood of resentment in the camp was worrying. An attempt to remedy the situation by having the men work together on further fortifying the town of Lampsacus was unsuccessful. Only in battle did it seem that they would pull together. And even this was uncertain.[38]

So it was something of a gamble when Alcibiades led them out, old hands and new arrivals, infantry and cavalry, and, while Thrasyllus sailed on ahead down-current through the Hellespont, marched out across the chilly bluffs south to Abydus, Sparta's headquarters in the Hellespont—a prize of infinite worth. For the Athenians to take the city would constitute a major victory and boost morale enormously.[39]

Thrasyllus arrived first and disembarked his troops. But—almost immediately—the dull thud of a thousand hooves on the hard earth, and the Persian cavalry were thundering across the fields towards them, with the dashing Farnavaz conspicuous at their head. Thrasyllus' men formed up in battle line, their round shields interlocked in front of them, their spear points bristling. While, behind the cavalry, the Persian infantry, too, fell into rank. And, from the city gates, poured Spartan hoplites. *Aulos*-flutes skirled. The paean hymns were sung. Determined not to yield, Thrasyllus' men awaited his command.

But even now there was an agitation in the Persian battle-line. No longer were they so assured. Instead, their heads were turning. First, uncertainty. Then fear. Then panic. And their ranks disintegrated. The soldiers ran in terror. Alcibiades and his cavalry were galloping towards them at full speed, spears raised to stab, swords drawn to slash, their armour dazzling in the winter sun.

Now Thrasyllus' troops advanced and, together with the hoplites who had marched with Alcibiades, pursued the Persians running for their lives, while the cavalry careered across the plain, harassing the fleeing enemy deep into hostile territory, reining in their panting horses only when daylight failed. In the adrenaline rush, no one had thought to try to take the city.

And now that they had failed, they would have been forced to mount a lengthy siege. Perhaps it had never really been the plan to take the city anyway. Instead, though, the Athenians had won a sweet and easy victory—Alcibiades' and Thrasyllus' men together—and their army was united in its celebrations.

So, with a renewed feeling of confidence and camaraderie, the Athenians turned their sights east. Towards the Bosporus. And in particular, two cities: Byzantium and Chalcedon, which lay on either side of the busy straits. Until recently, both had belonged to Athens. But in the unsettled months following the Sicilian defeat, each in turn had rebelled from her empire. And now the Athenians were determined to win them back.

Their first goal was Chalcedon, just outside the mouth of the Bosporus, a few miles south of their existing customs base at Chrysopolis. Why its Megarian founders had chosen to settle here, rather than much better-placed Byzantium across the channel, baffled many. Had those early colonists not been able to see its comparative disadvantages? In time, their choice seemed so shortsighted that Chalcedon won the nickname, "the City of the Blind." But its harbourage was good and its site so strategically significant that the Athenians could not ignore it.[40]

Already, Theramenes and the garrison at Chrysopolis had been conducting attacks on the territory of Chalcedon, and it was clear to everyone that it would not be long before the city, too, would be the focus of Athenian assault. So clear, in fact, that the Chalcedonians packed as many moveable belongings as they could into strongboxes and chests, loaded them on wagons, and sent them to their Bithynian neighbours for safekeeping. They would never set eyes on them again.[41]

Such a huge movement of property could not be hidden. The Athenians found out. And one of Alcibiades' first actions, when he arrived in theatre, was to lead the cavalry and infantry in a massive show of force across the border into the Bithynians' territory, while much of the navy—now nearly 190 triremes—glided up the coast beside him. The Bithynians were terrified. Their friendship with Chalcedon was not worth the casualties that defending Chalcedonian property would surely cause. So they meekly surrendered the goods and made a peace treaty. Without an arrow needing to be fired, the Athenians had won welcome booty.

Now for Chalcedon itself. Wedged into the Sea of Marmara, the city, with the River Chalcis, its shallows loud with the croak of frogs, flowing to its south, was built on a low-lying promontory. For Athens' tacticians, hampered by the lack of siege machinery, there was only one course of action they could take: just as at Potidaea more than twenty years before, and at Syracuse more recently, they would build a wall, cutting the city off by land, while their navy blockaded it by sea. They set to work with such efficiency and haste that, by the time that Farnavaz and his Persian army got there, a wooden wall ran from the Bosporus down to the River Chalcis, preventing his further approach. On the other side, safe between the palisade and city walls, were the Athenians. Waiting. And watching.[42]

Both the Chalcedonians and Farnavaz knew they must force a battle. They could communicate only by signalling. But communicate they did. And in a coordinated offensive, the allies launched their attack—the Persians on the palisade, the Chalcedonians opening the city gates and running out to form their lines of battle. From the top of their stockade, the Athenian defenders had no trouble beating back the Persians. But in the enclosed space between it and the city the fighting was fierce and feverish, as hoplite clashed with hoplite, shouting and shoving in a muddy, bloody scrimmage to the death.

And then, at last, their moment chosen perfectly, the Athenian cavalry, alert and fresh, and eager to engage, pounded in as if from nowhere, yelling their battle cry. And at their head was Alcibiades. Dispersed, the Chalcedonians scrambled for the safety of their city, and, as arrows rained down on the pursuing Athenians, the gates slammed shut behind them. It was an unsatisfactory ending to a trying day. Little had been achieved, and all that the Athenians could do now was wait and see how long it took before the city could be starved into submission. But if this were all they did, they would lose momentum and morale. Instead, they must push on with their mission to retake the Sea of Marmara.

The precise nature of the Athenian chain of command is uncertain. With several generals operating in theatre at the same time, there needed to be one commander-in-chief. Anecdotal evidence—the fact that he garnered the greatest praise for Athens' military successes at this time—would suggest that this was Alcibiades. However, this may simply be because of his knack of placing himself in the limelight and attracting praise, whether it was due to him or to others. More likely, Thrasybulus was in overall command. In land-based military encounters, it was Thrasybulus who tended to command the all-important hoplites, albeit with Alcibiades leading the flamboyant cavalry charges that turned deadlock into victory. Even at Cyzicus, Alcibiades' role had been subsidiary—to tempt the enemy to sail into the open sea, where Thrasybulus and the rest of the fleet could engage them. That this plan failed, and the outcome of the battle, including the killing of Mindarus, rested on men under Alcibiades' command, could not have been foreseen in advance.[43]

But Alcibiades was much more than a brilliant general. His mercurial imagination and magnetic personality, his passion and persuasiveness made him the ideal diplomat, the man of choice when it came to negotiating with reluctant cities, shoring up their loyalty and bleeding them of cash. So, while the remainder of the army stayed at Chalcedon, it was Alcibiades who was assigned the task of bringing the coastal cities of the Sea of Marmara back into the fold, augmenting the land army and gathering the money to pay them and the sailors in advance of the next main focus of the season, the recapture of Byzantium.[44]

With this in mind, Alcibiades sailed back to the Hellespont, not only visiting allied cities and collecting cash, but mobilizing his loyal Thracian fighters, for whom the time had come to prove their mettle. And so the journey east again began, the Thracians marching by the shore, while the Athenian triremes, their mainsails slapping in the breeze, kept leisurely pace at sea. Out from the Hellespont, the coastline was for the most part rolling farmland. Only once did a low chain of gnarled hills impede the army's progress. And so they made good time, their numbers and their coffers swelling by the day. Until they reached Selymbria.[45]

Alcibiades had visited Selymbria the year before, after the victory at Cyzicus. Then, while its citizens had given money, they had shown their reluctance by refusing to admit him inside their walls. At the time, it had been a snub that the Athenians could live with—cash was more crucial than a cordial relationship. Now, though, it was vital that Selymbria be brought into the fold. To fail would not just leave an untidy gap in the integrity of the coastline. Being only forty-five miles northwest of the Bosporus, an independent, hostile Selymbria could potentially cause problems for the

Athenians launching an attack on Byzantium. Moreover, speed was of the essence. With the new Spartan fleet now nearly built and ready, the window was closing on this rare period, when Athenians could criss-cross the Sea of Marmara unchallenged. There was no time for a long siege.[46]

So Alcibiades resorted to guile. He already had supporters in Selymbria, and they entered into secret negotiations. Plans were confirmed, a date agreed. At midnight, this small cabal of pro-Athenians would steal down to the city gates and throw them open, while one of their number raised a blazing torch high on the walls to signal that the way was clear. So, as the sun set, and night flooded the plains, Alcibiades and his army, encamped before the city, waited beneath the stars. There were still hours to go, but they were ready.[47]

And then—too soon!—the torch flame. Something had gone wrong! Alcibiades could not afford to hesitate. Yelling orders to his captains to fall in behind him when they could, he took the twenty light-armed troops and thirty hoplites, who happened to be nearest him, and sprinted through the darkness to the city walls. The gates were open. They ran through. And then, ahead, they saw, advancing down the broad street, in full armour, the Selymbrian army, helmets lowered, round shields raised, outnumbering them horribly. What to do? To fight was suicidal. To retreat unthinkable. Among Alcibiades' small squad of soldiers was his trumpeter. Whom he now commanded to blast forth a call for silence. While Alcibiades himself, his helmet raised, his shield and spear laid down, strode forward. Exposed. Alone.[48]

Baffled, the Selymbrians stopped in their tracks. And listened. As Alcibiades spoke. Confidently. Assuredly. Instructing them that they must lay down their arms. The city was already taken. Even now, whole quarters of Selymbria were occupied by the Athenians. There was no point in trying to resist. At his back, Alcibiades was aware that the rest of his army had, indeed, arrived and fallen in, ready to do battle. But it would be so much better to avoid bloodshed. Which the Selymbrians clearly were considering, too. For a moment, the outcome hung in the balance. Then the Selymbrians laid down their weapons. The immediate danger had passed.

But still another worry menaced Alcibiades: how his Thracian soldiers would react. Mercenaries most, their greatest love was booty, and the joy they dreamt of more than any was the moment they were unleashed on a defenceless city, to smash, to loot, to rape, to kill. Just six years earlier, a band of Thracian mercenaries, sailing home from Athens, had vented their bloodlust on the hapless villagers of Mycalessus, forcing their way into houses, breaking down temple doors, and killing everyone and everything they found: men and women, oxen, donkeys, everything. But it was the massacre of schoolboys that most shocked the Greeks. The village school, the largest in the neighbourhood, had been packed with children. Not one of them survived.[49]

For the plans already formulating in Alcibiades' mind, a repeat of such barbarity would be disastrous. So, he ordered his Thracian soldiers back, as far from the walls of Selymbria as possible. And he assured the citizens of his goodwill. All he required of them was their cooperation. And (of course) their money. Give him those, and they could live in peace without any penalty to pay for their hostility just now. Relieved, the Selymbrians agreed.[50]

Thanks to Alcibiades' quick thinking and *sangfroid*, Selymbria was now in Athens' hands. But it was not the only intriguing development. Over in Chalcedon, the generals had been enjoying a diplomatic triumph of their own. The siege was at an end. Unable to storm the Athenian palisade, and unwilling to commit his time and troops to monitoring a long siege, Farnavaz, acting on both his own behalf and that of the Chalcedonians, had entered talks with the Athenian generals.[51]

Their outcome pleased all sides. The Athenians received not just much needed money—from the Chalcedonians (who still retained nominal independence), this year's tribute plus arrears; from the Persians, twenty talents—but the granting of safe passage to a diplomatic mission to the Great King, so that they could put their case for support to him in person. At the same time, Farnavaz received assurances from the Athenians that they would attack neither the land and city of the Chalcedonians, nor (more crucially) the territories that he himself controlled. At least until the diplomats returned from Susa. Which could mean many months. If not years. He was quite literally buying time.[52]

To seal the deal, the negotiators held a ceremony, making sacrifice, and swearing oaths. But for Farnavaz, there was one Athenian general who was conspicuous by his absence: Alcibiades, who was otherwise engaged in capturing Selymbria. For the satrap, however, it seemed crucial that Alcibiades should make a public (and religious) show of agreeing to the peace terms. After all, experience had shown how slippery he could be. Farnavaz would be entirely justified if he suspected that, given half a chance, Alcibiades (whose relationship with democratic Athens was still not entirely clear) would argue that a treaty made by his Athenian colleagues did not apply to him.[53]

But, if Farnavaz expected that Alcibiades would simply go through the motions of taking the oath and adding his name to that of his colleagues in a low-key private ceremony, he was mistaken. Never one to be regarded simply as an addendum, and with his eye as always on appearances, Alcibiades insisted that Farnavaz observe exactly the same protocol with him as with the generals: if Alcibiades must ratify the treaty and swear the oath, so, too, must Farnavaz. In person.

And so it was, on his triumphant return from Selymbria, that Alcibiades sent Farnavaz a message. He would be delighted to ratify the oath, but only if Persian representatives travelled to witness him doing so at Chrysopolis—and only if he had first heard from his own delegates that Farnavaz had made his own pledge personally to Alcibiades in their presence. Farnavaz had no choice but to agree and, accordingly, two Greeks, both fine Athenian noblemen, made their way with all the pomp and ceremony that they could muster to the satrap's camp at Chalcedon; and, in their turn, two Persians duly turned up at Chrysopolis to witness Alcibiades' oath.

It was such a pleasing show of power, a dramatic demonstration to the world of Alcibiades' special status, that the representative of Persia's Great King should sign a treaty personally and swear an oath exclusively with him. It was also, arguably, a sign of the extent to which Alcibiades yearned for recognition. In truth, to Farnavaz, such symbolism mattered little in comparison to an undertaking to leave his lands alone. For already, as the Athenian ambassadors set off on their long journey to the heart of Empire, the Persians were playing a longer game.[54]

With the threats from Selymbria and Chalcedon now neutralized, the Athenians could turn their focus to the region's main prize: Byzantium. Founded more than two-and-a-half centuries before on a gently rising headland by colonists from mainland Megara, the city's chiefest joy and greatest asset was its harbour, which was sited on a lazy loop of water, called in later years the Golden Horn, stretching inland from the outflow of the Bosporus. Thanks to its position on the straits between the Black Sea and the Sea of Marmara, Byzantium had grown fat on trade and taxes, a steady source of revenue for the Athenians, while it stayed part of their empire but, when it rebelled and threatened to blockade the grain supply, an existential threat. For four years, the densely populated city had been subject to a Spartan governor, Clearchus. It was time to take it back.[55]

Even as Alcibiades was conducting his audience with Farnavaz, across the Bosporus, his colleagues had been hard at work. With the city walls impregnable, they resorted to tried and tested means: a palisade across the foreland from the Sea of Marmara down to the Golden Horn, an occasional assault against the walls (more as a show of strength than in any hope of real success), and the prospect of a lengthy siege.[56]

The weeks slipped by. As the city slumped into starvation, Clearchus slipped out one night in a small boat and rowed across the Bosporus to plead with Farnavaz to help with ships and money. But in his absence, anger grew against him. The Spartans had a reputation for an overbearing style of government that bred resentment and alienated those whose support they needed most. Clearchus was no exception. Despite being Byzantium's *proxenos* in Sparta, he had little understanding of its labyrinthine politics and took no care to ingratiate himself with the city's great and good, who, as a result, resented him. And not just him. His motley garrison of liberated Spartan Helots and Megarians, too. So much, in fact, that they sent a clandestine message out to Alcibiades that they were prepared to help him take back their city. News of his gentle treatment of Selymbria had impressed them. Only let him guarantee similar leniency to the Byzantines, and the city would be his. He did. And together they hatched a plan.[57]

It was a strategy as old as the taking of Troy. But it had worked then, and it could work now. Word was circulated round the Athenian camp of an emergency in Ionia. To address it, the fleet and army were urgently required. The siege of Byzantium must end! Within hours, the news had filtered back inside the city. And when, from their walls, they saw Athenian tents being struck, bags packed, chests loaded aboard triremes, horses led onto transport ships, oarsmen filing up the gangplanks and sitting ready on their benches, the Byzantines experienced a sense of great elation. At last they could bring in supplies! At last they could fill their empty bellies! And then the Athenian fleet put to sea, a light breeze caught the sails, and the ships were scudding west to vanish in the summer haze behind the headlands out towards Selymbria.

But that night, in the darkness, as Byzantium, relieved and joyful, slept, the black ships of Athens nosed back across the silent sea and glided into harbour. A sudden shout, the baying answer of a thousand throats, and the Athenians launched their attack, causing flamboyant damage to the boats tied up along the quayside, ramming some and dragging others out to sea with grappling hooks. In the city, the men of the garrison fumbled to strap on greaves and breastplates, snatched spears from wall-hooks, and clattered out into the night, down to the harbour and the sound of chaos.

Now it was that the conspirators ran to the walls on the city's landward side and raised the torch in signal. The gates were locked and guarded, but it was a moment's work to lower ladders, and now Athenian hoplites were swarming up and over. And leading them was Alcibiades. But they met stiff opposition. Not only Spartans and Megarians. Byzantines, too, who knew nothing of the deal that had been brokered and believed that they were fighting for their lives.

As at Selymbria, so here, carnage could be prevented only by diplomacy. As slaughter surged down through the city, the raucous sound of trumpets blared. Announcements were proclaimed to any who would listen: lay down your arms, and you will not be harmed. And, gradually, street by street, and square by square, resistance slipped away, as some citizens surrendered, and others, emboldened and enraged at the treatment they had suffered in the last four years, turned on the Spartan garrison and chased them down, until they ran in terror to the city's altars and asylum. Throughout Byzantium, the shouts of men were dying down—only the dogs were barking still—and the city awaited its fate.

But there was no need for anxiety. Alcibiades was true to his word. The Byzantines were spared. As for the Spartan and Megarian garrison, they were disarmed, and sent as prisoners of war to Athens. Reconciliation, not revenge, was Athens' watchword now. It was a policy so far removed from that which she had meted out on Melos only eight years earlier, or at Scione at the end of the first phase of the war. But it was working.[58]

Thanks to the panache of its commanders, Athens' operation to regain control of the Bosporus had proved successful. Not only that. An Athenian delegation was even now on its way to the Persian Great King. Many of these successes could be attributed undoubtedly to the military genius of Thrasybulus, Theramenes, and the other generals, but many, too, were due in no small part to Alcibiades' diplomatic skills and far-sighted strategy of clemency. Since his recall to Samos four years earlier, Athens had enjoyed a series of important victories, while Sparta had been driven from the seas. And as Athens' star waxed, so Alcibiades' brilliance shone ever brighter.

But now, out on the edge of empire in the badlands of the northeast, he had done everything he could. He was needed here no longer. He had ensured the safety of the grain supply. He had proved his loyalty to Athens. Surely there could be no better time for him to bid his helmsman set course for the west. And sail back home.[59]

11

DOG DAYS

Me, I can think of nothing sweeter than my native land.

Homer, *Odyssey,* 9.27–28

BY 407, many in the army, those veterans of the democratic mutiny on Samos, had not seen Athens for five long and eventful years. For Alcibiades, it had been eight. But, while his men looked forward eagerly to being reunited with their wives and families, and to seeing their homes again, for Alcibiades, the prospect was more daunting.[1]

Yes, the army had recalled him. Yes, he had blazed a phosphorescent trail of victory throughout the east—fighting heroically against the Persians and Spartans, keeping sea lanes open, ensuring that, like the sieves of the Danaids in Hades, the city's haemorrhaging coffers were kept constantly refilled. And yes, his kudos was colossal—greater, perhaps, than at any period before. But to the Athenian People, how would any of this success compare, when they considered all he had done to harm them? The list was damning: advising Chithrafarna to prolong the war by playing one side off against the other; fighting the Athenians at Miletus; encouraging rebellion in Ionia; suggesting a Spartan garrison at Decelea; counselling the Spartans to send help to Syracuse. Even if, in reality, these episodes could have happened just as well without him, Alcibiades could be held responsible for any of them. Or all of them. And frustratingly, the reason for this was that he, himself, had taken so much care to exaggerate his influence. Of course, he had had his reasons at the time. But now? And then there were the other charges he might face: encouraging an oligarchic coup in Athens; misleading the People into sending the disastrous expedition against Sicily; not to mention the lingering accusations of involvement in the profanation of the Mysteries and the smashing of the Herms.

There were so many reasons why Alcibiades might hesitate before returning home. But there were equally so many reasons why he must return. If he remained out in the east (even if he were to win more victories for Athens and amass more money), he would be sidelined; his enemies at home would feed the rumours, questioning his motivations for keeping far away; and the People would become suspicious.

Indeed, ever since his flight to Sparta, the absent Alcibiades had haunted Athens' memory. Almost immediately he was gone, Aristophanes staged *Birds,* a comedy that portrayed him as an ambitious young subversive who, abandoning Athens, rallies the birds around a strategy that sees them triumph over the gods while he transforms himself into their thunderbolt-wielding tyrant. More recent dramas, though, reflected a growing yearning for Alcibiades and the increasing hope that, thanks to him, Athens might be victorious. Just two years earlier, in 409, Sophocles had staged a tragedy that explored the bringing of a powerful exiled general back into the fold. In his *Philoctetes,* a noble Greek hero, banished because he has unwittingly offended the gods, is rehabilitated, since the army realizes that, without him, it will never win its war with Troy.[2]

With so much uncertainty surrounding his return to Athens, it was not surprising that Alcibiades put it off for as long as possible. Perhaps he was waiting until he heard the result of the annual elections to the post of general, a useful weathervane for public opinion. In the worst scenario, not only might Alcibiades be stripped of his command, his friends and allies might be, too, in which case he would be well advised to stay away. If, on the other hand, the generalship was split between supporters and detractors, he must weigh the dangers that might face him. Only with a clear vote in his favour could he set foot back in his homeland with any confidence. And even then, the situation might be fraught. The trouble was that the elections kept being postponed. Scheduled for March, they were still not held in April. And, with each day that passed, the tensions of uncertainty kept rising.[3]

If it was crucial that Alcibiades should judge the timing of his home-coming with care, it was equally important that it be stage-managed to achieve the greatest impact possible. And for that, he needed to bring with him as much money and flamboyant booty as he could. So, once the fleet had blossomed back into the Aegean Sea, leaving the Bosporus and the oppressive Hellespont secure behind it, the black ships scattered. One squadron headed southwest for Athens. A second curved northwest along the southern shores of Thrace; its mission: to win back Thasos and such other cities as it could, while at the same time accumulating money. The third, led by Alcibiades, swung south.[4]

The first hours of their journey were instructive. As they skirted the Troad on their way to Samos, nudging provocatively close to land, they could see all too clearly the well-organized activity in the shipyards of Antandrus, where the construction of the new Spartan fleet was nearly complete. It was a salutary sight. The Athenians' unchallenged mastery of the sea, enjoyed for the past year to such brilliant advantage, was quickly coming to an end. Unless they could win another victory as crushing as the victory at Cyzicus, it would not be long before, on any voyage, they must again be on the lookout for attack.

In what they knew would be a lull between the fighting of the past few years and the new realities ahead, the fleet could be excused if an air of indulgence pervaded this final uncontested voyage down the Asian coast. Yet it was not a pleasure cruise. After a brief stopover on friendly Samos, Alcibiades continued south with twenty ships towards the cities on the coast of Caria and the Ceramic Gulf. There were reminders everywhere of Athens' losses. Islands such as Rhodes and Chios, wealthy Ephesus, once-so-dependable Miletus: all were in Spartan hands. Everywhere they anchored, Alcibiades spent tireless hours rallying the steadfast to stay loyal to Athens, persuading sceptics to remain on side, identifying malcontents, tallying which cities were reliable and which were not. In all, he took pains to spread the news of his lenient treatment of Selymbria, how he had spared Byzantium, how it was better to embrace the empire than resist it. And from all he requested money, no doubt calibrated carefully to gain the greatest profit in return for the least possible offence. When he sailed back north to Samos, Athens was richer by a hundred talents.[5]

By now, it was high spring, and still no news of the elections. But Alcibiades could not stay in Samos any longer. He must make his way back west, even if his course were slow. And far from direct. A leisurely voyage saw him at last cruising off the southern Peloponnese. It was a massive detour, yet once more its purpose was hardheaded. Having inspected the progress of Sparta's new fleet at Antandrus, Alcibiades wanted to discover if the ships being built at Gytheum were almost ready, too. It was the one piece of intelligence still missing from the comprehensive survey that he had been conducting for the past few months. From out at sea, he counted them—thirty new triremes, all ready to be launched, with the jagged mountain peaks of Sparta rising high behind them.[6]

Then, as he sped away back around Cape Malea and along the shoreline of the eastern Peloponnese, it came: the news he been waiting for. The results of the elections of the generals were in. And they were so much better than he had hoped. Alcibiades himself was reconfirmed in post. And every one of his nine colleagues was a friend or ally. The People had sent a clear sign of their support. There was no longer any need to hesitate. The time for his homecoming was now.[7]

Ever since his youth, Alcibiades had been aware of the power of public opinion, and as the prospect of his return to Athens became ever more real, more concrete, he must have considered with increasing care how best to stage-manage an event that would inevitably prove of the highest significance to the city. And would set the mood for his subsequent reception. It was of crucial importance that the Athenians, both friends and enemies alike, should be left in no doubt of his leading role in the victories of the past four years, or that, without him, the war could have taken a very different path. It was vital, too, that his arrival should bolster the new mood of optimism that had gripped Athens ever since the victory at Cyzicus. Yet too triumphalist a tone was fraught with danger. Any sign of gloating, any hint that Alcibiades was revelling in his new-found power, and his enemies could accuse him of personal ambition, denounce him for hubris, reignite the rumours of his lust for tyranny. Whatever he did he would have detractors. What was important, though, was that he capture the current atmosphere of hope, that he win the immediate approval of the People, that he strengthen the morale not just of the city but of the fighting men whom he and his colleagues commanded. Undoubtedly, the other generals, his colleagues, were also monitoring reports, calibrating what they learned of the political climate, calculating how best to pitch the homecoming.

And when the time came, they agreed with Alcibiades: it must be done in style.[8]

And so at last, in mid-June, with anticipation in the city now at fever pitch, the news shot like a blazing arrow through the streets. The fleet was coming! It was just a day away! It would be sailing with the dawn! Even before cock-crow and the bark of waking dogs, even before the peacocks' mournful cry was echoing across the roof tops, the people of Athens were out of bed and thronging through the still-dark streets down to Piraeus. As dawn broke and shadows became shapes, there were already thousands on the move, men and women, citizens and foreigners and slaves, all pouring down the broad, straight road, the Long Walls towering high on either side. For many, memories came flooding back of that morning eight years earlier, when they had made this very journey to cheer the fleet as it sailed off for Sicily. Painful memories. Of sons and fathers lost. Of husbands never seen again. But now all in the past. Despite so much bereavement, most still had friends and family living, men who had served abroad for years, for whose safety they had prayed, for whose lives they had made offerings to gods. And the anticipation of their forthcoming reunion outweighed the pain of loss.[9]

Out at sea, too, expectancy was building. Already the ships' crews had adorned their vessels, proudly securing captured shields, and weapons, golden figureheads, and other trophies to the exoskeleton of outriggers, twined in a profusion of rich garlands. With the light winds of the morning, there was no need to row. Instead, on every trireme, sails were pregnant with the breeze, and bronze rams cut their furrows through the hissing foam. As the sun rose higher and the haze was burnt away, from his flagship's deck, his purple sail slapping and bellying behind him, Alcibiades could see the light catch on the spear tip of Athene's statue, high on the far Acropolis. And then the sails were furled, and the long oars dipped and rose: and each beat brought the flock of triremes closer to its home. By now, Alcibiades could make out the Acropolis itself, and the city clustering around it: houses, temples, and the lines of the Long Walls; the low hill of Piraeus with its geo-metric street plan, its houses, and its market, and its harbours of Mun-ychia and Zea; and then the entrance to the port itself, its sea-walls lined with onlookers. In, through the harbour mouth. The wharves and warehouses; the stoas; and the quayside thick with crowds, thousands upon countless thousands thronging the waterfront, packing the balconies, lining the flat roofs. As the ships entered the harbour, the cheering had begun. As they nudged ever closer, it was deafening.

This was the crucial moment, the moment for which Alcibiades had been preparing for so long. How he behaved now was critical. And so, while all Athens clamoured for him to come ashore, Alcibiades hung back. The tumult grew, but still he did not move. Which made the crowd roar louder. It was a charming hesitation, pitched cleverly to suggest anxiety, contrition, reluctance even—whatever self-effacing emotion an onlooker might wish to read into it. But it was, too, a moment of the most brilliantly staged theatricality. For, as Alcibiades stood motionless, his head cocked back at that so-familiar angle, the citizens could gaze at him as one.

And what they saw delighted them. Yes, he had aged in the past eight years. But he remained as handsome as they remembered him. "In child-hood, youth and manhood, his beauty blossomed with each season—desirable, and sweet. Euripides may say that 'beauty's autumn has a beauty of its own,' but this is not true of everyone. It was, however, true of Alcibi-ades." At forty-five, he was well into middle age, battle-hardened, and perhaps battle-scarred, but his youthful energy and his innate charisma were as electric as they had ever been. And as he slowly scanned the shore, the crowds lining the sea walls felt the warm glow of his gaze. And then he caught sight of a well-known face—his cousin, Euryptolemus—and he hesitated no longer. Along the gangway, down into the surging mass he went, and with cheering supporters clustering around him walked the five miles to Athens. And the spectators followed in his wake.[10]

It was all judged to perfection. For the next day was the annual festival of Plynteria, when the ancient olive-wood statue of Athene was ritually stripped of its robes, veiled, and hidden from view. Meanwhile, the priests in procession took the robes, so carefully woven with scenes showing battling gods and giants, out from the Temple of Athene Polias, down from the Acropolis, and through empty city streets, between the Long Walls, to the sea, where they were ritually washed and purified. So sacred was this ritual, and so taboo, that no business was transacted on this day: not only was the statue covered up, the goddess herself was thought to be absent from the city, and, without her, how could anything good be achieved? For many, it was the most ill-omened day of the Athenian year. For all, it meant a pause. A day to hunker down, take stock, prepare for the new year ahead. A day to stay at home with newly returned loved-ones. A day to think over the exhilarating consequences of Alcibiades' return. Twenty-four hours of enforced anticipation. But once the robes were purified, once the statue was again uncovered and the goddess, properly adorned, returned, Athens could breathe again, her great commercial heart could beat once more, and her citizens could look forward to a new year of success thanks to the gods' protection.[11]

So it was with a real sense of renewal that, within days of his arrival, Alcibiades found himself first in the Agora, addressing the members of the Council, then taking the steep road to the Pnyx, before climbing the familiar steps up to the Speaker's Platform. Above him, in the auditorium of the packed hill, five thousand citizens fell silent, waiting for the voice that had been silent for so long. Behind him, the Acropolis with its gaudy temples and its shrines thrust, proud, into the pale blue sky; beneath him stretched the Agora; and all around him, in the distance, the violet hills of Attica—Hymettus and Pentelicon—and the nearer cone of Lycabettus. For better or for worse, the errant Alcibiades was home. It was not surprising that the speech he gave to mark the moment was emotional.[12]

Fighting his tears he spoke of all that he had suffered personally since he last stood here. And all that the Athenians had suffered, too. For his part, he said, he was plagued by an evil spirit that was bent on sabotaging his success. Perhaps he genuinely did believe in this destructive daemon, a mirror image of the daemon that his mentor, Socrates, believed protected him. Or perhaps he meant to conjure up the old curse on the Alcmaeonid dynasty, his family execrated for two hundred years for having murdered prisoners protected by Athene. Or perhaps he simply intended to deflect the blame, to suggest that nothing he had done was his own fault, that he, like Athens, was the plaything of a force much stronger than himself. But, he proclaimed, if Athens' enemies believed that they would win, they were misguided. In a rousing peroration, Alcibiades rehearsed the victories that he and the Athenian army had enjoyed since his return to them on Samos, and the victories that surely lay before them—victories in not just single battles, but the war.[13]

If the troops who had been serving under him had heard it all before, it did not matter. Listening to his rolling cadences, his speech delivered with his famous traulism, which turned his *r*-s to *l*-s, his audience was spellbound. It was as if the past eight years had never happened, as if Athens basked still in her glory days. With his final rousing phrases, the Pnyx erupted in loud cheers, and even as he stood there, basking in the adulation, the proposal was put forward and approved that the city should award him golden crowns, exquisite, intricately fashioned garlands of delicately fragile golden leaves. And not just that. They voted to appoint him general-in-chief, *strategos autocrator,* with supreme command on land and sea, the most powerful man in Athens. It was his prize not only for four years of victories in battle and diplomacy, but for the clever way in which he had made sure that all reports enhanced his role in them. In democratic Athens, it was the greatest honour he could ever hope for, the pinnacle of his ambition.[14]

Unless he really did have his eye on tyranny. And there were still those who suspected that he did. For now, they might be keeping quiet, but Alcibiades' enemies had not gone away. And there was much to vex them—the return of his domestic property, confiscated when he was condemned for sacrilege; the removal from the Acropolis of the "stele of disgrace" (the inscription that proclaimed the charges made against him), its transportation to the sea, and its sinking deep beneath the waves; the renouncing of the curses by a reluctant Callias and his craven colleagues in the priesthood of Eleusis. Only one man refused, Theodorus, the high priest of the Mysteries, neatly sidestepping his obligations by maintaining that he had placed a curse on Alcibiades, only if Alcibiades did harm to Athens.[15]

It was not the only sour note to disrupt the cosy warmth and harmony. All too soon, Alcibiades' enemies were manufacturing a fresh outrage. Greek days were reckoned from sunset to sunset. And, while Alcibiades may indeed have sailed into Piraeus the day before the Plynteria, celebrations for the fleet's return lasted well into the night—well into the most ill-omened day in Athens' calendar. Surely, this was further proof of Alcibiades' deliberate contempt for all that the city held holy! Surely, to encourage partying and revelry on that most taboo of days was as serious a sacrilege as the imitation of the Mysteries, the revelation of their secrets to the uninitiated, or the vandalizing of the Herms! Surely, it was evidence, if evidence were needed, that nothing about Alcibiades had changed. Infected with the Alcmaeonid curse, perverted by the atheistic teachings of philosophers, cavalier in his attitude to the most holy festivals, it was just a matter of time before he and anyone associated with him attracted the gods' anger. And faced their punishment.[16]

Meanwhile, far off on the horizon, still more dark clouds were massing. On the international stage, events were taking a potentially alarming turn. In Persia, the Athenian delegation, which had set out with such high hopes under the patronage of Farnavaz, had made slow progress towards Susa. So slow, indeed, that they were forced to overwinter in the ancient Phrygian capital of Gordium, high on the Anatolian plateau. Here, on the frosty steppe, the delegates had kicked their heels for months with few amusements, distracted only when the priests showed them on their acropolis (as they showed every esteemed visitor) an ancient wagon, dedicated to their greatest god, Sabazius. The vehicle's pole was fastened to its yoke with a complicated knot, which the priests invited the Athenians to untie. But try as they might, they failed to make the slightest inroad.[17]

If they found the Gordian Knot complex and tortuous, however, it was as nothing compared to the workings of the Persian Court. With the coming of spring, the delegates set off once more. But they had not gone far before they met a cavalcade of horsemen and lavish coaches heading west. To their horror, they discovered that the riders were Spartans, a diplomatic mission fresh from an audience with the Great King, Dārayavahuš. Tired of dealing with the slippery Chithrafarna, they had gone above his head and secured a promise of the Great King's unequivocal support. Indeed, so weary was he, too, of Chithrafarna, that the Great King was removing him from post and confining his sphere of influence to Caria. In his place, he was appointing the young man, who was reclining even now in one of the rich carriages: the Great King's son, Prince Korush.[18]

A mere sixteen years of age, Korush was already the quintessential Persian nobleman. Modest and dutiful in dealings with his elders, he excelled in those crucial courtly skills of horsemanship and hunting. His encounter with a bear was legendary. Cornered in the closing nets, the frightened creature lunged at young Prince Korush and dragged him from his horse. But Korush would not be cowed. Bleeding profusely, yet ordering his comrades to stand back, he beat off the bear's attack and, in savage combat, killed it. He would forever show his scars with pride. He was skilled, too, in the arts of war, unerring with the javelin and deadly with the bow. His only weakness was impetuosity, forgivable in most young men, but dangerous in one as ambitious as Prince Korush.[19]

For, although he was the Great King Dārayavahuš' second son, his elder brother had been born before his father took the throne. Which, in Korush's opinion, rendered his brother ineligible to succeed. This was the opinion of Korush's doting mother, too, the cruel and scheming Pari Satis. She had little love for her first-born son, and only hatred for his wife, Estatira. And as it happened, Estatira was the sister of the satrap, Chithrafarna. So it was in large part thanks to Pari Satis' influence with her husband, Dārayavahuš, that the young prince, rather than an older, more experienced official, was now heading west. Not only would Chithrafarna's dismissal from his satrapy undermine and upset Estatira, but Korush could build a power base of his own, especially as his new bailiwick was vast, embracing Lydia and Phrygia, Cappadocia and Ionia. And with that power base, when the time came, he might conceivably secure the Persian throne.[20]

That the Great King had thrown his unequivocal support behind the Spartans, and thereby dashed all Athens' hopes, was not the only irksome news. After a succession of mediocre generals, the Spartans had sent as the commander of their new fleet in Ionia a man whom Alcibiades had no doubt met in Sparta and knew to be both brilliant and dangerous: Lysander. A member of an ancient dynasty, the now fifty-four-year-old Lysander could trace his lineage to Heracles. But, in more recent generations, poverty had struck. The family was stripped of its citizen rights and reduced to the rank of *mothax,* able to fight for Sparta but not to take part fully in public life. Yet this did not deter Lysander. As a young man, he was the lover of Agesilaus, whose half-brother, King Agis, was even now harassing Attica from Decelea. In his company, he proved his worth. He was, indeed, exceptional. Although ascetic and austere, Lysander possessed a dangerous charm, quick intelligence, icy ruthlessness, and vaulting ambition. Like Alcibiades, he was well aware of the power of appearances. "A fine head of hair," he insisted, "makes a handsome man more handsome, and an ugly man more terrifying." Throughout his life, he had been determined to succeed at any cost. His appointment to Ionia gave him the chance he craved.[21]

With his thirty freshly finished triremes, the scent of pitch still rising from their hulls, Lysander sailed from Gytheum by way of Rhodes and Cos until he reached Miletus, for the past five years the centre of Spartan operations in Ionia. But not for much longer. At a glance, Lysander found the city glaringly inadequate, not least because of its position. For one thing, Miletus lay south of Athenian-held Samos, which meant that, each time they sailed from there to Chios and the northern cities, Spartan ships must run the gauntlet of attack. For another, it was inconveniently far from Sardis, where Korush was already setting up his court. Now that the Persians were fully behind Sparta, it was essential that they maintain the closest contact possible. And not just that. For reasons of his own, and with his own aggrandizement in mind, Lysander was intent on forging his own personal relations with the prince.[22]

So, in a bustle of activity, the Spartan navy sailed out from Miletus north for Ephesus and a joyfully enthusiastic welcome. Once a commercial powerhouse, the city had suffered badly in the war. Thanks to its split from Athens, trade with the Aegean and the west had virtually dried up, and Ephesus was in danger of becoming an economic backwater. Moreover, the increasing Persian presence in the city—and, not least, Chithrafarna's zealous support of its Sanctuary of Artemis—meant that it was rapidly losing its proud Greek character and becoming (in the lingo of its old inhabitants) "barbarized." So, when Lysander announced his intention not just to set up shipyards but to transform the port into the region's economic hub, the Ionian Ephesians were euphoric. Soon, the city was resounding to the rasp of saws and clang of hammers while, at the quayside, stevedores once more were heaving sacks and crates aboard huge merchant ships, and, out in the wide, shallow bay, the full complement of Sparta's fleet—now seventy ships strong—was practising manoeuvres, its crews training to row as one, to pick up speed, to ram and to reverse, to kill.

And all the time, they did so unopposed, while the Athenians—in Athens—enjoyed a summer such as they had not experienced for years. For, even in the absence of good military reasons for the soldiery to stay so long in Attica, there were still sound social and political necessities. It was, after all, not only Alcibiades who had been absent for such a very prolonged time, but his oarsmen and hoplites, too.

Until recently, campaigns had tended to last no more than a few weeks or months at most, not least because many participants were small farmers who needed to get home to bring the harvest in. Yes, there had been longer operations, such as the Egyptian Expedition of the 450s, but these had been exceptions. Recently, however, with the campaigns first to Sicily and then to the Hellespont and Bosporus, vast swathes of the Athenian male population had been gone from home for years. Economically, this had been just about sustainable. With Attica under threat from the Spartans in their fort at Decelea, her agricultural base was shaky anyway. Rural dwellers had sought refuge behind city walls, and, by now, many of the necessities of urban life were imported from abroad.

But socially, the long campaigns had taken a huge toll, especially, of course, the Sicilian debacle, where thousands had been killed, though the absence of so many men since then had had an impact, too. Not least on family life. It was no coincidence that playwrights such as Euripides were experimenting at this time with a new genre of "return tragedies," dramas with unusually happy outcomes, in which long-lost family members were reunited, often in the most unexpected settings. The reality of a soldier's return from war, of course, was very different, and families were more likely to face loved-ones suffering from post traumatic stress than to experience a fairy-tale romance.[23]

Politically, too, the long years of absence had taken their toll. Since many of those now returning had last been home, events of seismic intensity had rocked the city—the coup of the Four Hundred and their summer reign of terror; the oligarchy of the Five Thousand; the return of full democracy—all of which had followed closely on the heels of that strange, disturbing time before the army sailed to Sicily, the uneasy months that followed, when Athens was gripped by the conspiracy theories that forced Alcibiades to flee. Adding to the potential for unease was the fact that, four years earlier, while Athens had accepted oligarchy, her soldiery in Samos had not. With the return of the fleet, those two factions—non-combatant city dwellers who had let the constitution be suspended, and the staunchly democratic navy—were reunited for the first time. Under the oligarchy, feelings had run high, and, despite measures taken to protect the democratic constitution in the future, there must still have been many who, rather than follow a path of reconciliation, would have preferred to settle scores. Even now, the mood in the Assembly was uncomfortable, and a fair proportion of the People—the majority, whose household incomes meant that they were only just surviving, or who survived thanks only to state handouts—viewed the better-off with resentment and suspicion.[24]

Alcibiades was not immune from the tensions inherent in reunions following long absence. Not least when it came to his two children. What became of them when he left Athens is unknown, but, given the circumstances of his flight, it is unlikely that Alcibiades himself played much of a role in deciding their fate. Or, given his personality, that he showed great interest in them during his exile. Whether or not he tried to make up for this now, he failed to have much impact on his son's growing wilfulness, or to strike up a rapport. As for his daughter, he was probably too busy to give her much thought.[25]

Other family members caused greater concern—and one especially, his erstwhile brother-in-law and friend, now bitter enemy, Callias. With the other powerful priests of the Eleusinian Mysteries, Callias had used his revered position to anathematize Alcibiades, constantly taking the moral high ground, relishing the opportunity for conspicuous high drama, which the ceremony of the curses on the Acropolis had provided, and seizing every chance he could to denounce him in the Assembly, as he reminded the People of his sacrilege and the crimes of his cankerous family. At the same time, Alcibiades had done what he could, albeit from afar, to undermine Callias and deplete his wealth. Thanks to the escape of so many slaves from Laurium to Decelea, Callias' income had diminished drastically. But he had failed to cut his cloth to match these newly straitened circumstances, and the riches of what once had been the richest house in Athens were fast running out. Which in itself was satisfying to Alcibiades. But there was more that he could do to humiliate his enemy.

Part of what united the People was the yearly cycle of their festivals. Athens boasted more than any other city. Perhaps the greatest was the Panathenaia, celebrated every August to mark the birthday of Athene. At its heart was a great procession, in which men and women, citizens and foreign residents, marched from Athens' Sacred Gate, along the broad road leading through the cramped industrial quarter of the Cerameicus, with its potters' kilns and blacksmiths' forges, across the broad Agora, and up the steep slope onto the Acropolis, where, after prayers and sacrifices, a new robe was presented to the olive-wood statue of the goddess, housed in her temple of Athene Polias. It was a time for the city to come together, to recognize the part played by every one of its inhabitants, be they her powerful generals or the little girls who helped weave the sacred robe. And this year, with the fleet home and the city reunited, it must have held a special poignancy.[26]

Undoubtedly, Alcibiades, *strategos autocrator,* was conspicuous at that August's Panathenaia. But, even as he celebrated, watching the sacrifices, joining the prayers, feeling the warm sun radiate from the Acropolis, his mind was on a different, fast-approaching festival, which he was determined more than any other to make his own: the celebration of the Eleusinian Mysteries. Just weeks away, in mid-September. The festival that Callias and his prim colleagues had used to smear his reputation and help bring him down. The festival, where he would now take his delicious—and so public—revenge.[27]

Like the Panathenaic Festival, the Mysteries involved a sacred procession. But not of a mere mile or so through city streets. Of fifteen miles, out from the Sacred Gate, past Athens' sprawling cemetery, along the wide dirt road, through olive groves and vineyards, across the low foothills of Mount Aegaleos, down into a broad, fertile plain, and on through wheat fields, until it came to one of the most sacred sites in all of Attica: Eleusis, with its sanctuary of the goddesses, Demeter and Persephone, and its Great Hall of Initiation, where, in a blaze of light, worshippers received the promise of eternal life. To walk from city cemetery to the sanctuary, where immortality would be bestowed, was to take part in a procession fraught with symbolism, a preparation for the journey that the blessed soul would make when the earthly body died.[28]

But ever since Agis and his Spartans had occupied their fort at Decelea, the Athenians had been too nervous to make it. Instead, intimidated by the prospect of attack, they had simply sailed around to Eleusis, from one walled harbour to another, and hoped that it would not matter to the gods if they ignored the ritual of procession. This year, however, Alcibiades made it known that, thanks to his protection, there was need to fear no longer. Callias and his fellow priests might be too craven to ensure the safety of the worshippers. But he, Alcibiades, was not. The procession would be conducted as the gods intended. Overland.

So it was with an air of nervous, heady expectation that the crowds of keen initiates assembled before dawn. They met inside the city walls beside the Sacred Gate. It was a towering edifice, through which passed both the well-packed road and the waters of the River Eridanus, in truth little more than a malodorous stream, the bearer of much of the city's waste and floating rubbish. Indeed, the whole area was insalubrious. Not only was the Cerameicus an industrial heartland, it was home to many of the city's brothels, where the cheapest of the cheap slave-prostitutes plied their dismal trade, turning tricks for meagre earnings in cramped, airless cubicles or in the shadows of the gravestones in the cemetery outside.[29]

But in the twilight, with the foundries and kilns still quiet, and the prostitutes still sleeping off the night before, the open square, where the pilgrims were assembling, could seem magical. All of Greek-speaking humanity was here—men and women, slaves and free, Athenians and foreigners—and all dressed in their finest robes, their heads crowned with wreaths of woven myrtle leaves. But this year, they were joined by hoplite soldiers, their weapons and their armour gleaming dully in the growing light. By now, too, other soldiers, sent on ahead under the cover of night, were occupying strategic heights along the Sacred Way, guarding the safe cordon along which pilgrims would soon pass. Maybe by cavalry, as well. If they really did think they might be attacked, they would need the speed of horsemen to launch lightning strikes against aggressors and chase them far from the procession. And, among them, Alcibiades, perhaps leading his horse, perhaps astride it, all the while letting it be known that it was he who was in charge.[30]

And then, with due ceremony, the gates swung open. And the procession was underway. At its head was Alcibiades. Beside him, borne aloft, was the ancient wooden statue of Dionysus Iacchus, the god who was thought to lead his snaking file of devotees to spiritual salvation. Beside him, too, the Eleusinian priests, Alcibiades' arch-enemies, nursing their hatred of him, while, puffed with their own pomposity, they waddled with self-importance, dressed in their gorgeous robes and carrying covered baskets containing objects of the utmost sanctity. And behind him stretched the eager throng, hushed, silent. Normally, the journey to Eleusis was no po-faced pilgrimage. Instead, the worshippers told ribald jokes or sang loud hymns to Iacchus as they danced the fifteen miles along the Sacred Way. But this year, a strange quiet had descended on the worshippers as they left the safety of the city walls behind them, not knowing quite what dangers they might face.[31]

As they left the gravestones of the Cerameicus, passing Alcibiades' own family plot, and entered the open countryside, the military escort was on high alert. For the Spartans to ambush them, perhaps with a view to taking high-profile hostages, would be disastrous. The most likely place for an attack was where the road climbed over the low wooded ridge of Mount Aegaleos, past an important sanctuary of Apollo, with nearby rock-cut niches sacred to Aphrodite. But still the procession was unopposed, and, as they descended onto the broad Rharian Plain, they could see that their way was clear. When they crossed the bridge over the narrow River Rheiti, the pilgrims paused while officials moved among them, tying saffron ribbons round the right hand and left leg of each, an ancient ceremony now performed again after an absence of seven years. Here, too, they lit the sacred torches that each initiate would carry to Eleusis, the procession relaxed now and relieved that they had come so far in safety. Past shallow ponds sacred to Demeter and Persephone, where only the Eleusinian priests possessed the rights to fish, they came at last to the bridge across the River Cephisus, its parapets lined with men, their heads and faces ritually covered to protect their anonymity. For it was their sacred duty to hurl insults and abuse at all the great and good as they squeezed their way across the bridge, a rite designed to ward off evil as the procession reached the precinct of Eleusis and the Great Initiation Hall itself.[32]

The parade was over. That it had gone so well, so safely, could be credited to one man: Alcibiades. And the implications were enormous. Eight years before, Alcibiades had been vilified and hounded into exile largely on the charge of holding these very Mysteries in such contempt, that he had profaned them with his friends, showing no concern for all their awesome sanctity. It had been the Eleusinian priests who led the spine-chilling ceremony on the Acropolis, shaking out their red robes towards the setting sun, calling down curses on his head. It was the priests, more than anyone, who opposed his return and rehabilitation. And it was the priests who must now acknowledge themselves in his debt.

By ensuring that the procession could come safely to Eleusis, Alcibiades had proved his piety to all of Athens. And, by doing so, by outplaying the priests at their own game, he had won the sweetest victory. Indeed, there were many who now declared that he was not merely a military general but a high priest, single-handedly responsible for initiating the neophytes into Mysteries that promised everlasting blessings. After such a public demonstration of devotion, how could anyone accuse him of impiety again? And, although he probably knew all along that the Spartans, an unusually pious people, would never dream of attacking a religious procession, that was irrelevant: the point was that only he had dared to take the risk.[33]

Eleusis: The Great Hall of the Mysteries, site of the initiation ceremony. (Photograph by the author.)

This was not the only sign of Alcibiades' newly discovered piety. In anticipation of his coming expedition against Ephesus, he caused a marble statue of Phrygian goddess Cybele, the alter ego of Ephesian Artemis, to be set up beside the Council Chamber, a site of great esteem. Surely, when the Athenians honoured her so publicly, the goddess would smile on their ambitions to retake her city and her sanctuary![34]

Thanks to this and the brilliance of Alcibiades' dramatic coup in protecting the pilgrimage to Eleusis, among the fighting men of Athens morale soared to unprecedented heights. With Alcibiades as their general, they felt they were invincible. The People, too, the city's democratic poor, were captivated. Surely, the best thing now, they thought, would be for Alcibiades to assume complete control, to take the role of tyrant, beneficent, efficient, like Peisistratus a hundred and more years before, a guiding shepherd to his flock. If only he were untouchable by those who envied him! Then he could pass executive decisions, untrammelled by the weight of law! Then he could rid the city of the windbag armchair generals and so-called politicians, who loved to debate, but were so blatantly incapable of producing tangible results! Then he could make Athens great again! In the streets, at market stalls, in barbers' shops, they talked of it openly, while braver citizens climbed the steep alleyways that snaked up to Scambonidae to hammer in person on Alcibiades' door, and beg him to accept the role of People's Champion—of tyrant.[35]

Far from endearing him to enemies, however, or healing dangerous rifts, the People's adulation and such high-profile success merely incensed Alcibiades' adversaries and rivals all the more. In his absence from Athens, a new generation of politicians had become used to dominating the Assembly, preening in their newfound power, and they took badly to the adulation being lavished on the returned prodigal. Indeed, if they wanted to find fault with him, they did not have far to look. For what was he doing loitering in Athens, scoring points off priests, luxuriating in his kudos, when the situation in Ionia was deteriorating by the day? Was the great *strategos autocrator* not aware of the dangerous alliance even now being forged between the Persian Korush and the Spartan general Lysander? Or the failure of the Athenians to make any diplomatic inroads whatsoever?[36]

Reports reaching Athens from the east were worrying in the extreme. Lysander had lost no time in discovering all he could about Prince Korush from the Spartan delegates, who had ridden with him on the road from Susa to Ionia, and, within weeks, Lysander and these same ambassadors were on their way to Sardis. It was a journey Alcibiades had made so often. But where he had found the oleaginous, smooth-operating Chithrafarna, Lysander discovered in Prince Korush a young man possessed (like him) of ruthless energy, determination, single-mindedness, eager to waste no time in reaching an agreement that would see Sparta well funded and well supported. The niceties of court ritual quickly dispatched, the two men got down to business. Lysander knew instinctively how he must handle the precocious prince, now flattering his ego, now pushing for the maximum support—while Korush, his eye always to the future and the Persian throne, shrewdly calculated just how much of an investment he must make to secure Sparta's loyalty, should he ever need to fight his way to power.[37]

Lysander knew already of churning jealousies and hatreds within Persia's ruling family, and he knew, too, how to use them to his best advantage. So, he took every chance to heap scorn on Korush's brother-in-law, the disgraced Chithrafarna, complaining of how devious the satrap was, and how erratic; how he had said he would provide a fleet, though no ships came; how he had even failed to carry out official policy and make payments Persia had promised to the Spartan oarsmen. In response, Korush made lavish undertakings of his own. He had with him, he boasted, five hundred talents earmarked for his Spartan allies. He had his private wealth. He even (without knowing it) echoed Chithrafarna's empty pledge that, if he had to, he would melt down his gold and silver throne and mint it into money for the Spartans.[38]

It was all very well. But when Lysander then asked him to double the oarsmen's pay, which would both boost morale and encourage wavering Athenians to defect, Korush backtracked. Lysander persisted. And at the farewell banquet on the eve of his return to Ephesus, the two men reached a compromise. Delighted by their burgeoning relationship, and expansive in his cups, Korush told the Spartan that he wished to send him on his way with a gift to mark their friendship—anything; whatever Lysander wanted; nothing was too much. At which Lysander requested a pay raise for his men. Not double, as he had asked before. Merely a third. Modest, in comparison to what he wanted, but significant nonetheless. And Korush, delighted at his impudent insistence, granted it.[39]

It was this news in particular that worried the Athenians. There was no way they could match these wages, and for their oarsmen, struggling to make ends meet, many of them now not even Athenian citizens, the lure of extra pay could well trump patriotism. Anxious meetings produced just one solution. They must enlist the help of Chithrafarna! They must persuade him to accompany a delegation of their own to Korush to make the boy see sense! How Alcibiades reacted to this plan can only be imagined. Even if he and his fellow generals knew nothing of Korush's loathing of his brother-in-law, experience had taught that it was folly to rely on Chithrafarna. Indeed, the last time Alcibiades had met him on a diplomatic mission, the Persian had arrested him and thrown him into prison! And would the fallen satrap really want to offer help to Athens, when Alcibiades had then gone on to smear his reputation, suggesting it was thanks to him he had escaped? Yet, somehow they agreed to send the delegates; and somehow they did manage to persuade the satrap to accompany them to Sardis, and intercede with Korush. But, when they got there, the prince refused to see them. Unlike Chithrafarna, he was not playing games, and the message he conveyed to Athens was clear. War meant war. There would be no more negotiations.[40]

Perhaps Alcibiades knew all along that this would be the outcome. Perhaps he wanted to put off renewing his campaign until the end of summer, simply so he could stage and savour his delicious victory over the Eleusinian priests—that he might engineer a personal revenge. But, now that it was done, he had no reason to remain in Athens any longer. Instead, he had every cause to make whatever haste he could. Autumn was fast approaching with its treacherous seas; the money the Athenians had raised was running out; and Lysander's fleet was growing more experienced with every day that passed.[41]

So, once more, the rosters were posted in the shadow of the plane trees in the Agora, and tearful farewells made; and the familiar procession of sailors, soldiers, and well-wishers trooped down the road between the Long Walls to the sea. With Alcibiades went his friend, the helmsman Antiochus, who all those years before—when Alcibiades was young—had caught the quail when it escaped to flutter, clucking across the crowded Pnyx, and ever since had been a close companion. Perhaps Antiochus had sailed to Sicily with Alcibiades. Perhaps he had shared his exile. Perhaps he had returned with him to fight at Cyzicus and in the Hellespont and Bosporus. If so, his presence there is not recorded. But it is crucial now. For, as the long oars beat in rhythm, and the gleaming fleet of triremes sped into the open sea, it was Antiochus, steering a course towards Ionia, who held the fate of Alcibiades and Athens in his hands.[42]

12
NEMESIS

> In all things we must look to see how matters turn out in the end.
> Yes! For the god leads many people to expect good fortune, and then
> destroys them, root and branch.
>
> Herodotus, *Histories,* 1.32.9

WITH THE HELLESPONT AND BOSPORUS SECURE, and revitalized by three months of rest and recreation back in Athens, Alcibiades and his generals had every cause for optimism. True, the Spartans had made progress of their own—newly built ships, a dynamic new commander, a guarantee of pay from Persia—but it would only take one victory for her new bravado to be crushed. Only let Lysander sail out from his lair at Ephesus with his untried fleet, and the Athenians had every reason to believe they could defeat him. And, if they did, if Korush saw sense and realized that his backing of the Spartans was ultimately futile, it would not be long before the Persian switched sides, transferred his patronage to the Athenians, and helped Athens win the war. Until then, of course, campaigning must continue as before: rebel cities must be brought back on side; while, just as crucially, money must be raised from still-loyal allies.

As they sped east across the late September seas, they came first to the island of Andros, which, two years before, had declared for Sparta. To reclaim it swiftly would not just get the campaign off to a good start, it would be prudent, too: with Euboea to the north in enemy hands, the Spartans could control the sea between the islands, a strait just six miles wide, crucial waters for the passage of the grain ships, soon scheduled to sail down from the Hellespont.[1]

So, without delay, Alcibiades put in at Gaurium, a deep, well-sheltered harbour on the northwest coast of Andros and, with his army disembarked, set out through mountain passes for the city. At once the Andrians came out to meet him, but, in a swift-fought battle, the Athenians routed them. Yet, even so, as they chased them down through scrubland, they could not catch them. The Andrians escaped. And, instead of a quick victory, the Athenians were faced with a potentially long-lasting siege. It was not what they had hoped for, but there was little they could do, and (just as at Chalcedon the year before) they resolved to split their forces. So, while his colleague, Conon, stayed with thirty triremes to supervise operations on Andros and ensure safe passage through the straits, Alcibiades and the remainder of the fleet pressed east.

But not immediately to Ionia. Hampered by lack of funds, and wary of defections to the cash-rich Spartans, the Athenians looped south to vent their violence on the islanders of Rhodes and Cos, pillaging their fields and homesteads, seizing whatever plunder they could find. It was a very different policy from the soft diplomacy that had won the support of Selymbria and Byzantium, and might well have won supporters in Ionia as well. But then again, the circumstances were very different, too: the urgency to pay the fleet; the need to channel the frustrations of the army's failure to take Andros into something that might be perceived as victory; the need to rebuild an aura of invincibility as they prepared to meet the Spartans.[2]

Then, with swashbuckling bravado, they sailed on up the coast past Miletus and the spectral hills of Samos until they came to the great bay of Ephesus. Just around the headland to the north lay the still-loyal town of Notium, its temples, its houses, and its agora spread pleasantly across a rounded hill above a shallow anchorage. With a clear view south towards the entrance to the bay, it was the perfect base from which to monitor the Spartan fleet at Ephesus. All the Athenians need do was wait a little while, let Lysander question their intentions, let his sailors' nerves begin to fray as they contemplated the approaching battle and, when the time was ripe, engage the Spartans and defeat them. For the moment, all that was required was to sail into the bay from time to time to conduct reconnaissance and ratchet up the enemy's unease. It was nothing that required great military nous. Indeed, it did not even merit leaving a general in charge, especially as all ten Athenian generals were—or were soon to be—tied up in conflicts elsewhere. Instead, insisting that he should do nothing to risk meeting the Spartan fleet in battle, Alcibiades entrusted the exercise to his old friend, Antiochus, the helmsman. Surely he could manage on his own.[3]

So, leaving Antiochus with eighty triremes, Alcibiades continued sailing north with a small fleet of troopships and cavalry transporters, collecting money on the way from cities such as the now-restored (but constantly harassed) Clazomenae, until he came to Phocaea. Ringed by low hills, its bay protected by a scattering of islands, this pleasant, wealthy city had been in Spartan hands for five years now, and the Athenians were determined to get it back. Indeed, it was precisely for the reclamation of cities such as this that Alcibiades had brought cavalry and hoplites. It was why, too, he had ordered Thrasybulus to meet him there. As his ships curved into the enchanting bay, he could see that his colleague was in place already, and that he had wasted no time in beginning the process of building siege walls, with which to starve Phocaea into submission.[4]

It was a good strategy. With Lysander penned in at Ephesus, reluctant to put out to sea lest he risk engagement with the more experienced Athenian fleet, Alcibiades and his generals were free to launch attacks on more northerly Ionian cities, picking them off one by one, as they had picked off the cities of the Bosporus and Sea of Marmara, and methodically restoring them to Athens' empire. All being well, it could have worked. But all was not well. The lure of Persian gold was already proving irresistible for many in the Athenian fleet. Every night, knots of oarsmen were slipping out of Notium to hike the few short miles across the hills to Ephesus and Lysander's well-stocked camp. With them they brought not only manpower but intelligence, which the Spartans could weigh carefully and use. Besides, it is a law of war that circumstances overtake even the best-laid plans. And—perhaps only a few days after Alcibiades arrived in Phocaea—a trireme sped into the bay with grim news.[5]

The precise details would be argued and discussed for many years to come, but in essence what had happened was this: following the rules of engagement already laid down, the impetuous Antiochus had sailed into the Bay of Ephesus. With two ships. Or ten. The number was disputed. But what was clear was that he sailed in closer to the harbour than he should— perhaps personally shouting insults at the Spartans, perhaps even making provocative, lewd gestures (he was, as his detractors took such pleasure in observing, "a vulgar sort of man"). And Lysander had responded by scrambling his fleet. At lightning speed, he and the first three Spartan triremes had shot out to sea. In an instant, they had rammed Antiochus' vessel. And even as the water spouted through the shattered hull, and oarsmen splashed up from the rowing benches, desperate to abandon the now-useless ship, Antiochus, standing at the helm, had made an easy target.[6]

By now, the rest of the Spartan fleet, too, was streaking across the bay— ninety triremes, their ivory eyes locked on the Athenian ships, which had turned in panic and were racing to round the headland and escape. From Notium, the lookouts saw them, and they saw the Spartans, too. But Antiochus was dead, and he had appointed no lieutenant. In the absence of any chain of command, trireme captains shouted to their crews to get on board and put to sea. But in no order. In no tight formation. Piecemeal, chaotically, the Athenian fleet met the well-drilled, well-disciplined Spartan line in a nightmare of unpreparedness. By the time they scattered and fled back to Notium, between fifteen and twenty-three Athenian triremes had been holed or captured.

What had Antiochus been thinking? Was he, as some suggested, deliberately flouting orders, vaingloriously trying to emulate the tactics that had led to victory at Cyzicus, by luring the Spartan triremes out to sea, before springing the trap and surrounding them? But if that were the case, why did he allow himself to be attacked so easily, and why was the remainder of the fleet so unprepared when the Spartans did come bursting out into the open waters? More likely, it was a horrible mistake, a spur-of-the-moment miscalculation, which led to an enormous, shameful, and unnecessary loss of ships and lives. But, whatever the truth, it was an unforgivable defeat, costly to Athens, potentially disastrous for Alcibiades, the *strategos autocrator*, who had entrusted to his friend—the untried, unelected, ignorant Antiochus—the city's precious fleet.[7]

The debacle at Notium trumped the siege of Phocaea. So, taking Thrasybulus and his triremes with him, and loading the hoplites and cavalry back into his transport ships, Alcibiades immediately tore south. Perhaps he could lure Lysander out again! Perhaps, this time, he could defeat him! But, despite rowing around into the bay to goad the Spartans, and drifting close to shore, there was nothing he could do. In the coolly clever, ruthlessly astute Lysander, Alcibiades had met his match. For the moment, there was no need for the Spartan admiral to do anything. He had made his point. He had thrown the Athenians into disarray. He had unnerved their sailors. And he had potentially caused the People back in Athens to question their good judgement in appointing Alcibiades to the supreme command.[8]

Of all this, Alcibiades was well aware. So, rather than be tied down waiting for Lysander to respond, he ordered the fleet to strike camp and make haste for Samos and the safety of a friendly city. But Alcibiades knew all too well that time was against him. Ever since leaving Athens, nothing had gone right. First at Andros, then at Phocaea, and finally at Ephesus, he had failed to win a single victory. Moreover, his personal appointee had been responsible for the loss of a significant proportion of the fleet. How ironic that, when still labouring under the curses of the city's priests, he had enjoyed an unblemished record of success, but now that those curses were revoked, everything seemed to be going wrong! Perhaps (he might have reflected) he had been misguided to try to get the better of those priests at the Eleusinian Festival. After all, the earliest scene in all Greek literature, when Agamemnon's plans at Troy were thwarted by an angry priest, showed vividly that, in the gods' eyes, priests were more valued than generals.[9]

So, with his entire fleet, he set out north again. This time to Cyme, a rich if somewhat lazy city in the far north of Ionia. It was a loyal Athenian ally. And if, four years before, fifty of its citizens—oligarchic hotheads to a man—had tried to help the islanders of Lesbos break away from Athens' empire, that was their responsibility alone. The rest of the Cymeans were entirely innocent. Or so they thought. Alcibiades, however, looking for a pretext on which to attack them, did not agree. Cyme was a wealthy city, as he well knew. The board that drew up Athens' tribute lists, the board on which Alcibiades himself had served, had assessed its wealth as double that of Ephesus. And, with the soldiery still needing to be paid, it seemed unpatriotic not to punish it for the part its citizens had played in helping the rebellious Lesbians. Especially when Athens needed to notch up an easy victory.[10]

No sooner did the Athenian fleet dock than its men were fanning out across the fields and pasturelands around the city. Houses were looted; homesteads, burned. Farmers, peasants, slaves were rounded up as prisoners and herded to the sea. But even as the smoke was drifting high into the wintry sky, from the city Cymean hoplites issued out, all fully armoured, helmets down, shields up, spears lowered, their phalanx advancing on the unprepared Athenians. If only Alcibiades had brought hoplites of his own! But, thinking Cyme a soft target, he had disembarked them all on Lesbos, intending to use his troop ships to transport prisoners. Faced with an advancing wall of bronze, the fleet's oarsmen were helpless. Rather than fight what all knew would be an unequal battle, they abandoned prisoners and booty and raced back to the ships. And, although Alcibiades returned the next day with his hoplites, the Cymeans refused his challenge. Just as at Ephesus, so here, the Athenians had been humiliated. And all thanks to Alcibiades' misjudgement. As he led his fleet back south to Samos for the winter, Alcibiades cannot but have been imagining the capital his enemies would make out of his failures.[11]

There were already malcontents among the soldiery on Samos, and so it was inevitable that they should send a delegation back to Athens to complain of Alcibiades' poor handling of the campaign. It was inevitable, too, that the hitherto loyal citizens of Cyme, so outrageously attacked by their own allies, should send a delegation, too. The atmosphere they found in Athens was already a far cry from the heady optimism that prevailed after the Mysteries.[12]

For one thing, the city had experienced the shock of an attack. Not long after the fleet had sailed, the Spartan King Agis had assembled a huge force of Peloponnesians and Boeotians—twenty-eight thousand infantry and twelve hundred cavalry—and, on a moonless night, had marched them down towards the city, slaughtering the guards who manned the outposts on the way. At dawn, when the Athenians awoke, they could see from their ramparts the hostile army, its shield-line a mile long and four men deep, drawn up in an arc around the city. There was no good military reason to give battle. Psychologically, however, there was every need. So, as the women and old men lined the battlements, the Athenian cavalry swarmed out from the city gates. Half a mile away, the Spartans and their allies watched, too, as their own cavalry responded. Across the fields and market gardens of the suburbs, the battle raged as horseman charged horseman, jabbing spears and slashing swords, until, to the enthusiastic cheering of the citizens, the Athenians, victorious, pursued the enemy back towards their lines. But then the infantry advanced, and the Athenians wheeled around and clattered back inside the city. That night, the Spartans and their allies encamped at the Academy, and, though, next morning, both sides drew up as if for battle, neither felt confident enough to mount the first attack. Agis withdrew into the gathering dusk, and Athens celebrated victory. Yet for many, it had been a frightening experience, a reminder of the reality of war, a foretaste of the siege to come, if the navy should be lost and supplies by sea cut off.[13]

So it was against this backdrop that the Athenians learned of the defeat at Notium and the loss of so many ships. And now they learned, too, not only that the policy of winning back the rebel cities of Ionia was in tatters but that Alcibiades was attacking allies! In the Assembly, one of the malcontents who had sailed from Samos for this very purpose launched a bitter tirade. The defeat at Notium, he thundered, was entirely Alcibiades' fault. The supreme commander had left the fleet in the hands not of a seasoned general, but of his helmsman, one of the many drunken sots, the spinners of tall tales, whose company he craved, whose poor advice he took, ignoring the experience of cooler-headed captains. And why had Alcibiades left the fleet at all? To go whoring in the cities of Ionia under the pretext of collecting money for his war chests![14]

Already the mood was heated. When the Cymean delegates condemned Alcibiades' unfair attack, some Athenians stood up and shouted out that it was shameful that he had failed to take their city; that here was proof, if any proof were needed, that Alcibiades was in the pocket of the Persian Great King! And not just of the Great King—of Farnavaz as well. Did the citizens not know that the satrap had offered Alcibiades the governorship of Athens, if Athens lost the war? Nor was his one-time friendship with the Spartans overlooked. Others who had sailed from Samos took to the Speakers' Platform to accuse Alcibiades of being a Spartan agent, of deliberately helping them to win. Against a barrage of accusations such as these, and with the People now calling for his blood, there was nothing that even the most fervent of Alcibiades' supporters could say to save him. A resolution was proposed and passed, and Alcibiades was stripped of his command. So were his appointees. And a trireme was launched to take the news to Samos.[15]

But when it reached the island, Alcibiades was nowhere to be found. Reports had come to him already, and he had lost no time. Already he was out at sea and racing northwards. Remembering his experience in Sicily, he could well have feared arrest. And he did not wish to face a trial in Athens. Yes, its judicial system was the envy of the world. But its jurors were only human: five hundred representatives of the Athenian People who had put such faith in him, who, just months before, considered him invincible— their saviour—who had trusted him to win back the lost cities of Ionia, only to see him suffer defeat after bewildering defeat. His magic had evaporated. His promise was a sham. And now that his dazzling victories in the Hellespont and Bosporus had been eclipsed by his more recent failures, still older memories and damning accusations rose to the surface once again. Jolted once more into reality, and facing the prospect of a hard-fought war without the wherewithal to pay for it, the Athenians blamed not themselves but Alcibiades for offering the mirage of easy victory. Once get him in the dock, and they would make him their scapegoat, irrespective of the justice of their case. And, if a public enquiry into his conduct as general failed, there were many citizens with private grievances who were all too ready to lay suits against him.[16]

So, it was just as well that Alcibiades had made contingencies. Even if the Athenians had turned against him, even if the Spartans hated him, even if the Persians had lost all faith in him, he still had friends in Thrace. He had a mercenary army, too—the soldiers with whom Alcibiades had taken Selymbria and Byzantium, loyal soldiers whose loyalty he had almost certainly retained through payments made even in the months gone by. And just as importantly, he owned property. And it was to his property at Pactye that Alcibiades came first.[17]

Well-sited where the Hellespont's northern shore curved round into the Sea of Marmara, Pactye had long been a meeting place for Thracian and Athenian culture. It stood on the borders of the Thracian Chersonese, the long spit of land which, a hundred years before, Athenian aristocrats, the family of Miltiades, had ruled as tyrants. Indeed, to protect his land from hostile tribes, Miltiades the Elder had even built a wall across the isthmus, enclosing Pactye within his territory. Since then, Athens had maintained her contacts both in the area—Sestus, her naval headquarters on the Hellespont, lay in the Thracian Chersonese—and in wider Thrace. In the hope of an alliance, the Athenians had even awarded citizenship to a Thracian prince.[18]

But the two societies were very different. Whereas democratic Athens used every means it could to prevent power from being concentrated in the hands of one man, the Thracians, whose lands stretched from the north Aegean north to the River Danube and from the borders of Macedon east to the Black Sea, were ruled unashamedly by powerful individuals. In the course of the fifth century, a dynasty of strong kings had emerged to unite the rival tribes of the Thracian heartland, enlarging their dominion to include many on the fringes, forming the powerful nation over which Amadocus I had now ruled for four years. Of late, in their dealings with the Thracians, no Athenian had dared to emulate the self-aggrandizing ambition of Miltiades, lest his fellow citizens accuse him of behaving like a tyrant. No Athenian, that is, until Alcibiades. Already, through his force of personality, he had found ways to win the Thracians' friendship and affection, and now—once again unfettered by the stifling niceties of the Athenian democracy—he could build a powerbase of his own. And transform himself into a Thracian princeling.[19]

Evidence for Alcibiades' years in Thrace is scarce, but it is still possible to build a picture of the life he led there. It is probable that he struck up a friendship and made personal alliances with Amadocus' lieutenant in the region, Seuthes, who was desperately trying to win back territories that had rebelled against his father years before. Only a few years later, another Athenian (indeed, another of Socrates' pupils), the commander Xenophon, who had dealings of his own with Seuthes, described a visit to the Thracian in his well-protected tower. Remembering how an ancestor had been attacked by lawless tribesmen, Seuthes was paranoid. Not only did he keep horses saddled all night long, in case he needed to effect a quick escape, he carefully monitored his visitors, barring their entourage from entering, allowing only those he trusted through his gates. But to those he did trust, and who agreed to fight for him, he could be generous, offering not only good pay for their troops, but the gift of cities strung along the coast. Which was how Alcibiades now found himself in control of a chain of towns and fortresses stretching from Pactye in the west along the northern shores of the Sea of Marmara to Bisanthe in the east.[20]

The price for these possessions was allegiance to the king and the promise to campaign on his behalf against rebellious tribes, a promise Alcibiades was pleased to honour. Soon, with his own loyal Thracian troops, he was pressing deep inland—further than any Greek had gone before—using his newly returned military good fortune to restore broad swathes of territory to the king's control. But these military incursions did more than ingratiate Alcibiades with the Thracian court and bolster his position as a faithful ally. They furnished him with booty. And before long, he was amassing an enviable wealth. Not that he kept it all for himself. Whereas, in Persia, rulers showered loyal subjects with gifts to strengthen their relationships, in Thrace, the opposite was true. Vassals were expected to prove their allegiance by presenting overlords with the most lavish offerings that they could find, in exchange for which the men in power bestowed their patronage. As Xenophon was later told, "The more you give Seuthes, the more help Seuthes will give you." And the setting for such liberal gift-giving was invariably a banquet.[21]

The chic, sophisticated democrats of Athens liked to portray the blond-haired pointy-bearded Thracians as unrefined barbarians, whose primitive society was more akin to that of Homer's epics than of contemporary Greece. There certainly were huge gulfs between their cultures, and many a Greek relished the opportunities for the sort of adolescent humour that these differences afforded. The Greeks drank wine from wide shallow cups, and to them, the Thracian habit of sucking beer through straws reminded them of nothing so much as fellatio. Equally bizarre to an Athenian audience was the Thracian practice of circumcision, to them as alien a disfigurement as the extensive tattoos with which they adorned their bodies, or the top-knots in which they tied their hair. Nothing, however, seemed further from the civilized Greek way of life than the Thracian banquet. Yet this must have been the setting for much of the diplomacy that enabled Alcibiades to flourish in his new environment.[22]

Like the Thracian king, powerful lieutenants such as Seuthes had no administrative capital but progressed constantly throughout their territories, choosing to stay the night at prosperous villages, which could most readily provide the food and drink required to entertain both them and their large retinue. The banquet was thus an important ceremonial, invariably attended by the most powerful men in the region. Once inside the banqueting hall, and seated in a circle, three-legged tables were brought in, laden with sliced meat on skewers and loaves of bread, which Seuthes would tear apart and throw to favoured guests. At the same time, great horns of wine were passed around, for heavy drinking was a Thracian tradition, and one which accompanied the next stage in the evening: the gift-giving.[23]

Seuthes' agents had already been busy, suggesting the kind of present that would be most suitable. One by one, the guests rose to their feet, proposed a toast, and demonstrated how his gift would prove of the greatest benefit to Seuthes. The possibilities were many and varied: a horse; a slave-boy; clothes for Seuthes' wife; carpets; a silver cup. With much obsequious ceremony, each was handed over with more toasts and the ritual spilling of the dregs over the wearer's robes. That done, it was time for the entertainment. Trumpeters would enter and strike up anything from a martial air to what passed in Thrace for more rhapsodic melodies. But this was not all. Seuthes himself might perform a war dance. Buffoons and jesters might arrive to clown and tumble. And all the while, the banqueters indulged in more wine and lewd humour.

In which, unsurprisingly, Alcibiades surpassed even his hosts. For, just as in Persia and Sparta, he had quickly adopted local custom, so, in Thrace, he effortlessly transformed into a Thracian. And it was not just the drinking that appealed. The Thracians were horsemen, skilled cavalrymen, avid flat-racers, equally adept in racing chariots. On such shared interests, it was more than possible to build close friendships. Perhaps Seuthes tried to cement his relationship with Alcibiades still further. He would later offer to make Xenophon not just his brother and official dining-mate but his son-in-law, adding that, if the Greek had a daughter of his own, he would buy her from him.[24]

There is no record of Alcibiades marrying a Thracian heiress, but it is not impossible. He did, however, summon his own son to join him. The youth, now about fifteen years old, was already treading in his father's footsteps, blazing a trail of precocious scandal throughout Athens, earning a questionable reputation for his sexual excesses. Tongues wagged. And clucked. The stories multiplied. A mere child, he had spent the night with the populist politician, Archedemus "the Bleary-Eyed," partying at his house, lying under the same cloak as his host, drinking until dawn. Although under age, he kept a mistress, and, in general, he was trying to emulate the worst excesses of his ancestors.[25]

But if Alcibiades hoped to be a moderating influence on his son, or simply wished to have him at his side to share his own dissolute activities, he was sorely disappointed. The two got on abysmally. The boy had been separated from his father from an early age—he was, he was later to remind a jury, only four years old, when Alcibiades went over to the Spartans, from which time he considered himself an orphan—and in Thrace he did all he could to rebel. So much so that almost at once he took a lover, a Greek called Theotimus, and plotted with him to seize one of his father's fortresses. But when they succeeded, Theotimus promptly threw the boy in prison and demanded a ransom from Alcibiades. How he had misjudged the situation! Alcibiades refused. He hated his son so much, he said, that he could die for all he cared. And even then, he would not bother to retrieve his bones.[26]

This was more than a rejection of his son and heir. It was grimly topical allusion. In the months that followed Alcibiades' dismissal from the army, the retrieval of the dead, or rather their abandonment, had cast dark shadows over Athens with strategically worrying implications. With Alcibiades gone, the Athenians were determined to wipe the slate clean of his influence. So they elected ten generals who had never been associated with him in any way, and were therefore untarnished. And they appointed Callias Archon Eponymous, the symbolism of which cannot have been lost on anyone. Not only had the impious Alcibiades been dismissed, but heading the city's administration was his bitterest enemy, the high priest of Eleusis. And since, in Athens, each year was named from its chief magistrate, history would forever mark the twelve months following Alcibiades' expulsion as the Year of Callias.[27]

At the same time, the Spartans, too, were making changes. With the end of his year in office, Lysander was recalled, and his replacement, Callicratidas, another *mothax,* sent out to theatre. Loath to toady to the Persians, Callicratidas wanted to bring the conflict to a swift conclusion. So, almost at once, he set about provoking the Athenian navy. Not least by sending Conon, who still commanded Athens' fleet, an insultingly coarse message implying Spartan dominance of the Aegean: "Stop fucking with my sea!"[28]

Within weeks he had driven home his message by chasing Conon and his fleet to Lesbos and the protection of the port at Mytilene, where he not only mounted a blockade by sea but settled down to a siege. Desperately, Conon sent for help to Athens. Frantically, the People responded. They were already working feverishly to build new ships, and, within a month of getting Conon's news, they had seventy new triremes ready, paid for by melting down the gold from statues on the Acropolis—the statue of Athene in the Parthenon; statues of the goddess Victory. As a portent, this could be interpreted in either of two ways: either the Athenians were being sacrilegious by destroying images inhabited by the divine, and so the gods would be against them; or the gods were themselves contributing to the city's war chest, which, in turn, would promise victory.[29]

But there was an even more practical problem than a lack of money facing the Athenians. They were running out of men. Twenty-two thousand were required to row the new ships, and, if they were to draw only from the unpropertied classes, which until now had almost exclusively furnished oarsmen, there would simply not be enough candidates to man the benches. So, in an act of unprecedented desperation, the People voted to enlist not only those from wealthier social classes, men more experienced in fighting in the ranks as hoplites or even cavalry, but slaves. Not that they would *serve* as slaves. To win their loyalty, the People offered any slave who rowed with them both freedom and Athenian citizenship.[30]

But it was not this sudden inclusivity that proclaimed the city's desperation. It was the sheer inexperience of this new cohort of oarsmen. Somehow, the untried crews of this untested fleet—110 ships setting sail to face 170 well-seasoned Spartan triremes—must, in a week or two, learn all the skills of hostile seamanship, which they would need to bring to bear within mere minutes of their first encounter with the enemy. If they did not, quite simply, they were dead.[31]

Yet somehow, they succeeded. On a squally morning, they met the Spartan fleet at Arginusae, a scattering of islands east of Lesbos near the Asiatic coast, and, in a hard-fought sea-battle, they routed them. It was an outstanding victory. Led by no fewer than eight Athenian generals, they not only incapacitated seventy-seven Spartan triremes, they killed Callicratidas, the Spartan admiral, and routed the surviving ships, pursuing them far south, until pursuit seemed pointless. And then they turned back for Arginusae. But as they did, they saw the dark clouds closing in. Then came the high winds and the lashing rain, the rolling waves, which slapped the triremes' hulls, the spray, which threatened to engulf them. Their ships lurching and shuddering, the captains gave the order to make course for the sheltered coves of Arginusae and ride out the storm. Meanwhile, in the channels between the islands, the crews of twelve holed Athenian triremes were clinging to upturned hulls, while survivors of another thirteen vessels, smashed into pieces in the battle, clutched desperately to bits of wreckage, trying to stay afloat. And all around them, corpses drifted in the heaving swell.[32]

By the time the storm had passed, it was too late. Most who survived the battle drowned. And many of the dead had disappeared, washed away by currents and the wind-swept waves. To lie on land, unburied, was considered terrible by any Greek. But far worse was to die at sea, the body nibbled at by fish and squid and octopus, the bones detached and separated, scattered who knew where.[33]

Hot on the heels of the report of victory, the news broke in Athens of the generals' failure to rescue the shipwrecked and collect the dead. Bitter accusations flew. Among those charged with negligence, some blamed one another. The generals were recalled and put on trial. But not in a lawcourt. In the Assembly, where passion ruled judgement, and judgement was so often flawed. And such was the wrath that now gripped the People, angered beyond measure by the failures of their generals—from Nicias to Alcibiades and now to the generals of Arginusae—that passion turned to vengeance. Only a few brave voices spoke up against the baying majority. Among them was Socrates and two of Alcibiades' family: his uncle, Axiochus, with whom he had shared youthful adventures, and his cousin, Euryptolemus, whose face, seen at Piraeus, had reassured Alcibiades that it was safe to come ashore.[34]

But the arguments put forward in the generals' defence fell on the deafest of ears. Interpreting their failure to rescue the drowning or collect the dead as a gross affront to crews comprising men from almost every social class in Athens, the People condemned the eight generals to death. No matter that these were some of the best military minds of their generation. Or that one of them was the son whom Aspasia had borne to Pericles, the war's architect, the last link with what they now considered the age of Athens' greatness.

Perhaps, though, that was in part the point. For too long, the city had listened enraptured to the promises of politicians, the vaunting visions of men like Pericles, who proclaimed that it was Athens' destiny to win, to rule the world. For too long, they had believed the dream. And now, distressed and disillusioned, impoverished and bereaved, they had awakened to reality. Little wonder that they turned against the generals, representatives of the ruling class they blamed for all their hardships. Or that, instead of celebrating victory, they chose to contemplate disaster.

And they were right to do so. For even now, with the Athenian treasury lying all but empty, money was pouring into the Spartan war chests. With the death of Callicratidas, Lysander had been sent back to Ionia. He quickly renewed his personal relationship with the Persian prince and made it known that he would stop at nothing to achieve his goals. His sayings became legendary. "Where the lion-skin [worn by Sparta's—and his own—ancestor, the noble hero Heracles] will not reach, we must augment it with a fox-pelt [a symbol of wiliness and guile]." "One cheats boys with knuckle-bones, but men with oaths." And as he ruthlessly tightened his personal hold on Spartan troops and allies, more than a few muttered that he was behaving very much like a tyrant.[35]

His dominance was only increased when Korush was suddenly recalled to Susa. Ruling over wealthy tracts of land, and courted by the most powerful players in the region, the young prince had been exhibiting increasing signs of megalomania. Persian courtiers were obliged, as a mark of honour, to conceal their hands inside their sleeves whenever they came into the presence of the Great King. But only the Great King. When two of Korush's cousins came to Sardis, the prince demanded that they show him the same respect. Quite rightly, they refused. Quite wrongly, Korush had them executed. For Dārayavahuš, it was the final straw. Not even the pleading of Queen Pari Satis could prevent him summoning the boy home for a dressing down. And maybe more. Scenting the downfall of his bitter rival, the serpentine Chithrafarna insisted on accompanying Korush on his journey east, ostensibly to help him, in reality to coil the prince around with all the venom that he could.[36]

As he prepared for his departure from Sardis, Korush held a meeting with his friend, Lysander. With this new twist, each man needed to preserve the trust and backing of the other as never before: Lysander for the Persian's ongoing financing of Sparta's war effort; Korush to ensure that his provincial power base remained loyal. So, in an act that was as unprecedented as it was unconstitutional, Korush appointed Lysander (for as long as he himself was absent) to the position of satrap of Lydia, Phrygia, Cappadocia, and Ionia, with the authority to raise and use the tribute from his provinces as he saw fit. All he asked the Spartan in return was that he should not end the war too soon. At least wait for his return to deal the final blow.[37]

In reality, however, for Lysander, this was not an option. War has its own momentum. Besides, with Korush's future in question, not to mention rumours that the Great King, Dārayavahuš, was dying, the Spartan needed to capitalize on his successes while he could. So he swept like a firestorm west through the Aegean, destroying hostile cities and cementing the loyalty of allies, before bringing his ships to shore in Attica, where he met in conference with King Agis. Constantly wrong-footed and confused, all that the Athenian fleet could do was straggle in his wake—which was precisely what Lysander wanted. For, even as the Athenians were setting course for Attica, he put to sea once more and, like a comet, shot northeast. For the Hellespont. Through which the grain ships from the Black Sea must soon sail. And, like moths drawn to flame, the Athenian fleet followed.[38]

Lysander's goal was Lampsacus, the wealthy wine-producing city on the southern Hellespontine shores near the entrance from the Sea of Marmara. In years past, its philosophers had disputed the events of Homer's *Iliad*, its heroes and its gods—were they factual or allegorical? Now, though, war's realities were unquestionable. Descending on the city like an inferno, Lysander seized and looted it, and settled back to wait for the Athenians. And sure enough, they came. First to their base at Sestus, then closer still. To a scrubby beach where brackish streams, which irrigated the flat farmland, debouched into the channel. On the opposite shore from Lampsacus. At a place called Aegospotami, "Goat's Rivers." It, too, had excited philosophical debate. It was here that, sixty-two years earlier, in 466, a blazing meteor had thumped into the earth, fuelling the belief of men like Anaxagoras that the heavenly bodies were not divine but natural. Which was admirably scientific. But it did not mean that it was not an omen.[39]

For days, the two fleets lay there: the Spartans in the luxury of well-stocked Lampsacus; the Athenians at Aegospotami, sleeping in cramped tents beneath September skies. Eying each other hungrily. Putting out to sea each morning. Drawing up in formation near the harbour mouth of Lampsacus. Hurling insults. Singing paeans. Daring each other to attack. And then, as if bored by the charade, peeling off and shrugging back to shore. But even as each watched the other, they were being watched in turn. From across the belly of the bay. From a fortress tower at Pactye. By Alcibiades. And what he saw disturbed him.[40]

It was not just the site that the Athenians had chosen, though that was bad enough. Twelve miles from Sestus and the nearest friendly market, their men were forced to send out ships to fetch their food, which meant that, while the Spartan oarsmen could keep focused on the prospect of a battle that was sure to come, the Athenians were thinking of their bellies as much as of fighting. Moreover, discipline was poor. When the Athenians returned from morning manoeuvres, the trireme crews would scatter, some to forage for supplies, others to stroll leisurely along the country lanes, others to the squalor of their tents to sleep, still others to light fires and prepare the evening meal. It was as if no one was aware of the enormity of what was facing them across the straits: Lysander and the Spartan fleet, greedy for victory, greedy to bring the war to a swift close, greedy to smash Athens' fleet and starve her city into submission.[41]

For four days, Alcibiades looked on, and his frustration grew. At last, he could bear it no longer. Saddling his horse, he galloped around the bay and down into the Athenian encampment: 180 triremes dragged up on the beach; a canvas city of thirty thousand men and more, bivouacked on the flat plains all around them; and, clear to see with its distinctive flags, the headquarters tent beside which the six generals, the supreme command rotating every day, were kicking their heels complacently. Urgently and passionately, Alcibiades addressed them. Could they not see what a dangerous, exposed position they had chosen here at Aegospotami? Where was the harbour? Where were their walls? And could they not appreciate how perilous it was to have to send for food each day to Sestus? Better for the whole fleet to sail to Sestus and make its headquarters there! And then, where were their land troops? The Spartans had strong regiments of hoplites. The Athenians had few. And at Cyzicus, Selymbria, and Byzantium, hoplites and light-armed infantry had been essential. At Chalcedon, cavalry had played a crucial role, too. Did the generals really believe that they could achieve anything significant with only ships? But he, Alcibiades, could help them. If they let him share command. He had his own army of Thracians at his beck and call. And more. He could enlist the help of friends, the local governor Seuthes, not to mention the Thracian King Medocus!

Together—with Athens' navy and his land troops—they were a more than match for Lysander. Alone, the Athenians were in peril.[42]

It was such good advice. But the generals did not want to hear it. Especially not from Alcibiades. Admittedly, there were still those back in Athens who longed for his return. Only months before at the Lenaea festival, in *Frogs,* his bitter comedy set in the Underworld, Aristophanes had caused the god Dionysus to exclaim of Alcibiades, "The city longs for him, but at the same time hates him, too. But on balance it must have him!" And in reply, the dead poet Aeschylus advised, "You should not rear a lion cub in the city—no, really! Do not rear a lion cub in the city!—but, if you do, bend to its ways." It had not been the only drama to explore the dangers inherent in being seduced by someone as charismatic as Alcibiades. In *Bacchae,* performed in Athens the same year, Euripides had explored the myth of Dionysus, the mesmerizing god, who makes all he meets fall under his powerful spell, before turning on them and destroying them. Like the audience on the theatre benches back home, the generals at Aegospotami believed that they had learned their lesson. They were determined that they would not be taken in again. They were determined that they would be unimpressed.[43]

Indeed, they had every reason to suspect Alcibiades. His track record was hardly reassuring. There were still those who suspected him of being complicit with the Spartans. So, how did they know that this was not a trap? And as for his promises to bring help from the Thracians, the Athenians knew all about how empty such assurances could be. He had once guaranteed that, through Chithrafarna, he could bring the Persians over to the Athenian side. And look what happened to that promise! And then there was the possibility—the probability, indeed!—that if they did take Alcibiades' advice, if Alcibiades did bring his Thracian troops and Thracian friends to help defeat Lysander, it would be Alcibiades, not they, who would be praised by the Athenians as their saviour. No! As one of their number tetchily replied, voicing his colleagues' sentiments, "We're in command now. You're not."[44]

At which Alcibiades wheeled his horse and trotted out of the camp. As he did so, crowds of well-wishers, alerted to his presence, ran after him. For a moment he reined in to a walk and spoke to them. If the generals had not insulted him, he said, he would either have destroyed the Spartan fleet in harbour or forced it to engage in open sea, where the Athenians would have enjoyed every advantage. Then he spurred on his horse and galloped home to Pactye.

From there, next day, he watched as his worst fears were realized. Again, the two fleets drew up at the mouth of Lampsacus' harbour. Again, neither attacked. Again, the Athenians returned to Aegospotami, hauled their triremes up onto the beach, and dispersed to spend the afternoon in lazy relaxation. But as their usual squadron of triremes sailed off south for Sestus to pick up provisions, Alcibiades saw, shooting out from Lampsacus, the Spartan fleet. Easily they intercepted the Athenian ships and drove them back to Aegospotami. As their grappling hooks made contact with the still-beached triremes and dragged them out to sea, the Spartans landed a detachment of their hoplites. They made straight for the camp, slicing down bewildered, unprepared Athenians. In the chaos, some Athenians ran to the ships. But the crews were too dispersed. With nothing like full complements, the triremes simply could not be launched. Only Alcibiades' erstwhile lieutenant, Conon, managed to put out to sea with ten ships and escape. The rest were taken by the Spartans: 170 warships, the entire Athenian navy. And as myriad oarsmen ran for their lives, pounding the lanes where so lately they had strolled in the late sun, racing through the fields in terror, the Spartans herded the rest together and lined them up on the beach. In Lampsacus, a summary court passed its decision. Not one of the three-and-a-half thousand captives' lives was spared.[45]

On that September afternoon, with the Hellespont in Spartan hands, the war effectively came to an end. No grain convoys would come to Athens now. But still its citizens held out, terrified that the fate that they had meted out on others—the massacre of free men, the enslavement of free women and free children—would be meted out on them. And as they waited, their numbers swelled. All over the Aegean, cities were capitulating, and in every city, Spartans corralled all the Athenians they could find and shipped them off to Athens to swell the numbers of her citizens already running low on food. And yet all autumn and all winter, the Athenians refused steadfastly to surrender, until at last, next March, they bowed to the inevitable.[46]

Sparta and her allies showed commendable restraint. Not for them the savagery that once-proud Athens had inflicted on defeated Melos and Scione. Instead, they commanded, perhaps on the very anniversary of Greece's victory over Persia at Salamis, the Long Walls to the sea must be torn down. No longer would a safe corridor allow the land-locked city to function like a sea-girt island protected by its fleet. No longer would there be a fleet at all. And to govern Athens, there would now be not the People, but a specially hand-picked committee, thirty loyal men, to rule as Sparta saw fit. As an oligarchy. At its head was Critias, once Alcibiades' close friend, the agnostic playwright-philosopher, who had vied to be considered the chief advocate of his recall from Persia. Now, though, disillusioned by the war, embittered by the capriciousness of the Assembly, and driven by an icy rationalism that allowed for no compassion, Critias embarked on a reign of terror far worse than anything the city had endured under the Four Hundred. Anyone who threatened the new order was hunted down and killed, including those in exile around whom opposition might rally. And chief among these was Alcibiades.[47]

Not that this came as a surprise to Alcibiades. Even before Athens fell, he had probably abandoned his fortresses in Thrace, too close to the sea for comfort, now that the sea belonged to Sparta—whose cuckolded King Agis still wished him dead, whose general Lysander, too, was tracking down his enemies and liquidating them. Logic might have suggested that, even if the lands controlled by Seuthes were unsafe, Alcibiades would push north, deep into Thrace, where (he had boasted to the generals at Aegospotami) he enjoyed the friendship of the powerful King Medocus. The Thracian heartlands, after all, were far from any Greek sphere of influence, and he should have been quite safe there. Instead, though, with no time to lose, he turned his sights east to the lush orchards of Bithynia and its lakes and plains and snow-peaked mountains south of the Black Sea and Sea of Marmara. His fortress compounds were a fluster of activity as gifts and booty, glittering treasures amassed through rapine or diplomacy, were packed in crates and shipped ahead. More were to travel with him. Yet more still must be left behind, perhaps buried as a horde in the hope that one day he would return.[48]

But when he reached Bithynia, his crates and the Thracians to whom he had entrusted them had disappeared. Frustrated and sensing danger, Alcibiades was edgy, and soon he was on the move again. This time to an even more unlikely destination: Dascyleum and the court of Farnavaz—to pledge his allegiance to the Persians and their new Great King. For, even as the War in the Aegean was drawing to its close, in Susa, King Dārayavahuš lay dying.

Laid down in Roman times, a Spartan mosaic commemorates Alcibiades. (Art Collection 2/Alamy Stock Photo.)

The succession went as had been planned to his eldest son, who took the royal name Artaxšaça. But coronations can be times to settle scores, and days into his reign, one of his satraps whispered accusations in the new king's ear: Chithrafarna denounced his enemy, the young Prince Korush, of plotting to murder Artaxšaça and claim the throne himself. The evidence was compelling. The imperial guards seized Korush. But, distraught, Pari Satis rushed to the royal chamber and begged Artaxšaça to release and pardon him. Which Artaxšaça did. And soon Korush and Chithrafarna (no doubt in separate convoys) were being driven back along the Royal Road west to their respective provinces, where they continued to be bitter rivals, and Korush dreamed of Artaxšaça's overthrow.[49]

News of the plot had already reached Alcibiades, and already the outline of a plan was taking shape: to bring compelling evidence before the Great King, offer his full military support and pledge personal allegiance to the crown. The scheme had so much to recommend it. History was full of Greeks who had received rich recompense for helping Persia. Moreover, to attack Korush was to attack Korush's greatest friend and ally, Lysander, the nemesis of Alcibiades and Athens; and to do that, to neutralize both the Persian and the Spartan, would bring great joy to Alcibiades. It was because of Lysander, after all, that Alcibiades had been forced into exile in the wake of the defeat at Notium; it was thanks to him, too, that he had lost his Thracian lands and treasures after Aegospotami. Helping friends and destroying enemies was at the heart of popular morality, and (for the moment) Alcibiades had no greater enemy than Lysander. Added to which, with Lysander and Sparta defeated, the way might just be clear for his return to Athens.[50]

In his cloistered palace at Dascyleum, Farnavaz greeted Alcibiades with studied courtesy. Years earlier, the two men had sworn personal oaths to one another, as the Greek no doubt reminded his host. For Farnavaz, however, Alcibiades was an awkward guest. Not just his history but his current status, too, was dubious. While it might not be advisable to shun so great a general who was freely offering his services to the Great King, he had proved himself so unreliable in the past. And questions still haunted his precise relationship with Chithrafarna, who, although an enemy of Korush, was no friend of Farnavaz. So the satrap chose a compromise, a delaying strategy that would allow him to fulfil his obligations as a host, while containing Alcibiades' activities in Persia.

With elaborate urbanity and apparent kindness, he agreed to Alcibiades' requests. And more. Claiming to be so charmed by his guest that he held no one in greater esteem, he presented him with lands of his own in Phrygia, the fortress town of Grynium and the territory around it, from which he could accrue an annual income of no less than fifty talents. And, as accommodation, he offered him Melissa, a satrapal compound high on the Phrygian plateau, where the steep cliffs of an acropolis erupted like a jagged molar from the vastness of plain, and strange rocks littered the rich pastureland.[51]

Here Alcibiades must wait, while arrangements were made for his permit to travel on the Royal Road east to Susa. Only those with official documentation could use this tightly guarded highway stretching sixteen hundred miles from Sardis to the heart of empire. Riders with urgent messages could gallop the distance in a week, changing horses at staging posts strategically positioned every fifteen to twenty miles. Royal processions, travelling at little more than walking pace, took longer, perhaps ninety days, stopping for the night at cool caravanserai and compounds such as Melissa, where Alcibiades was setting up his private court.[52]

He was not travelling alone. Among his entourage were not just loyal companions, but two of the most beautiful and educated women of the age, the courtesans Timandra ("Man-Honourer") and Theodote ("God's Gift"). Timandra's fate was curiously linked to that of Alcibiades. She was a Sicilian Greek from the small town of Hyccara, near Panormus. During Athens' Sicilian Expedition, weeks after Alcibiades was recalled, his fellow general, Nicias, eager to win military kudos, had sailed around the island in search of a soft target. He found Hyccara and, in a somewhat inglorious raid, he took the town, enslaving many of its women and children, among whom were Timandra and her young daughter, Lais. Both found their way to Athens, where, thanks to their good looks, wits, and sheer hard work, they succeeded in establishing themselves as exclusive and expensive courtesans, fussy in their choice of lovers, suggesting prohibitively high fees to any who did not take their fancy. As for the vivacious Theodote, one of Socrates' companions once described her as possessing the most delightful breasts imaginable.[53]

It was well that Alcibiades had such distracting consorts for, as winter gripped the Phrygian plain and still no travel permits came, time could have settled very heavy on his hands. He was not a man who relished inactivity. Everywhere he went at every stage of life, he needed constant stimulation— whether in Athens, playing the high-stakes game of politics, roistering with rowdy friends, doggedly fomenting war; in Sparta, treading a precarious course, fighting to win confidence, while seducing the King's wife; in Persia, professing such sincerity, while sowing suspicion among all sides; in the Hellespont and Bosporus, where, cavalier with his own safety, he won breathtaking victories and kept the sea lanes safe; or in Thrace, where he led his mercenary troops to battle in his lust for wealth and glory, before, in the last and grandest gesture of them all, offering once more to fight for Athens. And now he was desperate to be on his way once more on the long road east to new lands and new adventures and the fabled palaces of Susa and Persepolis and Ecbatana, with its seven rings of battlements, each rumoured to be painted in a colour of its own, white, black and scarlet, blue and orange, silver, gold.[54]

But even as Alcibiades was contemplating his audience with the Great King, envoys were arriving at Dascyleum. From Critias and Lysander. They had heard that Farnavaz was entertaining Alcibiades, detaining him (without his knowledge) in his gilded prison. But they wanted him detained no longer. Rather, they wanted him dead. Perhaps the stimulus had come from Athens, where the Thirty Tyrants threatened to rebel from Sparta if the Spartans did not ensure the People's darling, whom they had already banished from the whole of Greece, could never return to overthrow them. Perhaps it came from Agis—still aggrieved that Alcibiades had slept with his young wife—who ordered Lysander to convey the message to the satrap that, unless he liquidated Alcibiades, Sparta would consider her peace terms with Persia null and void. In the end, it did not matter where the incitement came from. What mattered was, it came. And Farnavaz, now with a clear political mandate to save the alliance with Sparta, and perhaps convincing himself that the duplicitous Alcibiades was, in fact, an agent of the Evil One, the Great Lie, Angra Mainyu, acted. It was to be an operation of the highest sensitivity. Failure was not an option. So Farnavaz entrusted it to his closest family members, in whom he had the greatest confidence: his brother, Mazajus, and his uncle, Susamithra. And the two assassins headed east towards Melissa.[55]

Later, some said that Alcibiades had dreamt that he was lying in Timandra's lap, dressed in her clothing as she cradled his head and rubbed his face with rouge and white lead makeup. Others maintained he saw nightmarish visions: searing fire and flashing knives. Perhaps Timandra and her colleague, Theodote, really did report such things. More likely, they were conjured up in hindsight. There was no real reason why Alcibiades should fear a plot. As far as he knew, Farnavaz was sympathetic, loyal. Yes, the delay in setting out for Susa was frustrating—increasingly so, as spring turned into summer, and the Phrygian plain baked under a relentless sun. Maybe, indeed, Alcibiades was starting to suspect that he was effectively being detained under house arrest. But the same had happened to others in the past—when Chthrafarna bundled him to Sardis from Dascyleum, it had even happened to him—and nothing bad had come of it.[56]

And then, one night, the compound silent in the all-consuming darkness, an acrid smell of burning woke him from his sleep. Already, from outside, the crackling of fire was getting louder. Already, brown smoke was pouring in beneath the door, and through the cracks beside the doorposts. Fully awake now, fully alert, Alcibiades leapt out of bed and threw the door wide open. Outside, stacks of dried wood had been piled high, and the flames were already tearing through them. Shouting to the people in the house to help, he dragged out rugs and mattresses and blankets, and flung them on the fire. The flames were smothered. At least for the time being. But now the smoke was bellying, and tongues of fire were licking at the edges of the blankets, and the orange heat was growing more intense. And then the arrows came. From all directions. Thudding into walls and roof and earth. Anonymous and deadly. The only warning of their approach, a soft sighing of air.[57]

The household was panic-stricken as Alcibiades, his instincts kicking in, reached for his weapons. But they had disappeared. Somehow, in the night, someone had taken them. All that he had now was a short knife, which a comrade pressed into his hand. But no shield. No armour. Just a blanket wrapped around his left arm as he stood, poised on the threshold. And then, calling to his friend to follow him, he bellowed his war cry and ran, naked and exposed, out into the darkness. Silhouetted against the burning house, he made an easy target. From all around him javelins rained and arrows thumped like hail as first one, then another, then another found its mark. All Alcibiades could do was run into the night, and run, and keep on running while he could, until the night engulfed him.[58]

When the new day broke, Theodote, and Timandra, and all the household were already grieving, the women scouring their long nails across their lovely cheeks and screaming in their sorrow as they laid out the corpse. And then they washed him gently and wrapped him in their finest robes. But they could not comb his hair or close his eyes. For, as they galloped to Dascyleum, the assassins carried with them, tied tight to a saddle, a heavy, dripping sack, a trophy to present to Farnavaz as evidence that they had done their work. And, when he opened it and lifted out the blood-drained head to look upon the face that once had been the handsomest in Greece, the satrap knew for certain: Alcibiades was dead.[59]

EPILOGUE

THE SHADOW OF THE DEAD

> And with our own eyes at Melissa we saw the tomb of Alcibiades as we
> were journeying from Synnada to Metropolis.
>
> Athenaeus, *The Partying Professors*, 574 f.

IN DEATH, AS IN LIFE, Alcibiades cast a long and troubling
shadow. And because, like an actor, he had changed his mask so often
and so convincingly, his shifting, mutating persona meant not just that
no one could be certain who he had really been but that his memory attracted a miscellany of anecdotes and stories, many of them invented but
most so plausible that they have ever since been more or less accepted as
the truth.

There was even an attempt to obscure the true circumstances of his death,
cut down by cowards in a shoddy ambush. Uncomfortable with the role he
played in it, Farnavaz put it about that it had not been a political assassination after all. Instead, he maintained that Alcibiades was murdered by a native Phrygian family: true to character, the playboy Athenian had seduced
a local girl, and, when her brothers found out, they sought revenge for her
dishonour. It was they, he said, who had surrounded the house where Alcibiades was staying and shot him down as he ran out from the flames. It
was a romantic tale, and one which absolved the Persians, Spartans, and

Athenians alike. But all it really did was confirm just how undignified Farnavaz believed the episode had been.[1]

Meanwhile, in Athens, the Thirty Tyrants, as the junta put in place by Sparta became known, ruled with increasing brutality. Death lists were drawn up. Death squads were formed. And families lived in fear of nighttime visitors. Wealthy citizens and metics, owners of factories and workshops, disappeared along with their strong boxes; and their airy homes were requisitioned for those loyal to the regime.[2]

But even among the oligarchs, some baulked at such unbridled violence. Theramenes was one. The general who had fought with Alcibiades at Chalcedon urged moderation. But, stripped of his citizenship, he was condemned to death without a trial and made to drink the fatal hemlock. As he did so, he proposed an ironic toast to the Thirty's ruthless leader, "my beloved Critias."[3]

It was left to another of Alcibiades' erstwhile colleagues to spearhead opposition to the regime. The next year, returning from self-imposed exile at the head of a thousand men, Thrasybulus faced the soldiers of the Thirty at Piraeus. In street fighting, Critias was killed; the oligarchs and their supporters fled for safety to Eleusis; and, in tense negotiations, the Spartans agreed to let Athens revert to its democratic constitution—which she did with gusto. Soon, she was re-emerging as an economic and military power, re-establishing her position as one of the most powerful cities in mainland Greece. Partly, this was because the Spartans had succeeded in alienating even their erstwhile allies. Just ten years after the wipe-out at Aegospotami, Athens, financed by Farnavaz, found herself part of an unlikely coalition with Corinth, Argos, and Boeotia. In 394, a joint Athenian and Persian fleet, led by Conon and Farnavaz, respectively, defeated the Spartans at Cnidus and dashed all hopes they might have held of ruling the Aegean waves. Bullish once more, the Athenians reconstructed their Long Walls and rebuilt their navy.[4]

Culturally, too, Athens reached new heights, with philosophers such as Plato and later the metic Aristotle laying the foundations of great seats of learning that would distinguish the city in the centuries to come. But the great upheavals had left their mark. Not least on the Pnyx—for a century, the crucible in which democracy had been tested. In the last years of the war, possibly because of safety issues surrounding the collapse of supporting walls, the People had ceased meeting here, but now with renewed enthusiasm they refashioned their seat of Assembly. But in the process, and perhaps symbolically, they reversed its orientation. No longer did voters crowd the hill above the Speakers' Platform, watching their politicians perform, as Pericles and Nicias and Alcibiades had once performed, with a backdrop of the Acropolis and Agora. Instead, the People thronged the hillside with their backs to that majestic view, looking up as orators thundered on a rock-cut podium above them.[5]

But despite the horrors suffered during the long months of the Thirty's rule, thanks to Thrasybulus' moderating influence, there were few reprisals. After decades of war and civil strife, the People were prepared to favour reconciliation over vengeance—with one notable exception: Socrates. In the public mind, the maverick philosopher was so closely linked to zealous, arrogant aristocrats (not only Alcibiades but Critias and many whose memories were blackened by their part in the recent reign of terror), that they turned their wrath on him. To some a dangerous agitator, to others an innocent scapegoat, like Theramenes he was bundled off to prison and forced to drain the hemlock cup. One of his chief prosecutors was Anytus, the man who once perhaps urged Aristophanes to attack Socrates in *Clouds,* and whom Socrates' then-darling, Alcibiades, had so humiliated by purloining his precious tableware.[6]

The ambivalence in which Athenians held Socrates was mirrored in their views of Alcibiades as well, as Alcibiades' son learned to his cost. When the boy was at last freed from his prison tower in Thrace, and with the fall of the Thirty Tyrants, who had inscribed his name on their proscription list, he returned to Athens to face a barrage of lawsuits. Many were clearly politically motivated, brought by men who had failed to wrest justice from the father and were now trying to score points against the son. Which forced young Alcibiades, perhaps against his will, to defend his father's memory.[7]

One charge that had smouldered for more than twenty years related to his father's victory in the Olympic chariot race of 416. In a speech written for him by Isocrates, Alcibiades the Younger responded passionately to the charge that his father had stolen the winning chariot and team from their rightful owner and wrongly raced them as his own. Much of his defence consisted of a eulogy. Countering the prosecutions' slurs, he protested that his father was innocent of any wrongdoing—be it in regard to the Mysteries or to the advice with which he was alleged to have helped Sparta. Rather, like Thrasybulus and the patriots who so recently overthrew the Thirty Tyrants, he had fought to reclaim Athens from the hands of men who wished her harm. Look at his achievements, his negotiations with the Persians, his victories with the Athenian fleet in the Bosporus and Hellespont! All that he did, be it in politics or on the battlefield, in his public generosity or on the race track at Olympia—everything was done in Athens' interests! Rather than being reviled, he should be awarded a posthumous pardon![8]

In another trial, the prosecutor employed Lysias, the clever speech-writer, to accuse the boy of trying to avoid military service. But rather than bring evidence, Lysias turned his invective on the memory of Alcibiades, dragging in every accusation he could think of, accusing him of fighting more often for the enemy than for Athens, revelling in conjuring a graphic picture of "such men as he . . . whoring, sleeping with their sisters, having children by their daughters, defiling Mysteries, smashing Herms, profaning gods, outraging the city, behaving unjustly and illegally in public and in private." In the trial about the chariot team, Alcibiades the Younger had suggested that tales of his father's personal excesses were exaggerated. Now, though, they were resurrected with a vengeance.[9]

Alcibiades the Younger, the prosecution fumed, was every bit as immoral as his father. He, too, was profligate! (Indeed, in the speech written for him by Isocrates, he did admit to having no more land or money.) He, too, was immoral! He was notorious for sleeping with his sister, which was why the girl's husband had divorced her![10]

The identity of this husband is, perhaps, of greater interest than the scurrilous accusation. For he was none other than Hipponicus, the son of Callias, who would succeed him as hereditary priest of the Eleusinian Mysteries. Callias' decision to marry his son and heir to Alcibiades' daughter is intriguing and reveals much about his character and determination. When Alcibiades, receiving a considerable dowry, had married Callias' sister, Hipparete, and subsequently demanded "birth-money" when she bore a son, Callias had publicly proclaimed his fear of him, pointedly proclaiming that he left his property to the People in the event of his sudden death. Shortly after Callias' proclamation, Alcibiades had—also very publicly—prevented Hipparete from divorcing him and perhaps been complicit in her death. Later, the scandal of the Mysteries, Callias' curse, delivered on the Acropolis, and Alcibiades' triumphant restoration of the Eleusinian procession on his return to Athens did nothing to reconcile them.[11]

So, why did Callias marry Hipponicus, his eldest son, to Alcibiades' daughter? The reason can only be her dowry. For years, Callias had resented paying such huge sums to Alcibiades and failing to claw any of them back when Hipparete's divorce fell through. Especially since, thanks to Alcibiades, his revenues from the mines at Laurium had plummeted so drastically that (by his own standards, if not by those of the average Athenian) he was beginning to feel impoverished. So now, in the next generation, he redressed the balance, funnelling money from Alcibiades' household (now equally impoverished) back into his own through his daughter-in-law's dowry.[12]

But the slur about Alcibiades the Younger's incest with his sister, and the failure of the marriage, suggest that all did not work out as Callias had wanted, that somehow the girl managed to escape her union with Hipponicus, and that perhaps, in the end, Callias' dreams were thwarted. Once more, a lack of evidence obscures the truth, and (although we hear of a squalid scandal, in which Callias first married an heiress and then, when the girl absconded after a failed suicide attempt, married her mother) like the outcome of the trials that plagued Alcibiades the Younger, the ultimate fate of the two families, squabbling as they sank further into poverty, has been obscured. The last we hear of Alcibiades the Younger, he is trailing his robes through the dust of the Athenian Agora, head tilted to one side, affecting traulism, the very image of his father, albeit faded and diminished. But there is one rather more enduring memorial. In the Cerameicus cemetery, gravestones survive of Alcibiades the Younger's daughter, Alcibiades' granddaughter, named after her grandmother, Hipparete. Beside her lie her husband, two sons, and a grandson. In Athens, then, the legacy of Alcibiades lived on.[13]

And not just in Athens. On Samos, the historian and sometime tyrant Duris, born in 340, boasted his descent from Alcibiades, doubtless just one of many whose grandmothers or great-grandmothers had encountered the bewitching Athenian on his travels. But in Sparta, the consequences of Alcibiades' alleged philandering took on constitutional implications. When King Agis died around 400, the succession was thrown into confusion thanks to widespread suspicion that Leotychidas, now in his early teens, was not the rightful heir but the son of Alcibiades. This was not the only hurdle standing in the way of the young prince. Complicating matters further was the support being given to a rival candidate by the now strutting victor of the war, Lysander. Scenting even greater power, Lysander threw his weight behind Agis' half brother, his own former beloved, Agesilaus. But when Agesilaus *was* appointed king, he turned against Lysander, depriving him of his Ionian command, and campaigning in his own right in both mainland Greece and Asia—against Sparta's former allies, the satraps Farnavaz and Chithrafarna.[14]

For, even by the time of Agesilaus' succession, the world had changed markedly. Not least in Persia. Here—as Alcibiades had predicted—Korush did indeed launch his bid for the throne, leading a mighty army deep inland to confront his brother, Artaxšaça. But at Cunaxa, on the left bank of the Euphrates, Korush was struck down as he impetuously spurred his horse into the thick of battle, hoping to dispatch Artaxšaça with his own hands. Back in Susa, the Queen Mother, Pari Satis, frustrated at the death of her favourite son, poisoned Artaxšaça's wife, her bitter rival, Estatira.[15]

Fighting for Korush at Cunaxa were more than ten thousand Greek mercenary soldiers. Among them was Xenophon, the Athenian, who had once studied at the feet of Socrates, and who now led his men back to safety on a gruelling march north to the Black Sea. In Thrace, Xenophon met Seuthes, who enlisted his support against his enemies. Cannily, Xenophon suggested that, in return, Seuthes grant him asylum, since the Spartans were now masters over all of Greece and life for an Athenian could be dangerous. Seuthes agreed. And more. Tellingly, he offered him the fortress at Bisanthe, which had once belonged to Alcibiades, "the best of all my coastal towns."[16]

But Xenophon was not to stay in Thrace. Joining the Spartan army, he fought at Agesilaus' side, raiding the lands of the Persian satraps. And, although they at last succeeded in cementing a peace treaty with Farnavaz, they found his colleague, Chithrafarna, characteristically unreliable. By now, even Artaxšaça had tired of his irresolute lieutenant. He sent out a loyal assassin, and somewhere beside the River Pactolus in his hushed, plush rooms at Sardis, as his bodyguards, loyal not to him but to their Great King, Artaxšaça, grounded arms and turned away, a sword blade flashed, and Chithrafarna was beheaded. He had already seen his dearest dream dissolve in ashes. In an earlier raid, Agesilaus had ravaged the plain of Sardis, taking special care to destroy the satrap's parklands and gardens, "which had been laid out so beautifully at such great cost with plants and other luxurious fittings, which one might enjoy in peacetime." Agesilaus surely took great pleasure in this act of vandalism. For this lush oasis was none other than the Paradise of Alcibiades. And now it was a wilderness.[17]

This was not the only way in which Agesilaus attacked Alcibiades' memory. The Spartan king, still bearing a grudge because his half-brother, Agis, had been cuckolded by Alcibiades, had already sought to humiliate him on an altogether more global stage. At the Olympic Games. The scene of Alcibiades' great triumph in the chariot race of 416. Twenty years later, Agesilaus arranged for his sister, the horse-mad Cynisca, whose charms Alcibiades had once passed over in favour of Queen Timaea's, to race a chariot of her own at the Olympics—for, although women could not compete in person at the Games, there was no rule to forbid them from owning and entering a chariot. And when Cynisca's horses thundered past the finishing post to victory, Agesilaus took the greatest satisfaction in proclaiming that this was surely evidence that to race a winning chariot required no manly virtue, merely wealth. And then, to underline the point, Cynisca competed at the next Olympics, too. And won again. Surpassing Alcibiades and further eclipsing his triumph. As not just statues of Cynisca and her horses at Olympia but a hero cult and sanctuary dedicated to her at Sparta proclaimed.[18]

Yet, as the decades unfolded, and the politics of Greece underwent ever more seismic changes, the memory of Alcibiades refused to die. Wars came and went. Exhausted, the Greek mainland states called on the Great King Artaxšaça to arbitrate, and, in return for peace, they happily surrendered to him the cities of Ionia. But then a new power rose in Macedonia, and a new king overran first Greece, then Persia; a king whose artists showed him ever handsome, ever young, lion-haired, clean-shaven, his head twisted slightly upwards in the pose that Alcibiades had made so much his own. The king was Alexander. Romantic and adventurous, a brilliant general and a skilful diplomat, the image of the Macedonian began to meld with that of Alcibiades. To such an extent that statues, paintings, and mosaics of Alcibiades now showed him, too, like Alexander, anachronistically clean-shaven.[19]

Already in his lifetime, the grateful islanders of Samos had honoured Alcibiades with a bronze statue—before doing the same a few years later for Lysander. And when his reputation reached the rapidly expanding Roman world, images of Alcibiades proliferated. In the early third century BC, the Romans asked the Delphic oracle what they should do to ensure victory in war. The oracle replied that, where they held their popular assembly, they must erect two statues. Without naming names, it went on to say that one should portray the wisest of the Greeks, the other, the bravest. For the subject of the former, the Romans chose Pythagoras. For the latter, they chose Alcibiades.[20]

In time, likenesses of Alcibiades appeared throughout the Roman empire. In the city's Forum, a sculpture showed him driving a four-horse chariot. Another pictured him as a young Eros wielding a thunderbolt, the image which had been emblazoned on his shield. In Sparta, a mosaic was laid, depicting Alcibiades as long-haired and swarthy, with beetling brows and staring eyes. In the Baths of Zeuxippus in Byzantium, the city where Alcibiades had once won a great victory, a statue represented him as a wise and learned counsellor, while, at Aphrodisias in Asia, in a marble tondo he was seen, young, beardless, beautiful.[21]

And far across the mountains and the shimmering plains, in the rocky landscape of Melissa, where once the lovely Theodote and Timandra buried his still warm, bleeding body in the crumbling soil, and his bones still lay unclaimed by the Athenians despite his growing repute, the Roman Emperor Hadrian caused a statue of Alcibiades in Parian marble to be erected on his tomb, and ordained that every year an ox be sacrificed to his undying memory.[22]

NOTES

INTRODUCTION

1. Parallels between Alcibiades and the shape-shifting sea-god Proteus, the subject of the advice given in this passage from the *Odyssey,* were drawn by the fourth-century-AD writer Libanius (*Declamatio,* 12.42), who writes of Alcibiades "changing his personality more readily than Proteus."

2. All dates are BC unless otherwise stated.

3. The sources range from the Sicilian Greek Diodorus and Roman Cornelius Nepos in the first century BC to the Greek Plutarch in the first and second century AD.

4. The question of the reliability of sources dogs all classical biographies, but is particularly problematic in Alcibiades' case. David Gribble's *Alcibiades and Athens* (London, 2011) provides a valuable discussion of the problems, but concludes that even in his own lifetime Alcibiades was so controversial that writers exaggerated or invented biographical episodes to use him as an exemplum in moral or political arguments, and that it is consequently impossible to discover anything of the "actual behaviour" of the real Alcibiades. As outlined in the present introduction, biographers must try to weigh the evidence based on what is known of the wider context, while being constantly aware of its insubstantiality and unreliability. Occasionally, to let narrative flow, choices—and sometimes assumptions—must be made on which not every reader will agree, but wherever possible this is indicated either within the body of the text or in notes. A useful modern summary of the evidence can be found in P. J. Rhodes, *Alcibiades* (Barnsley, 2011), 1–4, 72–74. Filmic: modern readers will note the parallels between Alcibiades' death and the last scene of *Butch Cassidy and the Sundance Kid.*

5. "The nature of power": S. Nevin, *Military Leaders* (London, 2017), 2; see also J. de Romilly, *Thucydides and Athenian Imperialism* (Oxford, 1963). Alcibiades' "spin":

P. A. Brunt, "Thucydides and Alcibiades," *Revue des Études Greques* 65, no. 304 (1952): 59–96 (reprised in his *Studies in Greek History and Thought* [Oxford, 1993]).

6. Alcibiades' presence: probably not quite as ubiquitous as Michael Vickers would suggest, e.g., in *Aristophanes and Alcibiades* (Berlin, 2015). Libanius: frag. 50.2.21.

7. Socrates' reputation: see, e.g., R. Waterfield, *Why Socrates Died* (London, 2009); B. Hughes, *The Hemlock Cup* (London, 2011). Xenophon serving under Alcibiades: M. A. Sears, *Athens, Thrace and the Shaping of Athenian Leadership* (New York, 2013), 278. Plato, Xenophon, and Alcibiades: M. Munn, *The School of History* (Berkeley, 2000), 8.

8. Diodorus: A. Momigliano, "History and Biography," in M. I. Finley (ed.), *The Legacy of Greece* (Oxford, 1981), 164. Plutarch: see, e.g., S. Verdegem, *Plutarch's Life of Alcibiades* (Leuven, 2010).

9. D. Briggs and M. Vickers, "Juvenile Crime, Aggression and Abuse in Classical Antiquity: A Case Study," in G. Rousseau (ed.), *Children and Sexuality: The Greeks to the Great War* (Basingstoke, 2007), 41–64; A. C. Salter, *Predators* (New York, 2003); H. Cleckley, *The Mask of Sanity* (St. Louis, 1941).

10. *Bacchae*: D. A. Stuttard (ed. and trans.), *Looking at Bacchae* (London, 2016).

11. "Dictatorship of the proletariat": P. Cartledge, *Thermopylae: The Battle That Changed the World* (Woodstock, 2006), 52; see also his *Democracy, a Life* (Oxford, 2016).

12. Surprisingly for such a controversial figure, Alcibiades has not attracted many modern biographies. Chief among those in English are P. J. Rhodes, *Alcibiades, Athenian Playboy, General and Traitor* (Barnsley, 2011), a hundred-page scholarly monograph written for a general readership; W. M. Ellis, *Alcibiades* (1989; reprinted 2013), tends to eulogize Alcibiades as an appealing rascal; and E. F. Benson's charming if now dated *The Life of Alcibiades* (1928; reprinted 2010). Outstanding foreign language biographies are: J. Hatzfeld's seminal *Alcibiade* (Paris, 1951) and J. de Romilly's *Alcibiade* (Paris, 1995). Alcibiades has also inspired several works of fiction, including Peter Green's absorbing *Achilles His Armour* (London, 1955), Rosemary Sutcliffe's engaging *The Flowers of Adonis* (London, 1969), and Steven Pressfield's swashbuckling *Tides of War* (London, 2000).

PROLOGUE

1. Scholars are divided over the date of Alcibiades' birth, but if he was born (as suggested here) in 452 BC he would have been just old enough to take part in the Potidaea campaign of 432 (see Chapter 1). P. J. Rhodes, *Alcibiades, Athenian Playboy, General and Traitor* (Barnsley, 2011), 21, suggests a date of 451. Those

suggesting a later date are forced to invent slightly implausible extenuating circumstances for his service in that campaign; see J. Hatzfeld, *Alcibiade* (Paris, 1951), 27–28, 62–65. That Alcibiades was active in the Assembly in 422/1 is shown by an inscription (*SEG* 145) discovered in 1988, showing that he proposed a decree honoring the support given to Athens by one Polypeithes of Siphnos; see Rhodes, *Alcibiades,* 30. Coronea: Plutarch, *Life of Alcibiades,* 1; Plato, *Alcibiades,* 1.112c; Isocrates, 16.28; see also V. Azoulay, *Pericles of Athens* (Princeton, 2014), 36. For a variant of Alcibiades' family background, see Rhodes, *Alcibiades,* 17–19.

2. Adoption: Rhodes, *Alcibiades,* 23. There is no record of Deinomache after the death of Cleinias, though her memory may be evoked in Aristophanes' *Clouds* (see Chapter 2), where she may be represented by Strepsiades' haughty wife. It is from the same play (l. 815) that we learn of Megacles' well-columned mansion.

3. Alcmaeon, son of Nestor: Pausanias, 2.18.7. The story of Cylon's revolt is contained in Herodotus, 5.71; Thucydides, 1.126; and Plutarch, *Life of Solon,* 12. Megacles I and his family: J. Davies, *Athenian Propertied Families* (Oxford, 1971), 368 ff. Alcmaeonids: S. Verdegem, *Plutarch's* Life of Alcibiades (Leuven, 2010), 101–102.

4. Curse: Azoulay, *Pericles of Athens,* 18. The effects of a curse upon a family are traced in a number of Greek tragedies. Most famously the curse placed on the dynasty of Oedipus is the subject of three plays by Sophocles (*Antigone, Oedipus Tyrannus,* and *Oedipus at Colonus*), while the curse upon the lineage of Agamemnon forms the basis of Aeschylus' *Oresteia.*

5. Alcmaeon I's Olympic victory in 592: Herodotus, 6.125; see Azoulay, *Pericles of Athens,* 17. Horses and racing as an aristocratic sport: L. G. Mitchell, *The Heroic Rulers of Archaic and Classical Greece* (London, 2013), 69. Alcmaeon at Croesus' court: Herodotus, 6.125.

6. 585 BC. Plutarch, *Life of Solon,* 11; Pausanias, 10.37.

7. Herodotus, 6.129.

8. Peisistratus: Herodotus, 1.59 f; [Aristotle], *The Athenian Constitution,* 15–17.

9. Herodotus, 5.62–63; [Aristotle], *The Athenian Constitution,* 18; Thucydides, 6.56–59.

10. 508/7. Cleisthenes' reforms: [Aristotle], *The Athenian Constitution,* 21. P. Cartledge, *Democracy, a Life* (Oxford, 2016), 61–75.

11. Herodotus, 3.80 (where in a constitutional debate a Persian is incongruously made to describe *isonomia* as "the most beautiful and powerful of all"), 5.69.

12. J. Roisman, *The Classical Art of Command* (Oxford, 2017), 12; Azoulay, *Pericles of Athens,* 29.

13. Athens' offer of earth and water: Herodotus, 5.73. The most accessible account of the Persian Wars is Tom Holland's brilliant *Persian Fire* (London, 2005).

14. Athenian reactions to Miletus: M. Munn, *The School of History* (Berkeley, 2000), 43. Ionian revolt and aftermath: Herodotus, 5.97 f. First invasion: Herodotus, 6.44. Second invasion: Herodotus, 6.95 ff. Third invasion: Herodotus, 7.5 ff.

15. Delian League to Athenian Empire: Thucydides, 1.96–7; P. Brunt, *Historia,* vol. 2 (1953/4), 135–163; B.D. Meritt, H. T. Wade-Gery and F. M. McGregor, *The Athenian Tribute Lists,* (Princeton, 1939–43), vol. III, 95–105, 183–187. Accusation of medizing: Herodotus, 6.115.

16. Pindar, *Pythian,* 7.

17. M. Scott, *Delphi* (Princeton, 2014), 138.

18. Deinomache's marital history is far from clear. This reading, which sees her as the wife of first Hipponicus, then Pericles, and finally Cleinias, follows scholars such as P. Brulé, *Women of Ancient Greece* (Edinburgh, 2003), 118–119; P. J. Bicknell, "Axiochus Alkibiadou, Aspasia and Aspasios," *L'Antiquité Classique* 51, no. 3 (1982): 240–250; R. D. Cromney, "On Deinomache," *Historia: Zeitschrift für Alte Geschichte* 4 (1984): 385–401. While arguing against this thesis, Rhodes (*Alcibiades,* 23) points out that Nepos' *Life of Alcibiades,* 2, calls Alcibiades Pericles' "step son" (*privignus*). As will become clear, this thesis, which I follow here (albeit with reservations), makes Alcibiades and Callias half-brothers, which might provide further reasons for their initial close connections and subsequent rivalries in adulthood. On the family of Hipponicus and Callias, see Davies, *Athenian Propertied Families,* 254 f.

19. Cimon at Sparta: Thucydides, 1.102. The rise of Pericles is well charted in, e.g., D. Kagan, *Pericles of Athens and the Birth of Democracy* (New York, 1991); Azoulay, *Pericles of Athens.*

20. Deinomache's separation from Pericles: Plutarch, *Life of Pericles,* 24.

21. Cleinias' family: see, e.g., Davies, *Athenian Propertied Families,* 9 f.; Cleinias and Solon: Plutarch, *Life of Solon,* 15. Today the story is discounted by many (see Davies, *Athenian Propertied Families,* 255).

22. *Proxenia:* Herodotus' statement (6.57) that in Sparta the kings appointed *proxenoi* from among the Spartan citizens is discussed by L. G. Mitchell, *Greeks Bearing Gifts* (Cambridge, 1997), 23–36, esp. 32–33; also Munn, *The School of History,* 68.

23. Herodotus, 8.17. Plutarch's account of Alcibiades' family in the fifth century BC is clearly flawed. According to him (*Life of Alcibiades,* 1.1) the same Cleinias fought valiantly at Artemisium in 480 and Coronea in 447. This is unlikely. More probably Plutarch has made the understandable mistake of confusing two men with the same name: Verdegem, *Plutarch's* Life of Alcibiades, 103–104. My account

follows the schema proposed by W. Dittenberger, *Hermes* 37 (1902): 1–13. Aristeia: Munn, *The School of History,* 24–25.

24. Ostracism: Rhodes, *Alcibiades,* 41.

25. This was first proposed by Bicknell, "Axiochus Alkibiadou, Aspasia and Aspasios," 240–250. Like the marital history of Deinomache, this reading of Aspasia's life is not universally accepted.

26. The dating of the "Cleinias Decree" (here assigned to 447 BC) is debated. For arguments suggesting an alternative date in the 420s, see C. W. Fornara and L. J. Samons, *Athens from Cleisthenes to Pericles* (Berkeley, 1991).

27. Thucydides, 1.113; Diodorus, 12.5–6; Plutarch, *Life of Pericles,* 18; see, e.g., D. Kagan, *The Outbreak of the Peloponnesian War* (Ithaca, 1969), 122–124.

28. Inheritance laws: Diogenes Laertius, *Life of Solon,* 9. Pericles as Alcibiades' guardian: Plutarch, *Life of Alcibiades,* 1.

29. Guardianship of Pericles: Plutarch, *Life of Alcibiades,* 1; Plato, *Alcibiades,* 1, 104b, 118c, 124c; Isocrates, 16.28; Xenophon, *Memorabilia,* 1.2.40. Ariphron: Plutarch, *Life of Alcibiades,* 1. Hatzfeld, *Alcibiade,* 30; W. M. Ellis, *Alcibiades* (London, reprinted 2013), 18; Verdegem, *Plutarch's* Life of Alcibiades, 105; Brulé, *Women of Ancient Greece,* 119.

30. Pericles' character: Plutarch, *Life of Pericles,* 7–8. Attitude to money: Azoulay, *Pericles of Athens,* 70–71.

1. REARING THE LION CUB

1. The ceremony possibly took place in 452. Apaturia: H. W. Parke, *Festivals of the Athenians* (London, 1986), 88–92. See also P. J. Rhodes, *Alcibiades, Athenian Playboy, General and Traitor* (Barnsley, 2011), 21.

2. Deme: Plutarch, *Life of Alcibiades,* 22.

3. Scambonidae: W. Smith (ed.), *Dictionary of Greek and Roman Geography* (Boston, 1854). Athene Promachos: Pausanias, 1.28.2.

4. Leos: Plutarch, *Life of Theseus,* 13; Leos' daughters: [Demosthenes], 60.29.

5. Thucydides, 1.114; Diodorus, 12.5; Plutarch, *Life of Pericles,* 22.

6. Plutarch, *Life of Pericles,* 22–23; Ephorus, frag. 193. Some scholars question the story of Pericles' bribing Pleistoanax; see D. Kagan, *The Outbreak of the Peloponnesian War* (Ithaca, 1969), 124–125.

7. Thurii: founded in 446 or 443. Strabo, 263.6.1.13; Diodorus, 12.9–11.

8. Plutarch, *Life of Pericles,* 11. D. A. Stuttard, *Parthenon, Power and Politics on the Acropolis,* (London, 2013), 123–125; A. Powell, *Athens and Sparta: Constructing*

Greek Political and Social History from 478 BC, 2nd ed. (London, 2001), 66. Marble was brought also from the subject island of Paros.

9. Aspasia: M. M. Henry, *Prisoner of History: Aspasia of Miletus and Her Biographical Tradition* (Oxford, 1995); V. Azoulay, *Pericles of Athens* (Princeton, 2014), 101–104. Aspasia's intellect was famous in Antiquity. In Plato's *Menexenus,* Socrates delivers a funeral oration that he says was written by her. According to Plutarch (*Life of Pericles,* 24), she possessed extraordinary political wisdom and taught rhetoric to many leading Athenians. He also includes Socrates among her admirers, while Cicero (*De Inventione,* 1.51–52) quotes a lost dialogue by Aeschines in which she counsels Xenophon and his wife about marriage. Pericles' citizenship law: [Aristotle], *Constitution of Athens,* 26.4; Plutarch, *Life of Pericles,* 37. Kissing Aspasia: Plutarch, *Life of Pericles,* 24.

10. Cratinus, frag. 241, quoted in Plutarch, *Life of Pericles,* 24.

11. Pericles' sons: Plutarch, *Life of Pericles,* 24; 37. Amycla: Plutarch, *Life of Alcibiades,* 1; S. Verdegem, *Plutarch's* Life of Alcibiades (Leuven, 2010), 106–108; Rhodes, *Alcibiades,* 22. The scholion on Plato's *Alcibiades* (I.121*d*) mentions a second Spartan nurse called Lanice. Amycla was technically Alcibiades' wet nurse, though she may have assumed duties as dry nurse when he and his brother no longer required her milk. On Spartan women see, e.g., S. Pomeroy, *Spartan Women* (Oxford, 2002); P. Cartledge, *Spartan Reflections* (London, 2001), 106–126; P. Cartledge, *The Spartans: An Epic History* (London, 2013).

12. These and similar anecdotes (some undoubtedly apocryphal) are recorded in Plutarch's *Sayings of Spartan Women.*

13. Treatment of Helots: Plutarch, *Life of Lycurgus,* 28; Athenaeus, 657D; see, e.g., Cartledge, *The Spartans,* 66. Zopyrus: Rhodes, *Alcibiades,* 22.

14. Plutarch, *Life of Alcibiades,* 1; Plato, *Alcibiades I,* 122*b.* M. A. Sears, *Athens, Thrace and the Shaping of Athenian Leadership* (New York, 2013), 100. A good idea of the relationship between nurse (here a dry nurse) and tutor can be gained from Euripides *Medea,* 1–95.

15. Extent of Thracian Empire: Diodorus, 12.50. Athens relationship with Thrace: Sears, *Athens, Thrace and the Shaping of Athenian Leadership,* 2; 32.

16. Obeying *paidagogos:* Aristotle, 1119b. Knucklebones: Plutarch, *Life of Alcibiades,* 2. Like many of the tales surrounding Alcibiades youth (and adulthood), including those that follow, this anecdote's authenticity is questioned.

17. Plutarch, *Life of Alcibiades,* 2. See also: Verdegem, *Plutarch's* Life of Alcibiades, 119–121.

18. Schooling, see, e.g., T. B. L. Webster, *Everyday Life in Classical Athens* (London, 1969), 46–50.

19. *Kalokagathoi:* M. Munn, *The School of History* (Berkeley, 2000), 52. Educating the *kalokagathoi:* Aristotle, *Nicomachean Ethics,* 10.7.1171b f; 8.1249a f.

20. Both anecdotes: Plutarch, *Life of Alcibiades,* 7.1; Verdegem, *Plutarch's* Life of Alcibiades, 151–152.

21. Athenian gymnasia: D. G. Kyle, *Athletics in Ancient Athens* (Leiden, 1993), 98.

22. "Like a lion": Plutarch, *Life of Alcibiades,* 2.2. Sadly, the anecdote is unlikely to be true: Plutarch elsewhere attributes the story to an anonymous Spartan: *Sayings of Spartans,* 234DE. Killing the slave-attendant: Plutarch, *Life of Alcibiades,* 3. Again, it is unlikely that the anecdote is true: Plutarch's alleged source, Antiphon, was considered unreliable even by him. See Rhodes, *Alcibiades,* 26.

23. Not taking part in athletics: Isocrates, 16.33. Alcibiades' beauty: Plutarch, *Life of Alcibiades,* 1. Pronomus as tutor: this is the conjecture of M. Vickers, *Aristophanes and Alcibiades* (Berlin, 2015), 91. Pronomus is pictured on the so-called Pronomus Vase, now in Naples' Museo Nazionale Archaeologico, playing the *aulos* during preparations for a *satyr* play.

24. Plutarch, *Life of Alcibiades,* 2. Verdegem, *Plutarch's* Life of Alcibiades, 126–128. Faddish popularity: Aristotle, *Politics,* 8.1341a.

25. Callias and Critias as *aulos* players: Athenaeus, 4.184d; see C. Dougherty and L. Kurke (eds.), *The Cultures within Ancient Greek Culture* (New York, 2003), 195.

26. Greek homosexuality: K. J. Dover, *Greek Homosexuality* (London, 1978; new edition, 2015); T. K. Hubbard, *Homosexuality in Greece and Rome* (Berkeley, 2003); V. Wohl, *Love among the Ruins: The Erotics of Democracy in Classical Athens* (Princeton, 2002).

27. Homosexual partnerships: Plato, *Phaedrus,* 227a.

28. Lovers keeping fathers informed: Xenophon, *Symposium,* 8.11. Democrates: see, e.g., D. Nails, *The People of Plato* (Indianapolis, 2002), 123. The anecdote: Plutarch, *Life of Alcibiades,* 3. Plutarch is inclined (probably rightly) to reject this story, since his source, Antiphon, is inimical to Alcibiades. He does, however, include it in his biography, perhaps since it is an early instance of Alcibiades abandoning his true home for that of another; see Verdegem, *Plutarch's* Life of Alcibiades, 129–130; Rhodes, *Alcibiades,* 26.

29. Cleinias to Ariphron: Plato, *Protagoras, 320a–b.* The MS's reading that Ariphron "gave him back to Alcibiades" must be an error for "to Pericles." "Mad" Cleinias: Plato, *Alcibiades* I, 118e.

30. Plutarch, *Life of Alcibiades,* 4; 6. Verdegem, *Plutarch's* Life of Alcibiades, 131–135. Alcibiades and Socrates: J. Hatzfeld, *Alcibiade* (Paris, 1951), 32–58. There are myriad books on Socrates. Good introductions include: C. C. W. Taylor, *Socrates: A Very Short Introduction* (Oxford, 2001); R. Waterfield, *Why Socrates Died*

(London, 2009); B. Hughes, *The Hemlock Cup* (London, 2011). The question of Socrates' involvement with Alcibiades is well summarized in Rhodes, *Alcibiades,* 26.

31. Socrates as astronomer: Plato, *Republic,* 528e. He also appears as a type of astronomer in Aristophanes, *Clouds,* 222 ff. Protagoras on Socrates: Plato, *Protagoras,* 361e.

32. Zopyrus, "The Physiognomist": Cicero, *On Fate,* 10–11. Zopyrus on Socrates: Cicero, *Tusculan Disputations,* 4.80.

33. Euripides, *Bacchae,* 860–861.

34. Socrates' alleged observation about Alcibiades' character was probably invented after his trial and death by the philosopher's admirers, keen to absolve him of malign influence.

35. Socrates glimpsing naked flesh: Plato, *Charmides,* 155d. Aspasia's poem (preserved at Athenaeus, 219c–d = *PLG*2.288) reads:

> Socrates, don't think that I've not seen how you're burning with desire
>> for the son of Deinomache and Cleinias! But if you want a good
>> relationship
> with such a boy, heed my advice, and don't ignore me.
>> If you listen to me, it will go so much the better.
> When I heard the news, my body glistened with delight;
>> tears wet my eyes; this was the news I'd longed for.
> So prepare yourself. Fill your heart with the persuasive Muse.
>> She'll help you conquer him, if you instill her in his yearning ears,
> for she is the beginning of a friendship for you both. With her help you
>> will have him,
>> as you present him through your speech with your heart's marriage gift.

36. Plato, *Protagoras,* 309a. Once again, little of the *mise en scène,* including its details about Alcibiades, should be taken at face value.

37. Hippias at the Olympic Games: Plato, *Hippias Minor,* 360b–d; Prodicus: Plato, *Protagoras,* 315d–316a; [Plato], *Hippias Major,* 282c; Aristotle, *Rhetoric,* 1415b15.

38. Plato, *Protagoras,* 336d–e.

39. Critias: J. Davies, *Athenian Propertied Families* (Oxford, 1971), 326–328; Nails, *The People of Plato,* 308–311.

40. Protagoras the first sophist: Plato, *Protagoras,* 311e. See, e.g., W. K. C. Guthrie, *The Sophists* (New York, 1977); J. M. van Ophuijsen, M. van Raalte, and P. Stork, *Protagoras of Abdera: The Man, His Measure* (Leiden, 2013).

41. Callias and sophists: Plato, *Apology,* 20*a.* Pericles and philosophers: Plutarch, *Life of Pericles,* 4–6.

42. "Man is the measure": H. Diels and W. Kranz, *Die Fragmente der Vorsokratiker,* 6th ed., rev. Walther Kranz (Berlin, 1903; Berlin: Weidmann, 1952), 80A1 (hereafter cited as Diels / Kranz); D. Stuttard, *A History of Ancient Greece in Fifty Lives* (London, 2014), 117–119.

43. Plutarch, *Life of Pericles,* 4.4–6.3. Pericles' fiends: Azoulay, *Pericles of Athens,* 92–93.

44. Anaxagoras: see e.g., W. K. C. Guthrie, *A History of Greek Philosophy* (Cambridge, 1962). Molten metal: Anaximander Diels / Kranz 59A42; Meteorite at Aegospotamoi: Aristotle, *Meteorology,* 344b31–34; Pliny, *Natural History,* 2.149.

45. Plutarch, *Life of Pericles,* 4.

46. Plutarch, *Life of Pericles,* 4; [Aristotle], *Constitution of Athens,* 27.4.

47. Plutarch, *Life of Pericles,* 13.

48. Plutarch, *Life of Pericles,* 31.

49. Pheidias' fate: Scholiast on Aristophanes, *Peace,* 605; Diodorus, 12.39 f; Aristodemus, *FrGH,* 104.16,1–2; Plutarch, *Life of Pericles,* 31. Azoulay, *Pericles of Athens,* 124.

50. Plutarch, *Life of Alcibiades,* 7. Other versions (e.g., Diodorus, 12.38) have him making the remark to Pericles' face. The veracity of the anecdote can be challenged by those who see it as providing too neat a contrast between the upright Pericles and the flighty Alcibiades. See Verdegem, *Plutarch's* Life of Alcibiades, 152–155; Rhodes, *Alcibiades,* 24.

51. Athenaeus, 407b–c. See Munn, *The School of History,* 171; Rhodes, *Alcibiades,* 24. Listing this and other anecdotes, Rhodes concludes: "The general picture which we receive is of an arrogant and violent man, who took no notice of the ordinary restraints on selfish conduct and positively enjoyed shocking people" (27). However the reliability of this and the other anecdotes (presented here in the present tense) is questionable.

52. Xenophon, *Memorabilia,* 1.2.40–46.

53. Exile: Diogenes Laertius, *Lives of the Eminent Philosophers,* 2.3; see Kagan, *The Outbreak of the Peloponnesian War,* 195. Burning books: Diogenes Laertius, *Lives of the Eminent Philosophers,* 9.8; Cicero, *de Natura Deorum,* 1.23.6.

54. Weeping in public: Plutarch, *Life of Pericles,* 32. Stirring up conflict: Aristophanes, *Acharnians,* 522–533. Kagan, *The Outbreak of the Peloponnesian War,* 255.

55. Thucydides 1.24 ff; Kagan, *The Outbreak of the Peloponnesian War,* 206–221.

56. Thucydides, 1.31–45.

57. Megara as a cause of the Peloponnesian War: Thucydides, 1.67; 1.139; Aristophanes, *Peace*, 609 (with an allusion perhaps at *Acharnians*, 518–525); Andocides,
3.8; Diodorus, 12.39.4; Plutarch, *Life of Pericles*, 29–30. The Megarian Decrees are
hotly debated by modern historians; Kagan, *The Outbreak of the Peloponnesian
War*, 254–258.

58. Ephebes: Aristotle, *Constitution of Athens*, 42, written a century after Alcibiades
became an ephebe. Ephebe means literally "on the threshold of youth."

59. Ephebic Oath: Plutarch, *Life of Alcibiades*, 15; Lycurgus, *Against Leocrates*, 77.
Verdegem, *Plutarch's* Life of Alcibiades, 207–208.

60. [Aristotle], *Constitution of Athens*, 42. H. van Wees, *Greek Warfare, Myths and
Realities* (London, 2004), 94.

61. Alcibiades and Axiochus as lovers: Athenaeus, 12.574e.

62. Xanthippus: Herodotus, 9.120. Hero and Leander: Ovid, *Heroides*, 19; they are
also the subject of a fifth- or sixth-century-AD poem by Musaeus.

63. Athenaeus, 12.534f, 535a, 574e. Hatzfeld, *Alcibiade*, 61; Sears, *Athens, Thrace and
the Shaping of Athenian Leadership*, 106. Athenaeus' source is Antiphon's now lost
Attack on Alcibiades, whose very title should make us suspect the objectivity
(indeed, the veracity) of its contents. Rhodes, *Alcibiades*, 26.

64. Thucydides, 1.56; Kagan, *The Outbreak of the Peloponnesian War*, 273–285.

65. Ambition for Greek hegemony: Van Wees, *Greek Warfare*, 24. Call-up lists: J. M.
Camp, *The Athenian Agora* (London, 1986), 118. Mobilization: Van Wees, *Greek
Warfare*, 102–104.

2. COMING OF AGE

1. The details of hoplite warfare continue to be debated; see H. van Wees, *Greek
Warfare, Myths and Realities* (London, 2004); C. Matthew, *A Storm of Spears,
Understanding the Greek Hoplite at War* (Barnsley, 2012); D. Kagan and G. F.
Viggiano (eds.), *Men of Bronze, Hoplite Warfare in Ancient Greece* (Princeton,
2013); and V. D. Hanson, *A War Like No Other* (London, 2005), 136–146.
Armour: Van Wees, *Greek Warfare*, 167–168; Hanson, *A War Like No Other*,
136–142.

2. Pre-battle sacrifices: Van Wees, *Greek Warfare*, 120–121.

3. Euripides, *Phoenician Women*, 1377–1385.

4. Van Wees, *Greek Warfare*, 134–135. "The sweetest thing": Tyrtaeus, frag. 10 (West).

5. Plutarch, *Life of Alcibiades*, 7; Plato, *Symposium*, 220d–e; J. Hatzfeld, *Alcibiade*
(Paris, 1951), 62–66.

6. Alcibiades' prize for bravery: Plato, *Symposium,* 220d-e; Isocrates, 16.29. M. Munn, *The School of History* (Berkeley, 2000), 54; Van Wees, *Greek Warfare,* 194.

7. Thucydides, 1. 57–61. Baggage and attendants: Van Wees, *Greek Warfare,* 68; 104–105.

8. Isocrates, 16.29, says that Alcibiades travelled to Potidaea with Phormio, but Plato (*Symposium,* 219e) appears to suggest that he was part of the first expedition. Also, although there were skirmishes throughout the campaign, the first encounter at Potidaea was the only really significant battle. W. E. Ellis, *Alcibiades* (London, reprinted 2013), 24–27.

9. Sharing tent: Plutarch, *Life of Alcibiades,* 7. P. J. Rhodes, *Alcibiades, Athenian Playboy, General and Traitor* (Barnsley, 2011), 27–28. Camping arrangements: Van Wees, *Greek Warfare,* 107. It is entirely possible that (like so many details of his life) Alcibiades' sharing of a tent with Socrates was a later fabrication. By the time Plato wrote *Symposium* (some sixty years after Potidaea), there were few veterans left who might contradict his account.

10. Chaste sleeping arrangements: Plato, *Symposium,* 219d; Nepos, *Life of Alcibiades,* 2. It should be noted that by the late fifth century BC, a homoerotic element had crept into perceptions of Achilles and Patroclus' relationship.

11. Plato, *Symposium,* 220c–d. R. Waterfield suggests that this was a turning point "to do with Alcibiades": "During these twenty-four hours Socrates first conceived the political dimension of his mission, to take this boy in hand and train him as a philosopher-king, and to find others too" (*Why Socrates Died,* 190).

12. Plato, *Symposium,* 220a.

13. Thucydides, 2.70. D. Kagan, *The Archidamian War* (Ithaca, 1974), 97.

14. Cost: Munn, *The School of History,* 54; Hanson, *A War Like No Other,* 27. Sieges: see, e.g., Van Wees, *Greek Warfare,* 138–145.

15. Theban attack on Plataea: Thucydides, 2.26; Diodorus 12.41–42. Kagan, *The Archidamian War,* 43–48.

16. A version of Pericles' speech is contained in Thucydides, 1.140–144. Strategy: Hanson, *A War Like No Other,* 29–30.

17. Thucydides, 2.10–23. Statistics: Hanson, *A War Like No Other,* 35; 38; Van Wees, *Greek Warfare,* 121. Sayings: *Supplementum Epigraphicum Graecum,* 21 (1966), 6.44.12–13.

18. Hanson, *A War Like No Other,* 53. The next year, in 430, the Athenians' reaction was different. Having experienced a second invasion, and weighed down by the Plague, they sent envoys to Sparta to seek peace, but were rejected (Thucydides, 2.59).

19. Three hundred thousand people in Athens: Hanson, *A War Like No Other,* 6.

20. Thucydides, 2.47–54. Hanson, *A War Like No Other,* 67–80; Kagan, *The Archidamian War,* 70–100. As outlined by M. Papagrigorakis in *Scientific American* (January, 2006), the plague is now thought to have been typhoid fever, but see R. J. Littman, "The Plague of Athens: Epidemiology and Palaeopathology," *Mount Sinai Journal of Medicine* 76 (2009): 456–467.

21. Thucydides, 2.58; Kagan, *The Archidamian War,* 78.

22. Family unreconciled: Plutarch, *Life of Pericles,* 36. "No Athenian": Plutarch, *Life of Pericles,* 38.

23. Statistic: Hanson, *A War Like No Other,* 80. The plague finally ended in the spring / summer of 426.

24. Pericles and the cavalry: R. E. Gaebel, *Cavalry Operations in the Ancient World* (Norman, 2002), 92–93; Hanson, *A War Like No Other,* 52; 224 f.; Munn, *The School of History,* 62. A horse's appetite: Van Wees, *Greek Warfare,* 58. Registering: G. R. Bugh, *The Horsemen of Athens* (Princeton, 2014), 54.

25. Alcibiades' shield: Plutarch, *Life of Alcibiades,* 16; Athenaeus, 12.534e. S. Verdegem, *Plutarch's* Life of Alcibiades (Leuven, 2010), 222; Van Wees, *Greek Warfare,* 54. P. J. Rhodes is among those who argue that in accepting the detail of Alcibiades' shield, Plutarch and Athenaeus take "too seriously what was alleged in a comedy" (*Alcibiades,* 25).

26. Xenophon's two treatises are *On Horsemanship* and *How to Be a Good Cavalry Commander.*

27. J. Roisman, *The Classical Art of Command* (Oxford, 2017), 129; Hanson, *A War Like No Other,* 208.

28. See, e.g., K. J. Dover, *Aristophanes'* Clouds (Oxford, 1989); (too) much is made of Alcibiades' presence in Aristophanes comedies by M. Vickers, *Aristophanes and Alcibiades* (Berlin, 2015). Contrast Hatzfeld, *Alcibiade,* 34–35.

29. "Drive to town": Aristophanes, *Clouds,* 69–70.

30. Argument of Rightful and Wrongful Reasoning: Aristophanes, *Clouds,* 889–1106. Getting off scot free: Aristophanes, *Clouds,* 1076–1082. "Crimes against the gods": Aristophanes, *Clouds,* 1506–1507.

31. Aelian, *Varia Historia,* 2.13. The suitably archaic translations are by Thomas Stanley (London, 1665). See also Dover, *Aristophanes'* Clouds, xix.

32. The extent to which dramatic characters "stand in" for real ones in Aristophanes (and, indeed, other playwrights) is hotly debated. While there are those who deny any correlation, Michael Vickers is messianic in trying to uncover as many links as possible. Alcibiades threatens jurors: *Hypothesis to Aristophanes'* Clouds ch. 5 in

V. Coulon (ed), *Aristophane Tome 1* (Paris, 1923). Despite the failure of *Clouds* in the theatre, Aristophanes revised his script in 417, and, although it was never performed, it was probably circulated in manuscript form.

33. Anytus and *Clouds:* Aelian, *Varia Historia,* 2.13; Diogenes Laertius, *Lives of the Eminent Philosophers: Socrates,* 38. On Anytus, see D. Nails, *The People of Plato* (Indianapolis, 2002), 37 f.; Plato, *Meno,* 90a. Anytus was one of those who subsequently brought the accusations against Socrates that would lead to his execution.

34. Plutarch, *Life of Alcibiades,* 4; Athenaeus, 12.47. Vergedem, *Plutarch's* Life of Alcibiades, 135–136. Another made-up tale?

35. Aristophanes, *Banqueters, PCG* III.2 fr. 1205.5f. [*PCG* = Kassel, R. and Autin, C. (eds.), *Poetae Comici Graeci.*]

36. Aristophanes, *Acharnians,* 716. Alcibiades as lawyer: Munn, *The School of History,* 98.

37. See, e.g., J. H. McGregor, *The Athenian Agora* (Cambridge, 2014).

38. Traulism: Plutarch, *Life of Alcibiades,* 1. Verdegem, *Plutarch's* Life of Alcibiades, 114–117; Munn, *The School of History,* 81; Rhodes, *Alcibiades,* 25; Vickers, *Aristophanes and Alcibiades,* 4. Ability as orator: Plutarch, *Life of Alcibiades,* 10.

39. Liturgies: Munn, *The School of History,* 57–58; 61–62; L. G. Mitchell, *Greeks Bearing Gifts* (Cambridge, 1997), 45. Alcibiades' liturgies: Thucydides, 6.16; Isocrates, 16.34–35. Audience figures for the fifth-century-BC Theatre of Dionysus are notoriously difficult to calculate. Estimates range from 3,700 to 15,000; see V. Bers, "Audiences at the Greek Tragic Plays," in H. Roisman (ed.), *The Encyclopaedia of Greek Tragedy* (Chichester, 2014); E. Csapo, "The Men Who Built the Theatres," in P. Wilson (ed.), *The Greek Theatre and Festivals* (Oxford, 2007).

40. Duties of the *choregus:* V. Azoulay, *Pericles of Athens* (Princeton, 2014), 23–24. Admiration of men and women alike: Athenaeus, 534c.

41. Plutarch, *Life of Alcibiades,* 14.4. Taureas' birth: Andocides, 1.47; his challenge and its consequences: [Andocides], 4.20–21; Demosthenes, 21.147; Hatzfeld, *Alcibiade,* 132–133; Munn, *The School of History,* 59.

42. Phallenius: Aristophanes, *Banqueters, PCG* III.2 frag. 244. Neither the fictional Phallenius nor the historical Alcibiades was ever, in fact, chief archon, but the joke is in the name, not the historical veracity. Enticing husbands: Bion, at Diogenes Laertius 4.49.

43. Alcibiades' estates: Lysias, 19.52; see J. Davies, *Athenian Propertied Families* (Oxford, 1971), 20. Agatharchus: Vitruvius, *Praef. ad lib.,* vii; see T. B. L. Webster, *Everyday Life in Classical Athens* (London, 1969), 168. Alcibiades and Agatharchus:

Plutarch, *Life of Alcibiades*, 16.4. The scholion on Demosthenes, 21.147 suggests that Alcibiades was punishing Agatharchus for sleeping with his concubine. Hatzfeld, *Alcibiade*, 132–133; Rhodes, *Alcibiades*, 27.

44. A *parapetasma*, or curtain, is mentioned in the auction-lists of 415, as are other items on which this description is based.

45. Alcibiades' estates: Davies, *Athenian Propertied Families*, 20; Hanson, *A War Like No Other*, 86. Erchia: Plato, *Alcibiades*, 1.123c. Hatzfeld, *Alcibiade*, 136. Stores: Webster, *Everyday Life in Classical Athens*, 30–31.

46. Aelian, *Varia Historia*, 3.28—a pretty anecdote that is probably not grounded in fact.

47. Androgynous: the fourth-century-AD writer Libanius (*Declamatio*, 12.42) delights in embroidering the imagery, writing of Alcibiades' attending symposia in women's clothes, "an equal to Omphale in his powers of seduction," and "a sodomite at symposia, effeminate when drunk, like a woman in the evening, and changing his personality more readily than Proteus." See also Plutarch, *Life of Alcibiades*, 23.5–6. Ruining clothing: Plutarch, *Life of Alcibiades*, 16. Shoes: Athenaeus, 12.534c (a style of shoe was later named after Alcibiades). Angle of head: Plutarch, *Life of Alcibiades*, 1. "It's just what I wanted": Plutarch, *Life of Alcibiades*, 9; *Sayings of Kings and Commanders*, 186D. Verdegem, *Plutarch's* Life of Alcibiades, 161–162.

48. Plutarch, *Life of Alcibiades*, 5. Verdegem, *Plutarch's* Life of Alcibiades, 135–136; Rhodes, *Alcibiades*, 26–27. It is impossible to prove or disprove the tale.

49. Plutarch, *Life of Alcibiades*, 5.

50. Age restrictions: Xenophon, *Memorabilia*, 1.2.35. Fighting in Sicily: Thucydides, 3.86; Diodorus, 12.53; see Kagan, *The Archidamian War*, 181–186.

51. Diodorus, 12.53. Kagan, *The Archidamian War*, 182.

52. Revising tribute lists: [Andocides], 4.11; Plutarch, *Life of Nicias*, 9, hints at Alcibiades' early entrance onto the political stage. Munn, *The School of History*, 75. Increasing the tribute: Kagan, *The Archidamian War*, 249. On the ground of his age, P. J. Rhodes (*Alcibiades*, 29) discounts Alcibiades' involvement in assessing the tribute lists as well as another detail in [Andocides], 4.11–14, suggesting that Alcibiades persuaded the assembly to undertake the assessment in the first place.

53. "Cruel and violent nature": Diodorus, 12.55; Thucydides, 3.36; 4.21–22, 27–29; 6.16. Kagan, *The Archidamian War*, 130.

54. Thucydides, 3.36–50; Diodorus, 12.55. Kagan, *The Archidamian War*, 156.

55. For a possible alternative reconstruction of *Babylonians*: G. Norwood, "The Babylonians of Aristophanes," *Classical Philology* 25, no. 1 (1930): 1–10.

56. Parrhesia: see R.W. Wallace, "The Power to Speak—and not to listen—in Ancient Athens' in I. Sluiter and R. M. Rosen (eds.), *Free Speech in Classical Antiquity* (Leiden, 2004), 222–223.

57. Fishing for eels: Aristophanes, *Knights,* 864–867. Agoracritus: see Vickers, *Aristophanes and Alcibiades,* 39.

58. Pylos campaign: Thucydides, 4.2–39; Diodorus, 12.61–2. Kagan, *The Archidamian War,* 193–249; Roisman, *The Classical Art of Command,* 152–163.

59. Assembly and Cleon's campaign to Pylos: Thucydides, 4.27–39.

60. J. M. Camp, *The Athenian Agora* (London, 1986), 71.

61. Thucydides, 4.58–65; Diodorus, 12.54. Congress of Gela: Kagan, *The Archidamian War,* 266–268.

62. Trial of generals: Thucydides, 4.65. Thucydides does not name Cleon as the instigator of the generals' punishment, but it is likely that it was he. Plan of attack: Thucydides, 4.76; Kagan, *The Archidamian War,* 278–281.

63. Hippocrates and Megara: Thucydides, 4.66–74. Hippocrates: Nails, *The People of Plato,* 224.

3. UNBOWED IN BATTLE

1. The account of the Delium campaign and its aftermath is contained in Thucydides, 4.89–101; Diodorus, 12.69–70. For useful discussions, see S. Nevin, *Military Leaders and Sacred Space* (London, 2017), 37–48; V. Hanson, *A War Like No Other* (London, 2005), 123–132; D. Kagan, *The Archidamian War* (Ithaca, 1974), 279–286; J. Hatzfeld, *Alcibiade* (Paris, 1951), 73.

2. I follow the route proposed by J. Frazer in *Pausanias' Description of Greece* (Cambridge, 2012).

3. Delium: the Greek form of the name is Delion. Cattle to Euboea: Thucydides, 2.14; the history of this statue is told in Herodotus, 6.118.

4. This is the first recorded instance of a hoplite phalanx of such depth. A similarly deep phalanx would be used by the Thebans to win victory over the Spartans at Leuctra in 371, and the formation was adopted to great effect by the Macedonians under Philip II and Alexander III ("the Great"). Kagan, *The Archidamian War,* 283.

5. Plato, *Symposium,* 220e–221a; Plutarch, *Life of Alcibiades,* 7. See also Plato, *Laches,* 181a; Plutarch, *De Genio Socratis,* 581e; Cicero, *De Divinatione,* 1.123. P. J. Rhodes, *Alcibiades, Athenian Playboy, General and Traitor* (Barnsley, 2011), 28.

6. Statistic: Hanson, *A War Like No Other,* 135.

7. Hanson, *A War Like No Other,* 76, suggests that the non-burial of the Athenian dead prompted Euripides' tragedy, *Suppliant Women,* performed in the following year, 423.

8. Hanson, *A War Like No Other,* 132. A reconstruction of the flamethrower can be seen in H. van Wees, *Greek Warfare, Myths and Realities* (London, 2004), 141, and in action: https://www.youtube.com/watch?v=Ca62CHhcQvw.

9. Psychological impact of Delium: Hanson, *A War Like No Other,* 134. Date of Alcibiades' marriage: P. Brulé, *Women of Ancient Greece* (Edinburgh, 2003), 119.

10. Endogamy: Brulé, *Women of Ancient Greece,* 120; L. G. Mitchell, *Greeks Bearing Gifts* (Cambridge, 1997), 97.

11. Hipparete as *aristeia:* Isocrates, 16.31. J. Davies, *Athenian Propertied Families* (Oxford, 1971), 260; Hatzfeld, *Alcibiade,* 23–25.

12. Plutarch, *Life of Alcibiades,* 8. This is another dubious anecdote, perhaps designed to show how Alcibiades' charm could excuse his antisocial behaviour. Peacocks: Plutarch, *Life of Pericles,* 4. Diplomat: Pyrilampes, step-father of Plato.

13. Marriage: Plutarch, *Life of Alcibiades,* 8.2; Nepos, *Life of Alcibiades,* 2. Death at Delium: perhaps a lazy scribe mistook the name "Hippocrates" for the so-similar "Hipponicus," and over time the error stuck. Rhodes, *Alcibiades,* 28. Callias finalizing the marriage: Plutarch, *Life of Alcibiades,* 8.2. Family of Hipponicus and Callias: see D. Nails, *The People of Plato* (Indianapolis, 2002), 68; Davies, *Athenian Propertied Families,* 254. For a vivid invocation of Alopece, see B. Hughes, *The Hemlock Cup* (London, 2011), 59–60.

14. Mining for three thousand years: http://greece.greekreporter.com/2016/02/17/newly -discovered-greek-silver-mine-rewrites-history/. Laurium and Themistocles: Herodotus, 7.144

15. Hipponicus' income: Davies, *Athenian Propertied Families,* 260. Slaves: Brulé, *Women of Ancient Greece,* 117.

16. On the Eleusinian Mysteries, see, e.g., H. Bowden, *Mystery Cults of the Ancient World* (Princeton, 2010); W. Burkert, *Ancient Mystery Cults* (Cambridge, 1987); G. Mylonas, *Eleusis and the Eleusinian Mysteries* (Princeton, 1961); D. Stuttard, *Greek Mythology, A Traveler's Guide from Mount Olympus to Troy* (London, 2016), 39–42.

17. Aeschylus as costume designer: Athenaeus, 22e–f. See H. W. Parke, *Festivals of the Athenians* (London, 1986), 58.

18. Callias II: Davies, *Athenian Propertied Families,* 259. The anecdote, including the description of Callias as "the most cruel and unlawful of men": Plutarch, *Life of Aristeides,* 5.

19. Herodotus, 6.122 (a chapter whose authenticity some doubt). Davies, *Athenian Propertied Families*, 255.

20. Herodotus, 6.121–2.

21. Chariot victories: Davies, *Athenian Propertied Families*, 258; Elpinice (and Pericles): Plutarch, *Life of Cimon*, 4; *Life of Pericles*, 10. Elpinice's character: see, e.g., L. O'Higgins, *Women and Humor in Classical Greece* (Cambridge, 2003), 113.

22. The existence of the Peace of Callias, mentioned in Diodorus, 12.4, is (like so many other events in antiquity) debated (see, e.g., G. E. M. de Ste. Croix, *The Origins of the Peloponnesian War* (London 1972); E. Badian, "The Peace of Callias," *JHS* 50 (1987): 1–39; L. J. Samons, "Kimon, Kallias and Peace with Persia," *Zeitschrift für Alte Geschichte* 47 (1998): 129–140. On Callias III, see Nails, *The People of Plato*, 68. Callias and sophists: Plato, *Apology*, 20a. Callias' high opinion of himself: Xenophon, *Hellenica*, 6.3.3–6.

23. Dowries: Brulé, *Women of Ancient Greece*, 122–126. See also S. Pomeroy, *Goddesses, Whores, Wives, and Slaves: Women in Classical Antiquity* (London, 1976).

24. Weddings: Brulé, *Women of Ancient Greece*, 142–150; M. Dillon, *Girls and Women in Classical Greek Religion* (London, 2002), 211. Girl's life, including Brauron: Aristophanes, *Lysistrata*, 641–647. Brulé, *Women of Ancient Greece*, 128–131.

25. Talking seldom to wives: Xenophon, *Oeconomicus*, 3.12. Women's duties in the house: Brulé, *Women of Ancient Greece*, 151–185.

26. Alcibiades' marriage to Hipparete, the failed divorce, and the rift it caused with Callias: Plutarch, *Life of Alcibiades*, 8.2–4. Birth bonus: Andocides, 4.4.13. "Birth bonus" is the term used by S. Verdegem, *Plutarch's* Life of Alcibiades (Leuven, 2010), 161, where he suggests that the "birth bonus" is evidence that the marriage was arranged not by Callias but by Hipponicus.

27. Solon's law: Plutarch, *Life of Solon*, 20; "It's hard for a wife": Menander, frag. 7.2; see also Brulé, *Women of Ancient Greece*, 157.

28. Alcibiades' whoring: Plutarch, *Life of Alcibiades*, 8. Paid proxy: Athenaeus, 12.534c.

29. Plutarch, *Life of Alcibiades*, 8. Divorce: Brulé, *Women of Ancient Greece*, 126–128; L. Cohn-Haft, "Divorce in Classical Athens," *JHS* 115 (1991): 1–14.

30. Hipparete's death: Plutarch, *Life of Alcibiades*, 8. Hipponax on women: frag. 68 (West).

31. Brasidas to northern Greece: Thucydides, 4.78. Kagan, *The Archidamian War*, 287–290.

32. Brasidas' character: Thucydides, 4.81; Brasidas and Perdiccas: Thucydides, 4.83.

33. Amhipolis: M. A. Sears, *Athens, Thrace and the Shaping of Athenian Leadership* (New York, 2013), 77. Brasidas' Amphipolis campaign: Thucydides, 4.102–107; Diodorus, 12.68; Kagan, *The Archidamian War,* 290–302.

34. Thucydides, 4.104–108; exile: Thucydides, 5.26.

35. Timber: J. R. Hale, *Lords of the Sea: The Epic Story of the Athenian Navy and the Birth of Democracy* (New York, 2009), 21. See also R. Meiggs, *Trees and Timber in the Ancient Mediterranean World* (Oxford, 1982).

36. The death of Cleon and Brasidas and the aftermath of Amphipolis: Thucydides, 5.2 ff. Proverb: Polybius, 12.26.2.

37. The more cautious: Thucydides, 1.80–85, puts their concerns into the mouth of their king, Archidamus. See Kagan, *The Archidamian War,* 333–336.

38. Nicias: Plutarch, *Life of Nicias.* Nails, *The People of Plato,* 212; Davies, *Athenian Propertied Families,* 403. Nicias' and Alcibiades' rivalry is well summed up by Rhodes, *Alcibiades,* 39–40.

39. Plutarch, *Life of Nicias,* 2–4.

40. Plutarch, *Life of Nicias,* 3. Some scholars have dated the Delian *archetheoria* to 417, seeDavies, *Athenian Propertied Families,* 404; Rhodes, *Alcibiades,* 40. Nicias' *archetheoria:* M. D. Gygax, *Benefaction and Rewards in the Ancient Greek City: The Origins of Euergitism* (Cambridge 2016), 151; D. Kagan, *The Peace of Nicias and the Sicilian Expedition* (Ithaca, 1981), 153–154; M. Munn, *The School of History* (Berkeley, 2000), 58; Hanson, *A War Like No Other,* 85.

41. Apollo's plague: Homer, *Iliad,* 1.8 ff.

42. Long-robed Ionians: Homeric Hymn 3, *To Delian Apollo,* 154.

43. Plutarch, *Life of Alcibiades,* 14; Thucydides, 5.14 ff.; Diodorus, 12.75. Negotiations and terms of Peace of Nicias: Kagan, *The Archidamian War,* 341–345.

44. *Proxenia:* Munn, *The School of History,* 68. Endius and Alcibiades: Mitchell, *Greeks Bearing Gifts,* 13. Rhodes, *Alcibiades,* 29–31. Spartan kings appointing *proxenoi:* Herodotus, 6.57.

45. Plutarch, *Life of Alcibiades,* 14. Plutarch wrongly says that Alcibiades was Spartan *proxenos,* in which error he is (curiously) followed by Kagan, *The Archidamian War,* 341. Mitchell, *Greeks Bearing Gifts,* 34.

46. Thucydides, 4.40. I owe the observation about spindles and Helots to P. Cartledge.

47. Thermopylae was fought in 480 BC. "Fight in the shade": Herodotus, 7.266. Survivors of Thermopylae: Herodotus, 7.229 f.

48. "With it or on it": Plutarch, *Moralia,* 241. Burial on battlefield: I owe this observation to P. Cartledge. Declining numbers: R. Osborne, *Classical Greece* (Oxford, 2000), 206–207. Hatzfeld, *Alcibiade,* 74.

49. Pericles muzzling public debate: Thucydides, 2.22.1; Cleon's views on Assembly: Thucydides, 3.38.7.

50. Tract condemning Athenian constitution: [Xenophon], *Constitution of Athens,* 1 f. This anonymous tract is sometimes attributed to the "Old Oligarch," but there is every likelihood it was written by a young, hotheaded aristocrat. It has even been suggested that its author may have been Critias. Although its date is unknown, the views it expresses are almost certainly in line with those of the "laconizers" of the 420s. Spartan constitution: P. Cartledge, *The Spartans: An Epic History* (London, 2013), 60.

51. Athenians and slaves: [Xenophon], *Constitution of Athens,* 10; "Wearing hair long": Aristophanes, *Birds,* 1281–1282.

52. Minimum age for generalship: C. Hignett, *A History of the Athenian Constitution* (Oxford, 1952), 224.

53. Plutarch, *Life of Alcibiades,* 10. The episode is discussed in the context of Plutarch's philosophy and ethics in Verdegem, *Plutarch's* Life of Alcibiades, 168. Rhodes, *Alcibiades,* 29, points out that, while the story of the quail is possible, its context cannot be regarded as certain, especially since "the kind of scenario assumed . . . is attested in the fourth century but not earlier." Quails as courtship gifts: Aristophanes, *Birds,* 705–707.

54. Rowdy Assembly: V. Azoulay, *Pericles of Athens* (Princeton, 2014), 152–153.

55. Aelian, *Varia Historia,* 2.1. Once again, an anecdote impossible to prove or to disprove, but more likely than not to be invented.

56. Alcibiades' awe of Socrates' skills as a speaker: Plato, *Symposium,* 215e.

57. Alcibiades' rhetoric: Plutarch, *Life of Alcibiades,* 10. Verdegem, *Plutarch's* Life of Alcibiades, 169–171.

58. Rhetorician: Demosthenes, *Against Meidias,* 145. Polymath: Theophrastus, recorded in Plutarch, *Life of Alcibiades,* 10. Speaking style: M. Vickers, *Aristophanes and Alcibiades* (Berlin, 2015), 20.

59. "In the same way . . .": Plutarch, *Life of Nicias,* 9.

60. Plutarch, *Life of Alcibiades,* 14. Peace of Nicias: among many others, see Hanson, *A War Like No Other,* 151; Kagan, *The Peace of Nicias and the Sicilian Expedition,* 17.

61. Fortress in Attica: Thucydides, 5.17; see Kagan, *The Archidamian War,* 342. That the Spartans were considering building a fort in Attica in 421 is significant, as it

suggests that, in giving his advice to occupy Decelea in 415, Alcibiades knew that this was already something which the Spartans had considered. Weariness: Hanson, *A War Like No Other,* 151.

62. Terms of treaty and names of those ratifying it: Thucydides, 5.22–24.

63. Chariot horses: Plutarch, *Life of Cimon,* 16. Achieving Pericles' war aims: I. Spence, "Cavalry, Democracy and Military Thinking in Athens," in D. Pritchard (ed.), *War, Democracy and Culture in Classical Athens* (Cambridge, 2010), 120.

64. Plutarch, *Life of Alcibiades,* 14.

4. STIRRING THE HORNETS' NEST

1. Thucydides, 5.25–31; Diodorus, 12.75. D. Kagan, *The Peace of Nicias and the Sicilian Expedition* (Ithaca, 1981), 33–59.

2. Xenophon, *Hellenica,* 7.4.10.

3. Myths of Argos: D. Stuttard, *Greek Mythology, A Traveler's Guide from Mount Olympus to Troy* (London, 2016), 159. Importance of Argos: V. D. Hanson, *A War Like No Other* (London, 2005), 152.

4. Argos' ambitions: Thucydides, 5.28. "Battle of the Champions": Herodotus, 1.82.

5. Herodotus, 6.78–80.

6. Thucydides, 5.30–33.

7. Thucydides, 5.36–38.

8. Scione: Thucydides, 5.32. Kagan, *The Peace of Nicias and the Sicilian Expedition,* 45.

9. Covering the episode, Thucydides (5.43) introduces Alcibiades for the first time, commenting that, although he was young compared with politicians in other Greek states, he was distinguished by his glorious ancestry. Alcibiades as opponent of Nicias: Plutarch, *Life of Alcibiades,* 14. J. Hatzfeld, *Alcibiade* (Paris, 1951), 76.

10. Plutarch, *Life of Alcibiades,* 14.

11. Argive embassy to Sparta: Thucydides, 5.40. Kagan, *The Peace of Nicias and the Sicilian Expedition,* 58–59.

12. Plutarch, *Life of Alcibiades,* 14.

13. Thucydides, 5.44–45; Plutarch, *Life of Alcibiades,* 14; *Life of Nicias,* 10. Hatzfeld, *Alcibiade,* 91–93; Kagan, *The Peace of Nicias and the Sicilian Expedition,* 67–70.; S. Verdegem, *Plutarch's* Life of Alcibiades (Leuven, 2010), 194–200. P. A. Brunt, "Thucydides and Alcibiades," *Revue des Études Greques* 65 (1952): 66–69 (reprised in his *Studies in Greek History and Thought* [Oxford, 1993]) probably correctly sees Thucydides' source as Alcibiades himself.

14. Friendship with Endius: Thucydides, 8.6. See A. W. Gomme, A. Andrewes, and K. J. Dover, *A Historical Commentary on Thucydides*, 5 vols. (Oxford, 1945–1981), 4:51–53; Kagan, *The Peace of Nicias and the Sicilian Expedition*, 69.

15. Alcibiades as Thucydides' source: The episode and questions it raises are well discussed by P. J. Rhodes, *Alcibiades, Athenian Playboy, General and Traitor* (Barnsley, 2011), 31–33.

16. Hatzfeld, *Alcibiade*, 91–92.

17. Thucydides, 5.46. Kagan, *The Peace of Nicias and the Sicilian Expedition*, 70–71.

18. Terms of treaty: Thucydides, 5.47.

19. Thucydides, 5.49.

20. Gymnopaediae: P. Cartledge, *The Spartans: An Epic History* (London, 2013), 56. Lichas: Pausanias, 6.2.2; Xenophon, *Memorabilia*, 1.2.61; Thucydides, 5.76. For a good discussion of this episode, see S. Hornblower, *Thucydides and Pindar, Historical Narrative and the World of Epinikian Poetry* (Oxford, 2004), 273.

21. Beating Alcibiades: Hermogenes, *On Invention*, 1.4.22–24. *Hubris* might be translated here as "sneering high-handedness."

22. Thucydides, 5.50. Kagan, *The Peace of Nicias and the Sicilian Expedition*, 76.

23. Plutarch, *Life of Alcibiades*, 15.1; *Life of Nicias*, 10; Thucydides, 5.52. S. Vergedem, *Plutarch's* Life of Alcibiades (Leuven, 2010), 201. Generals: J. Roisman, *The Classical Art of Command* (Oxford, 2017), 11.

24. Hanson, *A War Like No Other*, 140: "There is . . . not a single major Greek general from any city-state in classical Greek history . . . who was not put on trial, demoted, fined, exiled, executed, or killed in battle."

25. Generals' office: J. M. Camp, *The Athenian Agora* (London, 1986), 116. Nicias' character: Plutarch, *Life of Nicias*, 5. Pale face: Aristophanes, *Ecclesiazusae*, 428.

26. Ephebic Oath: Alcibiades' interpretation of the oath: Plutarch, *Life of Alcibiades*, 15. Hanson, *A War Like No Other*, 64; H. Wees, *Greek Warfare, Myths and Realities* (London, 2004), 33.

27. Thucydides, 5.52; Plutarch, *Life of Alcibiades*, 15.1. Hatzfeld, *Alcibiade*, 97–98; G. Busolt, *Griechische Geschichte* 3:2 (Gotha, 1893–1904), 1232–1233; *Forschungen zur Griechische Geschichte* (Breslau, 1880), 149–151; Kagan, *The Peace of Nicias and the Sicilian Expedition*, 78–79.

28. Thucydies, 5.55. Gomme, Andrewes, and Dover, *A Historical Commentary on Thucydides*, 4:74; Kagan, *The Peace of Nicias and the Sicilian Expedition*, 84–85.

29. Thucydides, 5.52; Plutarch, *Life of Alcibiades*, 15.

30. Kagan, *The Peace of Nicias and the Sicilian Expedition*, 79–82.

31. Thucydides, 5.53. Kagan, *The Peace of Nicias and the Sicilian Expedition*, 82–84. Rhodes (*Alcibiades*, 34) follows Gomme, Andrewes, and Dover (*A Historical Commentary on Thucydides*) in his disparaging assessment that the episode's "daring, such as it was, its theatricality, and its small practical value, were alike characteristic of Alkibiades."

32. Thucydides, 5.55.

33. Thucydides, 5.56. Rhodes (*Alcibiades*, 34) rightly emphasises that Alcibiades' proposal did not include ending the Peace of Nicias.

34. Kagan, *The Peace of Nicias and the Sicilian Expedition*, 90, with note discussing Alcibiades' failure to be re-elected general.

35. Thucydides, 5.57.

36. Thucydides, 5.61. Kagan, *The Peace of Nicias and the Sicilian Expedition*, 102.

37. Late arrival and Alcibiades' status: Rhodes, *Alcibiades*, 35–36.

38. Thucydides, 5.57–59; Diodorus, 12.78–79. "Finest Greek army": Thucydides, 5.60. B. W. Henderson, *The Great War Between Athens and Sparta* (London, 1927), 304; Kagan, *The Peace of Nicias and the Sicilian Expedition*, 91.

39. Thucydides, 5.59–60; Diodorus, 12.78.

40. Thucydides, 5.61; Hatzfeld, *Alcibiade*, 104.

41. Thucydides, 5.61.

42. Thucydides, 5.62–64. The Eleans did not accompany the rest of the force to Mantinea—they were peeved that the alliance did not immediately march to shift the Spartans from their southern border.

43. Thucydides, 5.63–64; Plutarch, *Life of Alcibiades*, 15.1. Hanson, *A War Like No Other*, 153.

44. Battle of Mantinea: Thucydides, 5.65–74; Diodorus, 12.79. Kagan, *The Peace of Nicias and the Sicilian Expedition*, 107–137; W. Woodhouse, *King Agis of Sparta and his Campaign in Arcadia of 418 BC* (Oxford, 1933), 111–113; Hanson, *A War Like No Other*, 154–159. Spartan shields and tunics: Wees, *Greek Warfare*, 54.

45. Hanson, *A War Like No Other*, 154–159.

46. Thucydides, 5.76; Diodorus, 12.80; Rhodes, *Alcibiades*, 36; L. G. Mitchell, *Greeks Bearing Gifts* (Cambridge, 1997), 102.

47. Plutarch, *Life of Alcibiades*, 15; Kagan, *The Peace of Nicias and the Sicilian Expedition*, 136.

48. Thucydides, 5.82; Diodorus, 12.80; Plutarch, *Life of Alcibiades*, 15.2; Pausanias, 2.80.2; Kagan, *The Peace of Nicias and the Sicilian Expedition*, 138–139.

49. Thucydides, 5.82; Kagan, *The Peace of Nicias and the Sicilian Expedition*, 140.

50. Plutarch, *Life of Alcibiades*, 15; Thucydides, 5.82. Rhodes, *Alcibiades*, 37.

51. Thucydides, 5.83.

52. Thucydides, 5.84. Kagan, *The Peace of Nicias and the Sicilian Expedition*, 142; Hanson, *A War Like No Other*, 121. Rhodes, *Alcibiades*, 37.

53. Evidence for this lies in the unprecedented support which Chios, Lesbos, and Ephesus provided for Alcibiades at the Olympic Games of 416. This cannot have come out of the blue, but must have been the fruit of significant networking on Alcibiades' part.

54. Casualty figures (200 Athenians and Aeginetan hoplites) at Mantinea: Thucydides, 5.74.

55. Thucydides, 5.83.

5. COURTING THE HYDRA

1. Archestratus: M. Ostwald, *From Popular Sovereignty to the Sovereignty of Law: Law, Society, and Politics in Fifth-Century Athens* (Berkeley, 1987), 430 n.75. Quotation: Plutarch, *Life of Alcibiades*, 16.5. S. Verdegem, *Plutarch's* Life of Alcibiades (Leuven, 2010), 223. Alternative quote: Athenaeus, 12.535d–e.

2. Date of ostracism: D. Kagan, *The Peace of Nicias and the Sicilian Expedition* (Ithaca, 1981), 145; M. Munn, *The School of History* (Berkeley, 2000), 109–110. P. J. Rhodes (*Alcibiades, Athenian Playboy, General and Traitor* [Barnsley, 2011], 42–44) suggests 415 for the date of the ostracism. Ostracism: J. Hatzfeld, *Alcibiade* (Paris, 1951), 108.

3. Cimon: Plutarch, *Life of Cimon*, 17; *Life of Pericles*, 9. Thucydides Melesiou: Plutarch, *Life of Pericles*, 14; Damon: *Life of Pericles*, 4.

4. Plutarch, *Life of Alcibiades*, 13.4; *Life of Nicias*, 11.4; *Life of Aisteides*, 7.3

5. Frequency of Assemblies: T. B. L. Webster, *Everyday Life in Classical Athens* (London, 1969), 63.

6. The number and identity of candidates: Kagan, *The Peace of Nicias and the Sicilian Expedition*, 145–146.

7. Phaeax in Sicily: Thucydides, 5.4–5. Rival to Alcibiades and Eupolis quotation: Plutarch, *Life of Alcibiades*, 13. Kagan, *The Peace of Nicias and the Sicilian Expedition*, 145–146. For opposing views on Phaeax's role in the ostracism, see Hatzfeld, *Alcibiade*, 112–118 and J. Carcopino, *L'ostracisme athénien* (Paris, 1935), 230–232.

8. Lamp-maker: Aristophanes, *Knights*, 1315. Successor to Cleon: Aristophanes, *Peace*, 657 f. Style: Thucydides, 8.73; Aristophanes, *Knights*, 1304; *Acharnians*,

846. Ambitions: Aristophanes, *Knights,* 1304; Kagan, *The Peace of Nicias and the Sicilian Expedition,* 61.

9. Hyperbolus proposes ostracism: Plutarch, *Life of Alcibiades,* 13. Curiously, Thucydides omits this most tumultuous and politically significant of ostracisms from the narrative of his history, though he does refer to it at 8.73 in his description of Hyperbolus' murder some five years later on Samos.

10. Plutarch, *Life of Aristeides,* 7.

11. Plutarch, *Life of Aristeides,* 7.

12. Hyperbolus' ostracism: Munn, *The School of History,* 97. Topography of Agora: see J. Camp, *The Athenian Agora* (London, 1986). Votes required: whether 6,000 was the total required, or whether a candidate needed to attract 6,000 votes to lose, is hotly argued, but both Plutarch (*Life of Aristeides,* 7) and Philochorus (frag. 30, book 3) can be read as supporting the former.

13. Hatzfeld, *Alcibiade,* 116. At the time of writing, the results of the Brexit Referendum, the U.S. Presidential Election of 2016, and the U.K. General Election of 2017 are recent reminders of how unpredictable voting can be.

14. Plutarch, *Life of Alcibiades,* 13; *Life of Nicias,* 11. For discussions of the possible permutations, see Hatzfeld, *Alcibiade,* 112–118. To this day, respected scholars continue meekly to accept that Nicias and Alcibiades colluded to have Hyperbolus ostracized. Whatever the truth, partly thanks to the result, and partly because Athenian politics would soon change beyond all recognition, this was Athens' last ostracism.

15. Melos' status: Thucydides, 5.84. Athens attacks in 426: Thucydides, 3.91; Diodorus, 12.65. V. D. Hanson, *A War Like No Other* (London, 2005), 121; 188. Aiding Sparta in 427: D. Kagan, *The Archidamian War* (Ithaca, 1974), 199.

16. Thucydides, 5.84. Kagan, *The Peace of Nicias and the Sicilian Expedition,* 149. Alcibiades' role at Melos: Hanson, *A War Like No Other,* 121.

17. Alcibiades' liturgies: Thucydides, 6.16; Plutarch, *Life of Alcibiades,* 16; Isocrates, 16.35. Hatzfeld, *Alcibiade,* 129–131.

18. Panathenaic Festival: H. W. Parke, *Festivals of the Athenians* (London, 1986), 33–50.

19. Site of hippodrome: D. Kyle, *Athletics in Ancient Athens* (Leiden, 1997), 97.

20. *Inscriptiones Graecae* I 3rd edn. Berlin 1981, ed. David Lewis, 41–60 lists 102 Panathenaic amphorae won by Alcibiades, presumably in the chariot race at the Games. Rhodes, *Alcibiades,* 40.

21. Olympic Games: see D. Stuttard, *Power Games, Ritual and Rivalry at the Ancient Greek Olympics* (London, 2012). The chariot race was first introduced in 680 BC.

22. Kudos of victorious athlete: Munn, *The School of History,* 25.

23. Plutarch, *Life of Alcibiades,* 11–12; Thucydides, 6.16.

24. Tent: [Andocides], 4.30; Plutarch, *Life of Alcibiades,* 12.

25. Pelops and chariot race: Stuttard, *Power Games,* 73–74.

26. The result: Thucydides, 6.16; Plutarch, *Life of Alcibiades,* 11. Curiously, Thucydides has Alcibiades tell the Athenian Assembly that his chariots came first, second, and fourth. The reason for the discrepancy is uncertain. If the epinician ode is genuine (even if its authorship is questionable), it should probably take precedence over Thucydides' account of Alcibiades' speech, which he was not in the Assembly to hear. Euripides ode: Plutarch, *Life of Alcibiades,* 11; Athenaeus, 1.3e. Note that Plutarch (*Life of Demosthenes,* 1) questions the authorship of the ode. Paintings: Athenaeus, 12.532d–e. Munn, *The School of History,* 60: "perhaps the first examples of self-commissioned portraiture at democratic Athens."

27. Plutarch, *Life of Alcibiades,* 12; Athenaeus, 12.47.

28. Andocides, 4.29; Plutarch, *Life of Alcibiades,* 13.

29. Pausanias, 5.11.1–10; Stuttard, *Power Games,* 14–18.

30. Drees, *Olympia,* 120–121.

31. Prytanaeum: A fine rotunda on the site of the old royal palace of Peisistratus, between the Council Chamber and the generals' headquarters, where an eternal flame was kept burning, the spiritual heart of Athens. Camp, *The Athenian Agora,* 44. Stuttard, *Power Games,* 178.

32. Plutarch, *Life of Alcibiades,* 12; Diodorus, 13.74.3; Isocrates, 16. That cities (as opposed to individuals) could own chariots is also attested to by the story of Lichas entering his chariot in 420 as if it had belonged to the city of Thebes.

33. [Andocides], 4.26.

34. Winning chariot: M. Vickers, *Sophocles and Alcibiades, Athenian Politics in Ancient Greek Literature* (Ithaca, 2008), 124. Teisias and Diomedes: W. Ellis, *Alcibiades* (London, reprinted 2013), 51; Hatzfeld, *Alcibiade,* 140; J. Davies, *Athenian Propertied Families* (Oxford, 1971), 502; Rhodes, *Alcibiades,* 40 n.8; 115–116. Speech: Isocrates, 16.

35. Fear of Alcibiades' tyrannical ambitions: Thucydides, 6.15.

36. Xerxes' tent: Herodotus, 9.82. Pericles' Odeon: J. M. Camp, *The Archaeology of Athens* (New Haven, 2001), 100–101.

37. Melos: Thucydides, 5.116.

38. Plutarch, *Life of Alcibiades,* 16; [Andocides], 4.22–23. Ellis, *Alcibiades,* 50. Rhodes (*Alcibiades,* 37–38), while accepting that Alcibiades may have supported the proposal to massacre the Melians, and that it would have been "in character" for

him to father a child with a Melian slave, questions the source of this detail on grounds of the timing of the speech from which it is supposedly drawn vis-à-vis the timing of the boy's birth.

39. Plato, *Symposium*; Webster, *Everyday Life in Classical Athens,* 40–41.

40. Hatzfeld, *Alcibiade,* 50.

41. Flute girl, etc.: Plato, *Symposium,* 212c. "I'll wreath my sword": frag. 10 and 25 Diehl. Celebrating tyrannicides: Munn, *The School of History,* 20–21.

42. Plato, *Symposium,* 212d–14d.

43. Plato, *Symposium,* 214e–22b.

44. Plato, *Symposium,* 216a.

45. "Violet crowned Athens": Pindar, frag. 64.

46. Peleus and Thetis: D. Stuttard, *Greek Mythology, A Traveler's Guide from Mount Olympus to Troy* (London, 2016), 145.

47. Thucydides, 6.6; Diodorus, 12.32 (where Segesta speaks on behalf on Leontini, but see Kagan, *The Peace of Nicias and the Sicilian Expedition,* 159–166).

6. BETWEEN SCYLLA AND CHARYBDIS

1. J. Hatzfeld, *Alcibiade* (Paris, 1951), 142.

2. Diodorus, 12.83. V. D. Hanson, *A War Like No Other* (London, 2005), 202; D. Kagan, *The Peace of Nicias and the Sicilian Expedition* (Ithaca, 1981), 159–163.

3. Thucydides, 6.6. The Spartans had already requested help from Sicily (and Persia) in 431, but none had been forthcoming. D. Kagan, *The Archidamian War* (Ithaca, 1974), 23.

4. Thucydides, 6.8; Diodorus, 12.83. The temple at Segesta, begun in this period, was never finished.

5. Thucydides, 6.8; Plutarch, *Life of Alcibiades,* 18. One general in command: P. J. Rhodes, *Alcibiades, Athenian Playboy, General and Traitor* (Barnsley, 2011), 45. Parsimonious Lamachus: Plutarch, *Life of Nicias,* 15. Nicias as *proxenos* of Syracuse: L. G. Mitchell, *Greeks Bearing Gifts* (Cambridge, 1997), 68. A truncated account of the debates is contained in Plutarch, *Life of Alcibiades,* 17. Hatzfeld, *Alcibiade,* 149; Kagan, *The Peace of Nicias and the Sicilian Expedition,* 167–190; Hanson, *A War Like No Other,* 206.

6. Thucydides, 6.9–11; Diodorus, 12.83.6; Plutarch, *Life of Nicias,* 12. For a good, if brief, discussion of the debate and Thucydides' account of it, see Rhodes, *Alcibiades,* 46.

7. Or so Thucydides, 6.12, has him say.

8. Thucydides, 6.13–14.

9. Thucydides, 6.16–18. Again, the question must be raised of how reliable are Thucydides' versions of speeches, especially those that he did not personally hear. My personal view is that many of the speeches are literary constructs, influenced as much by drama as by what we would call historical fact. At 1.22, where he disingenuously claims to be writing history, not romance, he writes that, where he does not have verbatim records, he will provide the kind of speeches which he deemed "the occasion demanded." This is startlingly similar to Aristotle's statement (*Poetics,* 1451b.8–9) that drama describes the kind of things "that a person of a certain character would inevitably say or do. That is the aim of poetry." (Aristotle states that history, on the other hand, is concerned with facts, giving the telling example: "a specific fact is what Alcibiades did or what was done to him.") Given Thucydides' creativity in his speeches, then, the reader must in large part rely on his assessment of the characters involved (admittedly characters whom he knew better than we can ever do, and—in Alcibiades' case—whom he may have interviewed), while constantly remembering that his version of any speech is written not only with the benefit of often considerable hindsight but possibly through the prism of personal prejudice as well. However, in the absence of verbatim records, scholars often analyze Thucydides' speeches as if they are accurate reports. For example, writing of this one, V. D. Hanson (*A War Like No Other,* 360 n.4) observes: "As in all of Alcibiades' reported speeches, the problem is not just that he distorted facts and analyses for his own personal interest but that so often his assessments were nevertheless astute, if for entirely different reasons from those he intended." M. Munn, *The School of History* (Berkeley, 2000), 96, comments that in this speech Alcibiades, the hero of Potidaea, seeks to unite his personal *arête* (bravery / virtue) with that of Athens. To me the speech reads almost like an "alternative truth," a eulogy of what might have been had events turned out differently, composed after Alcibiades' death. Kudos of Olympics: L. G. Mitchell, *The Heroic Rulers of Archaic and Classical Greece* (London, 2013), 47.

10. Thucydides, 6.18. That Athens' owes her success to her restless populace is a theme running through many of Thucydides' speeches.

11. Thucydides, 6. 20–23.

12. Thucydides, 6. 24–25. Kagan, *The Peace of Nicias and the Sicilian Expedition,* 189–191. Plutarch, *Life of Alcibiades,* 18.2, identifies Demostratus (whose name meant "The Army of the People") as the man who proposed giving the generals full powers.

13. Aristophanes' description dates from 426: Aristophanes, *Acharnians*, 545–554. Athenians' excitement: Plutarch, *Life of Alcibiades*, 17.

14. Socrates: Plutarch, *Life of Alcibiades*, 17. Adonis festival: Plutarch, *Life of Alcibiades*, 18; Aristophanes, *Lysistrata*, 387–397. See Kagan, *The Peace of Nicias and the Sicilian Expedition*, 192–193. Bad omens: Thucydides, 8.1; Plutarch, *Life of Nicias*, 13; Munn, *The School of History*, 105.

15. Date: I follow D. Kagan (*The Peace of Nicias and the Sicilian Expedition*, 193) and D. MacDowell (*Andokides and the Mysteries* [Oxford, 1962], 188). But see K. J. Dover (in A. W. Gomme, A. Andrewes, and K. J. Dover, *A Historical Commentary on Thucydides*, 5 vols. [Oxford, 1945–1981], 4:274–276) and P. J. Rhodes (*Alcibiades*, 46), who place it in late May.

16. Mutilation of Herms: Thucydides, 6.1; Diodorus, 13.2; Plutarch, *Life of Alcibiades*, 18; Nepos, *Life of Alcibiades*, 3; Andocides, *On the Mysteries*, 62; Aristophanes, *Lysistrata*, 1094. Hatzfeld, *Alcibiade*, 158–161; Kagan, *The Peace of Nicias and the Sicilian Expedition*, 193–195; Rhodes, *Alcibiades*, 46–7; S. Verdegem, *Plutarch's Life of Alcibiades* (Leuven, 2010), 248–256. Cimon's victory: Battle of Eion, 476/5. Cimon's Herms: Plutarch, *Life of Cimon*, 7; J. Camp, *The Athenian Agora* (London, 1986), 74–75. Herms in Athens: Munn, *The School of History*, 104. Hermes: D. Stuttard, *Greek Mythology, A Traveler's Guide from Mount Olympus to Troy* (London, 2016), 88–90.

17. Thucydides, 6.28.1; Kagan, *The Peace of Nicias and the Sicilian Expedition*, 195–196; Hanson, *A War Like No Other*, 207; D. Hamel, *The Mutilation of the Herms, Unpacking an Ancient Mystery* (Baltimore, 2012), 7.

18. Kagan, *The Peace of Nicias and the Sicilian Expedition*, 195. Phallic names: Munn, *The School of History*, 104. Wealth tax (*eisphora*): Munn, *The School of History*, 100.

19. Who did it?: Possibilities are discussed by Rhodes, *Alcibiades*, 48–49. Assemblies: Plutarch, *Life of Alcibiades*, 18.4. Commission of Enquiry: Thucydides, 6.27; Andocides, *On the Mysteries*, 14; Munn, *The School of History*, 105–106; Kagan, *The Peace of Nicias and the Sicilian Expedition*, 195.

20. Assembly: Andocides, *On the Mysteries*, 11; see, e.g., M. Gagarin, and D. M. MacDowell, *Antiphon and Andocides* (Austin, 1998), 104. Charges: Thucydides, 6.28; Andocides, *On the Mysteries*, 11; Plutarch, *Life of Alcibiades*, 19. Hatzfeld, *Alcibiade*, 163.

21. Thucydides, 6.28. Kagan, *The Peace of Nicias and the Sicilian Expedition*, 195; Munn, *The School of History*, 106.

22. Thucydides, 6.29; Pluarch, *Life of Alcibiades*, 19. Under Athenian law, slaves' evidence was acceptable only if given under torture. The Assembly, of course, was not a law court, and this was not a formal trial; but it might be argued that for the

Assembly to hear and act upon Andromachus' freely given evidence was seriously unconstitutional.

23. Critias: M. Wright, *The Lost Plays of Euripides* (London, 2016), 55.

24. Eros: Munn, *The School of History,* 111.

25. Eupolis: *Baptae* most likely staged in 415: see I. C. Storey, *Eupolis, Poet of Old Comedy* (Oxford, 2003), 103. Euripides: Munn, *The School of History,* 121. Drowning Eupolis: Juvenal, 2.92; Aelius Aristides, 3.8; Themistius, 8.110; Platonius, *On the Distinctions among Comedians,* 1.21–23. Eupolis' drowning at Alcibiades' hands is unlikely: see Rhodes, *Alcibiades,* 49. Euripides, *Trojan Women,* 48–97. Sailing with ungodly men: Antiphon, *On the Murder of Herodes,* 82.

26. *Hetaereia:* Gomme, Andrewes, and Dover, *A Historical Commentary on Thucydides,* 5:128–131; R. Waterfield, *Why Socrates Died* (Toronto, 2009), 62–65; Munn, *The School of History,* 90; Kagan, *The Peace of Nicias and the Sicilian Expedition,* 196; Mitchell, *Greeks Bearing Gifts,* 43.

27. Fake corpse: Polyaenus, *Strategemata,* 1.40, see also Hatzfeld, *Alcibiade,* 164; Kagan, *The Peace of Nicias and the Sicilian Expedition,* 196. According to Polyaenus, the only man who agreed to help Alcibiades was Callias, son of Hipponicus, thanks to which Alcibiades "discovered that he was a faithful friend; and ever afterwards he held him in the first place in his affections." While Callias may, indeed, have been involved in the episode, it probably occurred (if it occurred at all) before relationships soured. I question Alcibiades' later friendship with him. Sacrilege and tyranny: S. Nevin, *Military Leaders and Sacred Space* (London, 2017), 187.

28. Tension between "great men" and democracy: Mitchell, *The Heroic Rulers of Archaic and Classical Greece* 154–155; see also 47. Pact to pervert constitution: Munn, *The School of History,* 109.

29. Thucydides, 6.29.

30. Thucydides, 6.29.

31. Description of departure based on Thucydides, 6.30–2; Diodorus, 13.3.

32. Tomb of Themistocles: Plutarch, *Life of Themistocles,* 32. Thucydides, 1.138, writes of the repatriation of Themistocles' bones but says that it was done by Themistocles' family without the knowledge of the Athenian authorities.

33. Own expense: Rhodes, 50. Hammock: Plutarch, *Life of Alcibiades,* 16; T. D. Fosbroke (*Encyclopædia of Antiquities* [London, 1825]) goes so far as to attribute the invention of the hammock to Alcibiades.

34. Thucydides, 6.424. Kagan, *The Peace of Nicias and the Sicilian Expedition,* 211.

35. Thucydides, 6.31 ("It resembled a statement to the rest of Greece of Athens' power and wealth rather than an expeditionary force against her enemies"); 6.43–44; Diodorus, 13.2. Kagan, *The Peace of Nicias and the Sicilian Expedition,* 210; Hanson, *A War Like No Other,* 205–206.

36. Thucydides, 6.44; Diodorus, 13.3 (who disagrees with Thucydides about the extent of the Athenians' frosty welcome). Kagan, *The Peace of Nicias and the Sicilian Expedition,* 211.

37. Thucydides, 6.46. It is well to heed P. J. Rhodes' warning (*Alcibiades,* 45) that "it is hard to believe that what actually happened was as simple as Thucydides' account of it."

38. Thucydides, 6.47; Plutarch, *Life of Alcibiades,* 20. The debate: Hatzfeld, *Alcibiade,* 196–197; Kagan, *The Peace of Nicias and the Sicilian Expedition,* 212–217; Rhodes, *Alcibiades,* 50.

39. Thucydides, 6.49.

40. Thucydides, 6.48. For analyses of Alcibiades' strategy, see U. Laffi, "La spedizione ateniense in Sicilia del 415 a.C.," *Rivista Storica Italiana* 82 (1970): 295; K. J. Dover in Gomme, Andrewes, and Dover, *A Historical Commentary on Thucydides,* 4:491–421; Kagan, *The Peace of Nicias and the Sicilian Expedition,* 213–216. Once more, it is possible that Alcibiades was Thucydides' source here, but this does not mean that the historian's account is untrue. The three strategies reflect what we know of each of the three men.

41. Thucydides, 6.50. Kagan, *The Peace of Nicias and the Sicilian Expedition,* 217.

42. Thucydides, 6.50. Naxos as colony of Chalcis on Euboea: Thucydides, 6.3.

43. Etna: Pindar, *Pythian,* 1.20–26. Carcinus: *TrGF* 1.70 F5 quoted in Diodorus, 5.51. Wright, *The Lost Plays of Greek Tragedy,* 108.

44. Thucydides, 6.50.

45. Syracuse: P. Cartledge, *Ancient Greece, A History in Eleven Cities* (Oxford, 2009), 113–130.

46. Thucydides, 6.50. Kagan, *The Peace of Nicias and the Sicilian Expedition,* 218.

47. Thucydides, 6.51; Polyaenus, *Strategems,* 1.40.4. Kagan, *The Peace of Nicias and the Sicilian Expedition,* 223.

48. Thucydides, 6.52; Kagan, *The Peace of Nicias and the Sicilian Expedition,* 224.

49. Thucydides, 6.53; Plutarch, *Life of Alcibiades,* 21.

50. Andocides, *On the Mysteries.* Rhodes, *Alcibiades,* 48. Andocides' family: [Plutarch], *Lives of the Ten Orators: Andocides,* 1; Plutarch, *Life of Alcibiades,* 21. Trial: Plutarch, *Life of Alcibiades,* 21. Much has been written about Andocides and the

trials, including: Munn, *The School of History*, 106–118; Kagan, *The Peace of Nicias and the Sicilian Expedition*, 198–203.

51. Callias: Munn, *The School of History*, 113. Tyrants: Thucydides, 6.53–59. Herodotus: Munn, *The School of History*, 116.

52. Thucydides, 6.60–61; Plutarch, *Life of Alcibiades*, 21.6. Kagan, *The Peace of Nicias and the Sicilian Expedition*, 203.

53. Gods not letting army win: Diodorus, 14.67–69; see Nevin, *Military Leaders and Sacred Space*, 14. Indicting Alcibiades: Plutarch, *Life of Alcibiades*, 22.3. Hatzfeld, *Alcibiade*, 176. Avoiding disturbance: Plutarch, *Life of Alcibiades*, 21. See Kagan (*The Peace of Nicias and the Sicilian Expedition*, 203; 225) suggesting from Diodorus, 13.5, that the crew of the *Salaminia* informed Alcibiades of what had been going on in Athens in his absence.

54. Thucydides, 6.61; Diodorus, 13.5; Plutarch, *Life of Alcibiades*, 22.

7. SLEEPING WITH THE ENEMY

1. Plutarch, *Life of Alcibiades*, 23; Nepos, *Life of Alcibiades*, 11.

2. Route: Thucydides, 6.61; Plutarch, *Life of Alcibiades*, 23; Nepos, *Life of Alcibiades*, 4. Plutarch's assertion that Alcibiades went to Argos is possibly a confusion with Themistocles' journey in exile. J. Hatzfeld, *Alcibiade* (Paris, 1951), 206–207; P. J. Rhodes, *Alcibiades, Athenian Playboy, General and Traitor* (Barnsley, 2011), 50–51.

3. "Can't you trust your country?": Plutarch, *Life of Alcibiades*, 22. S. Verdegem, *Plutarch's* Life of Alcibiades (Leuven, 2010), 258–260.

4. Sparta's treatment of returning prisoners of war: Thucydides, 5.34. See D. Kagan, *The Peace of Nicias and the Sicilian Expedition* (Ithaca, 1981), 48.

5. Messana: Thucydides, 6.74; Plutarch, *Life of Alcibiades*, 22. Scholars (e.g., Hatzfeld, *Alcibiade*, 206) have been quick to accept Thucydides' account that Alcibiades *did* prevent Messana from siding with the Athenians. However, especially given the frosty response of Camarina and the lukewarm reception at Catana, I can see no reason why Alcibiades could reasonably have supposed that he could have influenced Messana now to change its stance.

6. Immunity: Thucydides, 6.88.

7. Spartan villages: P. Cartledge, *The Spartans: An Epic History* (London, 2013), 54. Alcmaeonids: the accuser was Agariste, wife of Alcmaeonides, and former wife of Pericles' music teacher and political advisor, Damon; Andocides, *On the Mysteries*, 16.

8. Curses: Lysias, 7.51; Plutarch, *Life of Alcibiades*, 22; 33. Theano: Plutarch, *Life of Alcibiades*, 22; see Hatzfeld, *Alcibiade*, 204 n.4.

9. One hundred talents: see V. D. Hanson, *A War Like No Other* (London, 2005), 86 n.35 (calculating that, in 2005, 100 talents would have been equivalent to $48,000,000). Inscriptions: now fragmentary, these so-called Attic Stelai were published in Hesperia, XXII, (American School of Classical Studies at Athens, 1953), 225–299; see Rhodes, *Alcibiades,* 48. Wild silk: see M. M. Lee, *Body, Dress, and Identity in Ancient Greece* (Cambridge, 2015), 91. "Stele of disgrace": Plutarch, *Life of Alcibiades,* 22; Philochorus, *FGrH,* 328, frag. 134; so-called by Kagan, *The Peace of Nicias and the Sicilian Expedition,* 225; see Hatzfeld, *Alcibiade,* 204 n.1. "I'm alive": Plutarch, *Life of Alcibiades,* 22.

10. For the best general introductions to Sparta, see P. Cartledge, *The Spartans: An Epic History* (London, 2013) and *Spartan Reflections* (London, 2001).

11. *Gerousia:* Like "Senate," *Gerousia* derives from the word for "old man." Voting by shouting: Thucydides, 1.87.

12. Education: See Cartledge, *Spartan Reflections,* 79–90. "Animal in nature": Aristotle, *Politics,* 1338b. Crypteia: Cartledge, *Spartan Reflections,* 88.

13. These were not the only purges carried out on Helots. During the Peloponnesian War, Helots who had fought conspicuously on Sparta's behalf were executed on their return from war, because they were deemed a threat (Thucydides, 4.80; Diodorus, 12.67).

14. Women: Cartledge, *Spartan Reflections,* 106–126.

15. Athenians and Syracusans seek help: Thucydides, 6.88. Kagan, *The Peace of Nicias and the Sicilian Expedition,* 249–251. General Spartan reluctance to become involved in foreign wars: Thucydides, 1.70.

16. Thucydides, 89–92, records Alcibiades' speech verbatim—or, rather, he gives a version of the kind of speech he believes Alcibiades would have made in the circumstances (see Thucydides' statement of intent, 1.22). In this case, he may be basing his report on conversations with Alcibiades when the latter was in his second exile from Athens after 406; see Kagan, *The Peace of Nicias and the Sicilian Expedition,* 256–257. Plutarch simply records the advice given: Plutarch, *Life of Alcibiades,* 23. Hatzfeld, *Alcibiade,* 209–211; Rhodes, *Alcibiades,* 51–52.

17. Moderating force: We might think of his moderate response to Nicias' diatribe about "younger men" in the Sicilian debate of spring 415. Democracy an acknowledged folly: Thucydides, 6.89.

18. Thucydides, 6.90. Hyperbolus had already been accused of wanting to defeat Carthage: Aristophanes, *Knights,* 1302–1305. Thucydides, 6.34, imagines Hermocrates suggesting that Carthage fears an Athenian attack. Hatzfeld, *Alcibiade,* 144–145; Hanson, *A War Like No Other,* 211.

19. Thucydides, 6.91. As J. T. Roberts writes (*The Plague of War, Athens, Sparta, and the Struggle for Ancient Greece* [Oxford, 2017], 201): "An ambitious program of world conquest led by *Nicias?* Surely not."

20. Thucydides, 6.88. See Lysias, 14.30.

21. Thucydides, 6.91. Unoriginal advice: M. Munn, *The School of History* (Berkeley, 2000), 123. Spartan fort: Thucydides, 5.17. Theseus and Helen: D. Stuttard, *Greek Mythology, A Traveler's Guide from Mount Olympus to Troy* (London, 2016), ch. 18. Special honours: Herodotus, 9.73.

22. Thucydides, 6.91. Hanson, *A War Like No Other,* 60.

23. Thucydides, 6.92.

24. Thucydides, 6.93.

25. Thucydides, 6.93. Hatzfeld, *Alcibiade,* 212; Kagan, *The Peace of Nicias and the Sicilian Expedition,* 257. *Mothax:* Cartledge, *Spartan Reflections,* 125. Gylippus and Thurii: Thucydides, 6.104. Alcibiades' effect on Spartan policy: Rhodes, *Alcibiades,* 52.

26. Reluctance to break oath: Thucydides, 7.18. Kagan, *The Peace of Nicias and the Sicilian Expedition,* 290.

27. Hyacinthia: Cartledge, *Spartan Reflections,* 18–19; *Gymnopaediae:* Cartledge, *Spartan Reflections,* 86.

28. Agora and Persian Stoa: Pausanias, 3.11.3. Tomb of Leonidas: Pausanias, 3.14.1. Brazen House: Pausanias, 3.17.2f. P. Cartledge, *Sparta and Lakonia: A Regional History 1300–362 BC* (London, 1979), 90.

29. Cynisca: Pausanias, 3.8.1–3. P. Cartledge, *The Greeks, Crucible of Civilization* (London, 2001), 141–150.

30. Timaea: Plutarch, *Life of Alcibiades,* 23.7; *Life of Agesilaus,* 3; Justin 5.2. Rhodes, *Alcibiades,* 58. Hair: Cartledge, *The Spartans,* 159. Timaea's youth can be implied from the fact that she had not yet borne Agis a son. The ephors fined King Archidamas for marrying a short, plain wife, implying that kings usually looked for the opposite in their queens. See, e.g., S. Pomeroy, *Spartan Women* (Oxford, 2002), 74. Timaea was probably not the only woman to whom Alcibiades paid court in Sparta. Athenaeus, 13.574d, talks of him breaking down the doors of Spartan prostitutes, though arguably this raises more questions than it answers. It may simply be a hyperbolic way of referring to his liaison with Timaea. P. Cartledge (*Spartan Reflections,* 125) notes the lack of reference to Spartan prostitutes before the third century BC. Fathering a Spartan king: Plutarch, *Life of Agesilaus,* 3.2. Adultery laws: Cartledge, *Spartan Reflections,* 124–125. Hatzfeld, *Alcibiade,* 217; L. G. Mitchell, *Greeks Bearing Gifts* (Cambridge, 1997), 108.

31. Thucydides, 7.19. Diodorus, 13.9, suggests that Alcibiades accompanied him in the initial stages of his fortification of Decelea, but this is unlikely.

32. Hanson, *A War Like No Other,* 60; Kagan, *The Peace of Nicias and the Sicilian Expedition,* 288–292.

33. *Hellenica Oxyrhynchia,* 12.3. Thucydides, 7.27. V. D. Hanson, "Thucydides and the Desertion of the Attic Slaves During the Decelean War," *Classical Antiquity* 11 (1992): 210–228. D. Kagan, *The Fall of the Athenian Empire* (Ithaca, 1987), 3.

34. The sorry tale of the failure of the Sicilian Expedition takes up most of Thucydides, book 7 as well as Diodorus, 13, 6–33, and is the subject of much modern scholarly debate. Opium: I owe this observation to Dr. M. D. Grant.

35. Thucydides, 8.6. Kagan, *The Fall of the Athenian Empire,* 16–23; Munn, *The School of History,* 129. Persian-Greek relations: Rhodes, *Alcibiades,* 55–56.

36. Murder of Khashayarsha: Aristotle, *Politics* 1311b; Ctesias, *FGrH,* 688, frag. 13; Diodorus, 11.69. Royal Road: Herodotus, 5.52–53; 8.98; Xenophon, *Cyropaedia,* 8.6.17–18.

37. Aristophanes:*Acharnians,* 65–94. Intercepting missions: Thucydides, 2.7.1; 2.67.1–2. "Concerning the Spartans": Thucydides, 4.50.3. Hatzfeld, *Alcibiade,* 215–216, D. Kagan, *The Archidamian War* (Ithaca, 1974), 257–258.

38. Humarga: Thucydides, 8.5. Munn, *The School of History,* 128; Kagan, *The Fall of the Athenian Empire,* 27–31; Rhodes, *Alcibiades,* 56.

39. E. R. M. Dusinberre, *Aspects of Empire in Achaemenid Sardis* (Cambridge, 2003), 1–6.

40. Chithrafarna's ancestry: Herodotus, 6.133. Chithrafarna: W. Smith (ed.), *A Dictionary of Greek and Roman Biography and Mythology* (London, 1873).

41. Ctesias, 53. Pišišyaothna: D. M. Lewis, *Sparta and Persia* (Leiden, 1977), 55. Dusinberre, *Aspects of Empire in Achaemenid Sardis,* 2.

42. Dascyleum: J. M. Cook, *Greek Archaeology in Western Asia Minor* (Cambridge, 1960), 34.

43. Education: Herodotus, 1.136. Farnavaz: *A Dictionary of Greek and Roman Biography and Mythology.*

44. Thucydides, 8.5–6. Kagan, *The Fall of the Athenian Empire,* 29; 32–33.

45. Thucydides, 8.5.

46. Thucydides, 8.6; Plutarch, *Life of Alcibiades,* 24. Kagan, *The Fall of the Athenian Empire,* 28.

47. Kagan, *The Fall of the Athenian Empire,* 33–34. Grain supply: Hanson, *A War Like No Other,* 35.

48. Thucydides, 8.6; Plutarch, *Life of Alcibiades*, 24. Kagan, *The Fall of the Athenian Empire*, 33; Rhodes, *Alcibiades*, 56–57.

49. Endius as ephor: Thucydides, 8.6. Hatzfeld, *Alcibiade*, 216 n.3.

50. Thucydides, 8.5; 8.8. Kagan, *The Fall of the Athenian Empire*, 25–28; 37–38.

51. "Bridge of restless sea": Pindar, *Nemean*, 6.40. Diolcus: B. R. MacDonald, "The Diolkos," *Journal of Hellenic Studies* 106 (1986): 191–195. Spiraeum: Thucydides, 8.10. Kagan, *The Fall of the Athenian Empire*, 36–39.

52. Thucydides, 8.12. Kagan, *The Fall of the Athenian Empire*, 39.

53. Timaea and Leotychidas: Plutarch, *Life of Alcibiades*, 23, *Life of Agesilaus*, 3; Xenophon, 3.3.1–2. Hatzfeld, *Alcibiade*, 217–218; 226. Alcibiades' relationship with Agis: Thucydides, 8.12; Plutarch, *Life of Alcibiades*, 24.

54. Thucydides, 8.12. Kagan, *The Fall of the Athenian Empire*, 41; Rhodes, *Alcibiades*, 57.

8. IN A PARADISE GARDEN

1. Thucydides, 8.14. D. Kagan, *The Fall of the Athenian Empire* (Ithaca, 1987), 43; P. J. Rhodes, *Alcibiades, Athenian Playboy, General and Traitor* (Barnsley, 2011), 57.

2. Chian constitution: O. Murray, *Early Greece*, 2nd ed. (London, 1993), 188; Kagan, *The Fall of the Athenian Empire*, 43. Athens' use of fleet: Thucydides, 3.10.

3. Thucydides, 8.14. Kagan, *The Fall of the Athenian Empire*, 43–45.

4. Thucydides, 8.14. Kagan, *The Fall of the Athenian Empire*, 46.

5. Thucydides, 8.15. Reserve fund: Thucydides, 2.24. Samian revolt of 440: Thucydides, 1.115–117.

6. Thucydides, 8.15. Unusually for the period, Chians used slaves as part of their trireme crews. There were more slaves per head of population at Chios than any other state except Sparta: Thucydides, 8.40.

7. Thucydides, 8.16. Kagan, *The Fall of the Athenian Empire*, 46.

8. Thucydides, 8.17.

9. Thucydides, 8.17. Alcibiades and Chithrafarna: Plutarch, *Life of Alcibiades*, 24. Kagan, *The Fall of the Athenian Empire*, 54.

10. Terms of provisional treaty: Thucydides, 8.18. J. Hatzfeld, *Alcibiade* (Paris, 1951), 221–222; M. Munn, *The School of History* (Berkeley, 2000), 129.

11. Thucydides, 8.19–23. Kagan, *The Fall of the Athenian Empire*, 56–57.

12. Thucydides, 8.24.

13. Thucydides, 8.25. Kagan, *The Fall of the Athenian Empire*, 61.

14. Thucydides, 8.26–27—if any passage is derived from interviews with Alcibiades, it is surely this. Kagan, *The Fall of the Athenian Empire,* 62–63. Talent on Alcibiades' head: *FGH* 328 Philochoros F134; Pollux, 10.97.

15. Operation to take Iasus: Thucydides, 8.28. Kagan, *The Fall of the Athenian Empire,* 69–70.

16. Thucydides, 8.28.

17. Pay to Spartans: Thucydides, 8.29. A. W. Gomme, A. Andrewes, and K. J. Dover, *A Historical Commentary on Thucydides* 5 vols. (Oxford, 1945–1981), 5:70.

18. Implications of Chalcideus' death: Hatzfeld, *Alcibiade,* 224–225.

19. Alcibiades with Chithrafarna: Thucydides, 8.45; Plutarch, *Life of Alcibiades,* 24; Kagan, *The Fall of the Athenian Empire,* 71–77. Sardis: E. R. M. Dusinberre, *Aspects of Empire in Achaemenid Sardis* (Cambridge, 2003).

20. "Count no man happy": Herodotus, 1.32. Astyochus' orders: Thucydides, 8.45; Plutarch, *Life of Alcibiades,* 24. Kagan, *The Fall of the Athenian Empire,* 71; Hatzfeld, *Alcibiade,* 226.

21. Alcibiades' magic: Plutarch, *Life of Alcibiades,* 24.

22. Kagan, *The Fall of the Athenian Empire,* 71–73. Timaea: Justin, 5.2.5.

23. Learning Persian: Athenaeus, 12.535e (which may refer to 406, post Notium, see M. Vickers, *Aristophanes and Alcibiades* [Berlin, 2015], 104). K. Vlassopoulos, *Greeks and Barbarians* (Cambridge, 2013), 48. Persian lifestyle: Dusinberre, *Aspects of Empire in Achaemenid Sardis;* perfumes, 210; clothing, 22–23 (see Athenaeus, 12.525d-e); gold foil ornaments, 148. Beards and manliness: L. Llewelyn-Jones, *King and Court in Ancient Persia 559 to 331 BCE* (Edinburgh, 2013), 59. Trousers: a good discussion of whether Athenians *did* consider trousers effeminate is R. Gorman and V. B. Gorman, *Corrupting Luxury in Ancient Greek Literature* (Ann Arbor, 2014), 108 n.61.

24. Table-mate as honour: Herodotus, 3.132; 5.24. Signet ring: Tantalizingly, a signet ring bearing Alcibiades' trademark device, the figure of flying Eros holding a victor's olive wreath in his outstretched right hand, has been discovered at Sardis (Dusinberre, *Aspects of Empire in Achaemenid Sardis,* 280, fig. 97). Tapestries: Dusinberre, *Aspects of Empire in Achaemenid Sardis,* 157. Concubines performing at banquets: Llewelyn-Jones, *King and Court in Ancient Persia,* 125. Food: Herodotus, 1.132; Athenaeus, 4.26G; Llewelyn-Jones, *King and Court in Ancient Persia,* 129; 173; 176; Xenophon, *Cyropaedia,* 8.2.6.

25. Court creating "a theatrical display of power": Llewelyn-Jones, *King and Court in Ancient Persia,* 9–10. Eight hundred stallions: Herodotus, 1.192. Llewelyn-Jones, *King and Court in Ancient Persia,* 83–85.

26. Hunt: Xenophon, *Cyropaedia*, 1.4.5–8; Chariton, *Callirhoe*, 6.4; Llewelyn-Jones, *King and Court in Ancient Persia*, 129–132.

27. Plutarch, *Life of Alcibiades*, 23.

28. Paradises: Diodorus Siculus, 14.80.2; Llewelyn-Jones, *King and Court in Ancient Persia*, 93; Dusinberre, *Aspects of Empire in Achaemenid Sardis*, 71–73.

29. Paradise of Alcibiades: Plutarch, *Life of Alcibiades*, 24. Miltiades' son: Herodotus, 6.41. Demaratus: Xenophon, *Hellenica* 3.1.6; Athenaeus, 1.29–30. Themistocles: Plutarch, *Themistocles*, 28; Diodorus, 11,57; Thucydides, 1.138.

30. Thucydides, 8.30–35; 43. Kagan, *The Fall of the Athenian Empire*, 77; 84–86.

31. Arguments over terms of treaty: Thucydides, 8.43: Kagan, *The Fall of the Athenian Empire*, 90–91; Rhodes, *Alcibiades*, 57–58.

32. Alcibiades' advice: Thucydides, 8.45–46. Once more, Thucydides provides a suspiciously full report of Alcibiades' private conversations with Chithrafarna, which might suggest that Alcibiades himself was his source. In which case, Alcibiades may have been claiming as his own policies which were subsequently followed but which he had not, in fact, suggested. The unexpected detail that he even gave this advice to the Great King rather smacks of typically Alcibiades-style exaggeration. See also: Athenaeus, 12, 534B; 535E; Nepos, *Life of Alcibiades*, 5.3; Justin, 5.2.5–8. Munn, *The School of History*, 130. Quotation: Aristophanes, *Lysistrata*, 1131–1134.

33. Rhodes, *Alcibiades*, 60.

34. Hatzfeld, *Alcibiade*, 228–229; Kagan, *The Fall of the Athenian Empire*, 76–77.

35. Great King's presence: Thucydides, 8.47. Persian roads: Dusinberre, *Aspects of Empire in Achaemenid Sardis*, 3. Travelling arrangements: Xenophon, *Cyropaedia*, 8.5.2–14; Curtius Rufus, 3.8.2; Llewelyn-Jones, *King and Court in Ancient Persia*, 88.

36. Rug and footstool: Athenaeus, 12.514C. Alcibiades' audience: Thucydides, 8.47. King enthroned: Athenaeus, 12.514C. King's appearance: Esther, 15.5–7.

37. Obeisance: Llewelyn-Jones, *King and Court in Ancient Persia*, 71–72.

38. Thucydides, 8.47.

39. Thucydides, 8.45. The extent of Alcibiades' influence with Chithrafarna is well discussed by Rhodes, *Alcibiades*, 59–60.

40. Thucydides, 8.48. Munn, *The School of History*, 131.

41. Rhodes: Thucydides, 8.44. Kagan, *The Fall of the Athenian Empire*, 92. Seeking Alcibiades' help: Thucydides, 8.48. Munn, *The School of History*, 131; Kagan, *The Fall of the Athenian Empire*, 132.

42. Communicating with Samians: Thucydides, 8.47.

43. Thucydides, 8.48.

44. Gomme, Andrewes, and Dover, *A Historical Commentary on Thucydides,* 5:124–125. Soldiery's views of history: S. Yoshitake, "The Logic of Praise in the Athenian Funeral Oration," and P. Low, "Commemoration of the War Dead in Classical Athens," in D. Pritchard (ed.), *War, Democracy and Culture in Classical Athens* (Cambridge, 2010).

45. Thucydides, 8.50. Rhodes, *Alcibiades,* 61.

46. Pisander as towering bear, or at least "pack-ass" (Hermippus, *Artopolides,* frag. 7) or "big ape" (Phrynichus, *Monotropus.* frag.21). D. Nails, *The People of Plato* (Indianapolis, 2002), 242.

47. Plutarch, *Life of Alcibiades,* 26.

9. TRADING PLACES

1. "The man who loves": Thucydides, 6.92.

2. Thucydides, 8.50–51; Plutarch, *Life of Alcibiades,* 25. J. Hatzfeld (*Alcibiade* [Paris, 1951], 235–236) questions whether the event happened at all, but see H. D. Westlake, "Phrynichus and Astyochus," *Journal of Hellenic Studies* 76 (1956): 99–100; D. Kagan, *The Fall of the Athenian Empire* (Ithaca, 1987), 125–130; P. J. Rhodes, *Alcibiades, Athenian Playboy, General and Traitor* (Barnsley, 2011), 59; 61–63.

3. Thucydides praises Phrynichus: Thucydides, 8.27.

4. Thucydides, 8.51.

5. Astyochus: C. Falkner, "Astyochus, Sparta's Incompetent Navarch?" *Phoenix* 53, nos. 3–4 (1999): 206–221.

6. *Probouloi:* F. D. Smith, *Athenian Political Commissions* (Chicago, 1920); Kagan, *The Fall of the Athenian Empire,* 5; V. D. Hanson, *A War Like No Other* (London, 2005), 236. The *probouloi* included the now-octogenarian poet Sophocles among their number.

7. Thucydides, 8.53–54. M. Munn, *The School of History* (Berkeley, 2000), 137–138; A. W. Gomme, A. Andrewes, and K. J. Dover, *A Historical Commentary on Thucydides,* 5 vols. Oxford: 1945–1981), 5:124–125; Kagan, *The Fall of the Athenian Empire,* 133.

8. Thucydides, 8.66. Kagan, *The Fall of the Athenian Empire,* 142–145.

9. Thucydides, 8.54. Munn, *The School of History,* 141.

10. Thucydides, 8.56. Kagan, *The Fall of the Athenian Empire,* 135; Rhodes, *Alcibiades,* 63.

11. Thucydides, 8.56. Whether there was a formal agreement with the Persians prohibiting their fleet from entering "Greek" waters is uncertain. Certainly, after their defeats at Salamis and Eurymedon, the Persians never again ventured into the Aegean.

12. P. J. Rhodes (*Alcibiades,* 64) believes that "however unjustifiably, Alcibiades continued to think that he had some influence with Tissaphernes."

13. See P. A. Brunt, "Thucydides and Alcibiades," *Revue des Études Grecques* 65 (1952): 80, reprinted in *Studies in Greek History and Thought* (Oxford, 1993).

14. Thucydides, 8.58. Kagan, *The Fall of the Athenian Empire,* 98–100.

15. Thucydides, 8.63–64. Kagan, *The Fall of the Athenian Empire,* 140–142.

16. Thucydides, 8.68; [Aristotle], *Constitution of Athens,* 32.3.

17. Killing rivals: Thucydides, 8.65. The Four Hundred: Thucydides 8.66–71; Munn, *The School of History,* 138.

18. Thucydides, 8.73. Samian coup: Kagan, *The Fall of the Athenian Empire,* 169–173; Munn, *The School of History,* 143; Rhodes, *Alcibiades,* 65.

19. Thucydides, 8.74. No democrat, Thucydides insists that stories of the horrors were exaggerated or invented.

20. Thucydides, 8.75.

21. Thucydides, 8.81; Plutarch, *Life of Alcibiades,* 26. Rhodes, *Alcibiades,* 65.

22. That Chithrafarna subsequently felt he had been outplayed and possibly betrayed by Alcibiades can perhaps be inferred from his subsequent arrest of his erstwhile guest at Farnavaz's capital, Dascyleum.

23. Thucydides, 8.81. Kagan, *The Fall of the Athenian Empire,* 175–178; Gomme, Andrewes, and Dover, *A Historical Commentary on Thucydides,* 5:277.
P. J. Rhodes (*Alcibiades,* 65) writes that it is hard "to be sure whether Alcibiades himself believed what he was saying to be true, but he was the kind of man who could believe his own propaganda."

24. Thucydides, 8.82.

25. Thucydides, 8.80. Kagan, *The Fall of the Athenian Empire,* 101.

26. Lampsacus: Thucydides, 8.62. Byzantium: Thucydides, 8.80. Kagan, *The Fall of the Athenian Empire,* 102.

27. Thucydides, 8.86. Plutarch, *Life of Alcibiades,* 26.4. E. F. Bloedow, *Alcibiades Reexamined* (Wiesbaden, 1973), 38–40; Rhodes, *Alcibiades,* 67.

28. Alcibiades to Chithrafarna: Thucydides, 8.82; Kagan, *The Fall of the Athenian Empire,* 179.

29. Astyochus: C. Falkner, "Astyochus, Sparta's Incompetent Navarch?" *Phoenix* 53, nos. 3–4 (1999): 206–221, n.491.

30. Thucydides, 8.83–5. Kagan, *The Fall of the Athenian Empire,* 179–180. Doreius as pancration victor: Thucydides, 3.8.

31. Thucydides, 87–88. Munn, *The School of History,* 144; Kagan, *The Fall of the Athenian Empire,* 212.

32. Plutarch, *Life of Alcibiades,* 26.6. Munn, *The School of History,* 152.

33. Thucydides, 8.87.

34. Diodorus, 13.46. Note that Diodorus constantly conflates Chithrafarna and Farnavaz, so here he misleadingly writes of Farnavaz. Rhodes, *Alcibiades,* 67–68.

35. Thucydides, 8.108; but Thucydides' claim here that Alcibiades sailed back to Halicarnassus, Cos, Caunus, and Phaselis *after* returning to Samos makes no geographical or strategic sense.

36. Opposed to the Four Hundred: Thucydides, 8.86. Galvanizing Athenians: Thucydides, 8.89.

37. Thucydides, 8.89–91. Kagan, *The Fall of the Athenian Empire,* 195.

38. Agis to Athens' walls: Thucydides, 8.71. Theramenes' role: Gomme, Andrewes, and Dover, *A Historical Commentary on Thucydides,* 5:300.

39. Thucydides, 8.90. Rhodes, *Alcibiades,* 68.

40. Murder of Phrynichus: Plutarch, *Life of Alcibiades,* 25 (a confused account). Betraying Athens: Kagan, *The Fall of the Athenian Empire,* 192; Munn, *The School of History,* 147.

41. Thucydides, 8.92.

42. Thucydides, 8.94–97. The Five Thousand: Aristotle, *Politics,* 13.1 f.; Diodorus, 13.38.1; Gomme, Andrewes, and Dover, *A Historical Commentary on Thucydides,* 5:323–328; P. J. Rhodes, "The Five Thousand in the Athenian Revolution of 411 B.C.," *JHS* 92 (1972): 115–127. Kagan, *The Fall of the Athenian Empire,* 201–203.

43. Lycurgus, *Against Leocrates,* 113; Craterus, *FGrH* III, 342 Fr. 17; Plut. *Moralia,* 834b. Kagan, *The Fall of the Athenian Empire,* 207–208.

44. Critias, frag.19.

45. Critias and the Four Hundred: H. C. Avery, "Critias and the Four Hundred," *Classical Philology* 58 (1963): 165–167.

46. Critias, 5. P. Wilson, "The Sound of Cultural Conflict: Kritias and the Culture of *Mousikê* in Athens," in C. Dougherty and L. Kurke (eds.), *The Cultures Within*

Ancient Greek Culture (New York, 2003), 197. Critias as architect of Alcibiades'
return: Rhodes, *Alcibiades,* 69.

47. Thucydides, 8.99–106; Diodorus, 13.39–40.

48. Eighteen ships: Xenophon, *Hellenica,* 1.1.5. Alcibiades' movements: I agree with
J. Hale, *Lords of the Sea: The Epic Story of the Athenian Navy and the Birth of
Democracy* (New York, 2009), 210. For contrary opinions see, e.g., Hatzfeld
(*Alcibiade,* 262), Rhodes (*Alcibiades,* 72), and Kagan (*The Fall of the Athenian
Empire,* 228), who interpret Thucydides, 8.108, as meaning that, rather than
sailing to Cos and Halicarnassus on his way back from Aspendus, as I suggest,
Alcibiades did so *after* he returned to Samos (see note 35 above), and that he
subsequently returned to Samos, where he remained "apparently inactive" for
some weeks. Kagan is forced to observe, "The ancient writers neither noticed nor
explained his inactivity."

10. RULING THE WAVES

1. Triremes and sea battles: V. D. Hanson, *A War Like No Other* (London, 2005),
236–246; J. Hale, *Lords of the Sea: The Epic Story of the Athenian Navy and the
Birth of Democracy* (New York, 2009), xxiii–iv; 20–27; H. Wees, *Greek Warfare,
Myths and Realities* (London, 2004), 206–212. *Rhuppapai:* Aristophanes, *Wasps,*
908–909.

2. Account of battle: Xenophon, *Hellenica,* 1.1.2; Diodorus, 13.45–46. Hale, *Lords
of the Sea,* 210–211; D. Kagan, *The Fall of the Athenian Empire* (Ithaca, 1987),
230–234. Hyacinths: Euphorion of Chalcis, frag. 40, Powell.

3. Mindarus at Troy: Xenophon, *Hellenica,* 1.1.4.

4. Diodorus, 13.46.

5. Syracusans: Diodorus, 13.45.

6. Diodorus, 13.46; Plutarch, *Life of Alcibiades,* 27. P. J. Rhodes, *Alcibiades, Athenian
Playboy, General and Traitor* (Barnsley, 2011), 74.

7. Farnavaz: Xenophon, *Hellenica,* 1.1.6.

8. Xenophon, *Hellenica,* 1.1.7; Diodorus, 13.47.

9. Xenophon, *Hellenica,* 1.1.8. Athenian finances: R. Meiggs, *Athenian Empire*
(Oxford, 1972), 370.

10. Chithrafarna to Farnavaz: Thucydides, 8.109. Xenophon, *Hellenica,* 1.1.9.

11. Alcibiades to Chithrafarna: Plutarch, *Life of Alcibiades,* 27. Dascyleum:
K. Vlassopoulos, *Greeks and Barbarians* (Cambridge, 2013), 249.

12. Plutarch, *Life of Alcibiades,* 27.

13. Xenophon, *Hellenica,* 1.1.10; Plutarch, *Life of Alcibiades,* 28.

14. Chithrapharna's motives: M. Munn, *The School of History* (Berkeley, 2000), 163. Alcibiades' motives for implicating Chithrafarna: Rhodes, *Alcibiades,* 75.

15. Alcibiades to Cardia: Xenophon, *Hellenica,* 1.1.11. Theramenes and Thrasybulus: Xenophon, *Hellenica,* 1.1.12.

16. Xenophon, *Hellenica,* 1.1.11. Cyzicus: F. W. Hasluck, *Cyzicus* (Cambridge, 1910), 1–4.

17. Xenophon, *Hellenica,* 1.1.11–13; 1.1.15; Diodorus, 13.49.

18. Xenophon, *Hellenica,* 1.1.14. Rain: Plutarch, *Life of Alcibiades,* 28; Xenophon, *Hellenica,* 1.1.16.

19. The following account is an amalgam of Xenophon, *Hellenica,* 1.1.16–18; Diodorus, 13.49–51; Plutarch, *Life of Alcibiades,* 28. J. Hatzfeld, *Alcibiade* (Paris, 1951), 269–273; E. F. Bloedow, *Alcibiades Reexamined* (Stuttgart, 1973), 46–55; Kagan, *The Fall of the Athenian Empire,* 236–244; Hale, *Lords of the Sea,* 212–217; Rhodes, *Alcibiades,* 75.

20. Xenophon, *Hellenica,* 1.1.18.

21. Trophies: Wees, *Greek Warfare,* 136–137. Booty: Diodorus, 13.51. Letter: Xenophon, *Hellenica,* 1.1.23; Plutarch, *Life of Alcibiades,* 28.

22. Endius to Athens: Rhodes, *Alcibiades,* 77. Reaction at Athens: Diodorus, 13.52. Reaction in Sparta: Diodorus, 13.52.1; Nepos, *Life of Alcibiades,* 5; Justin, 5.4.

23. Diodorus, 13.52. It is, he boasts, the speech "as Endius delivered it," but his record of speeches is no more to be trusted than that of Thucydides.

24. Diodorus, 13.53, disagrees—as, with the benefit of hindsight, have most subsequent historians.

25. Diodorus, 13.53, records that the opposition was led by the arch-demagogue, Cleophon.

26. Kagan, *The Fall of the Athenian Empire,* 248–249.

27. Aristotle, *Politics,* 34.1. Kagan, *The Fall of the Athenian Empire,* 252.

28. Legal specialists: Kagan, *The Fall of the Athenian Empire,* 255. Building project: Kagan, *The Fall of the Athenian Empire,* 260. The Temple of Athene Polias is now commonly called the Erechtheum.

29. Xenophon, *Hellenica,* 1.1.25. Gytheum: *Hellenica,* 1.4.11.

30. Xenophon, *Hellenica,* 1.1.22. Chrysopolis is the mediaeval Scutari, now Üsküdar, a residential district of modern Istanbul.

31. Munn, *The School of History,* 154; Kagan, *The Fall of the Athenian Empire,* 244; Rhodes, *Alcibiades,* 76.

32. Alcibiades and Thrace: Alcibiades' tutor, Zopyrus, was Thracian, while a close relation may have been Cleopompus, one of Athens' leading experts in all things Thracian. Not only that, Alcibiades' friend Theramenes, who helped lead the campaign for his recall, was the son of the Thracophile, Hagnon, the man who founded Amphipolis. See M. A. Sears, *Athens, Thrace and the Shaping of Athenian Leadership* (New York, 2013), 103.

33. Oaths of loyalty: Sears, *Athens, Thrace and the Shaping of Athenian Leadership*, 96.

34. Pylos: Diodorus, 13.64. Nisaea: Diodorus, 13.65.1–2. Corcyra: Diodorus, 13.48. Euboea: Thucydides, 8.95.

35. Diodorus, 13.43–44.

36. Xenophon, 1.2.1; Diodorus, 13.64; Plutarch, *Life of Alcibiades*, 29.

37. Or did he? The manuscripts of Xenophon, 1.2.13, read "*kateleusen*," which means "stoned him to death." With Kagan, I prefer the alternative reading, "*apelusen*," "set him free." Whichever reading is correct, Thrasyllus' treatment of Alcibiades' cousin does not seem to have cast a cloud over his relationship with Alcibiades. If he *did* put him to death, we can perhaps assume that Alcibiades and his cousin were not on the best of terms.

38. Plutarch, *Life of Alcibiades*, 29. Rhodes, *Alcibiades*, 79.

39. Again, it is necessary to piece together details; see Xenophon, *Hellenica*, 1.2.15–17; Diodorus, 13.64; Plutarch, *Life of Alcibiades*, 29.1–2. Kagan, *The Fall of the Athenian Empire*, 276.

40. Herodotus, 4.144. Chalcedon: modern Kadıköy, a suburb of Istanbul.

41. Xenophon, 1.3.2–4; Plutarch, *Life of Alcibiades*, 29.

42. Siege and battle: Xenophon, 1.3.4–7; Diodorus, 13.66; Plutarch, *Life of Alcibiades*, 30. Kagan, *The Fall of the Athenian Empire*, 277; Rhodes, *Alcibiades*, 79. River Chalcis: known today as the Kurbağalıdere ("Frog Stream").

43. Kagan, *The Fall of the Athenian Empire*, 279; Rhodes, *Alcibiades*, 75.

44. Xenophon, *Hellenica*, 1.3.8. Hatzfeld, *Alcibiade*, 282.

45. Plutarch, *Life of Alcibiades*, 30. Selymbria: Kagan, *The Fall of the Athenian Empire*, 281; Rhodes, *Alcibiades*, 80. Selymbria is modern Silivri.

46. Previous visit: Xenophon, *Hellenica*, 1.1.21. Current visit: Xenophon, *Hellenica*, 1.3.10.

47. Plutarch, *Life of Alcibiades*, 30; Diodorus, 13.66.

48. Plutarch (*Life of Alcibiades*, 30) tells us that Alcibiades "ordered one of those present" to make the proclamation, but it is difficult to see how, in the circumstances, he could have communicated his orders with sufficient speed and clarity.

Given his abilities as an orator, not to mention his pluck, it is much more likely that it was Alcibiades himself who delivered the speech.

49. Mycalessus: Thucydides, 7.29. D. Kagan, *The Peace of Nicias and the Sicilian Expedition* (Ithaca, 1981), 293; Sears, *Athens, Thrace and the Shaping of Athenian Leadership,* 80.

50. Plutarch, *Life of Alcibiades,* 30. Part of the agreement is preserved on an inscription in Athens; see Rhodes, *Alcibiades,* 80–81.

51. Xenophon, 1.3.8–12; Diodorus, 13.66; Plutarch, *Life of Alcibiades,* 31.

52. Xenophon, 1.3.8. Kagan, *The Fall of the Athenian Empire,* 280.

53. Xenophon, 1.3.11; Plutarch, *Life of Alcibiades,* 31. Hatzfeld, *Alcibiade,* 285; Rhodes, *Alcibiades,* 81.

54. Munn, *The School of History,* 163; Rhodes, *Alcibiades,* 82.

55. Clearchus and Byzantium: Thucydides, 8.80; Diodorus, 13.40. Rhodes, *Alcibiades,* 81.

56. Siege and capture of Byzantium: Xenophon, *Hellenica,* 1.3.14–22; Diodorus, 13.66; Plutarch, *Life of Alcibiades,* 31. E. F. Bloedow, *Alcibiades Reexamined,* 63; Kagan, *The Fall of the Athenian Empire,* 282–283.

57. Xenophon, *Hellenica,* 1.3.17–18.

58. Kagan, *The Fall of the Athenian Empire,* 284; Rhodes, *Alcibiades,* 82.

59. Plutarch, *Life of Alcibiades,* 32. Kagan, *The Fall of the Athenian Empire,* 285.

11. DOG DAYS

1. Date of return: M. Munn (*The School of History* [Berkeley, 2000], 335–339) offers a good summary of the problems of chronology for this period. While the evidence is contradictory, my inclination is to date his return and subsequent exile to 407.

2. *Birds,* 414: In Aristophanes' play, Peisthetaerus subverts conventional religion; his name can mean both "He Who Persuades his Companions" and "He Who Persuades the Political Clubs" (*hetaeriai*); the first avian "official" he encounters is an ephor—or rather, playing on the word, an *epops* (hoopoe)—and such is his ambition that, in the end, wielding the thunderbolt (like the Eros on Alcibiades' shield), he even ousts Zeus from his throne. See, for example, M. Vickers, *Aristophanes and Alcibiades* (Berlin, 2015). Munn, *The School of History,* 124–125. *Philoctetes,* 408: M. Vickers, *Sophocles and Alcibiades, Athenian Politics in Ancient Greek Literature* (Ithaca, 2008), 59.

3. Xenophon, *Hellenica,* 1.4.11; Aristotle, *Politics,* 4.44. J. Hatzfeld, *Alcibiade* (Paris, 1951), 292 n.5; D. Kagan, *The Fall of the Athenian Empire* (Ithaca, 1987), 287.

4. Xenophon, 1.4.9–10; Diodorus, 1.72.

5. Xenophon, 1.4.8–9. Reconnaissance / hearts-and-minds mission: unrecorded by any of the ancient historians, but Alcibiades would have been uncharacteristically lax had he failed to do this.

6. Xenophon, 1.4.11.

7. Hatzfeld, *Alcibiade,* 293–294.

8. Done in style: Diodorus, 13.68; Nepos, *Life of Alcibiades,* 6.3. Xenophon (*Hellenica,* 1.4.12) suggests it was more low-key. Plutarch (*Life of Alcibiades,* 32), noting the discrepancies between the sources available to him, many of which do not survive today, steers a middle course. Hatzfeld, *Alcibiade,* 294; 295 n.1; Munn, *The School of History,* 166; P. J. Rhodes, *Alcibiades, Athenian Playboy, General and Traitor* (Barnsley, 2011), 85. The following description favours Diodorus and Nepos, but includes elements from Xenophon and Plutarch.

9. Date: June 16 is suggested by Kagan, *The Fall of the Athenian Empire,* 290.

10. "In childhood," etc.: Plutarch, *Life of Alcibiades,* 1. Euryptolemus: Plutarch, *Life of Alcibiades,* 32.

11. Plynteria: Xenophon, *Hellenica,* 1.4.12; Plutarch, *Life of Alcibiades,* 34. H. W. Parke, *Festivals of the Athenians* (London, 1986), 152–155. Scholars have happily accepted Plutarch's explanation that Alcibiades miscalculated the day of his return. This, however, seems implausible in the extreme, and the present account seeks to find a more convincing explanation for why Alcibiades' detractors could use the Plynteria to smear him. B. Nagy ("Alcibiades' Second Profanation," *Historia* 43 [1994]: 285) goes so far as to argue that the Plynteria "appears to have been a festival that few Athenians knew very much about. The evidence suggests . . . that the crowd at the Piraeus, along with Alcibiades and his supporters, had all been unaware that this was the day of the Plynteria." While this is possible, especially given the fact that the Athenian calendar was notoriously flexible, it is surely improbable (unless, of course, Alcibiades' priestly enemies arbitrarily declared it the day of the Plynteria in order to make his return ill-omened).

12. Speech: Xenophon, *Hellenica,* 1.1.20; Plutarch, *Life of Alcibiades,* 33. Rhodes, *Alcibiades,* 86. Pnyx: The orientation of the Pnyx was the opposite of how it appears today, being deliberately changed by (or after) the Thirty. R. A. Moysey, "The Thirty and the Pnyx," *American Journal of Archaeology* 85, no. 1 (1981): 31–37.

13. Evil spirit: Plutarch, *Life of Alcibiades,* 33; Diodorus, 13.69; Justin, 5.4.13–18; Nepos, *Life of Alcibiades,* 7.6. Kagan, *The Fall of the Athenian Empire,* 289.

14. Plutarch, *Life of Alcibiades,* 33; Xenophon, *Hellenica,* 1.4.20; Diodorus, 13.69; Justin, 5.4.13–16; Nepos, *Life of Alcibiades,* 7. Hatzfeld, *Alcibiade,* 298; Kagan,

The Fall of the Athenian Empire, 290. Justin (2.5.4) goes further, saying that the Athenians awarded Alcibiades "not only all human honours, but divine ones too."

15. Plutarch, *Life of Alcibiades,* 33; Diodorus, 13.69. Munn, *The School of History,* 167–168; Kagan, *The Fall of the Athenian Empire,* 289.

16. Plutarch, *Life of Alcibiades,* 34. Munn, *The School of History,* 167.

17. Xenophon, *Hellenica,* 1.4.1. Gordian Knot: Arrian, 2.3–4; Curtius, 3.1.14–18; Justin, 11.7; Plutarch, *Life of Alexander,* 18. Delegates in Gordium: Kagan, *The Fall of the Athenian Empire,* 284.

18. Xenophon, *Hellenica,* 1.4.2–7. Hatzfeld, *Alcibiade,* 289; Kagan, *The Fall of the Athenian Empire,* 284. Korush: Also known as Cyrus the Younger. Munn, *The School of History,* 177; Rhodes, *Alcibiades,* 83; 88.

19. Korush's childhood and character: Xenophon, *Anabasis,* 1.9.

20. A. T. Olmstead, *A History of the Persian Empire* (Chicago, 1948), 356–376; J. M. Cook, *The Persian Empire* (New York, 1983); D. M. Lewis, *Sparta and Persia,* (Leiden, 1977), 134–155; Kagan, *The Fall of the Athenian Empire,* 294–298. Ctesias, 53–55. Pari Satis: *Parysatis,* in Greek. Estatira: *Stateira,* in Greek.

21. Xenophon, *Hellenica,* 1.5.1. Lysander: Plutarch, *Life of Lysander, passim.* See, e.g., P. Cartledge, *The Spartans: An Epic History* (London, 2013), 182–190; J. Roisman, *The Classical Art of Command* (Oxford, 2017), 187–226; Kagan, *The Fall of the Athenian Empire,* 297–298; Rhodes, *Alcibiades,* 88. Quotation: Plutarch, *Life of Lysander,* 1. Agesilaus: Plutarch, *Life of Agesilaus,* 2.

22. Xenophon, *Hellenica,* 1.5.1; Diodorus, 13.70; Plutarch, *Life of Lysander,* 3. Kagan, *The Fall of the Athenian Empire,* 301–302.

23. Euripidean happy endings: See, e.g., D. J. Mastronarde, *The Art of Euripides: Dramatic Technique and Social Context* (Cambridge, 2010); F. M. Dunn, *Tragedy's End: Closure and Innovation in Euripidean Drama* (Oxford, 1996).

24. I extrapolate this from the People's reaction to the generals after the victory at Arginusae the next year (406). See Chapter 12.

25. Alcibiades and his son: Lysias, 14; see Chapter 12.

26. Panathenaic Festival: Parke, *Festivals of the Athenians,* 33–50.

27. Munn, *The School of History,* 169; Kagan, *The Fall of the Athenian Empire,* 291–292; Rhodes, *Alcibiades,* 87.

28. Alcibiades leads the procession to Eleusis: Xenophon, *Hellenica,* 1.4.20; Plutarch, *Life of Alcibiades,* 34. Eleusinian Mysteries: Parke, *Festivals of the Athenians,* 55–72.

29. Aristophanes, *Knights,* 1398–1401; Xenarchus, 4; Eubulus, 67; 82; Aeschines, *Against Timarchus.* The Cerameicus is well evoked in B. Hughes, *The Hemlock Cup* (London, 2011), 72.

30. Processional Assembly Hall (Pompeion): The building whose foundations can be seen today was built seven years later, in 400; J. M. Camp, *The Archaeology of Athens* (New Haven, 2001), 135.

31. Plutarch, *Life of Alcibiades,* 34. Kagan, *The Fall of the Athenian Empire,* 291.

32. Route: Pausanias, 1.36.3 f. The monastery of Daphni is built on the site of Apollo's sanctuary.

33. High priest: Plutarch, *Life of Alcibiades,* 34. Hatzfeld, *Alcibiade,* 299.

34. Pausanias, 1.3.5; Arrian, *periplous,* 9. Munn, *The School of History,* 174.

35. Plutarch, *Life of Alcibiades,* 34–35. Hatzfeld, *Alcibiade,* 301.

36. Xenophon, *Hellenica,* 1.5.1.

37. Xenophon, *Hellenica,* 1.5.2; Plutarch, *Life of Lysander,* 4 (reporting that Korush took pleasure in hearing Lysander disparaging Chithrafarna).

38. Xenophon, *Hellenica,* 1.5.3; Plutarch, *Life of Lysander,* 9. A. W. Gomme, A. Andrewes, and K. J. Dover, *A Historical Commentary on Thucydides,* 5 vols. (Oxford, 1945–1981), 5:276.

39. Xenophon, *Hellenica,* 1.5.3–7; Diodorus, 13.70.3; Plutarch, *Life of Lysander,* 4. Rhodes, *Alcibiades,* 88.

40. Xenophon, *Hellenica,* 1.5.8–9. Lewis, *Sparta and Persia,* 131 n.134; Kagan, *The Fall of the Athenian Empire,* 307.

41. Kagan, *The Fall of the Athenian Empire,* 293; 307–308.

42. Antiochus: Plutarch, *Life of Alcibiades,* 10; 35; Xenophon, *Hellenica,* 1.5.11; Diodorus, 13.71.

12. NEMESIS

1. Andros: Xenophon, 1.4.22–23; Diodorus, 13.69; Plutarch, *Life of Alcibiades,* 35. J. Hatzfeld, *Alcibiade* (Paris, 1951), 306; S. Verdegem, *Plutarch's* Life of Alcibiades (Leuven, 2010), 352–353; D. Kagan, *The Fall of the Athenian Empire* (Ithaca, 1987), 308–309. Date of fleet's sailing: P. J. Rhodes, *Alcibiades, Athenian Playboy, General and Traitor* (Barnsley, 2011), 87.

2. Diodorus, 13.68. D. Kagan (*The Fall of the Athenian Empire,* 309 n.69) points out that the cost of Alcibiades' expedition was around fifty talents a month, "no small sum for the Athens of 407/6." See Plutarch, *Life of Lysander,* 35.

3. Xenophon, 1.5.10–11; Diodorus, 13.71; Plutarch, *Life of Alcibiades,* 35. Rhodes, *Alcibiades,* 89.

4. Clazomenae: Diodorus, 13.71.1 (only mentions Clazomenae, but it is *en route* from Notium to Phocaea). Phocaea: Xenophon, 1.5.11; Plutarch, *Life of Lysias,* 5.1. Thrasybulus: Xenophon, 1.5.11. Hatzfeld, *Alcibiade,* 309 n.6; Rhodes, *Alcibiades,* 89.

5. Defections: Diodorus, 13.71.3; Plutarch, *Life of Lysander,* 4.4. Kagan, *The Fall of the Athenian Empire,* 311.

6. Battle of Notium: Xenophon, 1.5.12–15; Diodorus, 13.71; Plutarch, *Life of Alcibiades,* 35.5–6; *Life of Lysander,* 5.1–2; *Hellenica Oxyrhynchia,* 4. The sources disagree about the course of the battle, with Diodorus providing perhaps the most coherent account. Kagan, *The Fall of the Athenian Empire,* 315–319; Verdegem, *Plutarch's* Life of Alcibiades, 356–359; M. Munn, *The School of History* (Berkeley, 2000), 178; Rhodes, *Alcibiades,* 89. Impetuous: Diodorus, 13.71.2. Rude gestures: Plutarch, *Life of Alcibiades,* 35.5. Abandoning ship: A trireme can be evacuated in twenty-four seconds; D. Hamel, *The Battle of Arginusae* (Baltimore, 2015), 40.

7. Cyzicus: Hatzfeld, *Alcibiade,* 312.

8. Alcibiades to Ephesus: Diodorus, 13.71.4. Rhodes, *Alcibiades,* 90.

9. Samos: Xenophon, 1.5.15. Agamemnon at Troy: Homer, *Iliad,* 1, 9 f.; S. Nevin, *Military Leaders and Sacred Space* (London, 2017), 194.

10. Attacking Cyme: Diodorus, 13.74.3–5. Kagan, *The Fall of the Athenian Empire,* 320. Wealth and tribute lists: R. Meiggs, *The Athenian Empire* (Oxford, 1972), 540–542. Pretext: Diodorus, 13.73.2. Cyme's character: Generally, the citizens of Cyme appear to have preferred a quiet life to making a principled stand, as attested by their readily handing over the rebel Pactyes to the Persians (Herodotus, 1.157), the speed with which they capitulated to the Persians during the Ionian Revolt, and the infamously oft-repeated assertion of their most famous son, the historian Ephorus, that, in any year, "the Cymeans kept quiet" (Strabo, 13.3.6). Rhodes, *Alcibiades,* 90.

11. Diodorus, 3.73; Nepos, *Life of Alcibiades,* 7. Kagan, *The Fall of the Athenian Empire,* 320–321.

12. Diodorus, 3.73; Plutarch, *Life of Alcibiades,* 36.

13. Diodorus, 13.72–73. Hatzfeld, *Alcibiade,* 316 n.1; Kagan, *The Fall of the Athenian Empire,* 320–321.

14. Plutarch, *Life of Alcibiades,* 36. Rhodes, *Alcibiades,* 90–91.

15. Xenophon, *Hellenica,* 1.5.16–17; Plutarch, *Life of Alcibiades,* 36; *Life of Lysander,* 5. Great King: Nepos, *Life of Alcibiades,* 7. Farnavaz, governorship of Athens,

Spartan agent: Diodorus, 13.73. Stripped of command: Diodorus, 13.73. Kagan, *The Fall of the Athenian Empire*, 322–323; Munn, *The School of History*, 179.

16. Departure: Diodorus, 13.74.4; Xenophon, 1.5.17; Plutarch, *Life of Alcibiades*, 36.3; Nepos, *Life of Alcibaides*, 7. Timing: Diodorus says Alcibiades waited to hand over command to Conon; Xenophon hints that he did not; Plutarch and Nepos maintain he left Samos on hearing of the vote to depose him. Given his experience in Sicily, the chances are that they are correct. Private grievances: Diodorus, 13.74.4.

17. Pactye: Diodorus, 13.74.2. Pactye = Callipolis ("the fair city") = modern Gelibolu / Gallipoli. Army: Plutarch, *Life of Alcibiades*, 36. Rhodes, *Alcibiades*, 95.

18. Miltiades: Herodotus, 6.30. M. A. Sears, *Athens, Thrace and the Shaping of Athenian Leadership* (New York, 2013), 59–71.

19. Hatzfeld, *Alcibiade*, 319–324; Sears, *Athens, Thrace and the Shaping of Athenian Leadership*, 141.

20. Seuthes: Xenophon, *Anabasis*, 7.2; Alcibiades' fortresses: Nepos, *Life of Alcibiades*, 7.4. Rhodes, *Alcibiades*, 95.

21. Fighting for king: Nepos, *Life of Alcibiades*, 7.4–5. Seuthes: Xenophon, *Anabasis*, 7.3. L. G. Mitchell, *Greeks Bearing Gifts* (Cambridge, 1997), 135–137.

22. Primitive society: Sears, *Athens, Thrace and the Shaping of Athenian Leadership*, 6. Pointy blond beards: Sears, *Athens, Thrace and the Shaping of Athenian Leadership*, 196. Straws: Archilochus, frag. 42 (West). Circumcision: Aristophanes, *Acharnians*, 158. Appearance: K. Vlassopoulos, *Greeks and Barbarians* (Cambridge, 2013), 178.

23. Xenophon, *Anabasis*, 7.3. Drinking: Mitchell, *Greeks Bearing Gifts*, 138; Sears, *Athens, Thrace and the Shaping of Athenian Leadership*, 146; 208–212.

24. Horses and chariots: Sears, *Athens, Thrace and the Shaping of Athenian Leadership*, 179. Surpassing hosts: Nepos, *Life of Alcibiades*, 11. Seuthes' offer to Xenophon: Xenophon, *Anabasis*, 7.2.

25. Lysias, 14.25.

26. Alcibiades IV as "orphan": Isocrates, 16.45. Alcibiades IV in Thrace: Lysias, 14.26–27.

27. Xenophon, 1.6.16–17; Diodorus, 13.74. Callias: Diodorus, 13.80. Kagan, *The Fall of the Athenian Empire*, 325–326.

28. Callicratidas: Xenophon,1.6.1–18; Plutarch, *Life of Lysander*, 6–7. Kagan, *The Fall of the Athenian Empire*, 329–335. Message to Conon: Xenophon, 1.6.15.

29. Conon's defeat: Xenophon, 1.6.15–18; Diodorus, 13.77–79. Message to Athens: Xenophon, 1.6.19–22. Melting statues: Aristophanes, *Frogs*, 720, with scholion.

Kagan, *The Fall of the Athenian Empire,* 335–339; Munn, *The School of History,* 180.

30. Xenophon, 1.6.24; Aristophanes, *Frogs,* 693–694, with scholion.

31. Inexperience: Xenophon, 1.6.31.

32. Battle: Xenophon, 1.6.28–33; Diodorus, 13.97–100. Munn, *The School of History,* 181; Kagan, *The Fall of the Athenian Empire,* 341–53; J. Hale, *Lords of the Sea: The Epic Story of the Athenian Navy and the Birth of Democracy* (New York, 2009), 225–229; Rhodes, *Alcibiades,* 96.

33. Public burial: Munn, *The School of History,* 36.

34. Trial of generals: Xenophon, 1.6.33–7.35; Diodorus, 13.100–103. Few previous trials have spawned as much scholarly debate as this one. See, e.g., Kagan, *The Fall of the Athenian Empire,* 354–375; Munn, *The School of History,* 181–188.

35. Lysander's return: Xenophon, *Hellenica,* 2.1.10–15; Diodorus, 13.104; Plutarch, *Life of Lysander,* 6–7. Callicratidas and Korush: Plutarch, *Life of Lysander,* 6. Lysander and Korush: Xenophon, *Hellenica,* 2.1.11–12; Diodorus, 13.104. Sayings: knucklebones, Plutarch, *Life of Lysander,* 8; lion-skin, Plutarch, *Life of Lysander,* 7.

36. Recall: Xenophon, *Anabasis* 1.1.2; Xenophon, *Hellenica,* 2.1.8–9; Munn, *The School of History,* 197; Kagan, *The Fall of the Athenian Empire,* 381.

37. Xenophon, *Hellenica,* 2.1.13–14; Diodorus, 13.104; Plutarch, *Life of Lysander,* 9.

38. Meeting Agis: Plutarch, *Life of Lysander,* 9. To Hellespont: Xenophon, *Hellenica,* 2.1.16–18; Plutarch, *Life of Lysander,* 9. Rhodes, *Alcibiades,* 98–99.

39. Debating Homer: Plato, *Ion,* 530d. Lysander to Lampsacus: Xenophon, *Hellenica,* 2.1.18–19. Athenians to Sestus and Aegospotami: Xenophon, *Hellenica,* 2.1.20–21. Meteor: See Chapter 1. Kagan, *The Fall of the Athenian Empire,* 385–388. Site of Aegospotami: Rhodes, *Alcibiades,* 99.

40. Standoff: Xenophon, *Hellenica,* 2.1.22–24. Alcibiades observations: Xenophon, *Hellenica,* 2.1.25; Plutarch, *Life of Alcibiades,* 36.

41. Kagan, *The Fall of the Athenian Empire,* 386–388.

42. Xenophon, *Hellenica,* 2.1.25; Diodorus, 13.105, Plutarch, *Life of Alcibiades,* 36; Nepos, *Life of Alcibiades,* 8. Munn, *The School of History,* 199. Advice: Rhodes, *Alcibiades,* 99. Sharing command: Hatzfeld, *Alcibiade,* 337.

43. Aristophanes, *Frogs,* 1425; 1431–1433. Euripides, *Bacchae;* D. Stuttard (ed.), *Looking at* Bacchae (London, 2016), 4–7. Munn, *The School of History,* 193; Rhodes, *Alcibiades,* 97.

44. Xenophon, *Hellenica,* 2.1.26; Diodorus, 13.105; Plutarch, *Life of Alcibiades,* 37.

45. Xenophon, *Hellenica*, 2.1.27–29; Diodorus, 13.106. Kagan, *The Fall of the Athenian Empire*, 391–394; Hale, *Lords of the Sea*, 236–243.

46. Xenophon, *Hellenica*, 2.2.3–19; Diodorus, 107. Kagan, *The Fall of the Athenian Empire*, 396–405; Munn, *The School of History*, 201.

47. Terms: Xenophon, *Hellenica*, 2.2.19–23; Diodorus, 14. Anniversary of Salamis: Munn, *The School of History*, 220. Critias: Munn, *The School of History*, 226; Kagan, *The Fall of the Athenian Empire*, 405–412.

48. Plutarch, *Life of Alcibiades*, 37. Hatzfeld, *Alcibiade*, 337.

49. Plots: Plutarch, *Life of Artaxerxes*, 3; cf. Xenophon, *Anabasis*, 1.1.3. Alcibiades to Farnavaz: Plutarch, *Life of Alcibiades*, 37; Nepos, *Life of Alcibiades*, 9.

50. Alcibiades and news of Korush's rebellion: Diodorus, 14.11; Nepos, *Life of Alcibiades*, 9. Munn, *The School of History*, 233; Rhodes, *Alcibiades*, 101.

51. Grynium: Nepos, *Life of Alcibiades*, 9. Sears, *Athens, Thrace and the Shaping of Athenian Leadership*, 3. P. J. Rhodes (*Alcibiades*, 102) stresses that the location of Grynium is unknown. Melissa: Athenaeus, 574e–f. Melissa is possibly modern Afyonkarahisar, but see Rhodes, *Alcibiades*, 103. Hatzfeld, *Alcibiade*, 342.

52. Herodotus, 5.52.

53. Timandra and Theodote: Athenaeus, 12.535c; 13.13.574e (where he calls Timandra "Damasandra"). Timandra: Plutarch, *Life of Alcibiades*, 39 (the strait-laced Plutarch leaves out Theodote—one courtesan is more than enough for him). Hyccara: Plutarch, *Life of Nicias*, 15; Thucydides, 6.62.3–4. Hycarra = modern Carini, near Palermo. Theodote and Socrates: Xenophon, *Memorabilia*, 3.11.1 ff.; Athenaeus, 588d. Rhodes, *Alcibiades*, 102.

54. Ecbatana: Herodotus, 1.98; Polybius, 10.27.

55. Wishing Alcibiades dead—Spartans and Lysander: Diodorus, 14.11; Plutarch, *Life of Alcibiades*, 38; Isocrates, 16.40. Critias and Lysander: Nepos, *Life of Alcibiades*, 10. The Thirty: Justin, 5.8.12–14. Majazus and Susamithra (in Greek, Magaeus and Sousamithras): Plutarch, *Life of Alcibiades*, 39; Nepos, *Life of Alcibiades*, 10. "People's darling": Plutarch, *Life of Alcibiades*, 38. Munn, *The School of History*, 234.

56. Dream: Plutarch, *Life of Alcibiades*, 39; Cicero, *de Divinatione*, 2.143. Hatzfeld, *Alcibiade*, 348–349; Rhodes, *Alcibiades*, 102. In the past: E.g., Histiaeus, Herodotus, 5.24.

57. Alcibiades' death: Diodorus, 14.11; Plutarch, *Life of Alcibiades*, 39; Nepos, *Life of Alcibiades*, 10. Also Justin, 5.8.14; Hieronymus, *Against Iovinian*, 1.44. Rhodes, *Alcibiades*, 103. Justin has Alcibiades being burnt alive; Hieronymus has him being suffocated. Hatzfeld, *Alcibiade*, 348 n.1.

58. Missing weapons: Nepos, *Life of Alcibiades,* 10.

59. Decapitation: Nepos, *Life of Alcibiades,*10. Nepos has Timandra cremate Alcibiades' body in the burning house. Burial: Plutarch, *Life of Alcibiades,* 39.

EPILOGUE

1. Phrygian feud: Plutarch, *Life of Alcibiades,* 39.5. Diodorus (14.11.2–4) suggests that Farnavaz himself was the instigator of Alcibiades' death. On the cast of suspects, see P. J. Rhodes, *Alcibiades, Athenian Playboy, General and Traitor* (Barnsley, 2011), 103.

2. The Thirty: Xenophon, 2.3.1–2.4.43. M. Munn, *The School of History* (Berkeley, 2000), 209–252; P. Krentz, *The Thirty at Athens* (Ithaca, 1982).

3. Xenophon, *Hellenica,* 2.3.56.

4. Long walls: Xenophon, *Hellenica,* 4.8.9–10. Cnidus: Xenophon, *Hellenica,* 4.3.10. J. R. Hale, *Lords of the Sea: The Epic Story of the Athenian Navy and the Birth of Democracy* (New York, 2009), 249–268. A good modern account of the ongoing war after (and before) 404 is J. T. Roberts, *The Plague of War, Athens, Sparta, and the Struggle for Ancient Greece* (Oxford, 2017).

5. Reorientating Pnyx: R. A. Moysey, "The Thirty and the Pnyx," *American Journal of Archaeology* 85, no. 1 (1981): 31–37.

6. Plato, *Apology.* Socrates' trial: Munn, *The School of History,* 284. There are myriad books on the subject, including: R. Waterfield, *Why Socrates Died* (London, 2009); B. Hughes, *The Hemlock Cup* (London, 2011).

7. Alcibiades IV: D. Nails, *The People of Plato* (Indianapolis, 2002), 20–22. Alcibiades' posthumous reputation: Munn, *The School of History,* 311; 322.

8. Isocrates 16 "On the Team of Horses": Mysteries: Isocrates, 16.6. Isocrates, Sparta: Isocrates, 16.10. Pardon: 16.12.

9. Lysias, 15.41.

10. No land or money: Isocrates, 16.46. Divorce: Lysias, 14.28; 15.28.

11. Lysias, 14.

12. Note that, although the money passed to Hipponicus, under Athenian law, it technically still belonged to Alcibiades and must be returned if the couple divorced.

13. Scandal: Andocides, 1. Callias served as a general in 392 and as a negotiator with Sparta in 371. He died shortly thereafter. Alcibiades the Younger copying his father's walk: Plutarch, *Life of Alcibiades,* 1; Archippus in Kock, *Comicorum Atticorum Fragmenta,* 1.688. Alcibiades' descendants: Nails, *The People of Plato,* 22.

14. Duris: Plutarch, *Life of Alcibiades,* 32. Leotychidas: Xenophon, *Hellenica,* 3.3.1–4; Plutarch, *Life of Alcibiades,* 23; *Life of Lysander,* 22.4–6. Agesilaus: Xenophon, *Hellenica,* 3.4 ff.; Plutarch, *Life of Agesilaus.* P. Cartledge, *Agesilaos and the Crisis of Sparta* (London, 1987).

15. Diodorus, 14.19 ff.; Xenophon, *Hellenica,* 3.1 ff. Cunaxa: Diodorus, 14.23; Xenophon, *Anabasis,* 1.8. Pari Satis and Estatira: Plutarch, *Life of Artaxerxes,* 6.5–6.

16. Xenophon, *Anabasis,* 7.2.38. The story of Xenophon's journey is the main subject of *Anabasis.*

17. Chithrafarna beheaded: Xenophon, *Hellenica,* 3.4.25. Paradise wrecked: Diodorus, 14.80.2.

18. Cynisca's chariot at Olympia: Xenophon, *Agesilaus,* 9.6. D. Kyle, " 'The Only Woman in all Greece': Cynisca, Agesilaus, Alcibiades and Olympia," *Journal of Sport History* 3 (2003): 183–203. Statue of Cynisca at Olympia: Pausanias, 6.1.6. Statue of her horses: Pausanias, 5.12.5. Hero cult and sanctuary: Pausanias, 3.15.1. L. G. Mitchell, *Greeks Bearing Gifts* (Cambridge, 1997), 70.

19. M. Vickers, "Alcibiades, a Classical Archetype for Alexander," in S. Chandrasekaran, A. Kouremenos, and R. Rossi (eds.), *From Pella to Ganhara: Hybridisation and Identity in the Art and Architecture of the Hellenistic East* (Oxford, 2011), 11–16.

20. Samos: Pausanias, 6.3.14–15. Honouring Lysander, the Samians went one step further, paying him divine honours. Rome: Pliny, 34.26.

21. Charioteer: Pliny, *Natural History,* 34.80. Eros: Pliny, *Natural History,* 36.28. It may be that this sculpture gave rise to the tradition that Alcibiades' shield bore the image of Eros and the thunderbolt. Munn, *The School of History,* 125. Sparta: H. A. Shapiro, *Art in Athens during the Peloponnesian War* (Cambridge, 2009), 236–264 (a chapter discussing "Alcibiades: The Politics of Personal Style"). Baths of Zeuxippus: Christodorus, *Ecphrasis,* in *The Greek Anthology.* Aphrodisias: R. R. R. Smith, "Late Roman Philosopher Portraits from Aphrodisas," *Journal of Roman Studies* 80 (1990): 127–150.

22. Athenaeus, 574 f.

TIMELINE

All dates are BC

490–79   Persian Wars

478–31   Delian League turns into Athenian Empire

461   Pericles consolidates hold on power, heralding 32 years as "first citizen"

452   Alcibiades born

447   Alcibiades' father Cleinias killed at Coronea; Alcibiades becomes ward of Pericles

434   Alcibiades comes of age as "ephebe"

432–29   Alcibiades campaigns at Potidaea

431–21   First phase of Peloponnesian War ("Archidamian War")

430–26   Plague at Athens

429   Pericles dies from plague

427   Aristophanes' *Banqueters* suggests Alcibiades is practising law

426   Nicias stages spectacular religious ceremony on Delos

425   Alcibiades serves on commission to review tribute lists, is satirized as "The Sausage Seller" in Aristophanes' *Acharnians;* Athenians capture Pylos

424–21   Alcibiades champions Spartan war prisoners held in Athens

424   Alcibiades serves on Delium Campaign; Congress of Gela in Sicily

423	Alcibiades satirized as "Pheidippides" in Aristophanes' *Clouds*
422	Eligible to hold public office, Alcibiades marries Hipparete; Brasidas and Cleon killed at Amphipolis
421	Peace of Nicias
420	Alcibiades engineers alliance with Argos
419	Alcibiades elected general, campaigns in Peloponnese
418	Alcibiades maintains support of Argive alliance; may be present as observer at Mantinea; probably wins Panathenaic chariot race
417	Alcibiades elected general
416	Alcibiades elected general, survives ostracism vote; according to Plato, attends Agathon's symposium (January); enters seven chariots at the Olympic Games, winning first prize (August); autumn massacre at Melos
415	Alcibiades elected general, proposes Sicilian Expedition; scandals of the mutilation of the Herms and profanation of the Eleusinian Mysteries; Alcibiades is recalled and escapes to Sparta
414	Alcibiades is satirized as "Peisthetaerus" in Aristophanes' *Birds*
413–04	Second phase of Peloponnesian War ("Ionian War")
413	Athens' Sicilian Expedition defeated; Spartan outpost at Decelea in Attica fortified
412	Alcibiades sails with Spartans to Ionia, foments revolt of Athenian allies; condemned to death by Sparta, Alcibiades winters in Sardis with Chithrapharna
411	Regime of the Four Hundred oligarchs in Athens; supplanted by the Five Thousand; Alcibiades recalled by Athenian fleet in Samos, raises funds and helps lead to victory at Battle of Abydus
410	Alcibiades helps recapture Cyzicus; is arrested by Chithrafarna but escapes; democracy restored in Athens
409	Alcibiades and Athenians set up customs base at Chrysopolis; Alcibiades cultivates relations with Thracians; his return to Athens explored in Sophocles' *Philoctetes*

408	Athenians take Chalcedon; Alcibiades takes Selymbria, swears oath with Farnavaz; Athenians take Byzantium
407	Alcibiades returns to Athens, ensures safe passage to Eleusinian Mysteries before sailing to Ionia for renewed hostilities
406	Alcibiades' helmsman Astyochus defeated at Notium, precipitating Alcibiades' self-imposed exile in Thrace; Athenian generals tried after Battle of Arginusae
405	Aristophanes debates recalling Alcibiades in *Frogs;* Euripides' *Bacchae* possibly characterizes Alcibiades as Dionysus; Athens defeated at Aegospotami; Alcibiades flees to Farnavaz
404	Alcibiades is detained at Melissa; Athens surrenders; government of the Thirty; Alcibiades assassinated
403	Overthrow of the Thirty; Athenian democracy restored
401	Korush killed at Cunaxa
399	Trial and execution of Socrates
396	Cynisca wins Olympic chariot race; Agesilaus sails to Asia Minor, fights Chithrafarna
395	Chithrafarna executed
394	Sparta defeated in Battle of Cnidus
387	Artaxšaça II concludes "The King's Peace" with warring Greek states; Ionian Greek cities ceded to Persia

ACKNOWLEDGEMENTS

The life of Alcibiades has intrigued me since I was an undergraduate. It has been the greatest privilege not only to have been commissioned to research and write about it, but to have received such warm support from friends and colleagues on every step of the way. My thanks go to all of them, including Robin Waterfield, for introducing me to my agent, Bill Hamilton; Bill himself, his assistants Becky Brown and Florence Rees, and all at A. M. Heath for determinedly championing both Alcibiades and me; and Ian Malcolm of Harvard University Press for commissioning the book and guiding me through the process with such charm and kindness. Also at the Press I am grateful to Olivia Woods and Stephanie Vyce for their stalwart work, including coordinating and gaining permissions for illustrations; manuscript editor Louise Robbins, for overseeing production and editing; Jill Breitbarth, who designed the cover, and Laura Shaw, who designed its interior, for such superb artistry; and Andrew Martin, Richard Howells, and Rebekah White, for spearheading the book's publicity. My thanks, too, to both Melody Negron at Westchester Publishing Services, with whom I worked closely throughout the proofing and indexing processes, and Robert Koelzer, the indefatigable copy editor, who scoured the text with a fine-tooth comb and made many helpful suggestions. I am indebted, too, to Isabelle Lewis for drawing such beautifully clear maps.

In addition, I should like to thank Alex Zambellas and Sam Moorhead for their excellent suggestions about the draft manuscript, the two academic readers for their valuable comments and recommendations, and especially Paul Cartledge, who allayed fears and whose meticulous annotations and generous advice saved me from many a blunder. It goes without saying that such errors and infelicities as remain are due entirely to my own intransigence.

Part of the process of research involved travel in Greece, Italy, Sicily, and Turkey, and I am grateful to the British Schools at both Rome and Athens for facilitating my journeying and site visits.

My heartfelt thanks go also to the "home team," my friends, my mother, and my wider family who have endured me throughout the process—but most of all to my wife, Emily Jane, whose love, encouragement, and companionship inspire me constantly. Finally, I must acknowledge the crucial role played at all times by our two cats, Stanley and Oliver, as handsome, demanding, and enigmatic as Alcibiades, but considerably more faithful.

INDEX

Alcibiades (*continued*)

daughter, legitimate, 85, 302–303; in debate over Sicily, 141–144; debates justice with Pericles, 39; at Delium, 73, 75; diplomatic attempts in Sicily, 158–160; early education, 28–32; enrolled in cavalry, 54; enters politics, 95; erases a legal document, 39; fake corpse at club initiation, 151–152; fights for Sparta in Ionia, 193–196; flees to Bithynia, 292; flees to Elis, 163–165; flees to Farnavaz, 292–294; flees to Thrace, 280; flogged at Olympic Games, 108; and Homeric tutor, 29; hunting dog, 64; as initiate in Eleusinian Mysteries, 79–80; interpretation of ephebic oath, 110; intervenes in Argos after democratic coup, 118–119; kills a slave-attendant at the *palaistra*, 30; knucklebones, 28; lamdacism, 60, 97, 259, 303; learns death sentence passed by Sparta, 193–195; at Magnesia on the Meander, 199–203, 207–208, 211–212, 216, 220; marriage, 77–78, 82–86; meets Dārayavahuš II, 201–202; and Melian slave girl, 136; in Melissa, 295–298; at Olympic Games, 129–133; at Panathenaic Games, 128; Paradise of, 197, 305; and Pericles' accounts, 39; Persian envoys to Sparta, 182; personal oaths with Farnavaz, 248–249; in Plato's *Protagoras*, 35–36; in Plato's *Symposium*, 136–138; practising law, 59–60; present at Argos and Battle of Mantinea, 113–116; property auctioned, 116; proposes an Athenian oligarchy, 203; protects the Eleusinian Mysteries, 266–268; punches Hipponicus, 77–78; recalled, 216, 226; receives Athenian ambassadors in Magnesia, 211–213; receives "birth bonus," 85–87, 302; receives dowry, 82, 86; receives Samian ambassadors in Magnesia, 202; returns to Athens, 256–260; rhetorical skills, 97; at Sardis, 193–198; scandal over the Olympic chariot, 133–134, 136, 302; sex tourism to Abydus, 43; shield, 55, 306; siege of Byzantium, 249–251; and Socrates, 4, 33–35, 48, 50, 58, 63, 75, 96, 136–139, 145, 167, 225, 259, 301; in Sparta, 165–167, 169–177, 181–185; and Spartan prisoners of war, 92–94, 165; and Spartan *proxeny*, 18–19, 92, 165, 170; and Sparta's envoys to Athens, 104–107; speech to Samian army, 217–218; stripped of supreme command, 279; takes Selymbria, 247–248; in Thrace, 281–284, 292; and Thucydides, 3, 105–106, 173, 202, 208–209, 213; townhouses, 62–63; treatment of admirers, 59, 64–65; as tribute commissioner, 65, 70, 77, 240, 277; as ward of Pericles, 20–21, 23–25, 32–33, 39, 52, 57, 97; wardrobe, 63–64

Alcibiades I, 18

Alcibiades II, 10, 19–20, 25, 82

Alcibiades IV, 85, 265, 283–284, 301–303

Alcmaeon, 11–12

Alcmaeon I, 12–13, 21, 166

Alcmaeonid curse, 12–15, 18, 38, 58, 150, 161, 259–260

Alcmaeonids, 11–18, 38, 55–56, 58, 71, 81, 150, 161, 166, 193, 259–260

Alexander the Great, 46, 305

Alopece, 78

Amadocus I, 281

Amorges. *See* Humarga

Amphipolis, 88–89, 98, 102–103, 107, 119–120, 169, 214

Amycla, 26–27

Amyclae, 174, 185

Anatolia, 1, 261

Anaxagoras, 36–37, 187, 288

Anaximander, 20

Anaximenes, 20

Andocides, 5–6, 161

Andromachus, 150–151, 153

Andros, 273–274, 277

Angra Mainyu, 180, 296

Antandrus, 240, 255–256

Antiochus of Miletus, 20

Antiochus the helmsman, 96, 272, 275–276

Antiphon, 214

Anytus, 58–59, 66, 242, 301

Apaturia, 22–23, 26, 41

Aphrodisias, 306

Aphrodite, 43, 55, 85, 141, 156, 268

Apollo, 7, 14, 16–17, 30–31, 46, 72–73, 75–76, 90–91, 101, 129, 149, 158, 174, 185, 268

Arabia, 222

Arcadia, 102, 110, 114–115, 144, 165

Arcadian League, 117, 119, 141, 164, 170, 204

Archelaus, 233

Archestratus, 121

Archidamus, 164

Arginusae, Battle of, 285–286

Argos, 99, 101–104, 107–108, 110, 112–120, 127–128, 134, 141, 144, 161, 164, 170, 300

Ariphron, 21, 32–33, 71

Aristeia, 19, 48, 77

Aristeides, 124

Aristogeiton, 137

Aristophanes, 3–4, 33, 56–60, 62, 67–68, 95, 98, 136–137, 145, 148, 150, 178, 199, 254, 290, 301; *Acharnians*, 59, 67; *Babylonians*, 67; *Banqueters*, 59, 62; *Birds*, 254; *Clouds*, 4, 56–59, 136–137, 150, 301; *Frogs*, 150, 290; *Knights*, 67–68; *Lysistrata*, 199

Aristotle, 300

Artabazus. *See* Artavazda

Artavazda, 180

Artaxerxes. *See* Artaxšaça I; Artaxšaça II

Artaxšaça I, 178–179

Artaxšaça II, 293–294, 304–305

Artemis, 83, 91, 156, 175, 263, 269

Artemisium, 15, 19, 48, 60

Aspasia, 20, 25–26, 32, 35, 40, 42, 54, 97, 188, 286

Aspendus, 221–222, 233

Astyochus, 190, 193, 198, 206–209, 220–221

Athenaeus, 6

Athene, 12, 31, 67, 101, 127–128, 150, 259, 265

Athene olive-wood statue, 128, 240, 258, 265

Athene Parthenos statue, 38, 132, 285

Athene Promachos statue, 23, 37, 257

Athenian embassy to Susa, 248, 261

Athenians at Samos debate Alcibiades' proposals, 203–205

Athens: Acropolis, 11–12, 23–25, 37, 41, 61, 78, 90, 95, 125, 128, 146, 166–167, 210, 238, 240, 257–260, 265–266, 268, 285, 301–302; Agora, 19, 23, 39–40, 42, 44, 56, 63–64, 66–68, 70–71, 87, 96, 101, 121, 124–127, 145–146, 169, 224, 259, 265, 272, 301, 303; Painted Stoa, 70, 92, 125; Parthenon, 24, 38, 51, 132, 285; Pnyx, 23, 66, 95–97, 121–122, 126, 145, 209, 225, 259–260, 272, 300; Sacred Gate, 127, 265–266; Temple of Athene Nike, 240; Temple of Athene Polias, 12, 240, 258, 265; Theatre of Dionysus, 7, 57, 61–62, 67, 96, 98, 148, 150

Athos, Mount, 15

Attic Stelae, 6, 167

Aulis, 101

Axiochus, 42–43, 83–84, 166, 286

Babylon, 179, 233

Bisanthe, 281, 304

Bithynia, 244, 292

Black Sea, 28, 181, 218–219, 226, 238, 249, 281, 288, 292, 304

Boeotia, 11, 20, 23, 42, 51, 70, 72–73, 89, 100, 103–104, 107–108, 113, 300

Boeotians, 20, 31, 72–76, 100, 103, 106, 113, 278

Bosporus, 28, 181–182, 218–219, 234, 239, 241, 244–246, 249–251, 255, 264, 272–273, 275, 280, 296, 302

Brasidas, 71, 88–89, 169

Brauron, 83

Byzantium, 15, 219, 235, 239, 241, 244, 246–247, 249–251, 255, 274, 280, 289, 306

Calabria, 156

Callias, Peace of, 178, 200

Callias I, 81–82

Callias II, 80–82

Callias III (Hipponicou), 31, 35–36, 78–79, 82–87, 92, 97, 161, 166, 173, 177, 210, 260, 265–266, 284, 302–303

Callias Calliadou, 48

Callicratidas, 284–285, 287
Camarina, 123, 160
Cape Malea, 256
Cape Spiraeum, 183, 187–188, 190
Cappadocia, 262, 288
Carcinus, 158
Cardia, 235
Caria, 255, 261
Carneia, 174
Carthage, 124, 145, 159, 242
Carthaginians, 169–170, 242
Catane, 123, 158–160, 162
Caunus, 222
Ceos, 35
Cephisus, River, 268
Cerameicus, 6, 86, 145, 265, 267, 303
Ceramic Gulf, 255
Chaeronea, 20
Chalcedon, 244–246, 248–249, 274, 289, 300
Chalcideus, 185, 187–188, 190, 193
Chalcidice, 43–44, 49, 88, 136
Chalcis, River, 245
Chios, 43, 131, 155, 181–184, 186–188, 190, 198, 202, 255, 263
Chithrafarna: Alcibiades recalled from court of, 216; arrests Alcibiades, 233–234; and Astyochus' letter, 207–209; attacked by Agesilaus, 304; brother of Estatira, 262; courts Sparta, 179, 182; death of, 304; family and background, 179–180; funds Spartan war effort, 184, 192, 210, 220, 233; and Humarga, 179–181; at Iasus, 192; initial war strategy, 181–182; lets Alcibiades act on his behalf, 202–203; at Magnesia, 199, 202–203, 207, 211–213, 216, 220; meetings with Dārayavahuš II, 202; meeting with Farnavaz, 233; at Miletus, 189–193; and Phoenician fleet, 221–222, 226; prospect of supporting Athens, 204, 207–208, 210–211, 213, 218–219, 222, 234, 271, 290; receives Alcibiades' advice, 199–200, 253; relationship with Alcibiades, 189–191, 193, 195–198, 207–209, 216–217, 233, 294; relationship

with Farnavaz, 182, 218–219, 233; relationship with Korush, 261, 271, 287, 293–294; removed from post, 261–262; at Sardis, 193–198; satrapal lifestyle, 195–197; supports Artemis Sanctuary at Ephesus, 263; terms for supporting Athens, 211–213; treaties with Sparta, 198–199, 214
Choaspes, River, 201
Chrysopolis, 241, 244, 249
Cimon, 17–18, 60, 81–82, 99, 122, 146, 162
City Dionysia, 56, 58, 61, 67, 119
Clazomenae, 37, 187, 190, 234, 275
Cleaenetus, 66
Clearchus, 250
Cleinias I, 18
Cleinias II, 19, 60
Cleinias III, 10, 18–20, 22–23, 26, 41–42, 44, 48, 59, 65, 73, 131
Cleinias IV, 10, 21, 25, 33
Cleisthenes of Athens, 14–16
Cleisthenes of Sicyon, 13
Cleon, 66–70, 88–89, 94, 96–97, 103, 124, 142
Clubs, 151–152, 211, 214
Cnidus, 300
Coesyra, 13
Colophon, 242
Congress of Gela, 70, 123, 140, 148, 157
Conon, 274, 284–285, 291, 300
Copaïs, Lake, 20
Corcyra, 40–41, 100, 155, 242
Corinth, 16, 40, 43–44, 89, 98, 100–103, 108, 111–113, 128, 141, 158, 169, 183, 189, 300
Coriolanus, 5
Coronea, Battle of, 10, 20, 23, 41, 73, 75
Coryphasion, 68
Cos, 222, 262, 274
Crimea, 181
Critias, 4, 31, 35, 150, 225–226, 292, 296, 300–301
Croesus, 13, 15, 21, 180, 193
Crypteia, 168
Cunaxa, Battle of, 304
Cybele, 269
Cylon, 11

Persia: administration, 179; Alcibiades'
   attempts to influence policy, 199–200,
   202, 207–208, 213–214, 302; alleged
   relationship with Alcmaeonids, 15–16;
   army burns Athens' temples, 23–24;
   Athenian embassy to, 249, 251, 261; court
   etiquette, 201–202, 211, 287; crushes
   Ionian Revolt, 15, 19; designs on Ionia, 15,
   200, 202, 211, 213, 218–219, 239, 262,
   305; designs on south coast of Sea of
   Marmara, 235; diplomatic relations with
   Greece in early Peloponnesian War, 178;
   education, 180, 261; enters Peloponnesian
   War, 178–179, 184; finances Sparta, 178,
   184, 192, 200, 217, 220, 233, 271, 273,
   275, 287; fleet, 15, 212, 221–222, 226;
   gift-giving, 195, 282; growth of empire,
   14–15; Hippias flees to, 14; hunting,
   196–197; invasions of Greece, 15–16, 19,
   27, 31, 43, 48, 61, 78, 80–81, 93, 135, 175,
   204; lifestyle, 195; peace with Athens
   (449), 82, 178; pleasure gardens, 9, 197;
   receives earth and water from Athens, 15;
   relationship with Athens and Delian
   League, 16–17, 126, 178–179, 188,
   203–204, 207–208, 210–211, 213,
   218–219, 222, 234, 271; revolts in empire,
   179–180, 192, 222; satraps, 179;
   Themistocles flees to, 154, 197–198;
   treatment of foreign turncoats, 197–198,
   294; treaty with Sparta, 184, 189, 198, 201,
   211, 214, 217, 296
Phaeax, 123, 125–126, 140, 152
Phalerum, 56, 128
Pharnabazus. *See* Farnavaz II
Pharnaces. *See* Parnaka
Phaselis, 222
Pheidias, 37–38, 132
Philaids, 13, 17
Philip II, 46
Phocaea, 275–277
Phoenicia, 222
Phoenician navy, 200, 212, 218, 221–222, 233
Phrynichus, 190–191, 204, 206–208, 211, 214,
   224–225

Phthonos, 7
Piraeus, 42, 52–54, 64, 79, 126, 145, 153, 159,
   182, 188, 215, 224, 242, 260, 267, 286, 300
Pisander, 205, 209–211, 213–214, 225
Pišišyaothna, 180
Pissuthnes. *See* Pišišyaothna
Pitane, 174–175
Plague, 53–54, 66, 88, 90, 98, 176
Plataea, Battle of, 15, 51, 93, 135
Plato, 4–5, 32–33, 35, 50, 136–139,
   300; *Protagoras*, 35–36; *Symposium*,
   136–139
Pleistoanax, 24, 98, 100, 173–174
Plutarch, 2, 5–7, 97, 105, 196
Plynteria, 258, 260
Polygnotus, 82
Poseidon, 154, 183
Potidaea, 43–44, 48–51, 53, 62, 75–77, 88,
   95, 100, 106, 119, 245; Battle of, 48–49
Probouloi, 209
Proconnesus, 235–237
Prodicus, 35
Pronomus, 30
Propontis. *See* Marmara, Sea of
Proskynesis, 202
Protagoras, 33, 35–36, 40, 56–57, 78
Pydna, 48
Pylos, 11, 68–70, 74, 88–89, 92–93, 98,
   103–105, 111–112, 142, 171, 238, 242
Pythagoras, 306
Pythian Games. *See* Delphi: Pythian Games
Pythonicus, 149

Rharian Plain, 268
Rhegium, 156–158, 182
Rheiti, River, 268
Rheneia, 91, 129
Rhium, 111–112
Rhodes, 203, 220, 255, 262, 274
Rhoeteum, 231–232
Rome, 306
Royal Road, 178, 201, 294–295

Sabazius, 261
Salaminia, 160, 162, 165–166

with Argos, 117; fifty-year alliance with Athens, 98; financed by Persia, 178, 184, 192, 200, 217, 220, 233, 271, 273, 275, 287; fleet, 183–189, 198, 208, 224, 226, 230–232, 240, 247, 255–256, 263, 285, 288–291; focuses on Hellespont and Bosporus, 218, 234; gains support of Dārayavahuš, 261–262; goaded by Pericles, 18, 41, 52; hairstyle, 35, 95; Helot revolt and repercussions, 17–19; hero cult of Cynisca, 305; historic enmity with Argos, 99, 101–102; imposes oligarchy in Argos, 116; imposes the Thirty in Athens, 4, 292; inability to meet peace terms, 98–100, 102–103, 106–107; interferes in late sixth-century BC Athenian affairs, 14–15; invades Attica (446 BC), 24; lifestyle, 169; loses Chios, 198; low reputation after Peace of Nicias, 102–103; and Melos, 126; messes, 169, 175; mosaic of Alcibiades, 306; negotiates peace with Athens, 89, 92, 98; negotiates with the Four Hundred, 223–225; occupies Decelea, 174, 176–177, 204, 264, 266; orders Alcibiades' death, 193–195, 198–199; Persian Stoa, 175; piety, 268; policy after Pylos, 70; population decline, 93, 165; presents war as struggle for freedom, 200; prisoners of war after Pylos, 70, 89, 92–94, 98, 103, 165; proposal to build forts in Attica, 98; raids Persia, 304; reluctant to make war, 51, 89, 119; resists Athenians at Abydus, 243–244; seeks peace after Cyzicus, 238–239; sends ambassadors to Athens after Peace of Nicias, 104–105; sends army under Agis against Argos, 113–114; sends Brasidas to northern Greece, 71, 88–89; sends Gylippus to Sicily, 174; suspected of poisoning Athens' wells, 53; suspicious of Alcibiades, 193–195; at Thermopylae, 15, 27, 93, 175; thirty years' peace with Athens, 24, 40; ties with Alcibiades' family, 18–19, 26; treaty with Persians, 184, 189, 198, 201, 211, 214, 217, 296;

urban topography, 174–175; victorious at Aegopotami, 288–291; victorious at Mantinea, 115–116; victorious at Notium, 275–277; women, 26–27, 93, 169, 175–176; wooed by Persians, 178–182

Sphacteria, 68–69, 103, 165
Stele of Disgrace, 167, 260
Strymon, River, 88
Susa, 82, 178–179, 201, 248, 261, 270, 287, 292, 295–297, 304
Susamithra, 296
Syracuse, 65, 123, 132, 140–144, 148, 157, 159, 160, 164, 171, 174–177, 182, 201, 217, 220, 242, 245, 253; Fountain of Arethusa, 159; Great Harbour, 159; Stone Quarries, 159, 177; Temple of Athene, 159

Tanagra, 74
Tarentum, Gulf of, 155
Taureas, 61–62
Taygetus, Mount, 165, 174–175, 181, 196
Tegea, 115–116
Teichiusa, 191–192
Teisias, 134, 136
Teos, 188, 190
Thales, 20
Thasos, 39, 131, 255
Theano, 41–42, 166
Thebes, 11, 51, 70, 98, 101, 103, 164
Themistocles, 15, 19, 154, 197
Theodorus, 260
Theodote, 295–297, 306
Theotimus, 285
Theramenes, 215, 223–224, 226, 235–237, 240, 244, 251, 300–301
Therapne, 175
Therimenes, 191–192
Thermopylae, 15, 27, 93, 175, 199
Theseus, 23, 101, 171
Thespiae, 74
Thesprotia, 123
Thessaly, 93, 123
Thetis, 138
Thirty, the, 4, 292, 296, 300–302
Thirty Tyrants. *See* Thirty, the